A HISTORY
OF
CLAN CAMPBELL

VOLUME I

From Origins to Flodden

A History of Clan Campbell

VOLUME 1
From Origins to Flodden

VOLUME 2
From Flodden to the Glorious Revolution
(to be published in 2002)

VOLUME 3
From 1688 to the Present
(to be published in 2004)

A HISTORY
OF
CLAN CAMPBELL

―――――――

VOLUME I

From Origins to Flodden

A<small>LASTAIR</small> C<small>AMPBELL</small> <small>OF</small> A<small>IRDS</small>
Unicorn Pursuivant of Arms

POLYGON
AT EDINBURGH

© The Clan Campbell Education Association 2000

First published 2000 by
Polygon at Edinburgh
An imprint of Edinburgh University Press Ltd
22 George Square, Edinburgh EH8 9LF

The right of Alastair Campbell of Airds to be identified as the author of this book has
been asserted in accordance with the Copyright, Designs and Patents Act 1988.

ISBN 1 902930 17 7

A CIP record for this book is available from the
British Library

Typeset in Bulmer
by Pioneer Associates, Perthshire
and printed in Great Britain by
The Bath Press, Bath

Contents

Foreword
by The Duke of Argyll

Only very occasionally, if at all, do all the right ingredients come together naturally to form the ideal recipe in whatever field. I would liken it to the so-called 'Primeval Soup' from which all life on Earth sprang. To this day we do not know if anything like it exists in the entire Cosmos, but these conditions have been met by the author. Others, with a profound thirst in the subject, realised what an opportunity there lay to produce this, a comprehensive history of the Clan of which I happen to be the extremely proud Chief, and to this end they prevailed on Alastair Campbell of Airds to undertake the mammoth task of which this is the first of an expected three volumes.

Here we have a man who has painstakingly collated and gleaned the knowledge with an enthusiasm for the subject that has since his youth seen him gathering small bits of a vast jigsaw. From his first few decades he kept meticulous notebooks, for no particular purpose other than his own pleasure, and these were to prove invaluable in this work of heroic magnitude.

The author has drawn together a myriad of strands, which in themselves took lifetimes to complete by extremely able historians in their own right.

People and manuscripts as well as authenticated stories from all five continents of the globe have been carefully scrutinised to build up the vast wealth of information which these books will contain.

I am delighted to commend this work to kinsmen and scholars alike, as well as to all who hold a special place for Scotland and all its peoples in their souls.

Argyll

List of colour illustrations

List of black and white illustrations

Introduction to the Organisation

The Clan Campbell Education Association, Inc.

The Clan Campbell Education Association was founded in 1992 by members of the Board of Directors of the Clan Campbell Society (North America). It is incorporated in California and has been approved as a tax-exempt charitable organisation by the US Internal Revenue Service and the state's tax authorities. Its present officers are Joseph McDowell Campbell, Jr., President, Wendell Campbell, Vice President, Beth Campbell Stoney, Secretary, and Kenneth B. Campbell, Treasurer.

The Association exists to educate its members and the public about the Scots and Scotland in general and about the Clan Campbell in particular. It seeks to promote the study, health and perpetuation of Scottish Culture, including music, dance, art, athletics, language and cuisine, and to support and conduct charitable and educational activities that advance this purpose. The Association also encourages the study of Scottish history and culture by financing scholarships, grants, loans and the award of incentives at Highland Games and competitions.

In 1997 the Association was able to commission the writing of a three-volume history of the Clan Campbell, and thus to fill a large gap in Clan – indeed Scottish – historiography. Funding for the project came from generous donations of Campbells world-wide as well as from other clans including the Clan Donald. The project has built on earlier research funded by the now inactive Jacob More Society, founded by the late Hugh Purfield Moore. This first volume has been written by Alastair Campbell of Airds: I am pleased to say that he has also agreed to write the remaining two.

Listed below for the recognition they so richly deserve are the major contributors who have made this history a reality. Special thanks go to the Patrons who have contributed $1,000 or more and to the Underwriters who have contributed $250 or more. Numerous others have donated lesser amounts.

Together they deserve our gratitude for making possible a legacy that will last forever.

Joseph McDowell Campbell, Jr.
President, CCEA

List of CCEA Patrons

Verda McClung Anderson
Dr & Mrs Stephen S. Bell
David & Mary Bernhardt
William H. Burns, Jr.
Cambelt International Corporation
Charles T. & Nancy J. D. Campbell
Clyde H. 'Bill' & Paula Campbell
Colin D. & Sherie Campbell
David R. & Mary E. 'Betsy' Campbell
Dewey G. & Rosemary H. Campbell
Mr & Mrs Donald Draper Campbell
Frederick H. Campbell
J. Richard & Barbara J. Campbell
Mr & Mrs Jerry Campbell
John A. 'Scotty' Campbell
Lt. Col. John W. & Mrs Marilyn A. Campbell, USMC (Ret.)
Col. & Mrs Joseph McDowell Campbell, USAF (Ret.)
Kenneth B. & Ruby G. Campbell
L. Allen & Eileen J. Campbell
Levin H. Campbell
Marc T. Campbell, Jr.
Michael J. Campbell
Richard L. Campbell
Scott W. Campbell & Amy E. Mueller-Campbell

Rev. Thomas W. & Elizabeth T. Campbell

In Memory of J. Lyle Campbell, Editor Emeritus of
the CCS(NA) Journal

V. Wilson & Ruth Campbell

Edgar T. Cato

Clan Campbell Society of Australia

David W. Campbell, President

In memory of Samuel Campbell, b. Tarbolton, Ayrshire 1809,
d. New York Mills, NY 1885

H. Cartan Clarke

In Memory of parents Donald & Betty Campbell

Alan K. & Isabelle Campbell DerKazarian

Mr & Mrs Richard L. Duplisea

Beverly Campbell Griffin

In Memory of Henry Alexander Campbell, Florida (1901–1977)

Mr & Mrs Carl A. Guilford, Jr.

Ellice & Rosa Hayward McDonald, Jr.

Honorary High Commissioner, Clan Donald, USA, Inc.

Charmion Randolph & Robert T. McKusick

Jennie Howe Merrill

Ms Helen Miser

Averill Q. & Ann Marie Mix

In Memory of Hugh Purfield Moore

Marian F. Moore

Michael & Mary Moore

Capital Management Group

Mr Wykoff Myers

Jeffrey & Susan Poulin

Roy Campbell Smith III & Annis G. Smith

William Campbell & Katherine Iliinsky Snouffer

Mr & Mrs Charles M. 'Tommy' Thomson

Mr & Mrs Rodney J. Tuttle

Elsie M. Whitmarsh

List of CCEA Underwriters

Lt. Col. Ervan L. Amidon, USAF
  (Ret.)
Richard & Aloma Blaylock
Bob & Karen Bruner
Mr & Mrs Douglas D. Caddell
Bob & June Campbell
Bruce & Karen Campbell
Clarence A. & Anita M. Campbell
Daniel B. Campbell
Dr Dennis E. Campbell
Diane M. Campbell
Diarmid A. Campbell
Mr & Mrs Donald F. Campbell
In appreciation of Flicky Campbell,
  Argyll, Scotland
  Douglas A. Campbell
Hyle & Joanne Campbell
James & Aimee Campbell
James A. Campbell
John & Bobbi Campbell
John A. L. Campbell
Lee E. Campbell
Lem W. Campbell
Leonard B. Campbell
Leonard R. & Erma D. Campbell
Niall Campbell
Patrick B. & Mary Jo Campbell
In Memory of Lt. Col. Robert L.
  Campbell (1921–1967), USAF,
  DFC
  Robert & Marjorie Campbell
Richard L. Campbell
Mr & Mrs Richard L. Campbell
Robert L. Campbell
Roland & Dianne Campbell

Judge Ross & Beverly Campbell
Seth A. & Fern V. Campbell
Timothy E. Campbell, TSgt. USAF
  (Ret.)
Helen Campbell-Lucas
Clan Campbell Society of Australia
  (Queensland)
Clan Campbell Society, Nova Scotia
Patricia & Michael Coller
Walter & Rosemary Campbell
  Dunden
Jane C. Graham
In Memory of William Elmer &
  Bertha Tuttle Campbell
Fauntella Campbell Hill
Prof. Jane Campbell Hutchinson
Mr & Mrs Glenn A. Kirchman
Robert Lamprey
Jean R. Ljungkull
Mariska P. Marker
Lois Mae (Miller-Tuttobene)
  Maulfair
George McQuilken
Mr & Mrs Thomas E. Murley
Dr & Mrs Thomas J. Quinlan
Elaine Reagan-Jones
Robert C. St. John, Jr.
Hugo & Marianne Schumacher
Bernard L. & Patricia H. Shaw
Beth & Tom Stoney
Mary J. Toerner
Mrs Clifford Withers Walker
James White
Helen Campbell Wiles
Jim & Betty Williams

Chronology

Campbell Chronology

1263 First documentary mention of a Campbell. Gillespic Campbell (father of Sir Cailean Mor) appears in Exchequer Rolls in possession of Menstrie and Sauchie.

1280 Reputed date of death of Gillespic.

1281 Sir Cailean Mor appears in Luss charter.

1291 Sir Cailean Mor named as one of the auditors for Robert Bruce, the Competitor.

1296 Sir Cailean Mor killed by the MacDougalls at the String of Lorne. A cairn now marks the spot.

1296 'Ragman Roll' – an oath of loyalty to King Edward I of England signed by most of the Scottish nobility, including several Campbells, among them Sir Neil Campbell.

1308 Battle of the Pass of Brander. Capture of Dunstaffnage.

1314 Sir Neil Campbell, one of the Scottish Commissioners, is sent to treat for peace with the English after Scottish victory at Bannockburn.

1314 Lands of forfeited David of Strathbogie, Earl of Atholl, conferred by King Robert on Sir Neil Campbell, his wife, the King's sister, Mary and their son John.

1316 Sir Neil Campbell of Lochawe dead by this date.

1316 Sir Colin Og Campbell, son of Sir Neil, receives Royal Charter of Lochawe and Ardscotnish, in free barony, 10 February.

1316 Sir Colin Og Campbell on Royal expedition to Ireland.

1318 Duncan Campbell and his wife Susannah Crawford receive charter for her family's former lands of Loudoun and Stevenson in Ayrshire.

1320 Letter to the Pope – 'The Declaration of Arbroath' signed, among other Scottish nobles, by Sir Donald Campbell, son of Sir Cailean Mor.

1322   Sir Arthur Campbell receives many lands in Lorne and Benderloch, including Dunstaffnage, for his services as Constable of Dunstaffnage Castle.

1324   Sir Dougall Campbell, son of Sir Cailean Mor, confirmed as Lord of Menstrie.

1329   Approximate date of creation of John Campbell, son of Sir Neil Campbell of Lochawe and Lady Mary Bruce, as Earl of Atholl.

1332   Balliol invades with help of English. Various Campbells change sides and are subsequently forfeited.

1333   Battle of Halidon Hill. Death of John Campbell, Earl of Atholl.

1334   Castle of Dunoon recovered from English. Keepership of the castle now hereditary in family of Campbells of Lochawe.

1343   Sir Colin Og is dead by May, succeeded by his son Gillespic or Archibald of Lochawe.

1346   Battle of Neville's Cross. Sir Andrew Campbell of Loudoun taken prisoner.

1369   Gillespic Campbell of Lochawe has charter from King David II confirming all former gifts of land, viz. Craignish, Melfort, Strachur, Upper Cowal and Kildalchane. 'We also confirm to the said Gillespic all the liberties and customs held and enjoyed by Duncan MacDuin, his late progenitor . . .'

1382   Gillespic Campbell of Lochawe together with his son, Colin, made hereditary Lieutenant of Argyll from Tyndrum to Loch Gilp and from Loch Melfort to Loch Long.

1394   Gillespic Campbell of Lochawe dead by this date. Succeeded by his son Colin Iongantach.

1414   Sir Duncan Campbell of Lochawe grants to Ronald of Craignish lands in Loch Avich together with the constabulary of the castles of Craignish and Loch Avich.

1422   Duncan Mor Campbell of Glenshira granted lands of Duntroon.

1423   Sir Duncan Campbell of Lochawe sent to England as hostage for the King's release.

1428   First mention of Colin Campbell, son of Colin Iongantach, as 'of Ardkinglas'.

1432   Colin, son of Sir Duncan, granted lands of Glenorchy.

1440   Death of Archibald Campbell, heir to Sir Duncan Campbell; buried at Kilmun.

1442   Sir Duncan founds the Collegiate Church of Kilmun, henceforth the burial place of the Campbell chiefs.

1445   Sir Duncan Campbell of Lochawe now created Lord Campbell.

1450 Approximate date of building of Kilchurn Castle.

1450 Approximate date of move to Inveraray.

1453 Death of Sir Duncan Campbell of Lochawe, Lord Campbell, succeeded by his grandson, Colin.

1457 Colin, 2nd Lord Campbell, created 1st Earl of Argyll.

1460 Sir Duncan Campbell at Siege of Roxburgh Castle with King James I.

1462 1st Earl of Argyll joint Justiciar of Scotland south of the Forth.

1464 1st Earl of Argyll created Master of the King's Household.

1465 1st Earl of Argyll marries Isobel Stewart, daughter of Lord of Lorne.

1470 1st Earl of Argyll, following deal with his wife's uncle, Walter Stewart of Innermeath, receives charter of Lordship of Lorne. Henceforth Earls known as Earl of Argyll, Lord Campbell and Lorne and galley quartered in arms.

1473 1st Earl of Argyll has grant of Keepership of Castle of Dunoon.

1473 1st Earl of Argyll has charter as Justiciar, Chamberlain, Sheriff and Bailie within King's lordship of Cowal.

1474 Erection of Inveraray into a Burgh of Barony.

1474 1st Earl of Argyll appointed with others as King's Lieutenant within Argyll, Lorne and Menteith.

1481 1st Earl of Argyll has charter as Keeper of Castle Sween.

1483 1st Earl of Argyll appointed Lord High Chancellor of Scotland.

1485 Reputed first mention of 'Campbell of Inverawe'.

1490 Name of Castle Gloom changed to Castle Campbell by Act of Parliament.

1493 Death of 1st Earl of Argyll, 10 May. Succeeded by his son, Colin as 2nd Earl.

1494 2nd Earl of Argyll has charter of the Castle of Gloom.

1499 2nd Earl of Argyll appointed Keeper of Tarbert Castle and Bailie of the Royal lands in Knapdale.

1499 Removal of Muriel of Cawdor for safe-keeping.

1501 Rescue of Donald Dubh from Innischonnell Castle.

1502 2nd Earl of Argyll granted Keepership of Castle of Skipness.

1504 2nd Earl of Argyll appointed King's Lieutenant within Argyll, Lorne, Knapdale, Kintyre, Discher and Toyer, Glenlyon and Balquhidder.

1502 Alexander 'Ciar' Campbell appointed Captain of Dunstaffnage.

1502 Sir Duncan Campbell of Glenorchy has grant from the King of lands of Glenlyon.

1510   Sir John Campbell, third son of 1st Earl of Argyll, marries Muriel, heiress of Cawdor.

1513   Death of 2nd Earl of Argyll, Sir Colin Campbell of Glenorchy and many other Campbells at Battle of Flodden.

Scottish Chronology

500   Traditional date of arrival of Scots from Ireland in Argyll.

565   Saint Columba, first Abbot of Iona, founds monastery.

762   Sacking of Scottish Capital at Dunadd by the Picts.

800   Sacking of Iona by the Norsemen in the first years of the ninth century.

843   Kenneth MacAlpine ascends throne of Picts as well as Scots.

1018   Battle of Carham.

1165   Death of Somerled at Renfrew.

1249   Death of King Alexander II on Kerrera.

1263   King Haakon of Norway's Expedition to settle question of the Isles.

1266   Treaty of Perth. The Isles to be Scottish.

1286   Death of King Alexander III. Succeeded by his granddaughter Margaret, 'The Maid of Norway'. Scotland ruled by six Guardians.

1290   Margaret dies at sea. Struggle over the succession commences.

1296   The signing of 'Ragman Roll'.

1297   English defeat at Battle of Stirling Bridge.

1305   Capture and execution of Sir William Wallace.

1306   Coronation of King Robert I at Scone.

1306   Bruce defeated at Methven. Skirmish at Dalrigh.

1308   Battle of the Pass of Brander.

1314   Battle of Bannockburn.

1318   Death of Edward Bruce at Dundalk.

1320   Declaration of Arbroath.

1329   Death of King Robert I. Succeeded by his son King David II.

1332   Invasion of Scotland by Edward Balliol.

1333   Scots defeated by English at Battle of Halidon Hill.

1346   King David taken prisoner at Battle of Neville's Cross.

1357   King David released from captivity in England.

1371   Death of King David II. Succeeded by his nephew Robert the Steward as King Robert II.

1388   Battle of Otterburn.

1390   Death of King Robert II. Succeeded by his son John, Earl of Carrick, as King Robert III.

1390 Burning of Elgin Cathedral by the 'Wolf of Badenoch'.

1396 The judicial Battle on the North Inch of Perth.

1406 Death of King Robert III. Succeeded by his third son King James I.

1406 Boy King James I taken prisoner by English while on way to refuge in France.

1411 Donald, Lord of the Isles, defeated at Battle of Harlaw.

1421 Franco-Scottish force under Earl of Buchan inflicts defeat on French at Bauge in France.

1424 King James I released from English captivity.

1425 Execution of Lennox and the Albany Stewarts. Escape of James Stewart 'the Fat'.

1427 Royal Expedition to the Isles. Summoning of Chiefs to Inverness and salutary executions.

1429 Lord of the Isles burns Inverness. Defeated by Royal Army. Submission of Lord of the Isles.

1431 Donald Balloch MacDonald defeats Royal Army at Inverlochy.

1437 Assassination of King James I. Succeeded by his son as King James II.

1452 Killing of Earl of Douglas by King James II at Stirling Castle.

1460 Death of King James II through bursting of a gun at siege of Roxburgh Castle. Succeeded by his son as King James III.

1462 Treaty of Westminster–Ardtornish between Lord of the Isles, Douglas and King Henry VI.

1475 Expedition against Lord of the Isles, who is defeated. Now left as a Lord in Parliament as Lord of the Isles, having lost Earldom of Ross, Knapdale and Kintyre.

1488 Death of King James III following Battle of Sauchieburn. Succeeded by his son as King James IV.

1493 Forfeiture of Lordship of the Isles.

1513 King James IV killed with many of his nobles at Battle of Flodden.

Early Campbell Relationships

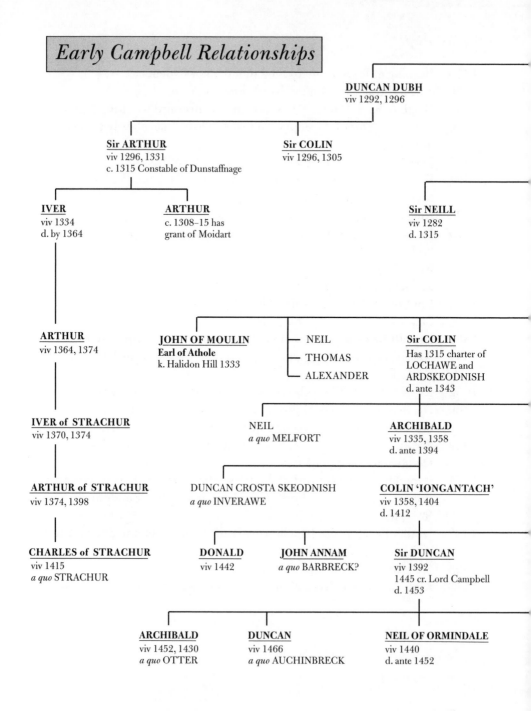

DUNCAN DUBH
viv 1292, 1296

Sir ARTHUR
viv 1296, 1331
c. 1315 Constable of Dunstaffnage

Sir COLIN
viv 1296, 1305

IVER
viv 1334
d. by 1364

ARTHUR
c. 1308–15 has
grant of Moidart

Sir NEILL
viv 1282
d. 1315

ARTHUR
viv 1364, 1374

JOHN OF MOULIN
Earl of Athole
k. Halidon Hill 1333

NEIL
THOMAS
ALEXANDER

Sir COLIN
Has 1315 charter of
LOCHAWE and
ARDSKEODNISH
d. ante 1343

IVER of STRACHUR
viv 1370, 1374

NEIL
a quo MELFORT

ARCHIBALD
viv 1335, 1358
d. ante 1394

ARTHUR of STRACHUR
viv 1374, 1398

DUNCAN CROSTA SKEODNISH
a quo INVERAWE

COLIN 'IONGANTACH'
viv 1358, 1404
d. 1412

CHARLES of STRACHUR
viv 1415
a quo STRACHUR

DONALD
viv 1442

JOHN ANNAM
a quo BARBRECK?

Sir DUNCAN
viv 1392
1445 cr. Lord Campbell
d. 1453

ARCHIBALD
viv 1452, 1430
a quo OTTER

DUNCAN
viv 1466
a quo AUCHINBRECK

NEIL OF ORMINDALE
viv 1440
d. ante 1452

Legend:
NAME historical reference.
NAME as per Scots Peerage.
NAME as per other sources.

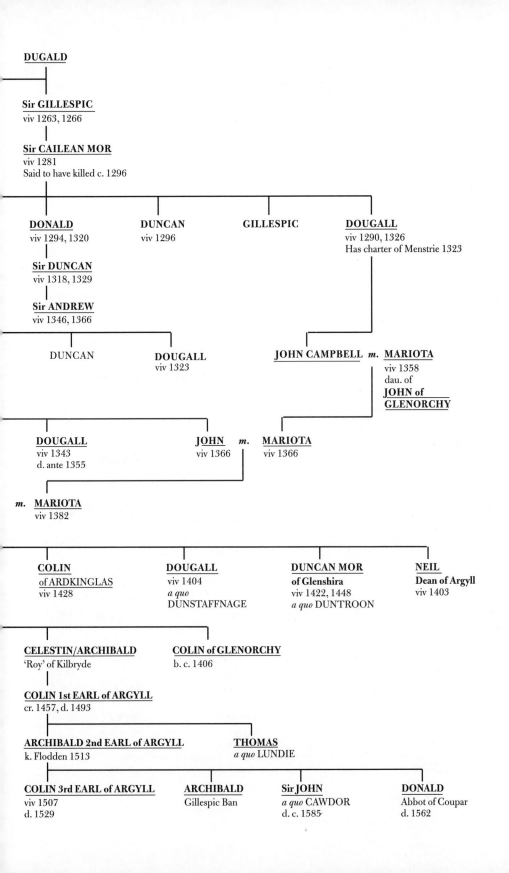

DUGALD

Sir GILLESPIC
viv 1263, 1266

Sir CAILEAN MOR
viv 1281
Said to have killed c. 1296

DONALD
viv 1294, 1320

DUNCAN
viv 1296

GILLESPIC

DOUGALL
viv 1290, 1326
Has charter of Menstrie 1323

Sir DUNCAN
viv 1318, 1329

Sir ANDREW
viv 1346, 1366

DUNCAN

DOUGALL
viv 1323

JOHN CAMPBELL *m.* **MARIOTA**
viv 1358
dau. of
JOHN of GLENORCHY

DOUGALL
viv 1343
d. ante 1355

JOHN *m.* **MARIOTA**
viv 1366   viv 1366

m. **MARIOTA**
viv 1382

COLIN
of ARDKINGLAS
viv 1428

DOUGALL
viv 1404
a quo
DUNSTAFFNAGE

DUNCAN MOR
of Glenshira
viv 1422, 1448
a quo DUNTROON

NEIL
Dean of Argyll
viv 1403

CELESTIN/ARCHIBALD
'Roy' of Kilbryde

COLIN of GLENORCHY
b. c. 1406

COLIN 1st EARL of ARGYLL
cr. 1457, d. 1493

ARCHIBALD 2nd EARL of ARGYLL
k. Flodden 1513

THOMAS
a quo LUNDIE

COLIN 3rd EARL of ARGYLL
viv 1507
d. 1529

ARCHIBALD
Gillespic Ban

Sir JOHN
a quo CAWDOR
d. c. 1585

DONALD
Abbot of Coupar
d. 1562

Comparative Table of Genealogies[1]

MS 1467	Kilbride MS	MacFirbis	Neil MacEwan	Ane Accompt
God	God			
Adam	Adam			*
Constantine	Constantine		Constantine	
Ambrose	Ambrose		Ambrose	
Uther Pendragon			Uther Pendragon	
Arthur	Arthur	Arthur	Arthur	Arthur
Smeirbi	Mervin	Smeirbi	Smervius	Smerevie
Eiranaid or Feradoig	Feradach	Feradoig	Ferither	Ferither Or
Duine	Duino	Duibne	Duinus magnus	Duibne Mor
			Arthur yr	Arthur Og
			Ferither Fion	Ferither
			Duine Tailderbus[2]	Duine Falt Dhearg
			Ferither Fionrua	Ferither Finruo
			Diarmid O'Duin	Duibne Dearg
			Duine Dedalus	Duibne Donn
Gillacolaim mic Duibne	Malcolm	Malcolm	Gilcalombus O'Duin	Diarmid O'Duine
				Duibne
	Duncan	Duncan		Malcolm
Gillespie	Gillespie	Eoghan	Archibald O'Duin *alias* Campbell	Archibald
			Colin Milma[3]	
			Archibald	
Dunnchach			Duncan[4]	Duncan
				Colin
				Gillespic
				Duncan
Dubgaill Cambeul	Dugall	Dugald	Dugald	Dougald
Gillespic	Gillespic	Gillespic	Archibald	Gillespic[5]
Cailin Moir	Cailein Mor	Colin	Colin jr	Colin Mor
down to	*down to*		*down to*	*down to*
Sir Colin Oig	*2nd Earl*		*9th Earl*	*5th Duke*

1. From Arthur onwards.
2. Said to be first Knight of Lochawe.
3. Said to be father of Tavis and Iver.
4. Said to be father of Ewan *a quo* Craignish.
5. Said to be father of Dougald *a quo* Craignish.
* intervening generations omitted

Introduction and Acknowledgements

This is the first of three projected volumes covering the history of Clan Campbell. It is the first time that an attempt has been made to cover the subject in some depth, and most of my friends on hearing of it have shaken their heads in sympathy and dismay.

This is not unjustified; it is an immense undertaking and it becomes quite plain why nothing quite like this has been done before. Starting from a small beginning, the story of Clan Campbell becomes inexorably intertwined not only with the story of Scotland but also, in due course, with that of the United Kingdom and of the British Empire, to say nothing of the United States of America.

A large number of people deserve thanks for their help. First of all are the Clan Campbell Educational Association in the United States who have funded the project, thanks to the generosity of many subscribers from around the world who include a number who are not themselves Campbells. Colonel Joe Campbell and his committee have spared no effort in getting the work started and in supporting it in every way.

I am much in the debt of our Chief, who, along with the late Hugh Moore, is ultimately responsible for making this whole thing possible. I have spent thirteen remarkable years working at Inveraray among the wonderful collection of archives there and have been allowed to make full use of them in this work.

And I would especially like to pay tribute to that remarkable scholar Niall, 10th Duke of Argyll, who spent a lifetime among his family papers and who, in particular, produced the fascinating series of *Argyll Transcripts* which shed so much light on the history of Clan Campbell. The late Sir Iain Moncreiffe of that Ilk, in the preface to his *The Highland Clans*, wrote of how he had visited Inveraray in the time of the present Duke's father where he had seen Duke Niall's work. 'Everything was unfinished and unpublished. It all seemed such a waste . . .'

As a small boy during the Second World War, I remember several visits to Inveraray and the old Duke who gave us tea in the present Armoury Hall which was then his sitting room and much cluttered. The great game was to point to one of the many, varied musical instruments hanging on the wall along with a fascinating mixture of weapons and ask 'Please Duke, blow that trumpet'. The old man, with great good humour, would climb upon a chair to unhook the instrument, out of which he would then produce a resounding blast. I hope he would approve of what has been written here in which his work has played a notable part.

Among many, I must also particularly thank three distinguished leading historians of today. Jean and Billy Munro and David Sellar, to whom, over the years, I have always turned in moments of stress, have been good enough to spend long hours going through this volume – just how long I hate to think, but I am immeasurably grateful to them for their kindness and hard work and for all their corrections and good advice. With all its faults, this book is very much better thanks to them than it would otherwise have been.

My thanks also go to the Royal Commission on the Ancient and Historical Monuments of Scotland (RCAHMS) for the outstanding photographs I have been lucky enough to have been allowed to cull from their archives.

I have been very lucky to have had so much help and support from knowledgeable Campbells on both sides of the Atlantic. Over the years, I have received an invaluable store of information from Dr Lorne Campbell, without doubt the greatest of a long line of Campbell genealogists. In the USA, Kenn Campbell of Baton Rouge has produced outstandingly professional maps, while I owe my cousin Diarmid Campbell, himself no mean historian, many thanks for much ongoing support.

We are very lucky in Argyll with the number of local sennachies we have; my thanks to Rae MacGregor who has assisted me in the Argyll archives over the years and whose store of local knowledge is unmatched, to Duncan Beaton, to Iain MacDonald, Clachan, and to the late Iain Stewart, Campbeltown, as well as to Angus McLean, late of Dunoon, all of whom have shared much detailed knowledge with me, as has Ian Fisher of RCAHMS, whose knowledge is encyclopaedic.

There are so many others: Professor Allan MacInnes of Aberdeen University, and Dr Jane Dawson with whom I have over the years enjoyed many useful discussions; Kenneth Nicholls of University College, Cork, who has provided much fascinating insight into the Irish dimension; Dr Steve Boardman, whose forthcoming study of the Campbells in medieval times is eagerly awaited and who has been very kind to me; Linda Fryer; Nicholas Maclean-Bristol, who has mingled great hospitality with his deep knowledge of Highland and Island history, both dispensed from his magnificently restored island castle in Coll – the list could go on and on. So many people have helped in one way or another; their names are not all here, but I would like them to know, one and all, how very grateful indeed I am.

One question I have been repeatedly asked is 'who is this book being written for?' It does not claim to be, nor is it intended as, an academic work, although I would hope it is an accurate one. Nor is it a 'pop' history replete with waving banners and gory details beloved of the tourist market. It is a serious and, I hope, readable attempt to tell all those who belong to the Clan Campbell – very many of them not called Campbell, as the book makes clear, but members of the clan no less – something of the deeds of their ancestors and to enable them to undertake more study in depth in areas which are of particular interest to them. I hope this interest will also apply to the many across Scotland whose forebears came into contact, comfortable or otherwise, with the Campbells.

It would be idle to pretend that such encounters were always pleasurable ones. I have been constantly warned against writing a partisan history. I am very sensitive to such an implied correction, since, for the last twelve generations of the Campbells of Airds, eight of the twelve have married other Campbells, my father and I being among the number; but I fully intend to tell the story 'warts and all'. I shall also do my best to restrain my pride in belonging to a truly remarkable clan, but cannot resist recounting the local tradition of the old woman in Inveraray who, on being told of the engagement of Queen Victoria's daughter, Princess Louise, to the Marquess of Lorne, remarked 'Och, it's a prood wumman the Queen'll be the day, wi' her dochter gettin' mairrit on the son of Mac Cailein Mor!'

It is often the custom, I have noticed, for the author to end these introductory remarks by thanking his wife for mowing the lawn while his book was being written. There are still another four years of this project to go, and I would like to thank her for hiring someone to do the job for her.

ALASTAIR CAMPBELL OF AIRDS
Unicorn Pursuivant of Arms

Inverawe Barn, Argyll

June 1999

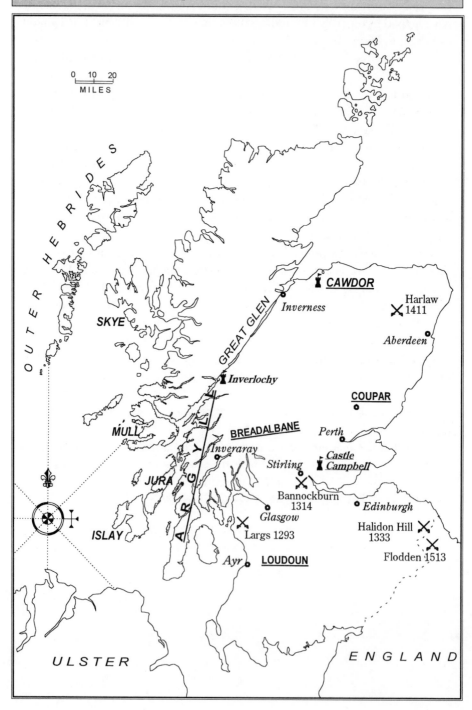

Map One: SCOTLAND

0   10   20
MILES

OUTER HEBRIDES

SKYE

GREAT GLEN

✠ CAWDOR

Inverness

Harlaw
✗ 1411

Aberdeen

✠ Inverlochy

MULL

BREADALBANE

COUPAR
◦

Perth
◦

Inveraray

Castle
✠ Campbell

JURA

Stirling

✗

Glasgow
◦

Bannockburn
1314

◦ Edinburgh

Largs 1293

Halidon Hill ✗
1333

✗

ISLAY

✗

Ayr ◦   LOUDOUN

Flodden 1513

ULSTER

ENGLAND

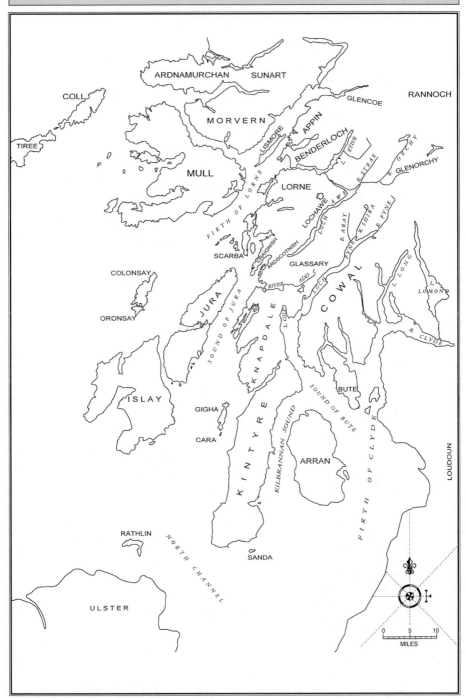

COLL

TIREE

ARDNAMURCHAN   SUNART

RANNOCH

GLENCOE

MORVERN   APPIN

BENDERLOCH

LISMORE

MULL

L. ETIVE

R. STRAE

R. ORCHY

GLENORCHY

FIRTH OF LORNE

LORNE

LOCHAWE

LOCH AWE

R. ARAY

R. SHIRA

R. FYNE

LOCH FYNE

SCARBA

CRAIGNISH

ARDSCOTNISH

GLASSARY

L. LONG

COLONSAY

JURA

RIVER   ADD

LOCH

L. GILP

COWAL

L. LOMOND

R. CLYDE

ORONSAY

SOUND OF JURA

KNAPDALE

BUTE

ISLAY

GIGHA

CARA

SOUND OF BUTE

KINTYRE

KILBRANNAN SOUND

ARRAN

FIRTH OF CLYDE

LOUDOUN

RATHLIN

NORTH CHANNEL

SANDA

ULSTER

0   5   10

MILES

COLL

TIREE

MACDONALD

M A C L E A N

MORVERN

MULL

MACLEAN

CAMERON

Inverlochy

MACDONALDS

STEWART

MACINTYRE

MACGREGOR

Oban
MACDOUGALL

MACARTHUR
M'CORQUODALE

LORNE

C A M P B E L L

MACNAUGHTON

MACFARLANE

Inveraray

COLONSAY

MACFIE

ORONSAY

MACLACHLAN

MACTAVISH

C O W A L

COLQUHOUN

MACEWANS

L A M O N T

JURA

MACNEIL

Loch Fyne

MACMILLAN

STEWART
Glasgow

BUTE
STEWART

MACDONALD

MACKAY

ISLAY

GIGHA

CARA

MACNEIL

MACALLISTER

MACKAY

ARRAN

CAMPBELL

MACDONALD

K I N T Y R E

Campbeltown

RATHLIN

MACEACHERN

SANDA

MACDONALD

ULSTER

0   5   10
MILES

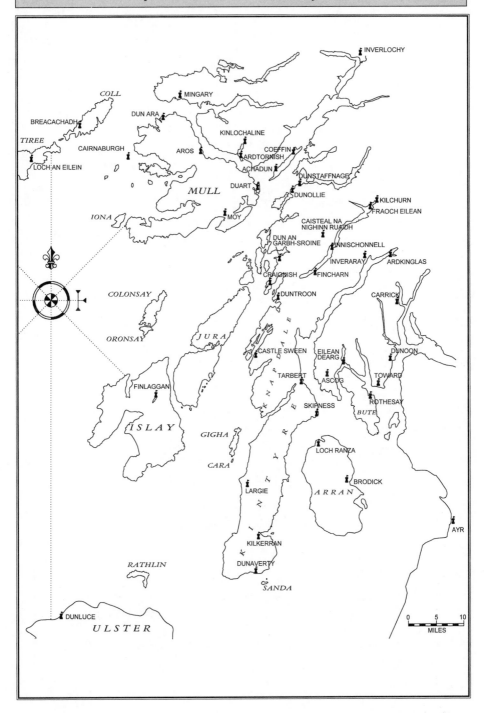

Map Four: *ARGYLL: castles by 1513*

INVERLOCHY

COLL

MINGARY

DUN ARA

BREACACHADH

KINLOCHALINE

TIREE

CAIRNABURGH

AROS

COEFFIN

ARDTORNISH

LOCH AN EILEIN

ACHADUN

DUNSTAFFNAGE

DUART

MULL

DUNOLLIE

KILCHURN

FRAOCH EILEAN

IONA

MOY

CAISTEAL NA
NIGHINN RUAIDH

DUN AN
GARBH-SROINE

INNISCHONNELL

INVERARAY

ARDKINGLAS

CRAIGNISH

FINCHARN

COLONSAY

DUNTROON

CARRICK

ORONSAY

JURA

CASTLE SWEEN

EILEAN
DEARG

DUNOON

FINLAGGAN

K
N
A
P
D
A
L
E

TARBERT

ASCOG

TOWARD

ROTHESAY

SKIPNESS

BUTE

ISLAY

GIGHA

CARA

LOCH RANZA

BRODICK

K
I
N
T
Y
R
E

LARGIE

ARRAN

AYR

RATHLIN

KILKERRAN

DUNAVERTY

SANDA

DUNLUCE

ULSTER

0   5   10
MILES

Map Five: NORTH ARGYLL

COLL

Breagacha

Dun Ara

Cairnaburgh

LUNGA

BAC
MOR

STAFFA

ULVA

IONA

COLONSAY

Mingary

MORVERN

Kinlochaline

Ardtornish

Aros

Sound of Mull

MULL

Duart

Moy

Firth of Lorne

LUING

SCARBA

JURA

Glen Coe

Loch Linnhe

Duror

APPIN

Castle
Coeffin

Loch Leven

Ardchattan
Priory

BENDERLOCH

Glenoe

BEN CRUACHAN

Kilburn

Fraoch Eilean

1308

Inverawe

Loch Nell

Torrinturk

Kilchrenan

Loch Awe

Achadun

Dunstaffnage

Dunollie

KERRERA

Oban

Degnish

Glenfeochan

Kilninver

Scammadale

Ardmaddy

Kilmelfort

Lerags

Carn Chailein

Innverinan

Sonachan

Innischonnell

Caisteal na
Nighinn
Ruaidhe

Dun an
Garbh-Sroine

Bartbreck

Ederline

Craignish

Duntroon

Dunadd R.

Kilmichael
Glassary

Inveraray

Ardverliever

Fincharn

PPV

Dundarave

Ardinglas

Carrick

Strachur

Castle
Lachlan

Loch Fyne

MILES

0   5   10

Map Six: MID ARGYLL and COWAL

Arrochar

Glen Croe

Ardkinglas

Dundarave

L. Goil

Loch Long

R. Clyde

Rosneath

Ardgarten (Gairnan)

Carrick

Blaitmore

Kilmun

Largs
1263

Innischonnell

Strachur

L. Eck

Stratbeck

Dunoon

Firth of Clyde

Inveraray

Fyne

Cruachan

Fincharn

Castle
Lachlan

Glendaruel

Auchenbreck

Ardlamont

L. Striven

Rothesay

BUTE

Dun an
Garbh-Sroine

Barrichbeyan

Bennan

Kilmartin

Torbhlaren

Kilmichael
Glassary

Ormidale

Otter

Loch Fyne

Skipness

Corivarow

Craignish

Duntroon

Poltalloch

Dunadd

Crinan

Oib

Dunardry

Learg na benison

Inverneill

Tarbert

K N A P D

Tayvallich

Castle
Sween

Keills

Danna

JURA

SCARBA

COLONSAY

ISLAY

Sound of Jura

R. Add

0   5   10

MILES

Map Seven: *GLENORCHY and BREADALBANE*

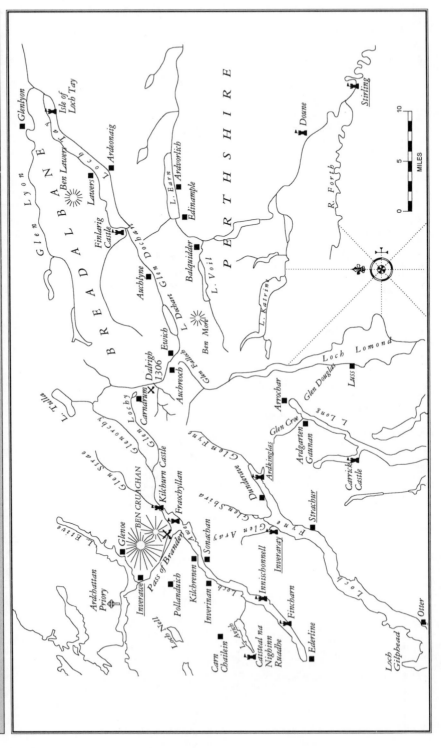

CHAPTER ONE

Out of the Mists

Beginning the story of Clan Campbell is not easy. There is no obvious starting point, there are a number of conflicting versions of our origins and there is a great deal more mythical legend than hard, historical fact. In this we are not alone; indeed, we fall in alongside most families. All that can be done is to try and trace the way and the reasons for which the genealogies were assembled and deduce what we can from them.

Pedigree has always been important to the Celts. When, in 1249, during the ceremony of Alexander III's inauguration as King of Scots, an old man with a flowing white beard, and clad in a long red robe, stepped forward and in sonorous tones declaimed the King's descent in Gaelic, he was carrying out a tradition which was already many centuries old. He was the Royal Sennachie, a role which has carried on to today in the person of the Lord Lyon King of Arms. Descent mattered, throughout society.

At the highest level, of important Chief or local King, it was necessary to be a member of the *derbhfine*, the inner family, from which the Chief was chosen by his predecessor during the former's lifetime, or, if for some reason that was impossible, elected by his peers. The *derbhfine* can be defined as the palm of the hand representing the common ancestor in the male line, with the segments of the fingers representing the generations who qualified as potential candidates – in other words, those who along with the ruling King or Chief claimed descent from a common great-grandfather. The fifth generation would fall outside this definition and could each start the process again on their own.

The system had its advantages as well as its drawbacks. While the Kingdom or the Clan would be more likely to have the best leader, competition for the position of *tanist* or appointed heir was intense and could lead to bloodshed and unrest. Succession was not from father to son but from uncle to nephew or from cousin to cousin, a fact which is of great importance when we come to consider the traditional genealogies.

All this older system was altered by the arrival of feudalism with its emphasis on primogeniture, the succession in each generation by the eldest lawful son. Introduced into England by the Normans, the system spread quickly into Lowland Scotland. Its progress into the Highlands was more gradual and is impossible to date, since it occurred in some areas before others. In fact, the two systems merged without too much trouble, with the basis of the social structure in the Lowlands feudal and that of the Highlands still based on the old, Celtic system. As Professor T. C. Smout, the Historiographer Royal, has put it, 'Highland society was based on kinship modified by feudalism, Lowland society on feudalism tempered by kinship.'[1] In fact, there was no definite changeover between the two systems, and in certain circumstances, when the eldest son was thought to be inadequate, even though the feudal system of succession had long been the normal one, the old system was preferred.

There are a number of complications which stem from the above in the interpretation of early pedigrees as we have them today. Because of the *derbhfine* system's replacement by feudalism with its insistence on primogeniture, the old pedigrees had to show the chief as descending from an unbroken line of chiefs – which, with the system of tanistry, just did not happen. There was also the problem of the incoming husband – a theme which went right back at least as far as the merging of the Pictish and Scottish thrones. Various theories have accounted for the apparent disappearance of the Pictish nobility; but, if the Picts had a matrilinear system of descent – reckoning through the mother rather than the father – then the marrying of Pictish heiresses by Scottish incomers with their system of patrilinear descent would produce a takeover of the old Pictish chiefdoms within a generation. But in certain cases it could be the mother's claim of descent that was the important one, and the differing male line had to be excused and accounted for. This is less bloodthirsty and more likely than the tale of the great feasting arranged by King Kenneth for the Pictish nobility, who each had a Scottish aristocrat standing behind them to minister to their every want. At a given signal, the Scots stepped forward and slit the throats of their unwitting guests.

Since then, there have been many examples of the usurping incomer. Many Highland Clans as we know them today have chiefs and names which are clearly foreign to the region in which they have their *duthus* or homeland; Chisholm and Gordon, to name but two, take their names from properties in the Borders and are probably of English (that is to say, Northumbrian) origin, while Murray descends from a Fleming, and Lamont and MacLachlan from an Irish incomer long after the arrival of the Scots in Dalriada in

AD 500. Yet all are clans which have long been based in their homelands. These interlopers, too, have presented problems to the Clan genealogist who has been concerned to present the Chief in the best possible light – as the descendant of a long and unbroken line of chiefs from father to son.

So it is that any genealogy which goes back earlier than the confirmation offered by contemporary written record has to be treated with considerable care, not to say distrust. On the other hand, they can be taken in broad terms to give general indications, but the detail should be treated with caution, and any attempt at detailed analysis is likely to be positively misleading.

The descent of the Campbell Chiefs has always given rise to a degree of uncertainty. This has been compounded by periods when certain descents were in fashion and by the political need for the Campbells to assert their authority in the region in which their power was based by claiming long descent from the ancient possessors of the soil there. So it is not altogether surprising that as far as the Campbells are concerned there seem to be three main theories, giving the name an early Irish origin, a Continental one and a descent from the Britonnic Celts of Strathclyde – the Ancient Britons. In order to achieve the maximum acceptability, all three strands are included in the 'official' version of the Campbell descent.

To this day, each has its uncritical supporters. In the main, this is due to modern writers merely copying the work of others without any critical appraisal, the version repeated depending purely by chance on which source they have come across. There is definite opportunity for confusion, since earlier authorities were by no means unanimous on the question. Douglas in his *Peerage of Scotland* is typical. Asserting that the name Campbell is 'of very great antiquity in Scotland', he then quotes Camden (origin with the ancient Kings of Argyll around the sixth century), Martin (French origin) and the Bards and Sennachies (in Argyll prior to 404 and descended from Diarmid O'Duine).[2]

More recently, Skene printed one of the reputed Irish genealogies back to the mythical Fergus Leith Dearg without comment, but his subsequent editor, Alexander Macbain, while admitting the popularity of the Norman theory, rebuts it in favour of an early origin based on the district of Garmoran, the area lying to the north of the modern county of Argyll.[3] Sir Thomas Innes of Learney, the late, great Lord Lyon, is hardly clearer: he gives Diarmid O'Dhuine as the generally accepted founder of the clan, with the heiress Eva marrying the first Campbell, to whom she brings the chiefship of the tribe.[4] The eighth Duke of Argyll had a slightly different idea: 'the purely Celtic family from which I am descended – a family of Scoto-Irish origin – that is to say, belonging to that Celtic colony from Ireland which founded the

Dalriadic Kingdom, and to whom the name of Scots originally and exclusively belonged.'[5]

The theory of a Norman descent is based on the claimed existence of a family by name of *de Campo Bello*, so-called from the Latin for 'of the Beautiful Plain'. *Campo bello* of course becomes Campbell, and, if transposed into Norman French, the name becomes *Beauchamp*, the same family as the Earls of Warwick who are also said to bear the same arms – the gyronny of eight – as borne by the Campbells. This theory can be dismissed on a number of grounds. The letter 'p' necessary to produce *de Campo Bello* is a later intrusion: all the early charters spell the name *Cambel*, and the 'p' does not appear until the fifteenth century. The name *de Campo Bello* seems to have eluded the attention of historians, although the name of *de Bello Campo* does appear. The earlier Beauchamps or the later Earls of Warwick, however, do not appear to have ever used the gyronny of eight, as has been claimed, as their coat of arms in any form. The theory of a Continental origin does have its adherents even today. The author has been told by one noted writer of historical novels that she has found irrefutable proof in French local archives of the Campbells originating in Normandy from the family named *de Campville*. Her opinions were unshakeable.

Equally strong, if on a rather different tack, is Mrs Beryl Platts, who claims a Flemish origin for the clan. She has produced three thought-provoking books on the links between Scotland and the Flemish which latter, she claims with some justification, have been underestimated by historians in favour of the Normans. Certainly a large number of distinguished Scottish Chiefs can be seen to derive from Flanders in the male line, but the use of heraldry as a main argument as propounded by Mrs Platts can be a dangerous game. Heraldry is hardly prime evidence but is nonetheless useful as circumstantial evidence – if not as to who people actually were, then at least to who they thought they were or who they would have liked to be.

Mrs Platts is firmly of the opinion that the Campbells are of Flemish origin. Her theory appears to be largely based on the Campbells' use of the *gyronny* – the heraldic coat used by the rulers of Flanders prior to their adoption of the Lion rampant – and on their early use of the name Archibald which, as *Erkenbald*, is claimed to be of Flemish origin. Archibald, as the Scots have it, for whatever reason, was taken to be the English version of the old Gaelic name Gillespic, 'Servant of the Bishop'.[6] This is thin stuff. No one nation, let alone a single family, however exalted, can claim to be the exclusive originator of such a basic coat as the gyronny and the earliest mentions of a Campbell give the name Gillespic rather than Archibald. But it does show how even today fresh theories are being put forward.

The Irish version – so-called because the Britons are also Celts – is in fact not one but several based on various versions put forward by the early Irish genealogists whose job, it would seem, was as much to produce lineages going back to Adam via all the most desirable figures of myth and legend as it was to produce reliable fact. No attempt will be made here to list all the various versions or to disinter what scraps of truth they may or may not contain. A further Irish complication is the existence of a famous war-leader named *Cathmhaoil* who gave his name to his descendants, who styled themselves *MacCathmhaoil*. The *Mac*-prefix was often dropped and the name *Cathmhaoil* was pronounced 'Cammle', as was the Scottish surname 'Campbell'. From the Irish surname a whole list of other variants derives, including such names as MacCawill, MacCavill, MacCowell, MacCall, MacCallion and even, on occasion, Caulfield.

Hence, it has to be pointed out, a considerable number of Campbells in Ireland have nothing to do with the Campbells in Argyll but come from a totally different stock. The Campbells of Tyrone are supposed to be of this alien descent. This would seem to be a plausible story; it would provide an entirely credible origin for the surname MacCampbell and also tie in with the apparently prevalent use of the name *Mac Calein* for Campbells who later went to Ireland as mercenaries and who wished to avoid confusion over their antecedents.

One popular Irish ancestor is 'Diarmid O'Dhuine', the mythical Fingalian hero of song and story who was a leader of one of the war-bands of youths called the *Fianna* under the command of the ageing Finn Mac Cool. Their deeds formed the body of a cycle of great tales recounted in both Ireland and the Highlands which flowered between the twelfth and fifteenth centuries and which enjoyed universal popularity in an age when the recounting of such sagas provided much of the entertainment offered by the television set today. Diarmid falls in love with Finn's girlfriend Grainn, who persuades him to elope with her. Finn sends men after them, and for seven years they are on the run until Finn pardons them and they return. But Finn's forgiveness was not genuine, and at a great boar-hunt he engineers the death of Diarmid, whose death, it was prophesied, would be due to such an animal. So it fell out, according to the tale. Either the boar kills Diarmid in the chase or he is commanded by Finn to measure its length along its spine after it has fallen. Diarmid is bare-footed and the stiff hairs of the boar's hide penetrate and infect his foot so that he dies of poisoning.

As with all great romances of this sort, there are many variations. Its location is placed in various spots; one Irish version is that it was the great boar of Ben Bulben in County Sligo, while a solitary monolith near the north end of Loch Nell in Lorne in Argyll goes by the name of Diarmid's Pillar and is claimed to have been the place where Diarmid died. So, too, is Ben Tuirc, the Hill of the Boar, in Kintyre, while another, popular version has his death occurring at the mouth of Glen Shee in Perthshire. But there are all sorts of sinister undertones attached to Diarmid; he is sometimes called not 'son of Duin' but son of *Donn*, the God of the Dead; the boar that kills him is a supernatural one, as indeed it has to be, since Diarmid has eaten the berries of the tree of immortality and cannot be killed by normal means. The boar itself was once Diarmid's foster-brother.[7]

As mythical, probably, are the claims for a descent from Niall of the Nine Hostages, the first historically recorded King of Ireland, who reigned in the fifth century, and from Conn of the Hundred Battles, two virtually obligatory ancestors for anyone seeking status in the Gaelic world. Certainly, the Irish versions make up in quantity what they may lack in clarity; they are extremely confused, as scraps of descent have been inserted in a number of different genealogies. A more detailed analysis as to any historical truth they may contain is beyond the powers of this author, and it is to be doubted whether such a task is either possible or worthwhile.

But a third version of the Campbell origin exists, which derives us from the Ancient Britons. It appears in various forms at greater or lesser length and detail, but certain figures are always included, notably that of Arthur, who is further identified as Arthur of the Round Table, King of the Britons. What appears to be the earliest of various known versions of this particular Campbell pedigree is titled, from the supposed date of its compilation, either 'MS 1467' or 'MS 1450'. This is printed in Skene's *Celtic Scotland*, where it is included in a number of 'Legendary Descents of the Highland Clans, according to Irish MSS'.[8]

David Sellar, discussed below, is scathing about the form in which this pedigree has been edited, while indeed the mass of early genealogies held in Dublin remains as yet to be fully scrutinised and reported on by modern scholars. MS 1467 commences with the fabulous *Fergus Leith Dearg*, son of *Nemed*, who is said to have led the early settlement of Ireland. From him, it descends to Arthur. It appears to end with Colin, 1st Earl of Argyll who died in 1493, but it manages, rather oddly, to get confused by several details in the last few generations which should have been relatively well known.

The Kilbride MS, one of the collection of documents formerly in the possession of the learned family of MacLachlan of Kilbride and later acquired by the Highland Society of Scotland, is printed in the Iona Club's *Collectanea de Rebus Albanicis*, where it has been edited by Skene.[9] It, too, leads the Campbell ancestry back to *Fergus Leath Dearg*, the son of *Nemed* via his son *Briotan*. It is more ambitious, however, and continues back via Noah to Seth the son of Adam the Son of God. The last Campbell to be mentioned is the 2nd Earl of Argyll, who fell at Flodden in 1513.

It need hardly be said that the earliest generations of the pedigree are purely mythical and not to be taken seriously, tempting as this is to the over-enthusiastic roots-seeker. Some years ago, I was invited to address a genealogical society in Glasgow, where the question came up of my own family. I gave the details of my antecedents and was a little startled by the rejoinder 'And ye'll have paper to prove it?' from an elderly member obviously soured by the imaginative claims to ancient birth of her colleagues.

Such paper is *not* forthcoming on these earlier claimed generations, although one can highlight the name *Briotan*, eponymous (so it is claimed) of the British race, and also the repeated inclusion of Arthur in these and later pedigrees.

It was this pedigree which was claimed some years ago by an American family of Campbells who were able to trace their descent from one of the major branches and so back to the main stem. They produced for sale a chart, magnificently set out and with heraldic illumination, showing this descent, accompanied by a commentary which ends by apologising for the fact that not all historians appeared to be convinced of the authenticity of the earlier information it contained, 'but as this cost us three hundred dollars to obtain we think it must be true'. Alas, if it were only this easy! Arthur appears again in the fragmentary pedigree produced by the famous seventeenth century Irish genealogist, Dugald MacFirbis, who was doubtless drawing on earlier sources.[10]

Of some interest is the pedigree stated specifically to be that given by Neil MacEwan, last of the MacEwan hereditary bards and sennachies to the Campbell Chiefs. The version in the Scottish Record Office is clearly a later copy, but it is stated to be *ut Nigellus MacKewnius . . . fide digno tradidit* 'as Neil MacEwan handed down in all good faith'.[11] Neil was the last member of a well-known traditional learned family in Lorne. They were the MacEwans who held the lands of Kilchoan (on Loch Feochan, south of what is now Oban) for their services, firstly to the MacDougall Lords of Lorne and then to the Campbell chiefs. This family has nothing to do with the MacEwans of Otter on Loch Fyne, who descend from the marriage of Anrothan, a Prince of the O'Neills, to the local heiress of Cowal and Knapdale. The sennachie MacEwans may have been MacDougalls by origin, but, with their repeated use of the unusual name *Arne* or, more correctly, *Athairne*, it has been suggested that they are a branch of the old Irish bardic family of *O hEoghusa* or O'Hosey who also use the name (see Appendix 3, 'Septs'). Like many traditional skills in the Gaeltacht which guaranteed both a position in society and the means to support it, their knowledge had hitherto been transmitted orally from generation to generation. But the increasing use of the printed word was threatening to make them redundant, and, around 1650, Neil's traditional version of the pedigree was committed to paper.

His Campbell genealogy commences with Constantine, King of Britain and grandfather of King Arthur. It ends with Archibald, the son of the 9th Earl, in whose time the pedigree has been written, thereby confirming its date to before 1685 when the earl was executed. As can be seen by comparing the various versions, while the earlier generations down to Duine and the later generations from Dugald are the same, the order of some intervening names has been reversed and a further nine generations have been introduced, among them the name of Diarmid O'Duine, which has not occurred in the earlier versions. This adding of generations occurs frequently in these Highland pedigrees in their later stages of evolution as it becomes apparent that more names are required to produce some semblance of sufficient generations to fill the gap between the earlier and later figures that appear.

We now come to what has been widely accepted as the definitive version of the Campbell pedigree. It was printed in volume 2 of the Scottish History Society's *Highland Papers*, where it is explained by the original, anonymous author that he has drawn on the pedigree as transmitted by Neil MacEwan, to which has been added the work done by Mr Alexander Colvin, 'who was better read in the histories of Scotland and in the particular papers belonging to the family under consideration.[12] This version ends with the 9th Earl of Argyll. There is a broadly similar version ('MS B') with some added details which brings the story down to the year 1776, and the two have been put together with the editor noting differences between the earlier and later versions, to form what is entitled *Ane Accompt of the Genealogie of the Campbells*, the fullest version of the family's early descent. This document has been expertly dissected by the noted Highland historian David Sellar, whose article 'The Earliest Campbells: Norman, Briton or Gael?' is required reading for anyone seriously interested in the subject.[13]

The evolution of this pedigree is further clarified by another article in volume 4 of the Scottish History Society's *Miscellany* on 'The Manuscript History of Craignish', whose earlier generations follow the same line down to the arrival of Dougal, first of Craignish. Its author, Alexander Campbell, who was an advocate and brother of George Campbell of Craignish, also throws light on the evolution of *Ane Accompt*. Neil MacEwan, he says, was the last of his line, dying around 1650. His account was revised by Mr Alexander Colville, Laird of Blair in Fife, at the behest of the Marquess of Argyll between 1650 and 1660, the second edition being known as *Colville's Genealogie*. This work was then added to under the influence of the 9th Earl between 1670 and 1676 by Mr Robert Duncanson, a member of a family long in the service of the Campbell Chiefs, who was minister of Campbeltown at his death. His work, known as *Duncanson's Genealogie*, forms the earlier basis of *Ane Accompt* into which the later account of 1776 has been merged.[14]

Over the years, I have seen a number of versions of the descent of the Campbells which all appear to be based on copies of one of the above, any alterations being relatively minor. Very occasionally, I have come across wildly fanciful accounts, one such being the work of Captain John Campbell of Achalick, who was to help Lady Charlotte Campbell in her *History of the Clan* which was commenced in the first decade of the nineteenth century but remained uncompleted. Another more interesting variation, published in 1862, was written by Donald Campbell, formerly Lieutenant in the 57th Regiment and later a claimant to the Breadalbane title. He claims that the ancient seat of the Campbells was in Ayrshire, where they were known as *Clan Duibhnidh*. *Duibhnidh* or Duibhne himself was buried, he says, on the banks of the Stinchar near the village of Barr, at a spot called *Cill Duibhnidh*. He gives no source for this statement, which is interesting in that the Campbells have indeed long had links with that part of Scotland since before a branch of the chiefly family became possessors of Loudoun.[15]

The essentials of the genealogy in *Ane Accompt* are as follows.

Arthur was son to Uther, King of the Britons by Igerna, wife to Gothlois, Prince of Cornwall. By his second wife, Elisabeth, daughter to the King of France, Arthur was father to

Smerievore, who was 'lurking and unknown'. He is said to have been born in Dumbarton on the south side in the Red Hall or *Talla Dheirg*. He was a wild, undaunted person who went by the name of 'The Fool of the Forest'. Smerievore married a sister of Aidan, King of the Scots, and was father to

Fferrither Uor (*Odhar*; Gaelic for 'dun-coloured' or 'pale'), said to have married a daughter of the Duke of Valentia and to have been father to

Duibhnemore, who, by his wife, daughter to Duke Murdoch of Moray, was father to

Arthur Oig ('Young Arthur'), father of

Fferrither Ele (*Eile*; Gaelic for 'the other'), said to have married the daughter of Diarmid O'Dhuine 'who was a great man in Ireland' and to have fathered

Dhuibhne Faltdhearg ('Red-haired'), said to have married a grandchild of Niall of the Nine Hostages, King of Ireland (the author of the pedigree is worried by the few generations between Niall and Dhuibhne Faltdhearg's wife). Their son was

Fferrither Finruadh ('Whitish-red', presumed from the colour of his hair). His son was reckoned to be

Duibhne Dhearg ('Red'), whose son was reckoned to be *Duibhne Donn* ('Brown'). The author of the pedigree does not make a specific statement about a son of

Duibhne Donn, but merely follows on with

Diarmid O'Dhuine, 'a great and eminent person in Ireland', whose wife was Grainn, daughter to Cormac son of Art son of Conn of the Hundred Battles, through which connection the Campbells were descended from the O'Neills.

From Diarmid, the Campbells are known as *Siol Dhiarmaid*, 'The seed of Diarmid'.

His sons were *Arthur Armdhearg* and

Dhuine Deudgheal ('White-toothed'), father of

Gillocollum or *Malcom O'Duibhn*, who was married twice. The author of *Ane Accompt* thinks it probable that his first marriage was to Dirvail, daughter of the Lord of Carrick, by whom he had three sons, *Gilmorie*, *Corcarua* and *Duncan Drumanach*.

Gilmorie had a natural son called *Nachtan*, from whom descended the Clan MacNaughtan (MS B adds the McNicholls, MacNivens and MacKenrigs); from Corcarua came the Clan Uilin in Ireland, and from Duncan the Drummonds.

Malcom then went to Normandy, where he married the heiress of Beauchamps, or 'Campus Bellus' in Latin, who was the daughter of William the Conqueror's sister and hence his niece.

Malcom had two sons by this marriage. The first was *Dionysius* or *Duncan*, who stayed in France, where his offspring were called Beauchamps or Campbell. MS B adds further information and says

Duncan had three sons; the eldest stayed in France and was the ancestor of Maréchal Comte de Tallard; from the third descended Beauchamp Earl of Warwick in England.

Malcom's second son was

Gillespig or *Archibald*, said by some to have been an officer in William the Conqueror's army who came from France to Scotland and married *Evah*, daughter of *Paul oduibhn* and of the heiress of Lochawe (see below).

At this point, we return to Diarmid O'Duibn's other son.

Arthur Armdhearg ('Red-armoured') was the father of four sons. The first was *Sir Paul oduibhn*, the second was *Arthur Urchanach*, the third *Arthur Cruachan* who was Tutor to his niece Evah and Depute of Lorne for the King, and the fourth was *Arthur Andrairan*. This last had two sons, *Patrick Drynach* from whom descend the MacArthurs of Innistrynich on Lochawe, and *Duncan Darleith*, progenitor of the MacArthurs of Darleith in the Lennox, who took the name of their property as their designation.

Paul odhuibn married Marion, daughter of Godfred King of Man. He was known as *Paul an Sparain*, 'Paul of the Sporran', from his being Pursemaster or Treasurer to the King, whom the author reckons to have been King Malcolm Canmore or his father King Duncan. (King Duncan reigned 1034–40; King Malcolm from 1058–93. The author of the pedigree has excluded MacBeth on the grounds of his being a usurper.) Their only child was *Evah*, the heiress of Lochawe, who, as we have seen, married Gillespic Campbell on his return to Scotland. Gillespic was the first to use Campbell as a surname, deriving it from the lands (of *Campus Bellus*) inherited by his father on his marriage.

Gillespic was succeeded by *Duncan* who married *Dirvail*, daughter to *Dugal Mcffiachar*, Thane of Over Lochawe. Lochawe was divided into the three parts of Over, Middle and Nether, and by this marriage all became united into the Lordship of Lochawe which the Campbell chiefs used as a designation until they were 'made Earles'.

Colin Maol Mhath succeeded Duncan. He was married to the niece of King Alexander. As Thane of Argyll, says the author, he took part in an expedition against the Norsemen in the Western Isles with the Earls of Atholl, Carrick and March and 'the Thane of Lennox' around the year

1254. For his services he was given three rewards, the positions of Justice General, Master of the Household and Lieutenant of the Isles.

He had two illegitimate sons. *Taius Coir*, from whom descend the Clan Tavish Campbells and who took Cowal from the Lamonts, was one, and the other was *Iver*, whose mother was the daughter of *Swineruo*, owner of Castle Sween and Thane of Knapdale. From this union came the MacIver Campbells, numerous in Glassary and Craignish.

His legitimate son and successor was

Gillespic or *Archibald*, who had three sons, *Duncan*, *Donald Don* ('Brown') and *Dugald Craignish*, progenitor of the Campbells of Craignish.

Duncan, who succeeded his father, had one son,

Dugald, who married *Ffindoig* (in other versions, '*Findorg*' or '*Finuaill*'), daughter of Nachtan MacGillmorie, who was a cousin of his, being also descended from Malcom Oduibhn as we have seen. They had three sons, *Gillespie*, *Duncan Dubh* ('Black') and *Eun* or *Hugh* and one daughter called *More Maith* ('More the Good'). From the second son, Black Duncan, descended the Clan Arthur Campbells of Strachur and from the third, Hugh, the Campbells of Loudoun.

Dugald was succeeded by his eldest son

Gillespic. Gillespic is on documentary record, and with him the pedigree moves from the realms of myth into historical reality.

At this point it is worthwhile taking a look at the genealogy above, about which it is possible to make some general statements. The first thing is that this is in no way a genuine pedigree in detail, but rather an impressionist picture. That it cannot be taken literally is even more clearly revealed by the obvious additions which have been made to the earlier versions: another three generations have been introduced to the male line, and characters have been included who did not exist at the time. The basic story is consistent throughout with its mention of Arthur, King of the Britons. Arthur himself can be discarded – Arthur of the Round Table, that is. So much was written about this fabulous monarch and his knights that it is a surprise to learn that the evidence for his historical existence rests heavily on no more than one passing near-contemporary reference to a shadowy figure who, whatever he was, was no king but a military leader around AD 500. On his resistance to the Saxons was built the whole wonderful cycle of romances which we know so well but which were mere literary invention many centuries later.

The question has been raised of a descent from another Arthur, famous enough for his name to have been remembered; one possible contender is Arthur, son of King Aedan of the line of Fergus Mor, son of Erc, one of the founders of Scottish Dalriada.[16] This Arthur was killed in 596 in a battle with a Pictish tribe, the Miathi, his death foretold by Saint Columba. There were other early Arthurs in the sixth and seventh centuries – strong circumstantial evidence for a recent role model after whom they had been named. The name itself is a quintessentially Celtic one, deriving from *artos* (bear). It is used frequently by other families who hail from the Lennox, notably the Galbraiths and the MacArthurs of Darleith, and it was also taken, as we shall see, by at least one early branch of the Campbell stock.

Smerievore, the next generation in the pedigree, is an apparent reference to Merlin the magician, who also plays a major part in the Arthurian romances – but never as a son of Arthur, to whom he is always a father figure. His identity is revealed by the references to him as 'The Fool of the Forest' and by his frequenting *An Talla Dheirg* – the Red Hall, near Dumbarton. It is not my purpose to enter into the realm of Arthurian controversy, on which alone it would be possible to add volumes to the myriad already written; but suffice it to say it is suggested that the inclusion of these figures is symbolic rather than literal. What the pedigree appears to be indicating is that while the exact origin of the Campbells is unknown, it is definitely from Brittonic Strathclyde, and they are of aristocratic – perhaps Royal – stock.

Neil MacEwan's version introduces another key figure – also mythical. Diarmid O'Duine is a major figure in the Fingalian cycle of romances which were developed during the twelfth century. The story of his death has already been given above. The reasons for the introduction of Diarmid into the pedigree can only be cause for speculation. The pedigrees all included a '*Duine*', '*Duino*', '*Duibhne*' or whatever the spelling used further dignified in the later two versions as being 'the great'. In MS 1467, the words *a quo* ('from whom') indicate that it is from this person that the Campbells took their early style of the *Clan O'Duine*. The mythical Diarmid was styled 'Diarmid O'Duine', and it may well have been this coincidence which led to the addition of his name to the pedigree. As a hero of the most popular series of stories that circulated round the fireside, he would do the Campbell name little but good.

Other fringe figures have also escaped the notice of history; Fferither Or is said to have married the daughter of 'The Duke of Valentia', which, if true, would have brought a dash of Anglo-Saxon blood into the line. But the major introduction into the story by the author of *Ane Accompt* is that of *Paul an*

Sparain, 'Paul of the Sporran', so called, the author informs us, because of his post as 'Treasurer to the King'. But the evidence for Paul is unimpressive. No such figure appears in written record. The post of Treasurer with his by-name referring to a sporran implies the guarding of cash, which was hardly a major feature at a time when it was seldom used. Some 300 years later, there was, it is true, a family by the name of MacSporran who are supposed to have carried out this task for the Lords of the Isles; and the son of Suibhne, builder of Castle Sween in the twelfth century, was *Maolmuire an Sparain*.

Unknown at the Court of the King of Scots, and before the emergence of Somerled, the only other likely court at which Paul could have gained his name would seem to have been that of the Norse ruler of Man and the Isles. Paul it seems, according to the story, was indeed the Knight of Lochawe and father of a daughter Evah, who marries her second cousin Gillespic or Archibald. Gillespic is the son of Malcolm O'Duine, who has been to France, where he marries William the Conqueror's niece, who is the heiress of Beauchamp. This convoluted relationship seems to have two main purposes: to allow the introduction of the de Campo Bello story (in the MacEwan version it is merely said that Archibald 'returned from France') and to deal with the question of the inheritance of the Lordship of Lochawe by marriage. For some reason, the compiler of the pedigree seems to think that the gaining of the Lordship of Lochawe by marriage was in some way less dignified than it might be and so we have this addition by which Evah the heiress is herself shown to be the heiress not only of the Lordship of Lochawe but also of the senior line of the family from which her husband himself comes. There is no explanation, if this is so, as to how the O'Duine line first obtained Lochawe, but the situation has changed: no longer is it a newly acquired possession due to inheritance by marriage, but it has already been in the family for generations past.

There is an interesting comment on this marriage in Alexander Macbain's edition of Skene's *The Highlanders of Scotland* which it is perhaps worth repeating

> While they say that their ancestor was a Norman de Campo Bello, they add that he acquired his Argyllshire property by marriage with the daughter and heiress of Paul O'Duin, Lord of Lochow. This story is so exactly similar to those in the other clans, where the oldest cadet had usurped the chiefship, that it leads to the suspicion that the same circumstance must have given rise to it among the Campbells. We have shewn it to be invariably the case, that when a clan claims a foreign origin, and accounts for their possession of the chiefship and property

of the clan by a marriage with the heiress of the old proprietors, they can be proved to be in reality a cadet of that older house who had usurped the chiefship, while their claim to the chiefship is disputed by an acknowledged descendant of that older house ... and the MacArthur Campbells of Strachur, the acknowledged descendants of the older house, have at all times disputed the chiefship with the Argyll family.[17]

While, as we shall see, Skene was in all probability correct as to the seniority by birth of the Strachur branch, they had not yet split from the common stem, so his comment is superfluous. Also, the reading of the pedigree is surely the exact contrary to what he says: there is no proof to support the idea that Paul an Sparain was the Chief and that the Lordship of Lochawe was previously in the family. Everything points the other way in this instance at least: the Campbells are incomers who have married a local heiress and thereby gained her local inheritance. And whatever the inheritance was, splitting it into two, thus necessitating two marriages before the whole of Lochawe is included in the Chief's property, seems to be an unlikely addition to the tale. The introduction meanwhile of the significantly named *Evah* or Eve, the ultimate symbolic name for a female, made possible the claim that the Campbells had been on Lochaweside since the dawn of time, which they clearly had not.

Although it can be little more than speculation, my suggestion would be that Evah and her father never existed and that there was only one marriage, the other heiress being Dervail MacFiachar. Again, the case for her is shadowy – we are reliant on tradition and on intelligent use of circumstantial evidence. According to the woodman John Dewar, collecting his local tales in the mid-nineteenth century, the MacFiachars themselves claimed descent from Niall of the Nine Hostages. It was a member of the family who is said to have built the Castle of the Red-haired Maiden – *Caisteal na Nighinn Ruaidhe* – on Loch Avich.[18] We will be returning later to this castle, which was definitely an early family possession for which the story of Dirvail's marriage gives an entirely credible *raison d'être*.

There is one other subject of interest which may also fit the picture. Successive Campbell Chiefs have always considered themselves to be hereditary 'Knights of Lochawe'. No such rank as 'hereditary' knighthood exists in the British Honours system, but it has existed in Ireland, where the Knight of Kerry and the Knight of Glynn are so recognised although the title is a purely courtesy one bringing with it no official recognition from the Crown, the Fount of Honour. This may just be the faint echo of an old, Celtic title. Duke Niall of Argyll reckoned himself to be the 44th Knight of Lochawe, which would make the present Chief the 46th Knight, while Cailean Mor would have been the 18th. Genealogists are wont to use the yardstick of three generations to 100 years, which, while somewhat rough and ready, is usually surprisingly accurate. This would date the first Knight of Lochawe back to around AD 700, which would fit in with an early Scoto-Irish descent soon after the establishment of the Kingdom of Dalriada. At that stage, however, the Campbells had not yet reached Argyll; the original Knight of Loch Awe must therefore have been an ancestor in the female line, and the marriage, which apparently brought with it the Lordship of Lochawe or whatever position first gave the Campbells a foothold in Argyll, would seem a prime candidate for also bringing with it the 'Knighthood of Loch Awe'.

One name is of particular interest – that of *Duine*, or *Duibne*. The earlier name for the Campbells was the *Clann Duibhne*, a style which lasted for many years even after the later introduction of the style *Clan Diarmid*. As noted above, it is not clear when and why the name of Diarmid was introduced to identify the clan, but it was probably due to the enormous popularity of the tales of Diarmid and the desire by the Chiefs to establish their descent from the great figures of Irish historical mythology. The clan has thus been largely identified for over 200 years with the mythical Diarmid rather than the probably historical Duine. The author of *Ane Accompt* notes that the style of *O'Duine* still existed alongside that of *Siol Diarmid* at the time he is writing; other evidence as to common usage may be found in the heraldic carving over the door of Carnasserie Castle near Kilmartin, built by Bishop Carswell for the 5th Earl of Argyll in the 1560s. An inscription reads *Dia le ua nDhuibhne* – 'God be with O'Duin' – and it is by this style that the Bishop referred to the Earl to whom he dedicated his Gaelic Liturgy of 1567. The fact that it was Duine who gave his name to the clan is a strong argument for his actual existence. As David Sellar has pointed out, in nearly every case the eponym of a Highland Clan can be shown actually to have existed.[19]

We have no details about the original Duine, although at least one genealogy refers to him as *Duine Mor* – 'Duine the Great'. He was clearly a man of renown. The name is an interesting one: it is extremely rare, and is not to be found in the Irish annals where one would have expected to find examples. In the late Middle Irish text *Acallamh na Senorach*, it refers to a legendary King of Bregia and Meath. The *Corco Duibne* were an early tribe in Munster and later in the Lennox. David Sellar quotes the case of another Duibne who (as *Duvene* and *Dufne*) witnesses several Lennox writs and who was the chamberlain of the Earl of Lennox in the early thirteenth century.[20] Another brief appearance of the name is in the *Book of Deer* in a charter of c. 1131, where among the witnesses is one *Dubni Mac Mal-Colaim*. It may or may not be of significance that among his fellow witnesses is Alguine Mac Arcill, ancestor of the Earls of Lennox.[21] But whoever he was, the Duibne of the Campbell pedigree was clearly a man to be remembered.

Ane Accompt also accounts for the identification as Campbells of various offshoots of the main stem. The MacTavishes and the MacIvers both descend from unions which, if temporary, were perfectly accepted in ancient Gaelic culture – the MacIver descent being from a daughter of *Swineruo* according to the pedigree, who is immediately recognisable as the historical *Suibhne Ruadh* who built Castle Sween. So, too, the great branch of the Campbells of Craignish are given descent from a younger son of the main stem. While all three were effectively branches of Clan Campbell both in behaviour and allegiance and also largely in blood through frequent inter-marriage, the question of their male line of descent remains unproven. It is not impossible that their identity as Campbells was politically motivated. But the modern attempt to group all MacIvers and every form of the name of 'Thomas's Son' together and to call them 'Clans' has no historical justi-fication any more than the grouping of all MacArthurs, regardless of the totally different stocks from which those of the name spring. The author of *Ane Accompt* is clearly aware of this problem of the diverse origins of the MacArthurs, and gets round it by producing a father called Arthur who has no fewer than three sons all also called Arthur, from whom the various MacArthur families derive. Other claims to parentage are made by the pedigree; the MacNaughtons and the Drummonds are both claimed as descendants, possibly for political reasons. A MacPherson tribe who certainly existed were nothing to do with the Clan Chattan MacPhersons but were the progeny of a son of a Dugald Campbell, a cleric whose descendants took the by-name of 'Son of the Parson'.

As to the arrival of the Campbells in Argyll, other versions suggest that it might have been during one of the Scottish Crown's several attempts to assert its authority over the western coast and isles. Alexander II's expedition of 1249 would probably have been too late, but there may have been earlier Royal invasions of Argyll, during one of which an O'Duin leader may have been left behind as a King's man to take over and bring order to the area. There is one other pointer to the genuine existence of a figure mentioned in the pedigree who predates the Gillespic of 1263: a later charter of David II to Gillespyk son of Sir Colin Cambel of Lochow, granted at Perth in March 1369, confirms all former gifts of lands, namely Craignish, Melfort, Strachur, Superior Cowal and Kildachanane. The charter continues: 'Concessimus etiam eidem Gillespyk omnes libertates et consuetudines quas habuit et quibus gaudebat quondam *Duncanus MacDowne*, Progenitor suus in baronia de

Lochaw et aliis terris quae fuerant dicti *quondam Duncani*'. 'We also con-
cede to the same Gillespic all the liberties and customary practices which the
late Duncan MacDuin, his (Gillespic's) progenitor, held and enjoyed in the
barony of Lochawe and in other lands which belonged to the late Duncan'.[22]
This would seem to validate the traditional pedigree back at least as far as
the beginning of the thirteenth century. Not only is Duncan named, but also
his patronymic *MacDowne* or *MacDuin* would also strengthen the virtual
certainty of an actual *Duin* who gave his name to his descendants.

We find Duncan given in the pedigrees as either the grandfather or the
great-grandfather of the Gillespic of 1263; his actual existence was clearly
known in 1369. He was either the father or the grandfather of one other
significant figure *Dugald* or Dougall, who was the first Campbell to use the
name – not, it is claimed, because of any dubious Norman connection but
because of a personal peculiarity which gave rise to the nickname *Cam Beul*
or 'Crooked Mouth'. It does seem a strange idea to take such a deformity,
although it may have been only a slight one, as a surname, but a similar claim
is made for the origin of the name Cameron, which is said to be due to a
Cam Shron or 'Crooked Nose' rather than to an incoming *de Cambron* or
Cameron from the Fife family of that name. If this is the case, then both these
men must have been remarkable ones. History has preserved nothing of their
doings, and yet their descendants wished to convert a personal blemish into
a proud surname.

One can only admire the construction of *Ane Accompt* which provides the
Campbell Chiefs with every possible claim to respectability. Ancient Irish,
Dalriadic and Norman descents are added to the Strathclyde British one;
ancient claim is laid to the Lordship of Loch Awe and to a social position
which permits marriage to the greatest in the land. Once stripped of all the
obvious additions, the added descents and the convoluted claim for possession of Loch Awe 'past memory of man', it would seem we are left with a
pedigree which indicates three things: a British descent, a descent of
respectably high degree, and the acquisition of a position in Argyll through
marriage with an existing heiress of a dynasty, who, while not necessarily of
any great importance, had been there for a long time. It was clearly of importance to the Campbells or, to be more particular, to the chiefly House of
Lochawe, as giving them the credibility which they needed. Throughout the
history of the Campbells, there is a recurrent feeling that they do not quite
belong. Much of this can probably be put down to their remarkable success,
which was not achieved without major discomfort to their neighbours and envy
among those less successful. But, for instance, the changing of the by-name
of the whole kindred from the genuine *Clan O'Duine* to the fictitious *Siol*

Diarmid was not only less than completely successful but hardly argues great self-confidence.

I suggest that the genealogy of the Campbells was used to overcome three obstacles. The first was when the line of Loch Awe was establishing itself, against competition as we will see, as the chiefly line of the Clan. The second was when the Campbell leaders, heads of what was a relatively new and not particularly important clan, were establishing themselves as the leading power in Argyll, and the third was when that power had expanded and was now seeking to dominate the West Highlands and Isles and beyond, mostly at the expense of the now forfeited Lords of the Isles. This demanded the establishment of a pedigree which would underline the position of Mac Cailein Mor as a great Highland Chief, a Gael among Gaels and a fit successor to the Lord of the Isles in that position. Such a pedigree would then support his claim for acceptance at the Scottish Court, where Norman or Flemish blood was considered desirable rather than that of wild and uncivilised savages from beyond the Highland line. These obstacles were overcome not without considerable difficulty; and the 'official' pedigree, with all its faults in content and with its composition in impressionistic rather than detailed representational terms, nevertheless gave the Campbell chiefs the respectability of descent which their ambitions required.

CHAPTER TWO

Setting the Scene

The main stage on which the story of Clan Campbell takes place is the old County of Argyll, now largely included in the new local-authority area known as Argyll and Bute. This new area has had a large part of what was Dunbartonshire added to it but has lost its old areas of Sunart and Ardnamurchan which now form part of Highland Region. It is a beautiful part of the world but it is not an easy one; the Campbells were moulded by its character. They were not original inhabitants but incomers, but they have been here for at least 800 years and possibly more. In time, they were to come to dominate nearly all of Argyll with much else besides.

In the early nineteenth century when the country lay under the imminent threat of invasion by Napoleon Buonaparte, the War Office issued an order that in the event of the French crossing the Channel, all horses, cows, sheep and other bestial that might be of help to the enemy should immediately be driven ten miles inland. This must have raised a smile or two in Argyll, since to obey the order is virtually impossible. For Argyll, the coastland of the Gael, is penetrated one after another by a series of fiords or sea-lochs that come far inland. From Ardnamurchan Point southwards, the county is mountainous for the most part. Only a few of its highest peaks approach 4,000 feet, a mere nothing when compared with most of the world's mountain ranges; but somehow, there is a majesty of scale about them that gives them a grandeur that few can surpass. Many of them are bare granite; for much of the landmass the topsoil is only skin-deep, a few inches at most, and the scrubby, wind-lashed trees hang on desperately with their shallow roots against the winter gales. Out in the islands they may not grow at all, so fierce is the perpetual gale. There is the tale of the new Minister on the Isle of Tiree who had the only tree on the island in his garden; he cut it down for firewood and is remembered still for that if not for his sermons.

But there is tremendous variety in a relatively small area, from the flat island *machair* to the high peaks, from the peat bogs and heather of the hills

20

to the gently rolling farmland of much of Kintyre. The coast faces the Atlantic to the west and the rainfall is high – for the most part around seventy inches a year – more on occasion and in certain areas. But along the coast it never gets very cold for very long since the Gulf Stream swings out across the Atlantic from the Caribbean and laves the rocky shores of western Ireland and the Western Isles and Highlands of Scotland. Just as well, for we are north of Moscow, on a level with Hudson's Bay and the southern part of Alaska, and if its welcome warmth were diverted as the weather prophets claim could happen quite easily and very suddenly, the result would be dramatic and highly uncomfortable. Not that the land has not undergone climatic changes before. It has spent long aeons under snow and ice, with the Ice Age engulfing it on more than one occasion. When the glaciers finally retreated, humans followed them up very soon after; the remains of the shellfish and other foods they ate are still to be found in caves along the coast.

The high winds and thin soil prevent the trees in Argyll from growing very large – apart from in the sheltered parks of great houses like Inveraray and Ardkinglas where, just to prove the exception to the rule, some of the highest trees in the United Kingdom flourish. But most of them cling to the hillside in a tangle of oak, alder and birch and, inland, the traces of the outliers of the ancient Caledonian Forest with scattered stands of twisted and gnarled Scots pine. Much of this is now submerged by great, dark, dank, soulless plantations of imported conifers – commercial plantation on a vast scale that deadens the landscape where birds sing no more in the close-packed, dripping woods.

In summer, the northerly latitude gives days so long that there is scarcely any night; in June the sun sets in the north-west leaving a golden glow which dips below the hills and then moves round to the north before it just fades for an hour or so before reappearing, this time in the north-east from where the new day once more rises in tranquil splendour. The price of these long, lazy days where the heat haze casts a sheen over the heather and the bees hum in the wild flowers that cover the grasslands is the dark of winter. Here the opposite occurs; the dark takes hold in the early afternoon and by three o'clock on a dreich day the light has gone. When the cloud is down and the rain falls horizontally rather than vertically, it is necessary to have the electric lights on throughout the day. During one recent year, we had over seventy inches of rain in the first three months and we never saw the sun from January to the end of March. But the price is worth paying for the long, golden peace of summer and the blue on the loch and in the shadow on the contours of the hills. 'One great day in Argyll is worth forty bad ones' they say, while the pessimistic point out that that is about the average balance. In

fact it is not anything like as bad as that, although rainfall does vary dramatically; in the shadow of the great mountains it can double the average while,
if you are out on low-lying Coll or Tiree, you can watch the Atlantic weather
stream overhead as you bask in the sunshine, watching the clouds build up
and the rain come down over the high hills inland.

Water is everywhere in Argyll, fresh or salt. Loch Awe is the largest inland
stretch of water in the county – indeed, it is one of the longest lochs in
Scotland, only surpassed by Loch Ness and Loch Lomond. But in all the
hills there are little lochs – little more than ponds in some cases – and much
of the ground is boggy all year round. The effect of the warmer climate before
1300 may have lasted for a few hundred years after the weather changed
when labour was plentiful and cheap, but these high furrows have long since
been abandoned and only sheep and deer and a few cattle graze over them
now. Indeed there is now hardly any arable left in Argyll – the crop is just
not worth the labour. The best land is out in the islands – in Tiree and in
the Ross of Mull – and in the south of Kintyre. Elsewhere it tends to be at
the head of the lochs where the rivers run into the sea. But the people are
long gone, and without them the rushes have been allowed to grow and retain
the water, turning what was once planted crop into boggy grazing shared
between the sheep and the deer – the great red deer that stay on the tops in
summer, descending when weather forces them into the woods which are
normally the haunt of the smaller roe that proliferate along the shores. There
are still cattle grazing as well, but since the end of the eighteenth century it
has been the sheep that have become the predominant denizens of the
landscape. Only here and there the remains of stone-walled dwellings, walls
a few feet high amid the rubble, clinging together for comfort, show the
footprint of past settlement. The emptying of the landscape is an old and
continuing story in this part of the world, and it is often hard to distinguish
the age of these ruins. They may be centuries old or a mere three or four
decades as the young decline the old life and seek better fortune in the big
cities or overseas.

Thank the Lord, the wolf is a terror of the past here, although a few well-
meaning town-dwellers talk of reintroducing it. It seems that the fear it bred
in generations of our forefathers, so that every area will point to the place
where the last wolf in the district met its end, was all misplaced and the wolf
was a loveable, cuddly friend of man after all! The present fashion is all for
trees, and all else must give way before the natural reafforestation of the
land. The trouble in restoring a landscape is that it becomes a question of
deciding to which period it is to be returned, since we are looking, wild though
the landscape is, at a man-made view. Ever since the hunter-gatherers that

trod on the heels of the retreating ice sheet were replaced by the first farmers, man has been altering the environment and clearing the trees for the grazing of his bestial and the planting of his crops. The original forest was anyway nothing like as dense as the apologists for the excesses of commercial planting would have us believe; the sunlight came in among the sparse trees and gave light and growth to the forest floor, and the skyline was only seldom out of view. Except in small areas, it was nothing like the dense forests that cover much of North America, which made people live with a view of twenty yards for much of their lives, sending some mad and giving a terrible shock to the pioneer settlers from places like the treeless Outer Isles of Scotland who had never wielded an axe and now found themselves faced by an impenetrable wall of tall timber.

But you are never very far away from water. Brown trout, sea-trout and salmon were plentiful, although many of the burns and lochs are too high and too peaty to allow the trout population to grow very large. Angling with a rod and line for sport only became the norm in the nineteenth century; before that, fishing was a serious business in the hunt for food, and fish were netted in the river mouth or upper pools or speared with the aid of flaming torches that attracted the fish at night. Sometimes the lord of the land had the right to a cruive or fishtrap on a river where the river flow was directed through a narrow stone-built channel which allowed the fish swimming upriver from the sea to spawn to be trapped within it.

Then there was the sea, the endless sea. At first feared and not without reason for its rocks and stormy currents, the ocean surrounds the hundreds of islands that litter the west coast of the Highlands from the Outer Isles which stretch all the way from the Butt of Lewis to Barra and which shield the great island of Skye with, to its south, the Small Isles – Rum, Eigg, Canna and Muck. They, and a host more, all lie to the north of Ardnamurchan Point, which juts further west into the Atlantic than any other part of mainland Britain. Off its rocks, the seas, unsheltered from the broad Atlantic, are as fierce as any around these shores, with one particularly notorious stretch known as 'the *Cailleach*' – the Old Woman.

The islands of Coll and Tiree are in the Inner Hebrides but on the outer fringe of Argyll. Tiree is treeless and so flat that it is possible to stand on the southern shore and watch the breakers throw white sheets of spray which catch the sun on the north shore of the island two miles away across the Reef which makes a perfect runway for the airport. Most of Tiree is shell-sand *machair* – studded with a myriad wildflowers in spring and in summer – which makes for superb grazing. Coll, only a few miles away, is very different: there is much less machair, and the West End has great sand dunes which, blown on a great storm, have engulfed much of the former pasture. In general it is very much more rocky, although the hills never rise to any great height. The Atlantic breakers come in against both islands – the surfing in Tiree is among the best in Europe, and even on a baking hot summer's day with the sea looking like glass there is still an underlying oily swell that is not for those afloat of a queasy disposition.

Coll and Tiree stand at the centre of a great circle of sea and far mountains that encompasses much of the Highlands and Isles. If you stand on the hill above Grishipol, you can look out on a clear day and see Barra, far to the north, and the hills of Harris as the Long Island stretches away to the Butt of Lewis. Further round the rim are the Cuillin peaks on Skye and nearer at hand the peaks of Rum and the islands of Eigg and Muck. Then it is inland to the tangle of mountains that is Moidart and the rocky promontory of Ardnamurchan. Next on the horizon comes the Isle of Mull to the east and south, with its high mountains divided from the mainland by the Sound of Mull, and, off the west shore of the island, a string of low-lying cliffed islands, the Treshnish Isles with the fortress of Cairnaburgh lying like a great ship in the stream. And far on the southern horizon, the low hills on Iona with, just visible in the haze, the far-off peaks of Jura.

The sea is a key feature of this part of the world, where it is the link that binds many lonely places. Once our forefathers had mastered it, it became a highway and not a barrier, although it could never be underestimated as a danger. It transforms the geography, and even the view from the deck of one of today's car-ferries can give one a totally different perspective.

If Coll and Tiree are very different to each other although lying side by side, so too are Islay and Jura. They are part of a string of islands that stretches from Kerrera by Oban to the Oa of Islay where Ireland is broad on the horizon. There are a number of passages inshore and between these islands which allow access to the seaway that lies inland of this chain, the northern one being the narrow tidal creek that divides Seil from the mainland, crossed by the graceful stone arch that for long has boasted itself to be the 'only bridge over the Atlantic', a claim which has surely now been destroyed by the controversial Skye Bridge. Further south, the openings are larger and easier of passage, but the tides that fill and empty the broad channel have to force themselves in and out of these narrow passages where the currents flow like rivers.

Nowhere is this more in evidence than in the gap between the north end of Jura and the mountainous small island of Scarba, where a deep dip in the seabed produces the fearsome Gulf of Corryvreckan which rages furiously as the tides pour in and out. At one point in the maelstrom of breaking water there is a standing wave, some twelve feet high, which, says the Yachtsman's

Guide, if wind is in opposition to the tide 'can double in height'. Brave or perhaps rash spirits who know the coast go through the Gulf at slack water, but those who attempt it in a small vessel when the current is running full will come to a bitter end, swamped by the mountainous breaking waves which, over the centuries, have caused the deaths of many hundreds of people.

Another narrow, watery defile separates Jura from the island of Islay to the south. This is the Sound of Islay – *Ilasund* to the Norsemen – where the tides also run strongly between the islands. Even in one of today's sophisticated ferries, I have done five circuits before the new captain of the vessel was able to bring us in alongside the pier at Port Askaig. Islay has everything – great sweeps of sandy machair, high dunes, woods, towering cliffs and serious mountains as well as much good pasturage that once was arable of excellent quality. It has long been a strategic centre of both the Norse Kingdom of the Isles and the later Lordship when the MacDonald Chiefs set up their headquarters on a couple of small islands in an inland loch at Finlaggan in the east of the island.

On the mainland, east of Islay, the long peninsula of Kintyre stretches away to the south-west. It, too, has wonderfully varied terrain. On the west, or Atlantic coast, the sea borders good pastureland which rises to open moorland and high, lonely hills, while on the eastern, inland side, the view is across Kilbrannan Sound to the island of Arran with its high peaks, and to the coast of Ayrshire, surprisingly close. Here the ground is much more typically Highland, with the hills falling steeply into the rock-girt sea through a tangle of scrub oak, birch and bracken. Kintyre boasts great sweeps of agricultural farmland which are more like Ayrshire than anywhere else, although the proximity of sea and mountain combines to give the peninsula an island feel. It is a very special place.

At its southernmost tip, the peninsula ends in a massif of wild rock and heather, a lonely place with deserted settlements and now only a few lonely sheep and a narrow twisting road that leads to the lighthouse at its end. The final descent is barred to casual visitors, who must stop several hundred feet above the turbulent waters of the North Channel, the eleven miles or so of stormy waters that separate Argyll from Ireland. This is the actual Mull of Kintyre. On a clear day, the view is superb. This is another pivotal point as one turns through the arc of the compass. Islay and the cliffs of the Oa are to the right, the north and eastern coasts of Antrim lie ahead with the low shape of Rathlin Island and, around to the south, the headland of the Rhinns of Galloway, the Ayrshire coast with the rocky eminence of Ailsa Craig rising from the Firth of Clyde and then, inland from Arran, the low promontory of Cowal in Argyll.

Someone living in Campbeltown once said to me, 'Of course we are so cut off where we are, at the end of Kintyre – we're in the middle of nowhere'. 'Middle of nowhere? You're at the crossroads of history!' For that is what it is, from the Roman fleet nervously feeling its way round the shores of Ultima Thule to the coracle that brought Columba over to Iona to the fleets of the Viking longships and then to great wartime convoys or their remnants coming in to final haven in the Clyde or the Mersey through the narrow gap of the North Channel that separates the Mull from Ireland. This was the old sea-road of the Norsemen who sailed from Norway across to Orkney, around the northernmost coast of Scotland – they called it Southland or Sutherland – and then with a slight turn bringing their ships into the Minch. From then on, much of the route was sheltered by islands inshore of Skye and once round Ardnamurchan Point sheltered nearly all the way to the Mull of Kintyre. Once through the North Channel, the coastlands on all sides were open for plunder or for settlement right down to the Isle of Man and then on to the great Norse city of Dublin.

Back inland across the long arm of Loch Fyne is the district of Cowal. There is something mysterious about Cowal. It, too, has low, relatively fertile farmland at its extremity, the green Kerry, but most of it is rugged mountain country pierced by a succession of fiords, from the Holy Loch to Loch Long to Loch Striven and Loch Riddon with the island of Bute separated from the mainland by the Kyles. From the Kyles of Bute southwards, the waters open on the Firth of Clyde – indeed the whole area is very close as the crow flies to the great urbanised Clyde and Glasgow, but its glens are lonely, there are few roads and they lead nowhere, and there is a brooding savagery about the tangle of mountains here that guards a secret still.

Such is the extent of old Argyll, the area with which Clan Campbell is associated above all other and from which its Chiefs have long taken their proud title. It is not a rich land, but it is one of remarkable variety and great beauty – heart-rending beauty which is, however, deceptive, for this is not a soft land. It gives people a living but at the price of much hard work and no riches at the end, for it is for the most part a desert – a wet desert, but a desert none the less. Here our forefathers had their being, living in stone or wattle-and-daub cottages, thatched with heather, shared with the cattle which needed protection through the long winter nights and which produced warmth as well as food for their owners. Here they wrenched a living from the unwelcoming soil, small crops of bere, barley and oats – later there were potatoes – supplemented by the fish that were plentiful in the surrounding waters and perhaps flavoured by the herbs that were grown in the small, sheltered gardens that produced peas, beans and kale to give some variation to the diet.

As the name *Earraghaideal* – the 'borderland of the Gael' – suggests, Argyll is a coastal strip, clinging to the British mainland with difficulty since it is firmly gripped by the sea which engulfs its glacial valleys far inland. The grain of Britain is north-to-south, and, taken as a whole, that is the general drift of its main arteries of communication. But Argyll is not like that. The hinterland is narrow, reaching to the dorsal fin of Drumalbyn, the watershed of Scotland, which is so short to the west and long to the east. All the ancient land routes here go ultimately from west to east through this wild tangle of deserted country. The great tangle of mountains around Glencoe is flanked by the glacial moon landscape of the vast Moor of Rannoch. It is twelve miles from the foot of Glenorchy at Dalmally – its alternative name *Dyseart*, quite simply the Gaelic for 'desert' – nothing now as we fling the miles behind us in our warm motor car, but a real barrier in winter for a lonely foot-traveller picking his way along the twisting path among the bogs on the valley floor with every small summer burn a raging grey torrent to be negotiated at peril. Only the great gash of the Great Glen offers a ready exit, and this leads not to the Lowlands but to the alien kingdom of Moray far to the north and east.

Argyll is cut off from the rest of Scotland. The grain of the country is from north-east to south-west, and everything leads into the sea and to Ireland, so close across the North Channel. From the Mull of Kintyre, the coast of Antrim is quite visible on a clear day, with its pattern of fields and the cars creeping along its roads, their windscreens reflecting the sun. From a surprisingly large area of Argyll, the smudge of hills on the horizon is Ireland, its coast no more than a full day's sail from as far north as Oban.

And of course it was from there in Ulster that, around AD 500, the sons of Erc – Fergus, Loarn and Angus – led a great expedition of their people to set up in Argyll an overspill for their Irish kingdom of Dalriada which was being sorely squeezed by their encroaching neighbours. Nomenclature becomes difficult, for these people were the original *Scotti* or Scots who came from Ireland. It was not until after the treaty of Drumceat around 575 which split the old kingdom of Dalriada that one can talk of 'Scottish' and 'Irish' Dalriada, and even then the terms are hardly accurate to the purist.[1] As it was, the two parts of the kingdom kept very close to each other, and it is hard to overestimate the influence on this new Scotland of the old, now left across the sea but closely in touch and with its culture still very much the same.

The date of AD 500 seems a good one to start our history; the Roman occupation never reached Argyll and its direct influence was not great. Of course, with the shores of Argyll so enticingly close on the horizon, there was in all probability a scattering of settlement from Ulster along its shores already. But the arrival of the sons of Erc was obviously an incursion in some force. Loarn was given what was to become North Argyll, Angus had Islay, and Fergus received Kintyre and mainland Argyll. Fergus's sons were Gabhran and Comghal, the latter giving his name to his patrimony of the district of Cowal.

Such an invasion leads one to envisage the disposition of the existing occupiers of the more fertile lands, of slayings and burnings and, at best, expulsion. Such, however, need not have been what happened. People were sparse, and manpower as ever was needed to work the land. Fresh blood invigorated the breeding stock. There might well be demotion and a new face might grace the head of the table, but that was all that was necessary. Sometimes even that would not happen, but the head of the house would merely pay his service to a new lord.

The incoming Scots are said to have set up four strongholds: at Dunaverty in Kintyre, at Tarbert on Loch Fyne, at Dunolly overlooking what is now Oban, and, their capital, at Dunadd, not far from Kilmartin in Mid Argyll where the broad glen holds a ritual landscape, a long vista of ceremonial burial cairns and standing stones of which the earliest predates the Pyramids and which formed a centre of mystery and wonderment and worship for nearly 4,000 years. Dunadd itself is built on a rocky outcrop that rises out of the fringe of the great Crinan Moss, a wide stretch of bog and heather and peat which now covers the saltmarsh and shallow inlet of the sea which once lapped the rim of Dunadd itself. The River Add unwinds itself in lazy undulations through the landscape; it was once navigable as far up as Bridgend, a couple of miles above Dunadd. Over the ridge of Dunamuck and down to Cairnbaan, where once a loch stretched nearly all the way to Lochgilphead and another expanse of mud and saltflats, seafarers avoided the long and stormy passage around the Mull of Kintyre and portaged their boats across the isthmus. Dunadd was therefore not only a position of great natural strength but also it stood on a well-used crossroads with routes from Loch Fyne to the Atlantic in the Sound of Jura joining others into the hinterland and even linking with Ireland via Islay and Jura by the short sea-crossing to Keills in Knapdale. Pottery and coins found here show that the Kings in Dunadd traded with the continent as well.

Around the mid-500s, a new figure appeared in Argyll: Columba, born a Prince of the Ui Neill, a self-imposed exile from Ireland and inspired missionary of the Church, eventually settled in Iona where he could no longer be tempted by the distant sight of his beloved homeland. There he set up a centre of Christianity whose light, in time, was to extend over much of continental Europe. Columba himself made a priority of converting the local Pictish rulers, travelling with a few devoted companions through this wild and savage land.

The Scottish tribes fought both with themselves and with their neighbours. In 736, so the annals tell us, Dunadd was besieged and taken by the Picts. They invaded the most holy place of the Kings' inauguration and defiled it by incising their symbol of a boar in the rock which held the footprint. It still remains today as a boast of conquest – people have asked why the Scots, when they once more reoccupied the fort, should have left the enemy sign in place. Closer inspection, however, reveals that the boar has had all evidence of its masculinity carefully removed.

Not long afterwards, the Scots kings left Dunadd, it would seem. They moved north, and, if legend is to be believed, it was at Dunstaffnage that they set up their headquarters, with their fortress on a promontory looking out across the Firth of Lorne to Mull and the great sea-route, with a well-sheltered anchorage at their back. It may have been the ill-omen of the desecration of their inmost sanctuary, it may have been the loss of the sacred significance of Kilmartin as Christianity finally established its hold, but Dunadd became a shadow of what it had been, with only metalworkings left on the hill.

But an ill wind was blowing, this time from the far north-east. The Norseman was on the move, his longships cleaving the ocean billow, their crews joyful for slaughter, for booty, women and slaves. No coast in Atlantic Europe was safe. Their great journeys took them up the rivers of Russia and down as far as Constantinople. People nervously watched the seas for these birds of ill-omen. Iona was merely one of many monasteries sacked and plundered. The monks kept coming back even though they knew that sooner or later fate would descend on them once more.

Church and temporal power stood it for a time, and then it all became too much. In 843, Kenneth the son of Alpin, King of Scots, moved east to what became Perthshire; through his mother and thanks, it may be, to the Pictish matrilinear system of inheritance, he was also King of the Picts, and the two peoples were henceforth to be united. With him from Dunstaffnage went the symbols of his royalty, and so too did the seat of the Church, now set up at Dunkeld and taking with it some of the relics of Saint Columba, since Iona was now so very unsafe. Other relics were taken to Kells well inland in Ireland and safe – or relatively safe – from Norse attack, among them the famous Book of Kells which had been produced in Iona. Many of the nobles of Dalriada, who saw their future along with their King, also now accompanied him to the more sheltered east.

Once their blood lust was sated, the Norsemen came to settle; to people used to the snows and precipitate landscape of Norway, the Northern and Western Isles were a welcoming change. They settled in all the islands of Argyll and away past the Mull of Kintyre, on both sides of the Irish Sea and in the

Isle of Man. They built the city of Dublin in Ireland, which became a centre of trade. Strangely enough, no trace has been found of their inhabiting the Argyll mainland, although there are plenty of placenames of Norse origin there and surely they must have settled, at least along the shorelands facing the sea.

Once more Argyll lived up to its name, the borderland of the Gael, but this time the border was looking the other way as Argyll found itself facing the Norsemen out to sea rather than the Picts in the hinterland. The Isles were now to all intents and purposes part of Norway although they did not always acknowledge the fact, as the ruling dynasty asserted its independence from any superior authority. But quarrels persisted between the Kings of Scots and those of Norway over the ownership of the Isles. There was an expedition in 1098 by Magnus Barelegs, who claimed Kintyre and the Isles on behalf of Norway and had himself dragged, it is said, in his galley, with oars and rudder shipped, across the narrow isthmus from West to East Loch Tarbert to make good his claim that Kintyre with its rich lands should be reckoned as one of the Isles.[2]

In the 1100s, there arose another claimant to the rule of the area: the famous Somerled, a warlord of mixed Norse and Gaelic blood, who led a revolt which established his rule over nearly all of Argyll and its islands possibly together with Arran as well. His expedition with the aim of attacking even more ambitious targets was brought to a halt by his death at Renfrew in 1164. But his realm lived on, split among his three sons, Dougall, Ranald and Angus. Dougall, the eldest, was given Somerled's lands in mainland Argyll and the islands of Mull, Coll and Tiree. Ranald got the northern part of the kingdom and possibly land in the Uists. Angus had Islay but he soon lost his patrimony to Donald, son of Ranald, who shared his father's lands with his brother Ruari who received the northern share of Moidart, Rum, Eigg and Canna. This new rule was no more acceptable to Scottish Royal authority, and various expeditions were mounted against the Western Isles to no real avail, in 1222 and 1249. On the later expedition, King Alexander II sickened and died on the island of Kerrera off what is now Oban, cursed by a witch whose death sentence he had confirmed.

By now, the sons of Somerled and their descendants were clearly in command of much of Argyll and its islands. Further south, in Cowal and in Knapdale and Glassary, the dominant families were those descended from the Irish *Anrothan*, a Prince of the O'Neills, who around 1000 had tried for his fortune in Argyll, and, probably through marriage with the Dalriadic heiress of these lands,[3] took over this large area. The saga of his clan, on the other hand, claims it was through conquest.[4] It was most probably a combination of the two.

His descendent *Suibhne* built the castle that bears his name in the form of Castle Sween in Knapdale towards the close of the 1100s,[5] while his son built the castles of Skipness and probably Loch Ranza on the island of Arran opposite it, thereby dominating the Kilbrannan Sound. MacLachlans, Lamonts, MacEwans, MacGilchrists, MacSorleys, MacDunsleaves and possibly MacNeils are all descended from this union, which produced what must have been about the most powerful family grouping in Argyll of its day – one unaccountably neglected by most historians.

Castle Sween was the first proper stone-built castle in Scotland. It sits overlooking Loch Sween gazing out across the Sound to Jura. The original castle was a rectangular curtain wall no doubt enclosing interior buildings; there have been later additions. Just below the castle is a boat noost – a small, artificial harbour – which gives shelter for a galley or just possibly two but no more. A hundred yards below the castle is a bay with a fine sandy beach, but it is open to the prevailing westerlies which blow straight on shore, and it seems likely that while the MacSween fleet was in being, their ships may have been moored in the tidal inlet of Linnhe Vuirich a couple of miles away on the other side of Loch Sween. Here there are signs of a dockyard, for want of a better word, with deep water enough to float a galley close inshore and the site dominated by the old fort of Dun Vuirich. There is a tale of fires being lit here, as well they may have been if this idea is correct, as a means of signalling between here and the castle.

But by 1262, the MacSween family were out of favour. In that year, Walter Stewart, Earl of Menteith, confirmed a grant to the Monastery of Paisley made to them by Dugall son of Suibhne who had also transferred the Castle of Skipness to Walter. Although not mentioned, it would appear that the MacSweens had lost Castle Sween at about the same time. The reason for this is unknown, but it is suggested that a MacSween foster-son of the King was banished as a result of his killing a son of the Earl of Mar, also the King's foster-son. As so often happens with tales of this sort, there is no historical evidence to support it, but it is not impossible that something of the kind may have happened.[6] In any case, the MacSweens were now out of favour and, as will be seen, although they made strenuous efforts to regain their former position, their hold in Argyll became ever more tenuous and, although they lingered for several decades yet, they eventually moved their centre of activity across the water to Ireland where they became noted gallowglasses and great chiefs again in another land. Their kindred clans stayed on in Cowal and Glassary, but they never achieved the dominance once held by the MacSweens.

This period now saw the first phase of castle-building in Argyll – proper castles, that is – that came to join the myriad forts, duns, earthworks, brochs and crannogs of bygone ages that spread across the landscape. It is claimed[7] that, apart from Castle Sween itself, Achadun, Caisteal na Nighinn Ruaidhe, Castle Coeffin, Dunstaffnage, Innischonnell, Dunoon, Fincharn, Dunaverty, Skipness, Tarbert, Cairnaburgh, and Duart castles can all be dated from the period 1200–50. The MacSween lands extended right across Knapdale from the Sound of Jura to Loch Fyne and south into what is geographically Kintyre, the north-east corner of which, however, has ever since been considered as Knapdale. Here, overlooking Kilbrannan Sound, the stretch of water that seperates Kintyre from the Isle of Arran, Suibhne's son Dougall built the castle of Skipness. It stands on flat meadowland without any hint of a natural defensive position. But its whole outlook is across the water: as with so many of these castles on the western seaboard, it is to sea that they look and this is the area they seek to dominate – the landward threat is minimised and they virtually disregard it. Dougall, as mentioned, is thought to have built the castle of Loch Ranza on Arran, thus giving effective domination of the waterway that lay between.

Achadun is on the island of Lismore and was the headquarters of the Bishops of Argyll. In 1240, 'two pennylands at Achacendune' were among lands granted by Ewen, son of Duncan de Ergidia, to Bishop William. Caisteal na Nighinn Ruaidhe has already appeared in our story as the reputed seat of the MacFiachar family whose heiress married Duncan, father of Colin Maol Math in the traditional account of the Campbell genealogy. It stands today on a small, rubble-strewn islet at the west end of Loch Avich. No more than the remnants of its walls are still to be seen, but nevertheless it manages to convey an aura of considerable strength. Its position covers the route to Loch Awe via Loch Avich by way of Craignish and Glen Domhain, and it is conveniently placed for the hill track that crosses the watershed to Scammadale over the String of Lorne, of which more below.

Castle Coeffin is also on Lismore, perched on a jutting promontory looking out over Loch Linnhe to Morvern. Tradition gives it a Norse origin, but it is thought to have been built by the MacDougall Lords of Lorne who may earlier have had a residence on the same site. There is a sheltered bay just below the castle, a small but well-sheltered anchorage while the site is well situated to cover the seaward entrance to the Great Glen.

Dunstaffnage has already entered the story and it, too, gazes out across the sea lanes to Mull and the southern end of Lismore, with, under the castle walls, the splendid sheltered anchorage for a galley fleet that is still a favoured yacht haven today. The present castle was built by Duncan (MacDougall) Lord of Argyll around 1220 before, having guaranteed his safety on earth, he went on to insure his well-being in Heaven by the building of Ardchattan Priory which dates from around 1230.

On Mull, facing Dunstaffnage, is Duart Castle on its cliff promontory, famous later as the seat of the Maclean chiefs. Its exact date of construction is not known but its builders were, once again, the Lords of Lorne who held Mull as part of their patrimony, until it was granted by Bruce to the MacDonalds and then by them to the Macleans.

Innischonnell was built, it is thought, soon after 1200. There is argument whether it was built by the MacDougall Lords of Argyll or by the Campbells whose base it was to become during the following century. There are three reasons why I incline to the first rather than the second theory: I think it doubtful the Campbells at the time it was built were of sufficient importance or had sufficient resources to be able to have built such a mighty castle; secondly, I do not believe that the Lords of Lorne, their near-neighbours with whom their relationship was never very close, would have permitted them to do so; and thirdly, there exists a letter from John of Lorne to King Edward of England in which he refers to his 'three castles upon a lake'. The lake is Loch Awe, and since Kilchurn, as far as we know, did not exist at the time, the three castles must have been Fraoch Eilean, Fincharn – and Innischonnell.

Fincharn belonged to the MacGilchrist Lords of Glassary who may well have been its builders. The earliest known charter of lands in Argyll is one of 1240 in which the fifteen pennylands of Fincharn are granted by King Alexander II to Gillascop MacGilchrist.[8] When and under what circumstances its ownership passed to the MacDougall Lords of Argyll is unknown.

Dunoon also dominates a waterway, but this time it is the entrance to the River Clyde. It is on record as early as the second quarter of the thirteenth century when John, 'Constabularius de Dunnon', witnessed a charter in association with Walter Stewart. It is unclear whether the castle was originally a royal one or whether it was built by the Stewarts. In any case, it would seem to have been early in the hands of the latter and it may well have served to provide the firm base on the Argyll side of the Clyde for the Stewart move into Argyll, of which more below.

Tarbert is another castle long associated with royalty, although the actual builder of the castle which was improved and rebuilt by King Robert I is unclear. It is reckoned to have been the site of one of the original castles of the incoming Scots in AD 500, as was Dunaverty. Situated on a hill overlooking the East Harbour, its importance lay in its dominance of the short land portage that separated East Loch from West Loch Tarbert. It would appear that this was a well-used route for mariners, allowing them to avoid the long and dangerous journey around the Mull of Kintyre. The fact that it does not feature as one of the castles owned by the MacSween Lords of Knapdale makes it probable that it was built as a royal one.

The final castle, that of Cairnaburgh, is a remarkable one. Set on the Treshnish Isles to the West of Mull, it is designed to cover the west-about passage round Mull, dominating the route past Ardnamurchan Point, which, instead of taking the more sheltered inland seaway through the Sound of Mull, heads due south directly for Islay and for Ireland. Its builder is unknown, but it is on record as early as 1249 when it is probably one of the four castles held by Ewen of Argyll from King Haakon of Norway.

Such is the list of the early castles of Argyll. One other should be added, that of the Castle of Rothesay on Bute, which also dates from the same period. Although it is in Bute rather than Argyll, it forms an integral part of the system of power and control in the area for which this list of early castles serves as a useful indication. Castles themselves, although they are fortified, are not meant to be besieged; if they are, they have failed in their purpose, which is to dominate their surroundings and to reflect the power and status of their owners. It will be noticed how, right from the start, most of these castles were seeking to impose their presence on the seaways – not just the local traffic that used them but also those that voyaged the great sea-route which stretched all the way from Scandinavia to the Isle of Man and to Dublin. But there were also a number inland, usually placed on inland waters, and again, dominating the routes which led through the glens.

The fact that such edifices should appear so early in this part of Scotland is also a remarkable one. True, there was plenty of available raw material and unskilled manpower. But the architects and masons must have come from outside and they must have gained experience of castle-building elsewhere, possibly from the Borders with England, or, more likely, from Ireland and the Norman castle-builders there. Or had they even come from the Middle East? How were they obtained in the necessary numbers and how were they paid? Currency hardly existed in the area, and one can only surmise that it took some getting. We have already noted in Chapter 1 that Suibhne's other son was called Maelmuire *an Sparain* – 'of the purse' – and it may be that this was his role as far as the MacSweens' castle-building was concerned. This, however, is mere speculation.

One other class of fortification should be mentioned here – the mysterious series of *mottes* of which there are a number in Argyll. A motte is a man-made or man-assisted mound on top of which would be a defensive palisade. They are said to have been very much used as a form of swiftly erected strongpoint to exercise dominion over an area. They are relatively numerous in the Lowlands but few in Argyll, where identification is not helped by the number of glacial moraines which often look remarkably like them. But apparent mottes have been identified at Dunoon, three at Strachur, one at Ballimore near Otter Ferry, two in Glendaruel, one in Glen Fyne at the head of Loch Fyne, one at the mouth of the River Awe and one in Kintyre. Their usual dating is early but it is uncertain, and quite possibly they were still being constructed during the twelfth century at least.[9]

One possible attribution is that several if not all of them owe their existence to the Stewarts, whose main lands were in Renfrew and Ayrshire across the Clyde from Dunoon. The Stewarts were early given Bute, Walter the first Steward of Scotland who died in 1093 being said to have been granted the island by King Malcolm,[10] and before they became royal it very much looks as if the Stewarts were given lands in Argyll as the chosen instrument for imposing royal authority on the area. In due course most of these lands, as we shall see, were passed to their connections, the Campbells.

Mottes were numerous in the Stewart homeland, and if Dunoon, just across the Clyde, was a bridgehead which needed a firm base, then the three at Strachur are conveniently placed to cover the far end of the route from Dunoon up the side of Loch Eck and across to Loch Fyne. If this then became the centre, it is covered at the head of the loch and to the south both by the Ballimore motte covering Otter Ferry and by the Glenfyne motte covering the route round the head of the Loch and the inland track over to Loch Lomond. So too, the route from Bute up Glendaruel is also covered by the two sites there.

The Stewarts also held lands in Kintyre, which might fit in with the existence of the motte at Machrie, although it is harder to fit in the site at Inverawe which guards ferry points across both Loch Etive and the River Awe into the possible pattern. And, not only are there other probable sites in the area which have not been identified, but there were many previously fortified sites from former days which might well have been brought back into service where required, since their siting is frequently in exactly the right spot to exert dominion.

As will be seen, many of these lands previously in Stewart hands belonged to the branch of the family who took the name Menteith. Walter Stewart, third High Steward of Scotland, had a younger son, also Walter, who married Mary, daughter and heiress of Maurice, Earl of Menteith, through whom he inherited that earldom. Their descendants used the name Menteith instead of Stewart. It was this Walter who acquired the former lands of the MacSweens in Knapdale prior to 1262 while his son, Sir John Menteith, is mentioned among the main landowners in Baliol's newly erected sheriffdom of Kintyre in 1292.

But the Menteith connection with Argyll goes back before the Stewart marriage, it would appear. According to Sir William Fraser, the earlier Celtic Earls of Menteith had jurisdiction over Kintyre and Cowal as far back as the reign of King David I (1124–53), as mentioned in the *Regiam Majestatem*.[11] The jurisdiction appears to concern *Claremathen*, 'an ancient regulation concerning the warrandice of stolen cattle or goods.'[12] 'Warrandice' refers to asserting proof of ownership – somewhat clarified in the third chapter of the Assizes of King William the Lion (1165–1214), where it is laid down that if any man be challenged 'gif his warrand be wonnande in Kintyre or in Cowalle, in that ilk manner, the Erl of Meneteth sall send his men with hym that is callyt to ber witnes to the foresayd assise . . .'.[13]

So there may have been two avenues of entry into Argyll for the Stewarts, both through the Menteith marriage and through their own employment by the Crown as part of an early attempt by the Scottish Crown to impose its authority on this fringe area of the kingdom. This struggle was a continual one for the crowns of both Norway and Scotland. In 1221, according to Fordun, King Alexander II raised an army from the men of Lothian and of Galloway and launched an expedition against Argyll and the Isles. A storm blew up and the expedition had to put back in some difficulty and danger before arriving at Glasgow. The following year he returned after Whitsunday

> for he was displeased with the natives for many reasons . . . The men of Argyll were frightened: some gave hostages and a great deal of money, and were taken back in peace; while others, who had more deeply offended against the King's will, forsook their estates and possessions and fled. But our Lord the king bestowed both the land and the goods of these men upon his own followers, at will; and thus returned in peace with his men.[14]

Wyntoun's version is slightly different because it fuses the two expeditions, if two there were, into one. Whichever version is correct, this expedition is of some considerable interest since it is thought that it may be the occasion of the arrival of the Campbells to settle in Argyll.

The Kings of Norway were also having trouble in the Isles, events culminating in 1229 when King Haakon sent an expedition under one Uspak to settle affairs. Uspak's identity is disputed, but he may have been a MacDougall. There was internal trouble between the Norse and the Hebridean elements of his force, but they sailed round Kintyre and arrived at Rothesay in Bute where they besieged the castle, apparently hewing away at its soft rock foundations with their fearsome axes. They managed to kill the garrison commander whose men then surrendered, but the approach of

Alan of Galloway with a large fleet and the death of Uspak decided them on retreat to the Isle of Man, where they wintered. The following spring they returned to Norway, pausing only to ravage Kintyre on the way.[15]

In 1249, it was the Scottish King himself who came, Alexander II, exasperated by the negotiations with the Norse to buy the Isles. He came with a great fleet but fell ill and was taken ashore to the Isle of Kerrera, just opposite modern Oban. As he lay dying, so the story goes, King Alexander was visited by the vision of three men who came to dissuade him from his endeavour. From their description, it was said that they must have been Saint Olaf, King of Norway, Saint Magnus, Earl of Orkney and Saint Columba. But the King would have none of them, and his fate was sealed.

But these royal expeditions in no way brought Argyll and the Isles to heel, and, in 1263, King Haakon of Norway came in all his might to settle once and for all the question of the suzerainty of the Isles which had continued to give trouble. Collecting a fleet from across Norway, he arrived in July in Shetland where they spent fourteen days at anchor in Bressay Sound. Guides from the Hebrides joined them there and they moved south to Orkney, where again they stayed, until 10 August when the fleet sailed for Lewis. On the 12th, at Raasay, they were joined by King Magnus of Man and his fleet. King Dougall MacRuari with his ships joined them in the Sound of Mull as the expedition moved on southwards, his ships awaiting the Norse King under the lee of Kerrera. By now the force totalled some 120 ships and, says the saga, a total of 20,000 men.

News of the Norse arrival had galvanised the Scots into reaction – it may not have been far short of panic. Garrisons were put on alert along the coast at Wigtown, Rothesay and Dunaverty and at the main Scottish base at Ayr. Castles as far away as Inverness and Stirling were put in a state of defence. An advance force of fifty ships under King Magnus of Man, King Dougall MacRuari and Brynjulf Jonsson was sent ahead to Tarbert – West Loch Tarbert, that is – to gain the submission of Angus (McDonald) Lord of Islay and of Murchadh MacSween.[16] This submission was obtained and hostages and 1,000 head of cattle taken; Angus resigned Islay for a regrant by King Haakon.

Dunaverty Castle then surrendered while a detachment of fifteen ships under Ruari MacRuari sailed ahead to Rothesay in Bute, over which the MacRuaris had a claim; once again the castle was under siege and forced to surrender. Ruari apparently killed off the garrison and then went on to ravage the nearby mainland. Meanwhile the invasion fleet was based at the anchorage at Gigha, the main refuge on that inhospitable coast. Ewen of Lorne, another King in the Sudreys and forebear of the MacDougall Lords of Argyll, came here to pay his respects. He was in a dilemma since he held his mainland possessions from the King of Scots and his island ones from Haakon. In spite of the latter's blandishments, Ewen refused to join the Norwegian expedition and relinquished his island domain. But Angus of Islay and Murchadh MacSween arrived in person to give their submission and stayed on; a fresh garrison was put into Dunaverty and Saddell Abbey was granted a letter of protection. At this time, too, a delegation arrived from Ireland to ask for help against the English.

The fleet now sailed round the Mull of Kintyre and came to Lamlash in Arran. Manoeuvres to show off the strength of the expedition were carried out off Ayr and off Bute while an ambassador from the King of Scots arrived to negotiate. Ewen of Argyll departed on friendly terms while the negotiations with the Scots dragged on, Arran, Bute and the Cumbraes being the sticking points which prevented agreement. On 8 September, the weather worsened. King Haakon and his fleet stood closer in to the mainland and anchored between the Cumbraes and Largs. A further meeting at Kilbirnie proved abortive and the truce was declared at an end. A strong force of some sixty ships, both Norse and Hebridean, was now detached under the command of King Dougall, Alan, his brother, Angus MacDonald of Islay, Murchadh MacSween and Vigleik Priest's-son. They sailed up Loch Long to Arrochar and there dragged their ships across to Loch Lomond, the name Tarbet on the freshwater side signifying an isthmus where such portages were made. Once afloat on the fresh water of the loch, they spread terror along its banks and plundered far inland, right up, so it has been claimed, to the walls of Stirling Castle itself.[17]

Sated with plunder, the detachment then returned to the main body. As they retraced their steps, dragging their boats through the glen that separated Loch Lomond and the sea, the locals attacked them, causing severe casualties. The leader of this party of local MacGilchrists was the young son of the Chief, Parlan. His kindred long remembered his bravery and took his name as the 'sons of Parlan' or Macfarlanes.[18] But on 1 October the weather blew up a storm and caused havoc among the fleet on a lee shore. Ten ships were wrecked, and in trying to extricate some of the grounded vessels the Norse became caught up in the so-called Battle of Largs and were attacked by a strong force of Scots, with the main army following up behind.

Largs was decisive. The year was drawing on and Haakon realised he had achieved little or nothing. The weather was worsening and winter was approaching. He decided on a withdrawal and retired once more to Lamlash in Arran and then to the anchorage behind the Isle of Sanda. The Fleet made the passage round the Mull of Kintyre and again dropped anchor at Gigha before crossing to the Sound of Islay where they lay from 12–14 October. That day they sailed north and arrived at Kerrera. Here, King Ewen MacDougall's island possessions were shared out. Mull, Coll and Tiree went to King Dougall MacRuari and his brother Alan. King Dougall was also granted Dunaverty while Ruari was granted Bute. Murchadh MacSween was given Arran.

Having rewarded his followers, King Haakon set sail once more via the Calf of Mull (Calve Island opposite Tobermory) to Raasay whence a storm blew them to Loch Snizort and Loch Eriboll where they lay from 27–29 October. Setting off once more, they had trouble getting through the stormy Pentland Firth. King Haakon decided to winter at Kirkwall where, on 15 December, worn out by the strain of the expedition and by disappointment, he died. His successor had no such desire to restore Norse rule. The following year, the Scots King sent an expedition under the command of the Earls of Mar and of Buchan and Alan Dorward. Norse supporters were punished and several were hanged. After lengthy negotiations, matters were finally settled in 1266 when, at the so-called Treaty of Perth, in return for a financial settlement, Norway gave up all claim to the Western Isles.

The story of the 1263 invasion is given in some detail and not only because – for once – we have some detail as to what happened. It was an extremely important event in the history of both Argyll and Scotland, as a result of which the Isles definitely became part of Scotland, although the later Lords of the Isles engineered their own downfall by their reluctance to accept this. Coincidentally, the period was also the first in which a Campbell appears in documentary record, Gillespic Cambel appearing as the recipient of the lands of Menstrie and Sauchie, in central Scotland. Of this, more below.

If these lands are far from Argyll, the family must have been well established by now on Lochaweside and it is possible to begin to outline the identity of their neighbours. We have already mentioned the sons of Somerled who by now are divided into three distinct divisions, the MacDougalls, the MacRuaris and the MacDonalds. The descendants of Anrothan were also beginning to follow the same pattern as they evolved into the various clans with which we are familiar. The leading kindred, the MacSweens, had already lost their great castle and the lands that went with it to the incoming Menteiths, but their MacGilchrist cousins still had most of Glassary. Their kindred, the Lamonts, MacLachlans, MacEwans and MacSorleys meanwhile controlled much of Cowal along with the Stewarts and the Menteiths.

In north Argyll, in Ardgour and Morvern the MacInneses and MacMasters, apparently both of one stock related to the Macgillivrays on Mull, seem to have been the leading families. It has been suggested that the Angus from whom the MacInneses take their name may even have been the original son of Erc who settled in Argyll in AD 500,[19] but this would seem very unlikely. The MacNaughtons were settled around the upper end of Loch Awe and over to Loch Shira; like the Campbells, their arrival in Argyll has been attributed to King Alexander II's expedition of 1222.

There was a strong concentration of power round the head of Loch Awe and extending over the neighbouring glens. This was the Glenorchy family, members, it is thought, of the kindred of Saint Fillan. Their main base was over the long pass to the east over Drum Albyn, and their leading clan the MacNabs. This Glenorchy family in due course were to attain fame if not notoriety as the MacGregors. From the above list, there are many omissions of names which were to become famous in the area. But this seems to have been a formative period as regards the clans as we know them today. It was a fluid period, both geographically with the movement of kindreds around the country and with the change in status which for some could be severe.

If there was movement, so too there was continuity, and many of the older kindreds must have stayed on the ground, their identity diminished and masked by more powerful newcomers. Certainly the pattern of the imposition of earlier powers is still to be found in the myriad forts, duns and crannogs that bestride the landscape, dating back to before the era of Our Lord. One or two of the earlier power groups may have survived, but more may, I would suggest, be found among what now became the lesser families – people like the MacEachrans of Kintyre who held land for their services as Mairs of Fee or administrators of South Kintyre, while their neighbours, the Mackays of Ugadale, performed the same function in North Kintyre. I think there is little doubt that they once were the lords of these lands, although the placing by the second-century Roman geographer Ptolemy of a tribe he calls the *Epidioi* ('horse-lovers') in what is taken to be Kintyre and the fact that the name in Greek means much the same as MacEachran does in Gaelic ('Son of the Horse-Lord') is no doubt mere coincidence.

Few if any of these people appear in the written records, although, like the Campbells, they are known to be there. They were soon to be joined by important newcomers, Macleans, MacMillans and the like. Meanwhile, the clan structure coagulated around the figure of the Chief, increasingly now part of the structure of feudalism, and the history of Clan Campbell at last becomes one for which there is contemporary written evidence.

CHAPTER THREE

Companion to the King

Even though we are now sure beyond doubt as to the existence of Gillespic Campbell, the actual evidence remains extremely slight and we are given no idea of his life and achievements. The Account for Stirling given in for 1264–6 by John de Lamberton, Sheriff of Stirling, mentions an inquiry at which the rate for the lands of Menstrie and Sauchie, given to Gillespic Cambell, is assessed at £40.[1] These lands lie far from Argyll, underneath the line of the Ochil Hills to the east of Stirling. The entry shows that if the Campbells of Loch Awe were now firmly tied to Argyll, they were by no means confined to that area and were also involved much closer to the centre of things in Scotland, something which few if any of their West Highland neighbours could claim.

Gillespic appears again, this time as *Agillascopper Cambel* – the scribe clearly had trouble with uncivilised Gaelic names – in 1266, when he is a witness to a charter of King Alexander III to the monks of Lindores Abbey erecting Newburgh as a burgh.[2] And Duke Niall makes mention of having seen an undated charter in which John of Arincrauche, Lord of Knapdale, grants Gillespic Cambel the lands of Arincraw, another spelling for Arincrauche, which Duke Niall thought might have been Ford at the southern end of Loch Awe. John, Lord of Knapdale was in all probability John of Menteith.

And that is all as far as documentary evidence is concerned. But if we return once more to *Ane Accompt* which otherwise gives no detail of Gillespic's life, we find a detail which has been overlooked by most historians. Gillespic is said to have been married to Effric, daughter of Colin, Lord of Carrick. The influential *Scots Peerage* has written out Colin of Carrick, denying he ever existed, which has probably accounted for this oversight. In the article on the Dukes of Argyll, the author goes so far as to state quite firmly 'There was no Colin of Carrick known to history'.[3] The article on the Earls of Carrick in the same series gives the clue; not for the first time, historians

41

became confused by the Latin names used as equivalent for local names in official documents, *Nigellus* for Neil and *Nicolas* for Colin being all combined by them in one.[4] In fact, there is plenty of evidence for there being both a Colin and an Earl Neil of Carrick, sons of Duncan, Earl of Carrick and his wife Avelina, daughter of the High Steward of Scotland and grandsons of Gilbert, younger son of Fergus, Prince of Galloway.[5]

Earl Neil married another Stewart, this time Margaret, daughter of Walter, the third High Steward. They had four daughters, only one of whom has been named. She was Margaret or Marjory, who had been left a young widow on the death of her first husband, 'Adam de Kilconcath' (Kilconquhar), who fell under the walls of Acre in 1270 as a Crusader. One day while out hunting, she met by chance a handsome young man. A lady of decided views, she took him, not without a struggle, back to her castle of Turnberry where, a few days later, it was announced that they had married! Having proceeded without the King's consent, her lands and castle were forfeit but she escaped with a fine, and her new husband, through right of his wife, became Earl of Carrick. His name was Robert Bruce, a name which his son was to make one of the most famous in all Scotland's history.

The eventual significance of this marriage can hardly be overestimated, linking the Campbells to two of Scotland's greatest families who were each in turn to become Royal. By it, Gillespie would have been a first cousin once removed to the future King Robert the Bruce. The King's contemporary ally and supporter, Sir Neil Campbell, who was in due course to become his brother-in-law, was already his second cousin once removed. It has been suggested that in fact the relationship was even closer, Effrica being one of the four unnamed daughters of Earl Neil, which would have made Sir Cailean Mor and the future King first and not second cousins. The separate identity of Colin and Neil of Carrick having been established, there seems no reason to believe this.[6]

At the same time the marriage raises intriguing questions, strengthening Campbell links with Ayrshire, an area with which they seem to have had early links, and strongly implying yet again that, although of insufficient importance at this time to appear in any of the accounts relating to Argyll, they were nevertheless able to make marriages of this status. As Professor Geoffrey Barrow has said, 'The precise origin of the Campbells is not known . . . but they were certainly not landless adventurers '.[7] Against this, the Campbells were still of insufficient importance to figure in what accounts we have of the contemporary history of the West Highlands and Isles, which in the years following the acquisition of the Isles by Scotland from Norway are dominated by the jockeying for power between the three main kindreds descended of Somerled; the MacDougalls, the MacRuaris and the MacDonalds.

The order in which they are placed here is deliberate since the MacDonalds, who were in due course to emerge as the most important and successful of the three kindreds in the guise of the Lords of the Isles, had by no means attained that pre-eminence at this stage. In fact, if compelled to assign an order of importance at this period, the MacDonalds would certainly rank behind the MacDougalls, probably behind the MacRuaris and also, albeit somewhat earlier, certainly behind the neighbouring MacSweens until the latter lost their holdings to the Menteith Stewarts.

It is perhaps just worthwhile making this point, since MacDonald historians tend to imply that there was an unbroken succession as ruler of Argyll and the Isles from Somerled to the MacDonald Lords of the Isles, when in fact this was not so. The MacDougalls are the chief losers by this; the MacDonalds have always been sensitive to Dougall's seniority by birth and his being not only the oldest son, but also a generation senior to that of Donald, who was Somerled's grandson. The record of the MacDougalls during the Wars of Scottish Independence was such as to make them easy targets in popular history, and it tends to be forgotten that the dreadful crash in their fortunes was the stepping stone on which was to be built the future greatness, not only of the Clan Campbell, but that of the MacDonald Lords of the Isles as well.

Two other players in the game now have to be taken into account – England and Ireland. England had moved into Ireland in 1169 and, based on the former Viking city of Dublin, had gradually extended its holdings over the land from behind the protection of the Pale, a move hotly contested by the Celtic warlords of the interior who sought help from their ancient kinsmen and allies across the water; as early as 1258 the *Annals of Connacht* report that *MacSomurli* – one of Somerled's descendants – came out of the Isles with a great fleet. In Connemara they captured a merchant ship and her cargo; the Sheriff of Connacht, Jordan d'Exeter, went after them with his own fleet but was roundly defeated by the Scots, who went on their way rejoicing.[8]

Of course, the inhabitants of Ireland were well used to the Norsemen and their ships, but this was a fleet from Scotland – almost certainly from the mainland if the identification of *MacSomurli* as Ewen MacDougall of Argyll is correct. No doubt such raids had been going on for centuries – in both directions – but at this period, the attraction for the warlords of Ireland of being able to increase their strength by the addition of well-armed fighting men – the *galloglach* – became apparent and was to last for succeeding centuries.

In 1286 there took place an event that was to lead to the transformation of the story of Scotland in general and the Campbells in particular. Keen to return to his new, young, French wife, King Alexander III insisted on his journey back from Edinburgh across the Forth and eastward into Fife, although the night was dark and stormy. His small escort missed him in the tempest and he went over the cliff edge on his horse without a sound. When day dawned, his lifeless body was found lying on the shore.

Alexander's three children were already dead, David in 1281, Alexander in 1284, and Margaret, who had married King Eric of Norway, in 1283. The only survivor of his line was his granddaughter, the young Princess Margaret of Norway, 'The Maid of Norway'. In her absence, the ruling of Scotland was entrusted to a body of six notables, the 'Guardians', made up of the Earl of Fife, the Earl of Buchan, the Steward, Comyn of Badenoch and Bishops Fraser and Wishart. By 1290, after protracted negotiations, agreement was reached on the marriage of the six-year-old Queen Margaret to Prince Edward of Caernarvon, the son and heir of King Edward I of England. The treaty cementing this alliance which would have seen the crowns of England and Scotland united was signed at Birgham in July that year.

But once again, death intervened; in October came the news that the infant Queen had died in Orkney on her journey, and her body had now been taken back to Norway. Scotland was without a Sovereign but not without competitors for the Crown. No fewer than fourteen people put forward claims. Unfortunately for the Scots, the situation allowed the entry of the English King Edward, who moved decisively to establish his position as the Overlord of Scotland. On 13 June 1291, at Upsetlington, the Guardians and the representative Barons and Knights of Scotland swore fealty to Edward as direct Lord and superior of Scotland.[9]

It was his choice that was to establish the rightful King of Scots – a contest which soon narrowed to one between four competitors. From David I's son, Earl Henry, had descended his sons Kings Malcolm IV and William I and their younger brother, David, Earl of Huntingdon, and sister Ada who had married Florence III, Count of Holland. Of the four final competitors, Count Florence V of Holland was Ada's great-great-grandson: five generations from Earl Henry. The others all descended from David, Earl of Huntingdon. John Balliol was the grandson of Earl David's eldest daughter Margaret and her husband Alan, Lord of Galloway, whose daughter, Devorgilla, had married John Balliol's father, John Balliol senior. He was four generations from Earl Henry but descended from him through the female line. Robert Bruce was father of the Earl of Carrick and grandfather of the eventual King Robert I. His father had married Earl David's younger daughter, Isabel, which meant he was only three generations from Earl Henry. John Hastings, the fourth competitor, was grandson of Earl David's youngest daughter, another Ada, and therefore, like John Balliol, was four generations from Earl Henry.

Edward decreed that a court should be set up of 104 Auditors, twenty of them being members of the English King's Council, forty being chosen by Balliol and forty by Bruce. Among the latter was Gillespic's son Sir Colin Campbell, Cailean Mor, said by some to have been accompanied by his son Neil and by Master Neil Campbell, the cleric.[10] In the event, it was decided that Balliol had the strongest claim.

One of the few positive moves in the short and ill-starred reign of John Balliol was a serious attempt to bring the Western Highlands and Isles under control by the erection of three new sheriffdoms. These were, respectively, the sheriffdoms of Skye, Lorne and Kintyre. Skye included, as well as Skye itself, Lewis, Uist, Barra and the Small Isles, Kintail and Wester Ross, all of which were placed under the Earl of Ross as Sheriff. Kintyre was joined with Arran, Bute and the Cumbraes under the Steward as Sheriff, while the rest of Argyll was incorporated into the new sheriffdom of Lorne under Alexander (MacDougall) of Argyll.

The ordinance which incorporated the new shires also listed the leading lords of Argyll and Kintyre. The lists are as interesting for the names omitted as for those included, and are given below with the identification of each, as far as is certain, set against the actual name as given in the list.

Lorne consisted of the lands of:

Terrae Kinnel Bathyn, Ardenmurich, Bothelehe	Morvern, Ardnamurchan etc.
Terrae Alexandri de Argadia	Alexander (MacDougall) of Argyll
Terra Johannis de Glenurwy	John of Glenorchy *a quo* the MacGregors
Terra Gilberti MacNaughton	Gilbert McNaughton of that Ilk
Terra Malcolm M'Ivyr	Malcolm (MacIver) Campbell
Terra Dugalli de Craiginis	Dugald (Campbell) of Craignish
Terra Johnnis M'Gilchrist	John MacGilchrist of Glassary
Terra Magistri Radulph de Dunde	Master Ralph of Dundee
Terra Gileskel M'Lach(lan)	MacLachlan of MacLachlan
Terra Comitis de Menteth de Knapedal	Earl of Menteith, lord of Knapdale
Terra Anegusii filii Dovenaldi Insularum	Angus MacDonald of the Isles

Kintyre consisted of:

Terra Lochmani M'Kilcolim M'Erewer	Lawman son of Malcolm son of Ferchar (Lamont)
Terra Enegus M'Erewer	Angus son of Ferchar (Lamont)
Terra de . . .	?
Insula de Boot	Island of Bute (the Steward)
Terra Domini Thomae Cambel	Sir Thomas Campbell *a quo* MacTavish?
Terra Duncani Duf	Duncan Dubh (father of Sir Arthur Campbell)

As can be seen, most of those included can be readily identified. The two M'Erewers in Kintyre are forebears of the Lamonts. Master Ralph of Dundee had married into the MacGilchrists of Glassary and had thereby inherited a share of the lands of Glassary; his descendants took the name *de Glassary* until their heiress eventually married the Royal Banner-Bearer and Constable of Dundee, Sir Alexander Scrymgeour. The de Glenorchy family later became better known under the name of MacGregor.

The omissions are also interesting. The lists may not have been meant to be complete, but there is no mention of Cailean Mor at this time – he may not have actually possessed land in his own right at this time, or, at least, not of sufficient extent to merit inclusion. There are a number of Campbells included: Duncan Dubh was the brother of Cailean Mor's father, Gillespic, probably the elder brother. His son was Sir Arthur from whom descended the MacArthur Campbells of Strachur. In early days, this branch of the Campbells was probably the pre-eminent one, more important than the Lochawe line.

Of Sir Thomas Campbell, we also know something. Whether or not he was a descendant of Taius Coirr, illegitimate son of Colin Maol Math, he must be a candidate for being the eponym of the Clan Tavish. He is a historical character, and his period is a much more likely one for the formation of a clan with a continuous surname than that of his possibly mythical ancestor.

Malcolm M'Inyr is Malcolm MacIver, descendant no doubt of Iver, whom Ane Accompt also claims as an illegitimate son of Colin Maol Math, fathered on the daughter of Suibhne Ruadh, the builder of Castle Sween. Colin is said to have quarrelled with him, possibly because he did not marry the girl with the full rites of Holy Church; had he done so, the MacIver landholdings might have included most of Glassary. Dun Mor, the impressive hill fort just behind what are now the county offices at Kilmory Castle, Lochgilphead, is said to have be an early seat of the MacIvers,[11] so perhaps Suibhne did not totally fail to provide for his daughter's child. As it was, they held extensive lands at what is now Arduaine at the mouth of Loch Melfort, south of Oban, where, overlooking the roadside, a rocky crag reveals falls of rubble to the sharp-eyed, the remnants of ancient ramparts where they had their strong-hold, Dun an Garbh-sroine, at the heart of what was known as 'MacIver's Lordship'. The former name for the area was Asknish, and the chieftains of this branch of the Clan used Asknish as their territorial designation even after they had agreed to exchange their lands for property on Loch Fyne whither they moved, taking the name of Asknish with them to their new estate.

But the waters have been muddied around the origins of the MacIvers, notably by Principal Campbell of Aberdeen University, who harboured a personal motive and for a long time petitioned the Lord Lyon for recognition as 'Chief of the Clan Iver', arguing that it was a separate clan altogether who had taken the name Campbell for political reasons. He wrote a book entitled merely *Account of the Clan-Iver*, which is excellent in parts but which needs a sharp eye to distinguish between definite fact and the political arguments he was seeking to make in furtherance of his own petition, which the Lord Lyon in due course rejected (see Appendix 3 on septs).

Principal Campbell denies the Campbell origins of the name and says that the MacIvers originate in Glenlyon, being part of the invading force of 1222, as a result of which they were settled in Argyll. His arguments would have been more convincing had it not been essential to his case for the Campbell connection to be replaced by one which left the MacIvers as an entirely separate clan. Unfortunately, this modern game of clan-constructing is again being played, with the claim being made for a Clan MacIver which appears to group together under one umbrella all those of the name regardless of their origins – a dubious concept in view of the popularity of the Norse name Ivar in its various forms wherever in Scotland the Norseman penetrated.

And then we come to the Campbells of Craignish, *MacDougall Craignish* from their eponym Dougall, said in both *Ane Accompt* and 'The Manuscript History of Craignish' to derive from Dougall, son of Gillespic, the legitimate half-brother of Tavish Coirr and of Iver above. Dougall – or Dugald, as 'The History of Craignish' spells it – was sent to be fostered by MacEachairn, the *Toiseach Ban* or Fair Thane of Nether Craignish; he married the daughter of Donald of Islay, a match which was engineered by Dougall's foster-father who encouraged the girl to elope from Islay with him. Her father, setting out after her with a strong force, camped at the north end of Jura, opposite Craignish where his numerous camp-fires were seen from the mainland. But the Toiseach decided on a stratagem; he had fires lit on all the hilltops around and kept them burning all night, which caused Donald of Islay to pause and think. At the instigation of his wife, who was the young girl's stepmother, he decided to treat on the morrow. All turned out well and the wedding was agreed on, the final happy ending being that MacEachairn, having no children, settled his estate of Craignish upon the young couple, whose descendants became the Campbells of Craignish. So goes the tale.

The author of 'The Manuscript History of Craignish' says that Dougall was born 'much about the year 1130'; this sounds like his own guess. It could hardly be exact, if the girl was Somerled's great-granddaughter with her father active in attacking Derry in 1214. But the point is merely an aside since it would be unwise to take the story as a whole as gospel, typical as it is of the good stories which abound in Highland genealogies where they are so often more of an art-form than strict history. This is particularly so in view of the very different accounts given in other sources of the family's origins. According to a note taken by Duke Niall from the Rev. J. MacDougall, Duror, it was MacEachairn's daughter and heiress whom Dugald Campbell married, while according to the Rev. A. Maclean Sinclair, Dougall himself was a MacEachairn, a younger son of the Chief of the clan we have already come across as being the ancient inhabitants of Kintyre. He makes no distinction between the spelling of MacEachran and MacEachairn or MacEachern which are one and the same, a point also made by G. F. Black.[12]

It is somewhat puzzling to find such a distinguished Kintyre family so far north as Craignish; 'The Manuscript History of Craignish', aware that an explanation is necessary, claims that this was the Chief's original residence. Having handed it over to his foster-son and his wife, he found himself more and more an encumbrance and eventually decided to set out for Ireland with his goods and chattels on horseback, declaring that he would settle where a beast first shed its load. In fact, he had got as far as Killellan in Kintyre when one of the ropes broke – incidentally a theme often repeated in Highland legend – and there set up his new home, which he took from the existing inhabitants by the sword. He married again and set up a new family who became the MacEachrans of Killellan. This version of course spoils the idea that the MacEachrans were the early inhabitants of Kintyre and descendants of the tribe of the *Epidioi*. There is, however, no doubt of their early existence in Craignish.

We are once again left with no very clear answer; either the Campbells of Craignish were indeed of the Blood and obtained Craignish through marriage, or they are an alien tribe who became Campbells *de facto* out of political expediency. This first Dougall was succeeded by a son and a grandson both by the same name; the first was said to have married Brigid, daughter to *Dugal MacCaurre*, Toiseach of Lochavich, by which he inherited those lands and also *Caisteal na Nighinn Ruaidhe* – the Castle of the Red-haired Maid on an islet in Loch Avich. His son, the third Dougall according to 'The Manuscript History', was married to a daughter of MacSween of Skipness, son of Sween the Red who built Castle Sween. With their son, yet another Dougall, the fourth in succession, we are back on firmer ground since he is the Dougall of Craignish mentioned as holding lands in the sheriffdom of Lorne. Although of concern to genealogists, to historians the origin of these various supposed branches of Clan Campbell are of lesser account since, from wherever they came, they all eventually thought of themselves and behaved as Campbells.

Balliol's reign, apart from this attempt to move into the Western Highlands, gave little of distinction. King Edward made it plain that he regarded the King of Scots as his subordinate. In 1294, he quarrelled over Aquitaine which he held of the King of France, who wanted it back. The English feudal host was called to muster on 1 September and the English King also demanded the presence of the King of Scots, the ten Scottish earls and sixteen barons, headed by the Steward and by Bruce the Competitor. None of the Scots in fact turned up, having made excuses of one sort or another. The following year, the Scots appointed a Council of Twelve who took the government out of Balliol's hands. A treaty was signed with the French and the country placed in a state of defence.

In March 1296, Edward invaded Scotland. Berwick was besieged and fell, surrendering on terms which were later ignored; the ground was littered with corpses of those who had given themselves up on promise of quarter. The thirty Flemings in their Red Hall fought until suffocated or burnt to a man. In no hurry, the English moved on the following month to take Dunbar, by now in Scottish hands although Earl Patrick of Dunbar was a supporter of Edward. The Scottish host moved to meet them and to succour the garrison, but, under the misapprehension that de Warenne's troops were in retreat, they broke ranks and were themselves roundly defeated. A large number of Scottish nobles were taken prisoner and held for ransom.

Among them, it would appear from entries made the following year, were *Nicolas Duncandowesone*, or Colin, son of Duncan Dubh, from his patronymic, a brother of Sir Arthur Campbell. He was imprisoned in Hardelagh Castle,[13] and may or may not have later been released; in any case he appears to have died before 1304 when John de Dovedale, to whom King Edward had granted Colin's land in fee, now succesfully petitioned for the ward and marriage of his son and heir who was then under age.[14] Thomas Campbell, also a prisoner, was to be liberated the following year with his fellow captives,[15] while Master Neil Campbell as Master Nigelaus Cambell, a prisoner in England, was given safe conduct to go to Scotland 'until the Feast of the Chains of Blessed Peter' together with John Comyn, Earl of Buchan, Alexander de Balliol, Alexander, Earl of Menteith, Reginald de Crawford and William Byset.[16]

Master Neil had previously appeared on record as an envoy of the Earl of Carrick.[17] From his Ayrshire connections and his use of the name Neil which was subsequently to become one of the Campbell family Christian names, it seems a safe bet to suggest that he was another descendant of the marriage of Sir Gillespic Campbell with Effrica of Carrick who brought the names Colin and Neil to the Campbells. His title of 'Master', often written 'Mr', denoted one who had matriculated at a university and was very often the title of a minister of the church. Neil was therefore almost certainly a younger brother of Sir Cailean Mor. There are few other local names among the Dunbar prisoners, but John de Menteith was among their number, as was John de Glenorchy.

These intermittent glimpses of early Campbells are frustrating – they are few and far between, and there is so much more one would like to know. Of no-one is this truer than of Sir Colin Campbell, Gillespic's son, who as *Cailean Mor* gave his name as patronymic to the later Chiefs of the Clan Campbell. 'Sir Colin' (so he must have been knighted by this date) appears on one of the Earl of Lennox's charters in 1281.[18] The following year he is again listed as a witness, this time one of Badindath, given as a gift to Cambuskenneth Abbey by William de Kininmonth.[19] An undated charter but thought to be some time around 1290 records him as the recipient of a grant of the lands of Kamesnamuckloch from John, son of Lagman or Lamont.[20]

In 1292, the first Campbell armorial coat-of-arms on record appears: the plain gyronny shield on the seal of 'Nicholas Cambel', otherwise Sir Colin, held in the chapter house, Westminster. That same year, Cailean Mor is to be found once more as one of the witnesses to a charter by Richard de Burgh of the gift of 'my Castle of Roo and Burgh' to James the Steward of Scotland who is marrying his sister Egidia, the charter being confirmed by King Edward I of England.[21] Here Cailean Mor appears as *Nicholas de Chambelle*, a version of his name which is not instantly recognisable. His son Neil also appears on the Badindath charter of 1282 as 'Neil son of Colin'. It will be noted that the style 'of Lochawe' does not yet apply to members of the family. In 1293 he received or acquired from Sir William Lindsay the lands of *Symontoun* – Symington – in Ayrshire, paying rent to the monks of New Battle who now have the superiority.[22] That year he made a gift to the same

Abbey[23] and also handed over a reddendo due for the lands of Symington.[24]

Ane Accompt says that Sir Colin married Janet, daughter of Sir John Sinclair, by whom he had two sons, Sir Neil and Gillespic, while others mention another son, Dugald, or Dougall, a parson from whom descend the Argyllshire *Sons of the Parson* or MacPhersons, not to be confused with the other Dougall, also son of Sir Colin. According to a traditional history of the MacDonalds, Sir Colin's daughter was married to Angus of the Isles and was therefore mother to Angus Og.[25] The only other Campbell on record prior to 1292 is Dougall Campbell, who appears as rendering account for his part in the management of affairs in Dumbarton 1288–92, along with William Fleming, who is Constable under the Sheriff, the Earl of Fife. Dougall's identity is given by a later charter of 1323 when he (assuming him to be the same Dougall) appears as 'Dugall son of Colin' and therefore a younger brother of Sir Neil.[26] Having been beaten at Dunbar, Scotland surrendered to Edward, who made a triumphal progress that spring and summer through the north-eastern shires. Balliol was made to surrender his crown, and at a ceremony at Montrose he finally resigned the kingdom to Edward, the Royal Arms of Scotland being formally stripped from his tabard. Thereafter he was known to his own people as 'Toom Tabard' – 'Empty Tabard'. The next month, he went to the Tower of London.

There is a most interesting note of instructions having been given at this period to Colin Campbell as 'Nicholaus Cambel, bailie of Leghor and Ardescothyn', that is to say Lochawe and Ardscotnish, the adjoining district round Kilmartin. It is of considerable significance that he is not described here or in any other document as being 'of Lochawe' and here is specifically described not as *Dominus* or 'Lord' of Lochawe but only as Bailie or Steward, presumably for the King.[27]

This poses a number of questions as to the claim made in *Ane Accompt* over the early holding by the Campbells of the whole Lordship of Lochawe which, it will be remembered, came to them by two marriages. Is this story false and were successive Campbells King's officers only? Did Cailean Mor hold the Lordship of Lochawe only and act as the King's agent for Ardscotnish which has not previously been mentioned? Or was he deposed by King Edward due to having taken up arms against the English King and only allowed to remain on his lands in the lesser capacity? There is no clear answer, but the failure to use the designation 'Campbell of Lochawe' or 'Lord of Lochawe' has to be taken into careful account.

The extent of Scotland's subjection was made plain when Edward prepared to leave the country in August. Cailean Mor signed the oath of fealty to King Edward – known as 'Ragman Roll' – among a group of leading earls and knights dated at Berwick-upon-Tweed on 28 August. Whether he and the others actually attended or not is to be questioned; more probably the oaths and signatures were collected by the local Sheriff and sent in to the King before he left Scotland. 'Master Neel Cambel' was among others from the county of Ayr; 'Thomas Cambel' was among the King's tenants in Perthshire; also from that county, which, it will be remembered, included most of Argyll until Balliol's attempts to set up new sheriffdoms which seemingly were now ignored or were unknown to the English, were listed 'Dougal, Arthur' and 'Duncan Cambel'. From the Western Isles came 'Duncan Cambel' – possibly the same as the foregoing – while 'Dovenal' (Donald) 'Cambel' came from the County of Dumbarton.[28]

The names are by now familiar ones, with the exception of Duncan of the Isles and Duncan of the County of Perth – they may be one and the same – and Donald from Dunbartonshire. They are assumed to be brothers of Sir Neil, and we shall meet them again. But that year, 1296, Sir Cailean Mor was killed, in a skirmish with the MacDougalls at the String of Lorne. A cairn named for him marks the spot today, situated by the side of a lonely track that climbs from the shore of Lochavich over the hill to the descent into Scammadale and so to Kilninver and the mouth of Loch Feochan. The route is an ancient one, leading from Dalavich on Loch Awe opposite where the castle of Innischonnel was to be built, away out to the Atlantic shore. The cairn is on the watershed, a lonely pile of stones surrounded by grass and heather, with no companions except grazing sheep and the lonely cry of birds wheeling under the scudding clouds.

Quite how this affair came about is unknown. *Ane Accompt* says that Sir Cailean had put the MacDougalls to flight and was following them up across the ford called *Ath Dhearg* or 'the Red Ford' when he was killed. The *Allt Dhearg* is obviously referred to, 'the Red Burn' so called, it is claimed, for the blood that stained its waters that day. This is several hundred yards to the west, on the MacDougall side of the watershed on which the cairn now stands. Other accounts say that Sir Cailean met his end shot in the back by an arrow. What is interesting is the stone enclosure on the hillside above the burn next to a tributary which goes by the name *Allt a Chomhairle* – 'Burn of the Council'.

This is reputed to be the site of a much earlier meeting place where the tribe of Loarn and the tribe of Gabhran, formed from the original Scottish settlers, met and quarrelled. The mention of the 'Council' may provide the clue. In various parts of Argyll there were ancient boundary meeting places – another such is Accurach on the watershed between Loch Awe and Loch Fyne close to the present road between Inveraray and Dalmally – where neighbouring communities met and thrashed out disputes over the marches of their respective territories, arguments over strayed cattle and the like. It very much looks as if this is one of them, in which case it could be that Sir Colin had been holding a meeting with the MacDougalls, no very friendly one, and at its conclusion had been returning home by way of the track which crossed the ford. Meanwhile, a MacDougall or MacDougalls could have taken the direct route over the heather and could have been waiting to ambush Sir Cailean at the point where his cairn now stands. This would at least make sense of the terrain.

So fell Cailean Mor who was to give his name to the title of future Chiefs of the Clan Campbell who take their title of *Mac Cailein Mor* from him. (The name is *Cailean* in Gaelic which becomes *Cailein* in the genitive.) Gaelic speakers point out that in that form it means 'Great Son of Colin' rather than 'Son of Colin the Great'. This is technically correct; as it happens we do not know if Colin was ever so named for being 'the Great' or merely for being large in size, in which case *Cailean Mor* would merely mean 'Big Colin'. From the scanty record of his doings it is not easy to see why he should merit the compliment 'the Great', but that is at least as likely to be due to lack of record of the period as to any lack of worth on his part. His body was taken by his people to the church at Kilchrenan, where it was buried. Years later, the most impressive stone in the churchyard was assumed to be his; when, however, its inscription was deciphered, it was found to commemorate someone quite different, so the Duke of the day had a new tombstone made in memory of his illustrious ancestor. It is to be found set up by the present church there today.

After Edward's departure, Scotland lay momentarily stunned under the heel of the invader. The English administration was under command of Hugh Cressingham and seemed all-powerful. But the following year, 1297, Scottish resistance revived, this time with its leading light one William Wallace, a man of good if not great social standing but one possessed of total dedication to his cause and the charisma to inspire the Scottish people. Much has been made of Wallace's relatively humble origins – he was the younger son of a minor laird – and of the dubious loyalties of the Scottish nobility. In fact, while the majority had bowed to the virtually inevitable in signing Ragman Roll, there were few indeed who were actually on the side of the English. A considerable number were, however, on the side of Balliol, whose claim to the Scottish Crown would still seem to be the best, while Bruce himself had for a time been on the side of the English. There is no contemporary mention of the Campbells taking part in the campaigns of William Wallace, which is not to say they did not do so. Master Neil, as we have seen, was given a temporary release from English captivity at this time.

An interesting sideline is provided by the epic poem 'Wallace' produced much later, around 1478, by the mysterious 'Blind Harry'. Thought to be written partly for entertainment and partly as a political diatribe against a too-subservient royal policy towards the English, it is splendid stuff. Unfortunately, however, much of it is clearly inaccurate, several incidents having obviously been lifted from the later exploits of Robert the Bruce. Among these is an entirely fictitious account of an earlier battle in the Pass of Brander where Loch Awe empties to the sea. According to the poet's version, a figure unknown to history, one 'MacFadzean', an Irish robber, is given Argyll, a gift which is acquiesced in by John (MacDougall) of Argyll since he has been given so much land in England by Edward I but which is resented by his uncle Duncan, who joins 'Campbell, the knight, that witty was and smart'. Together, MacDougall and Campbell manage to bottle up MacFadzean in the Pass of Brander while Wallace marches to their aid. The actual locations are somewhat confused in the poem, but the defeated MacFadzean takes refuge in a cave with a body of his men, where Duncan of Lorne despatches him. MacFadzean's head being then cut off and displayed on a pole (this is entirely according to ancient Celtic practice and, as a detail, does ring true), Wallace then moves to Ardchattan where he sets up his headquarters. Duncan, who, rather than being John's uncle as 'Blind Harry' has it, was in fact his brother, is given Lorne. All ends happily.

There is, however, an interesting twist to the tale. Several hundred yards from the site of the later and historical conflict in the pass, there is a pool in the River Awe, known to this day as 'MacFadzean's', marked by 'MacFadzean's Stone' now displaced by recent floods, while up on a neighbouring hillside is 'MacFadzean's Cave'. This is unusual in that history usually is confirmed by placenames, but here we appear to have a case of placenames invented to fit an apocryphal tale.

Wallace's story, having climbed the heights of triumph and the depths of disaster, was to come to a brutal and bitter end at the hands of the vengeful King Edward. After the defeat of the English host at Stirling Bridge in September 1297, the body of the hated Cressingham was flayed and, according to one account, Wallace had a sword-belt made out of the result. Under his command the Scots made a triumphal foray into England, burning and slaying in their turn and driving off a rich plunder. Early the next year, Wallace was made Guardian of Scotland. But the pendulum swung again. On 1 July 1298, the English host assembled at Roxburgh and on the 22nd it met the much smaller Scottish army at Falkirk, where the Scottish *schiltron* or close-packed formation of pikemen proved no match for the English longbows. Wallace and most of his subordinate commanders melted away into the woods.

It is not the purpose of this book to go in detail through the story of the years that followed. Wallace resigned as Guardian and went to France, seeking the support of the French King who, eventually, at the end of 1300, gave him a letter to the Pope. His departure did not meet with universal approval in Scotland, now under the command of three guardians, Bishop Lamberton, Bruce and Comyn. Bruce, however, soon resigned, being replaced by Sir Ingram de Umfraville. Early in 1301, all three resigned and Sir John de Soules assumed the position of sole Guardian. That summer, the Scots won their case before the Pope. Balliol was still the King of Scots, although there was no question of his returning to Scotland. Meanwhile, a series of invasions of Scotland by the English virtually extinguished resistance. In 1302 a truce was signed, at which point Robert Bruce went over to the English side.

This move may seem astonishing if not incredible to the modern popular view of Bruce. It was probably prompted by a number of factors. The Battle of Courtrai that year led to a truce between the English and the French, a prelude to the treaty which removed the French as potential allies. Balliol had once more entered the lists as the recognised king of Scots, thereby re-erecting the barrier to Bruce's gaining the throne which all along he coveted. Finally Bruce had just remarried, this time to Elizabeth, daughter of Richard de Burgh, Earl of Ulster, one of Edward's staunchest subordinates. Whatever the reason or reasons, Bruce now joined those – and they were many – leading Scots who were to be numbered among the ranks of the English adherents. By early 1304, all the Scottish leaders save Soules, Fraser and Wallace had succumbed.[29] And, so it would appear, did several if not all the leading Campbells.

In 1302, on 13 February, King Edward granted the lands of the late Hubert de Multon to his widow Margaret, to hold them until Hubert's son and heir was of age, with permission to marry Sir Neil Campbell. Orders were given to the Chancellor to produce a letter under the Great Seal to this effect.[30] The English King planned a great campaign for 1303, and in July that year the Earl of Ulster crossed to Scotland to join the King with a force of men-at-arms, light horse and 4,000 infantry. Detachments captured the Castles of Inverkip and Rothesay, but the main body were left to their own devices and to support themselves off the country as best they could until, at the end of September, they returned home, leaving only their leaders to remain with Edward. Among those summoned to join the Earl of Ulster's Knights was Sir Neil Campbell,[31] who in due course was given the marriage of Andrew Crawford's two heiress daughters to dispose of, a potentially profitable gift.[32]

Whether or not Sir Neil married Margaret de Multon seems doubtful. He may have done, but the attraction of Andrew Crawford's rich estates in Ayrshire, in an area in which the Campbell family were particularly interested, proved irresistible. At Martinmas 1303, Richard de Keith complained to King Edward that the marriage of Andrew's heiress daughters, now claimed by Sir Neil Campbell, had already been given to him. From an endorsement on the document, it would appear that the gift to Sir Neil had in fact been made, but the matter was placed before the King's Council, who took over the girls' ward and forbade Sir Neil to marry the younger daughter before they had come to a final decision. Sir Neil was in trouble, however, since he had already married the girl. In danger of being held in contempt of the Council, he pleaded that, at the time, she was not under their jurisdiction.[33]

It is of course just possible that, as in the case of Sir Donald and the elder Susannah Crawford, 'married' meant 'arrange the marriage of' and that she might have become a daughter-in-law or niece of Sir Neil over whose marriages, for there were certainly more than one, much uncertainty exists. Another persistent tradition has him married to the daughter of Cameron of Locheil who did not then exist as such; use of the name Cameron may represent a member of one of the chieftainly families of Lochaber or one of the Flemish families of the name Cameron or *de Cambrun* who held lands in Fife.

It may have been as a punishment that in 1304, Alexander MacDougall, instead of Sir Neil, uplifted the rents of Lochawe and Ardscotnish. Not all Campbells appear to have been in favour with King Edward, however. That same year, Sir John de Dovedale, to whom King Edward had given Sir Nichol Cambel's lands in fee since his son and heir is under age, now begs that the king will give him ward of the lands and the marriage of the infant.[34] This would seem to refer to the young son of Sir Colin, son of Duncan Dubh, who must have recently died.

One Campbell does, however, appear to have been in English service at this time: in 1304, on 9 January, John Botetourt, Justiciar of Galloway, Annan and Nithsdale, about to go on foray against the enemy, has with him a force which includes 'Sir Dovenald Cambel' with two esquires. He demands pay and also victual for his force from King Edward and the same for Sir Robert de Brus Earl of Carrick, for garrison of Ayr Castle.[35] The following year, 1305, on 8 April, there is mention of James de Dalilegh, King's Receiver in Scotland, paying out £65 – a sum he had received from Sir Donald Campbell, Sheriff of Wigtown, out of the King's rents in that county.[36]

A further list is given of men at arms in the following of John de St John in the King's service in Scotland. Sir Roger de Kirkpatrick has five horses and Sir Donald Campbell has two. The names of five other knights are given among a list of thirty-five names in all. The source is dated as being 1306–7, but this seems much too late. Sir John de St John was Warden of Galloway in 1301 and became the King's Lieutenant in 1302, and this seems a much more likely dating.[37] But it would seem that Sir Donald got into trouble along with his brother Sir Neil. This is suggested by a later letter of 1307–8 from Robert de Keith in Norman French to an unknown addressee which again mentions the Crawford heiresses whose marriages, he points out, were bought by him from King John Balliol and confirmed by King Edward, Sir Neil Campbell and Sir Donald Campbell being distrained to produce them. The girls' names were Susan and Alyse and their lands were those of Loudoun, Loncmertenan and Stenstoun in the county of Ayr and Draffan in the county of Lanark. But as we have already seen, this was too late; Sir Neil would seem to have married the younger girl while Susannah the elder had been married to Duncan, Sir Donald's eldest son and heir. Thus was founded the great Campbell House of Loudoun in Ayrshire, whose heads bore for arms the Campbell gyronny in Susannah's Crawford colours of ermine and red.

In 1305, disaster again hit the Scots with the capture of Wallace somewhere near Glasgow. He was captured by the servants of Sir John de Menteith who was at the time Edward's Governor of Dumbarton Castle, to which Wallace was taken. The vilification of Sir John for his part in Wallace's fate seems unjustified, but, in spite of his loyalty at the time being to the English King as was that of so many other Scots, neither that nor his subsequent conduct has ever excused him in popular estimation. Far more inexcusable was the personal venom with which Edward pursued Wallace, whose fate was almost unbearable for our modern eyes to contemplate – dragged as he was through the streets of London behind a horse on a hurdle, hung, drawn and quartered and his head impaled on a spike on London Bridge while his four quarters were displayed to the people's view in Newcastle-upon-Tyne, Berwick, Stirling and Perth.

There are various versions of another event of major importance which took place shortly afterwards. It would appear that Bruce and Sir John 'the Red' Comyn met and quarrelled and Bruce stabbed his erstwhile colleague to death. One version is that they had been plotting a rising against King Edward which, if successful, would have led to Bruce taking the throne and Comyn receiving Bruce's former lands. Comyn had then revealed the plot to the English King and Bruce had now killed him in revenge. It may be more likely that Bruce unveiled his plans to Comyn at their meeting and that the latter would have none of them. The Bruce's right to the throne was never without its opponents. Probably the two men quarrelled and Bruce lost his temper. Tradition has it that Comyn was mortally wounded. His uncle Sir Robert Comyn who came to his aid was himself killed by Bruce's brother-in-law Christopher Seton. There was a confused scuffle. Comyn may still have been alive in the hands of the monks when the King's follower Kirkpatrick uttered his famous promise 'I'll mak siccar' and, drawing his dagger, despatched the dying man. Whatever actually happened in detail, the killing was true enough. It took place in the Kirk of Greyfriars at Dumfries on 10 February 1306 and its repercussions would be felt for years to come.

The die was now cast and Bruce moved quickly. The fiery cross was out, and all over Scotland, adherents of Comyn and the English scuttled for cover. With the aid of his immediate circle of friends and relatives, Bruce consolidated his position in the south-west. The castles of Ayr, Dalswinton, Tibbers and Dumfries were taken, as was Rothesay. A deal with the custodian of Dunaverty meant that the Firth of Clyde approach was well under control apart from Dumbarton whose Captain, Sir John de Menteith, was not yet ready to come over. Bishop Robert Wishart of Glasgow gave his full support.

On 25 March, Robert the Bruce was crowned King of Scots at Scone. King Edward had taken the sacred Stone of Destiny to Westminster and the Earl of Fife, who as represcnter of arguably the senior line of the old Scots Royal Family had an essential part to play in the coronation of any King of Scots, was only 15 and firmly in English power. But his aunt Isabel, wife of the Comyn Earl of Buchan, slipped away from her husband's household – he himself was luckily enough on their English property at the time – and rode triumphantly to the King's inauguration where she placed the crown upon his head. Stone of Destiny there might not be, but the ancient Moot Hill of Scone that had seen the same ceremony repeated for centuries provided validation enough.

It would seem that until shortly before this this time Sir Neil Campbell was in England, quite possibly at the English Court, since on 20 June of the same year King Edward granted two parts of the manor of Ishall in Cumberland during the minority of the heir of Hubert de Multon to Robert de Carlisle, the said custody now being in the hands of the King due to 'Nigel' (i.e. Neil) 'Cambel', to whom the custody had previously been gifted, 'having taken himself to Scotland against the King'.[38]

Later that year, the matter of the ownership of the young de Multon's custody was still in doubt. On 22 November, at Lanercost, a commission of inquiry was granted at the request of Richard le Breton, to whom Neil Campbell had apparently transferred the custody. This was to establish whether the transaction had taken place when Neil was still in the King's Peace, thus making the deal a legal one and negating the King's later action.[39] It is clear that the projected marriage with Margaret de Multon had not happened; she had been passed over in favour of the Crawford sister, Alyse, whose name does not appear in the genealogies. It also seems that Neil Campbell, on hearing of the killing of Comyn and the uprising, fled back to Scotland to the side of his cousin Robert the Bruce. It would also seem likely that his brother Sir Donald, previously in King Edward's service, also in trouble for having married the elder Crawford heiress, went with him.

The Scots Peerage indeed says that Sir Neil was present at King Robert's coronation at Scone and was with him, too, at the disaster at Methven in mid-June when King Edward's Lieutenant, Aymer de Valence, Comyn's brother-in-law, caught King Robert and his men encamped in a wood some miles west of Perth in an unexpected dawn attack which sent the King of Scots and a few adherents scampering westward to the shelter of the great hills.[40] With him, we think, went Sir Neil, the Earl of Lennox, Sir James Douglas – 'the Good Sir James' – and Sir Gilbert Hay, Bruce's close companions through the years to follow. Bruce first seems to have gone to try and reorganise his forces, based on the area around Crianlarich and Tyndrum, in the area where Saint Fillan had lived and where the monastery devoted to his memory was to be built. For all his life, Bruce showed particular devotion to this saint and it seems that he was well looked after here when his fortunes were at a low ebb.

At this point, it is worthwhile reviewing the general situation in Argyll. This was as confused as regards changing loyalties as was the rest of Scotland. The MacSweens had long since lost their power base, although they were still in the area and keen to regain their former lands. The main theme was the struggle between the descendants of Somerled in what had become the major dynasties of MacDougalls, MacRuaris and MacDonalds. As the leading figure in the area, Alexander (MacDougall) of Argyll had been appointed sheriff of the new county of Argyll by Balliol in 1292. He fell out of favour with King Edward of England, however, and in 1296 Alexander Earl of Menteith had received a commission to take the fortresses, castles and lands of Alexander of Argyll and his son John.[41]

That same year, Alexander of Argyll took the oath of fealty to King Edward, but he was clearly out of favour since a 'statement of the Injuries committed by Alexander of Argyll upon the English' of June 1297 speaks of his having been imprisoned after he had taken the oath to the English King. Thereupon he set forth and devastated the MacDonald lands, burning and slaying as he went. The author of this letter is revealed, since he apologises for the fact that he has lost his seal and is having to use that of his wife Juliana, as being Alexander (MacDonald) of Islay. A major bone of contention had continued to exist between him and the MacDougalls ever since he had married Juliana, who was either a sister or just possibly a daughter of Alexander of Argyll.

With her, he claimed, had come her tocher of the island of Lismore which he had been prevented from possessing. Tempers ran high, and this continuing quarrel probably provided the main motivation for much of the political manoeuvring of both parties.

Alexander of Islay went on to complain of the MacRuaris in his letter to the King. Ruari MacRuari had been pursued and had been forced to agree to obey Edward's authority; his brother Lachlan,[42] who had sworn obedience, had nevertheless killed many of the King's followers, and the two brothers had ravaged and burnt most of Skye and Lewis and had burnt several ships in the King's service. Alexander ends by begging the King to order the nobles of Argyll and of Ross to come to his aid.[43] A further letter tells of Lachlan MacRuari also causing troubles, while Duncan (MacDougall) of Argyll, Alexander's son, rather than hand over two powerful galleys, the largest in the Isles, to Alexander (MacDonald) of Islay in his capacity of King Edward's Captain of the Coast of Argyll and Ross, burnt them as they lay under the walls of Inverlochy Castle.[44]

In 1301, John MacSween complains that having been granted his lands again, he is being prevented from occupying them by John (MacDougall) of Argyll and by Sir John Menteith. That same year, on 6 June, King Edward issues an instruction to his Admiral of the Cinque Ports to receive into the King's Peace Alexander (MacDougall) of Argyll, John and Duncan, his sons and Lachlan MacRuari his son-in-law.[45] In 1304, the King writes to John (MacDougall) of Argyll who is sick, excusing him from attending the parliament and excusing him *pur ce que nous nous fions molt de vous et de votre loiaute* – 'because we have much trust in you and your loyalty'.[46] That year, Alexander of Argyll, as we have seen, rendered account for the lands previously in Campbell charge in Argyll. In September of the following year, he was appointed a member of the advisory council to the new Governor of Scotland, John of Brittany. By now, he and his family were firmly on the King of England's side, and the killing of John Comyn, Alexander's nephew, by Bruce in 1306 only cemented them more strongly to that cause.

Alexander (MacDonald) 'of Islay' or 'of the Isles' – both designations are used – meanwhile pursued a different course. In 1296 he is King's Bailie for Kintyre, and in that capacity carried out orders to seize Kintyre and hand it over to 'Malcolm le Fitz Lengleys of Scotland', whose identity is unclear although he would seem to be a Highlander who has spent some time south of the Border.[47] Alexander rather plaintively does dare to point out that it is not right to depose existing tenants except by lawful writ – hardly surprising if he were among them.[48] Perhaps as a sop, in September that year, King Edward, who describes him as 'our beloved' Alexander, orders him to be granted lands rated at £100 for his past and future services.[49]

But all was not well within the family. Alexander had a rival in his younger brother Angus Og, who supplants him. There is some argument about the fate of Alexander, but the *Irish Annals of Connacht*, later echoed by the *Annals of the Four Masters*, under the year 1299 report: 'Alexander Mac Domnaill, the most generous and bounteous man of Scotland and Ireland together, was killed by Alexander Mac Dubgaill and a countless number of his men were slaughtered with him'.[50] The *Annals of the Four Masters* describe Alexander as 'the best man of his tribe in Ireland and Scotland for hospitality and prowess'.[51] This, surely, must be Alexander (MacDonald) of Islay. The links between the cultures of Ireland and Argyll were close, and it is interesting to note that Alexander's hospitality was ranked alongside his ability as a soldier.

The leadership of the family of Islay was now taken over by Angus Og, from whom the later Lords of the Isles descend. Alexander had several sons whose exact subsequent history is unclear. They were probably the origin of the *Clann Alasdair* or MacAlister branch of Clan Donald. We are still very much in the period before the general adoption of feudalism and its customs of succession in the Western Highlands and Isles. So it is Angus Og who writes to King Edward in 1301, describing himself as 'humble and faithful' and asking for orders. He also asks for protection for the MacRuaris, whom they have held for some time, so that they too can serve and obey the King.

This letter is written at the same time as two others in the same vein from Hugh Bisset and from John MacSween. Bisset reports that he is with his fleet together with Angus and MacSween, awaiting the King's directions as to Kintyre and Bute. He inquires as to the status of John of Argyll, namely whether he is in the King's peace or not. MacSween complains that he has visited his lands of Knapdale conferred on him by the King but has been turned away by John de Menteith and John of Argyll. He warns the King that John de Menteith is no friend of his. Should he be in the King's peace, he asks that Edward should command him to hand over Knapdale. As it happened, Sir John de Menteith at this time was still in the service of the English King, as events would show. Quite what happened to Angus Og to make him come over to the Bruce's cause some time in the years that followed is unknown – again, it is likely to have been his enmity to the MacDougalls rather than to the English that was the deciding factor.

So it was that, some weeks after his arrival in Strathfillan, Bruce and his small party found themselves at Dalrigh, near Tyndrum. Here they were intercepted by John of Argyll, Lord of Lorne, cousin of the murdered Comyn and King Robert's implacable foe. For an account of what followed, we turn to the great epic poem *The Bruce* by John Barbour, Archdeacon of Aberdeen. Although written around 1370, it is the nearest to a contemporary source for the story of the Bruce that we have, and most later accounts draw heavily upon it. According to Barbour, the Lord of Lorne had with him 1,000 men and the chief of the MacNaughtons. Bruce's small force was outnumbered but fought bravely. The men of Lorne, however, did great execution with their axes, and Sir James Douglas and Sir Gilbert Hay were both among the wounded.

> The king his men saw in affray
> And his ensenye can he cry
> And amaing thaim rycht hardyly
> He rad that he thaim ruschyt all
> And sele off thaim thar gart he fall . . .

But there were too many of the enemy, and Bruce ordered a withdrawal. It was now that he was attacked by three men, two of them brothers by the name of 'Mac na Dorsair' – 'sons of The Doorward', probably a hereditary appointment in the household of the Lord of Lorne. They managed to lay hands on the King, who was in great danger but who managed to fight them off, killing all three.[52] It was during this episode, according to popular tradition, that the King lost his brooch, which was given to John of Lorne and kept in the family of the MacDougalls of MacDougall to this day, after a period during which it was lost to the Campbells in the seventeenth century. Barbour makes no mention of the incident, and it has to be said that the elaborate brooch of today, which consists of a crystal stone set in a silver mount, is almost identical to the Lochbuie brooch, long in the possession of the Maclaines of Lochbuie. This, in its present form, is known to have been made in the sixteenth century. It seems likely that, as with the Ugadale Brooch, reputedly given by Bruce to Mackay of Ugadale in Kintyre, it is the crystal which forms the original brooch which has been later reset, perhaps more than once (see Appendix 5).

For the second time in a few weeks, after the triumph of his coronation and early campaign, Bruce now found himself on the run with only a few companions. The Royal party was split up, the Queen going with the ailing Earl of Atholl under the conduct of Neil Bruce to the relative safety of Kildrummy Castle in Aberdeenshire. This safety was to prove illusory all too soon and the Queen's party moved on to Ross, where they took refuge in the Chapel of St Duthac at Tain. Even this traditional sanctuary proved unavailing against the Earl of Ross, who took them prisoner. The wretched Earl of Atholl was sent south under guard to London, where he was executed on a special gallows thirty feet higher than the usual one, an acknowledgement of his royal descent. The Countess of Buchan who had crowned

Robert the Bruce was given special treatment, being confined in a cage within the castle of Berwick, a similar fate being inflicted on the King's sister, Mary, also imprisoned within a cage built for her in Roxburgh Castle. The King's brother Neil was soon besieged at Kildrummy by the Prince of Wales and the Earl of Pembroke until forced by treachery within the walls to yield the castle. He was taken south as far as Berwick and executed along with sixteen other adherents of King Robert.

Meanwhile, since the King had decided to seek refuge in Kintyre, Sir Neil Campbell was sent off on detachment to raise boats and victual for the King with a rendezvous in twelve days' time. According to Barbour, he left one of his brothers with the King, whose party seems to have gone down the eastern shore of Loch Lomond which they had to cross in order to make the agreed meeting with Sir Neil. The location of the rendezvous would seem likely to have been Lochgoilhead, but in any case Sir Neil had had no difficulty in fulfilling his mission and the King and his few followers slipped away to sea. The fugitives appear to have gone beyond Kintyre and the dubious safety of Dunaverty and to have made their base in Rathlin, the rocky island just off the north-east corner of the Ulster coast.

For the next four and a half months, the King lay low. Whether he was accompanied all this time by Sir Neil Campbell and his brother is unknown, but Sir Neil, who had already shown his usefulness in that part of the world, was no doubt at least in touch with the King. And whether the King remained in Rathlin is also questionable; it seems likely that he moved around the Inner Hebrides and the northern coasts of Ireland. The story, however, that he went to Orkney and Shetland and even to Norway, seems less probable. But in February 1307 he came back to the mainland – first, it is said, to Kintyre (when he may have given Mackay of Ugadale his brooch in gratitude for help received) and then on to his own earldom of Carrick, where he met up with his allies, Sir James Douglas and Robert Boyd of Noddsdale. A detachment of eighteen galleys sent with his two brothers, Thomas and Alexander, to Galloway was less fortunate. The brothers were captured and taken before King Edward at Carlisle, where they were executed.

The next two years were to see a transformation in King Robert's fortunes from this very low point. Making his base in the wild hill country of Carrick and Galloway, the King embarked on a campaign of guerilla warfare. An enemy force sent after him was ambushed and suffered heavy losses in Glen Trool in May, relieving the pressure sufficiently for the King to feel able to move out from his base. On his way he encountered Aymer de Valence, Earl of Pembroke, at Loudoun Hill in Ayrshire. An astute choice of position by Robert negated the superiority of the English force, who were soundly defeated. This victory following on the Glen Trool success was sure evidence of the Bruce's returning ascendancy, and his supporters throughout the country gained heart once more, in spite of the capture and execution of Sir William Wallace's brother.

The momentum in favour of the Scots King was further encouraged by the terminal illness of the dreaded King Edward of England, whose death was to take place in due course on 7 July 1311. This relaxation of the English grip on the middle of the country allowed more freedom of movement to Bruce, who launched an overland expedition against Comyn's castle of Inverlochy. This was supported by a galley force which effectively isolated John (MacDougall) of Lorne. The King and his army advanced up the Great Glen, burning the castles of Urquhart and Inverness and also the town of Nairn. A somewhat inconclusive encounter took place between the King's force and that of John Comyn, Earl of Buchan, David de Strathbogie, Earl of Atholl and John Moubray at Slioch near Huntly during the last days of December.

Further operations in the area culminated in May, the next year, 1308, when Comyn was completely routed at Inverurie; the victorious King then ranged through the Comyn earldom, burning, killing and destroying in the orgy of revenge known as 'The Herschip of Buchan'. That summer, Edward Bruce, the King's brother, subdued Galloway in a savage campaign which paid off many an old score, leaving, however, the English castle garrisons in place. Next objective on the King's list was his inveterate enemy the Lord of Argyll. Alexander by now was clearly an old man, and it was his son John who had been appointed the previous October by the new King Edward as Sheriff of Argyll and Inchegall and guardian of these parts against 'the enemy'.[53] Both father and son were among the leading clergy and nobles of Scotland adjured by King Edward, on his way to France in December, to keep his peace.[54]

Their position is set out in a letter to King Edward from John of Lorne. Its date is thought to be March 1308. In it, the writer explains that he has been ill for six months. Robert the Bruce had approached his territories both by land and sea with a force of between 10,000 and 15,000 men. To oppose him the writer has only 800 men, of whom 500 are kept constantly in pay to guard the borders of his territory. He receives no help from the Barons of Argyll. He had negotiated a truce with Bruce but is disturbed to hear that the latter is boasting that the Lord of Lorne came into his peace, this to encourage others to join his cause. This is not the case, and if the King should hear it from others he should ignore it, for Lorne shall always be ready to carry out the King's orders with all his power, whenever and wherever the

King wishes. 'I have three castles to keep as well as a loch twenty-four miles long, on which I keep and build galleys with trusty men to each galley.' He does not trust his neighbours in any direction. But as soon as the King or his army shall come, then, health permitting, the Lord of Lorne shall not be found wanting where lands, ships or anything else is concerned, but will come to King Edward's service. Should sickness prevent him, he will send his son to serve with the King's forces.[55]

Controversy surrounds the ensuing battle as to its location and to its date, as well as the identity of the three castles mentioned above. To the latter we will return, but, as regards the former, opinion seems to be weightiest on the battle having taken place in the Pass of Brander itself, in August 1308. The pass is a narrow gorge under the flank of Ben Cruachan, thought in Bruce's time to be the highest mountain in Scotland, where Loch Awe discharges its waters to the sea in Loch Etive some two miles away. Originally Loch Awe, whose chief source is the River Orchy, clearly emptied at the other end of its length, at Ford, down what is now Kilmartin Glen and so to the sea at Loch Crinan. But at some distant time in its geological past, a violent convulsion – or possibly the melting of a glacial barrier – opened up the Brander exit so that the loch both empties and fills at the same end.

The pass is a daunting one. At one point where the loch narrows to scarcely 200 yards, the slopes of Cruachan are nearly vertical and plunge dramatically into the dark waters of the loch. When, in the 1960s, the modern road was built through the pass, it was found necessary to construct piles on which to support it. Local legend has it that these are 300 feet deep and that all sorts of unexpected objects including bodies were discovered in the murky depths during its construction. Be that as it may, this location just next to the modern Hydro-Electric Visitor Centre forms an ideal point where the narrow path could effectively be blocked indefinitely by only a few men.

Here it was that the men of Lorne lay in wait. As the King's men entered the pass, they tried to crush them by rolling great boulders down the steep slope onto them; but the King had anticipated them and sent 'the Good Sir James' Douglas, with Sir Alexander Fraser, Sir William Wiseman and Sir Alexander Gray with all the archers to take the high ground, climbing high on Cruachan to outflank his enemy.

John of Lorne, meanwhile, was observing the fight from one of his galleys 'apon the se weill ner the pais' according to Barbour, who thus starts a considerable argument as to the fight's location. If, as Professor Duncan avers, the location of John's galleys was Loch Etive, then he would have seen nothing of a battle in the pass. Professor Duncan therefore relocates the battle on the shores of Loch Etive; but, while the slope of the hill is steep in places, it in no way provides such an obstacle, and the route used to arrive there is not nearly as direct or obvious as the one which would have led to the spot suggested above. The size of Loch Awe is such that it would be easy for a writer to confuse its fresh water with salt water.[56]

Barbour's account tells of a desperate attempt to destroy the only nearby bridge over the swift-flowing, deep and wide water which offered the only route of escape. This again ties up with the local tradition of a bridge over the River Awe which the men of Lorne would have to cross to get back to their homeland. According to tradition, their attempt to destroy the bridge was unsuccessful and their foes, following up, caught them in the low ground just over the far side of the river from today's main road between the hydro barrage and Brander Lodge where numerous cairns of scattered rubble are said to mark the place where they were cut down as they fled. There seems no reason to doubt this attribution: the cairns lie spread across the whole area and, if intended for field clearance, are clearly ineffectual.

Finally, John of Lorne could well observe the battle from Loch Awe if it took place, as suggested, in the pass; the water is sufficiently broad for him to be able to lie out of arrow shot while watching events, and when the battle was obviously lost he could sail safely away down the loch. The details of this battle have been set out in some depth. Although it will be noted that there is no mention of any Campbells in the King's force, it seems highly likely that they were there, and the fortunes of the later Clan Campbell were certainly much affected by what took place. Having displaced the enemy, the King's army followed up and besieged the main enemy stronghold of Dunstaffnage, which duly surrendered. According to local tradition, the King took up residence at Ardchattan Priory built by the MacDougall chief a century before on the other side of Loch Etive from Dunstaffnage. Here, it is claimed, he summoned 'the last Gaelic Parliament', which met in a room still used by the present owners today.

This last is complete nonsense – no such body as the 'Gaelic Parliament' ever existed – but it is perfectly possible, indeed probable, that the King took up his abode in the most comfortable quarters which the region could offer and that he summoned there the local warlords in order to read the riot act before he departed. By now the King had dealt with his main enemies in Scotland. The Earl of Ross submitted in October, and it is from this time that we find the King beginning to exercise the role of a reigning monarch with the issue of charters and edicts.

In his letter to the English King, John of Lorne had written of his uncertainty over his neighbours. Clearly, the rising star of Bruce had attracted those whose feelings towards him had been at best dubious. Among the most important conversions was that of Sir John de Menteith, holder of many lands in Knapdale and Kintyre, one-time Governor of Dumbarton Castle, and the person held responsible for Wallace's capture. Only two years before, he had been given the title of Earl of Lennox by Edward. All this was now behind him and he was to become one of King Robert's most doughty supporters. Angus Og of Islay had joined Bruce's side after the murder of Comyn, which had pushed his main foes, the MacDougalls of Argyll, into the English camp. The laird of MacNaughton, who had been with the Lord of Lorne at Dalrigh, was now with Bruce; wherever Alexander of Argyll looked, he was surrounded by foes.

The actual sequence of events is somewhat confused, since King Robert came back to Argyll the following year. Before he did so, he held his first Parliament – not at Ardchattan but at St Andrews. Among the business transacted was the composition of a letter to the French King, who was asking for Scots help in the forthcoming Crusade. The Scots answer was to the effect that Scotland was at war and could not be diverted. Among the Scottish magnates who signed this letter were Sir Neil Campbell and his brother Sir Donald,[57] Thomas Campbell, Gillespie MacLachlan and also, surprisingly, Alexander of Argyll. There are sixteen signatories in all, including two Earls and the Steward.[58]

Alexander of Argyll's apparent compliance with the Bruce regime was only temporary, however. The St Andrews parliament had taken place in March; by June, Alexander and his son John were at Westminster where, after consulting with them and with Alexander de Abernethy, Ingram de Umfraville and other Scots loyal to the cause of Balliol, King Edward ordered Aymer de Valence to assemble his army at Berwick-upon-Tweed in preparation for the invasion of Scotland and to come himself to Westminster to plan events.[59]

From now on, Alexander of Argyll and his son were out of Argyll, leaving a power vacuum behind them. By December 1309 they were in Ireland in King Edward's service. Alexander was dead by January 1311,[60] but John played a leading part in English affairs, being appointed in 1311 to command the fleet raised in English and Welsh ports by King Edward, to which no doubt he was able to add his own galleys. The appointment of Jean Dargael as *Admirallum et Capitaneum Flotae nostrae Navium* – 'Admiral and captain of our fleet of ships'[61] – has resulted in John of Lorne being listed among the earliest holders of the rank of Admiral of the Fleet of the Royal Navy – a remarkable feat for a West Highland Chief.[62] In this capacity he captured the Isle of Man for the English King in 1315, the governorship being later handed over to 'Sir Dougal Makouri'. He campaigned in Ireland in King Edward's interest, being well rewarded for his services both in lands and money.

On his second visit to Argyll, in 1309, the King commenced his campaign in the north at Loch Broom and covered the area south. At this time, he set in hand the rebuilding of the castle at Tarbert, Loch Fyne, which dominated the narrow neck of land between East and West Loch Tarbert across which mariners had long been accustomed to drag their boats rather than undergo the perils of the rough and treacherous passage round the Mull of Kintyre. Here the King had himself pulled overland between the two arms of the sea, sitting in his galley with its sails unfurled, a deliberate reproduction of Magnus Barelegs' famous exploit.

The next few years, largely uneventful, can be briefly summarised as Bruce consolidated his hold on the kingdom with forays into northern England which took place in spite of an invasion by the English in 1310. The mounting pressure of Edward's forces in Scotland in due course culminated in one of the great episodes of Scottish history – the Battle of Bannockburn in 1314. During this period there are few mentions of Campbells, although it seems that Sir Neil, at least, was in close touch with King Robert as one of his most trusted companions. In August 1309, Sir Neil, the King's envoy, along with John de Menteith, was given safe conduct by King Edward II to treat with the Earl of Ulster, his representative.[63] The following year, Sir Neil is again on record along with two others of King Robert's companions, Alexander Seton and Gilbert Hay, who swear to protect the lately crowned Robert against allcomers, French, English and Scots.[64]

While it is clear that Sir Neil is a man of considerable importance and influence, it is worthwhile commenting on the fact that there is no still no evidence as to what lands – if any – he possessed in Argyll. The King's regard for him is not in doubt. After the Battle of Bannockburn and the negotiations which then led to her release, King Robert gave his sister in marriage to Sir Neil. What happened to the unfortunate Alyse Crawford we do not know. Whether she was swept aside on some pretext in the face of the irresistible lure of such a close connection with the King or whether Sir Neil was wrongly accused of having married her, we do not know. She may of course have died, but, marriages of the time being as flexible as they were, it is hard to avoid the suspicion that she was merely deposed in order to make room for this even more glittering prize. By his new bride, Sir Neil had another son, John, to whom his royal cousin King David II was to grant the Earldom of Atholl, forfeited by David de Strathbogie.

Then in 1313, King Robert granted to Sir Cailean Mor's son, Dougall, the lands of Kilcongen, Degnish, Auchinaclosh, Auchinsaule, Caddiltoune, Garpynging, Ardincaple, Ragray, Kilninver, Esgeallan, Clachanseilach, Leternacrosh, Scamadil, Kilveran, Letternamuck and the isle of Toresay

(Torsa), all in Lorne, for services of a ship, fully manned, of twenty-six oars.[65] The original of this charter is lost, but its terms are included in a 1680 inventory of charters at Inveraray. Its provenance and the lack of the original might throw some doubt on its precise dating. The labelling of the grantee as 'Dougall Campbell of Lochawe' is surely a later gloss, although Dougall is clearly a figure of some importance in spite of his relative obscurity in the records. We last came across him as one of the signatories of Ragman Roll in 1296. As well as these lands in Argyll, he, rather than Sir Neil, also held the lands of Menstrie[66] originally granted to his grandfather Gillespic in 1263, and he was later to hold the important appointments of Sheriff of Dumbarton and of Argyll and Bailie of Athole.[67]

Whatever the date of their being granted, the lands in question were made up from a considerable portion of former MacDougall territory south of what is now Oban, extending from the borders of the old Lordship of Lochawe at the String of Lorne, where Sir Cailean met his end, down to the sea where the island of Torsa dominates the north end of the inland sea-lane from Islay to the Firth of Lorne. Of Bannockburn there is little to recount as far as Clan Campbell is concerned, and the story is already well known. There is no mention at all of Sir Neil or any other Campbell having taken part in the battle, although it is hard to believe that they were not there, either as individuals with their own particular following or as part of the division commanded by King Robert himself, made up of the men of Carrick, of Bute, of Argyll and of the Isles, the last under Angus Og MacDonald. The battle won, however, there was much to be done in consolidating the victory, and a lasting peace had to be negotiated. In September a message was sent by King Robert, referred to by the English as merely 'Sir Robert de Brus', requesting a safe-conduct for six weeks for his four envoys to come to King Edward to thrash out terms. They were Neil Campbell, Roger Kirkpatrick, Robert Keith and Gilbert Hay, four knights who had been the King's loyal companions and trusted councillors.[68] This was one of the last services he was able to perform for his beloved cousin and king; by February next year, 1316, Sir Neil Campbell was dead.

CHAPTER FOUR

The Springboard is Established

Sir Neil was a significant figure in the story of Clan Campbell. Connected by blood to the King, his services to his monarch were considerable, and for them he reaped rich rewards. Although he was contemporary with several Campbells who were men of note, it is chiefly due to him that the name Campbell was one to be reckoned with, not only in the West Highlands but in Scotland itself.

His position among his own kin is not entirely clear – the whole concept of chiefs and clans as we imagine it today was scarcely in its infancy. There is little evidence that the Campbells at this time thought of themselves as a coherent force, nor, even if they did, that they considered Sir Neil to be the head of it. His brother Sir Dougall, not Sir Neil, was the holder of the old Campbell lands of Menstrie which had been in the possession of his grandfather Gillespic back in 1263, as well as of many lands in Argyll. The fact that Sir Neil never appears with the designation *Dominus de* or 'Lord of Lochawe' is to be noted, although the non-use of the term 'Dominus' at this stage is perhaps less significant than it was to become. At the same time, it has to be put alongside Balliol's instructions to Sir Cailean as Bailie, not Lord, of Loch Awe and Ardscotnish, which we have already seen.

Another brother whose importance appears to have been little if any less was Sir Donald, one-time Sheriff of Wigtown and possessor of 'many lands' in Argyll, whose descendants inherited by marriage the rich lands in Ayrshire of the Crawford family and who became the important Campbell House of Loudoun. And then there is Sir Arthur Campbell, son of Duncan Dubh, who may well have been the elder brother of Sir Cailean Mor. He, too, was given many lands in Argyll and was appointed the Constable of Dunstaffnage with the lands that went with the castle. He was the progenitor of the family known as the MacArthur Campbells of Strachur, whose head was known in Gaelic quite simply as *Mac Artairr* – 'Arthur's son'.

There is a certain mystery about this family. For a time they seem to have

70

rivalled the Campbells of Lochawe in standing. The fact that they may have descended from an elder brother meant relatively little at a time which predated the formation of a clan as such and when, anyway, the feudal insistence on primogeniture – succession by the eldest son – had not totally displaced the older Celtic method of succession by selection. But there was certainly rivalry between the two branches, symbolised in one old traditional tale – one of the many collected by John Dewar – in which it is MacArthur as head of the oldest family in Argyll who occupies the chief seat in the Inveraray courthouse until Campbell of Lochawe reminds him of his origins and persuades him that he should resume the name of Campbell. This is agreed, and when, the next day, they assemble and MacArthur is about to take his accustomed seat, he is prevented by Campbell of Lochawe since, as he says 'although you were the oldest MacArthur in Argyll yesterday, I am the oldest Campbell in Argyll today'.[1]

This rivalry is probably the origin of the two well-known and oft-repeated sayings 'Hills, Ills and MacAlpines, but when did the MacArthurs come?' and 'The Hills, the Devil and MacAlpine, but whence comes forth MacArthur?' – two further digs at the relative seniority not of the later MacArthurs over other clans but of the two leading branches of the Campbells.[2] The existence of this family has caused and still causes considerable confusion among historians – and among MacArthurs themselves. There were several unrelated families who used the name MacArthur as a surname, notably the Lochaweside family descended from the same stock as the Campbells, who became landed in the sixteenth century when their leader became MacArthur of Terivadich, so called from his newly granted lands. His Gaelic patronymic was *Mac Mhic Artair* – 'Son of the Son of Arthur'.[3] It is of interest, if not exactly evidence, that Duke Niall in all his notes never refers to any of the Strachur Campbells as MacArthurs, although it may be pure fancy to suspect that he may have felt some sensitivity on the subject!

Apart from their ownership of lands in Argyll and to the north of Loch Lomond, this particular branch of the Campbells may nearly have brought off a spectacular marriage when Sir Arthur's younger son Arthur became, it seems likely, betrothed to Christina MacRuari, heiress of Garmoran, and former ally and help – some say the relationship was considerably closer – to King Robert on his wanderings in the Western Isles. In fact this marriage did not take place; it aroused too much political opposition. Had it done so, the Campbells would have brought off another spectacular acquisition of territory, and Arthur *jure uxoris* would have become Chief of one of the most important branches of the sons of Somerled.

Although we have no precise evidence of such a marriage, the charter still exists in which Christina grants to her husband-to-be the full extent of her lands; they include the lands of Moidart, Arisaig and Morar, the islands of Rum and Eigg and the Small Isles. The grant is to Arthur with remainder to their joint heirs for the services of a galley of twenty oars for the King's army.[4] There is no date on the charter; the witnesses include Sir John de Menteith, Sir Donald Campbell, Alexander MacNaughton, Iver MacIver, Duncan, son of Sir Thomas Campbell, and Neil and Donald Maclean.

In the event, opposition appears to have been too strong; whether or not the marriage did take place, the lands were claimed by her half-brother and remained in the hands of the MacRuaris. This did not go without a contest, it would seem, and over a century later the quarrel was still going on when the two leading claimants to the lands, including Arthur's descendant John MacArthur, were summarily executed. At that time, he was described as *Magnus princeps apud suos et dux mille hominum* – 'A great prince among his own people and leader of 1,000 men'. It would seem that, even if the figure of 1,000 men – a very significant following for the day and age – is not taken literally, the Campbells of Strachur were a major Campbell kindred. The noted historian W. F. Skene goes even further and states unequivocally that they were at this time the Chiefs of Clan Campbell.[5] The Campbells of the Lochawe branch, however, were not to be discounted.

John, son of Sir Neil and Lady Mary Bruce, referred to as 'John of Moulin' from the principal stronghold in Atholl at that time, up in the hills behind Pitlochry, was to be granted the earldom of Atholl by his cousin King David II some time between 1329 and 1333. This was the first peerage title to have been granted to a Campbell, and, had he survived, the Campbell Chiefship might well, indeed almost certainly would, have come down through him and not through his elder brother, while from the relative size of their holdings at the time, the centre of Campbell activity would have been a good distance further east in Atholl and not in Argyll.

But it was to *Colin Og* – 'Young Colin', son of Sir Neil by an earlier marriage – that, shortly after Sir Neil's death, King Robert made a most significant grant. On 10 February 1316, the King granted, conceded and by this charter confirmed to Colin, son of Sir Neil Campbell, for his homage and service, the whole lands of Lochawe and Ardscotnish in a free barony, in return for the service of a fully manned and equipped ship of forty oars for forty days whenever required and for forinsec service in the King's land army as performed by the other Barons of Argyll for their baronies.[6] This charter highlights the question of the previous status of the Lochawe line. The story in 'Ane Accompt' was that Gillespic married Evah, heiress of two thirds of Lochawe, and that their son Duncan's marriage to Dirvail McFiachar

brought the lordship of the whole of Lochawe to the family. This is contra-
dicted by the command to Sir Colin by Balliol which is addressed to him as
Bailie of the King's lands of Lochawe and Ardscotnish. As Bailie, he was no
more than the administrator of the lands for the King. The new charter is
in the form used for a new grant and would seem to imply that the traditional
genealogy's account had inflated the early importance of the family – a not
unlikely hypothesis. But, finally, as we shall see, a later grant adjures the
recipient to hold his lands as freely as had done his ancestor Duncan
O'Duine.

This is perhaps a convenient moment to discuss the question of the
main early Campbell stronghold in Argyll. Some would have it that this was the
mighty castle of Innischonnell, which was actually built by the Campbells.
This brings up the question of the status and wealth required to put such a
major work in hand and whether at the time the Campbells were capable of
it. If they were, the means to undertake such a task must surely have depended
on ownership of rich lands outside Argyll of which we have no record –
apart from Menstrie. The MacDougalls of Lorne would seem to be more
likely builders, and supporters of this theory point to John of Lorne's letter
of 1308 to King Edward in which, it may be remembered, he says 'I have
three castles to keep as well as a loch twenty-four miles long, on which I keep
and build galleys with trusty men to each galley'.

Loch Awe is taken to be the loch in question and Innischonnell, Fincharn
and Fraoch Eilean to be the three castles referred to, since Kilchurn did not
exist at this date. Innischonnell was almost certainly out of Campbell hands
at this date, and the suggestion that the Campbells first built then lost then
regained their main stronghold seems an ungainly one. The MacDougalls
could however claim three castles without involving any of the contemporary
ones on Loch Awe in the shape of a selection from Dunstaffnage, Duart, Aros,
Cairnaburgh and Castle Coeffin on Lismore, all of which are reckoned to have
been in existence at this period; Dunollie Castle, which was to become the
seat of the later chiefs of MacDougall, was not yet built at the time, although
it was the site of the former stronghold of the tribe of Loarn.

So the question remains unanswered for certain, although the restriction
of MacDougall castles to three perhaps means that those on Loch Awe are
the only ones referred to. If Innischonnell at this stage seems too grand for
it to have been the Campbell base, then an alternative solution must be the
much smaller but nevertheless substantial Caisteal na Nighinn Ruaidhe,
'The Castle of the Red-haired Maiden', on Loch Avich just over the hill from
the watershed where Sir Cailein Mor met his end in what was probably a
border dispute.

The castle was owned, it is claimed, by a family called MacCaurre. 'Dugal MacCaurre' was Toiseach of Lochavich according to the *Manuscript History*, and his daughter married Dougall of Craignish at the end of the twelfth century.[7] This marriage has to be added to the apparently earlier one between Gillespic of the Lochawe line to his cousin Evah, 'heretrix of Lochow' which ensured that two thirds of the lordship of Lochawe remained in the family's hands, the final third being acquired by the marriage of Gillespic's son Duncan to Dirvail, daughter of Dougall MacFiachar, Toiseach of Over Lochawe.[8] But it was an ancestor of this Dougall – one Mungan MacFiachar – who is, according to Dewar in his manuscripts, the builder of the castle on Loch Avich.

From this confusion of Campbell marriages into families of whom no more is ever heard, no clear truth is likely to emerge. In spite of the version which makes it an inheritance of the Craignish rather than the Lochawe Campbells, Caisteal na Nighinn Ruaidhe still seems a strong candidate as the early Campbell base; no mention is made in charter evidence of its being owned by the Campbells of Craignish before 1414, when Sir Duncan Campbell of Lochawe grants to Ronald of Craignish lands in Loch Avich together with the constabulary of the castles of Craignish and Loch Avich.[9] Finally, although not hard evidence, it is interesting that within a relatively short distance of this castle the place name Kilmun, *Cell of St Mun*, is to be found, as it is in close proximity to the succeeding bases of the Campbell chiefs both at Innischonnell and at Inveraray as well, while, as we shall see, the Campbell of Lochawe family burial place was for generations at Kilmun on the Holy Loch. Kilmun is not a common name in Argyll by any means, and the coincidence is a highly intriguing one.

During the period between his coronation in 1306 and his death in 1329, King Robert made a series of grants of lands to Campbells. In few cases is it possible to date them, but the periods following the defeat of the Lord of Lorne in the Pass of Brander in 1308 and after Bannockburn in 1314 would seem to be likely. So it was that Sir Dougall, whose extensive grant of lands we have already noted, was confirmed as Lord of Menstrie in 1324. He received a further grant of lands in Argyll[10] and had an interest in the twenty-merkland of Ardscotnish, the district lying between the south end of Loch Awe and the sea, where, as Dougall son of Sir Colin Campbell, he came to an agreement with his nephew Dougall, son of Neil Campbell, over these lands together with the advocation of the church of Kilmartin.[11]

Sir Arthur Campbell, progenitor of the Campbells of Strachur, was made Constable of the former base of the Lords of Lorne, Dunstaffnage Castle, and given the mains of the castle – the lands attached to it – for the sustenance of the castle itself.[12] He was also given a great list of lands in Benderloch and the neighbouring districts in 1322 – '3dl [pennyland] of Torrinturks, 1dl Stronsoleir, 2dl Lettirnanella with its island, 6dl Glencricceris, 3dl Blairhalchan and Blarenanerchennach. 4dl Alcanalkelich and Achinvachich, 2dl Kilmore, 2dl Achinfure, 1dl Dunolich, 3dl Ardstofniche near lands of Dunollich in free barony, and 3dl Inneraw 5dl Achennaba, 5dl Fearlochan, 5dl Achennacreich 5dl Archendekath in Benderloch, in free barony'.[13] Of particular note are the lands of Dunollie, Lochnell (Lettirnanella) and of Inverawe on the far side of the River Awe. The return for all this was the fourth part of the service of a knight, a very common reddendo in the east of the country but much less so in Argyll and the Isles where, as will be seen, the rent very often consists of the services of a fully manned ship when required. A further grant to him is recorded, of Kinlochlane (possibly Kinlochlean, Glassary) 'with many other lands'.[14]

In 1318, Sir Donald's son and Susannah Crawford received a charter for her family's former lands of Loudoun and Stevenston in Ayrshire. These were to be a barony with Loudoun as its *caput* or headquarters, all for the services of a knight.[15] Sir Donald himself received a grant of lands in Benderloch[16] on the forfeiture of John of Lorne and his father for the service of a ship of forty oars when required.[17] This is a major battleship by local standards, and would have been a fearsome vessel. One further grant should perhaps be highlighted – that of *the lands of Moyleags* and *Dunaghethe* (Moleigh and Dunach) to a Duncan Campbell.[18] These lie at the head of Loch Feochan in Lorne. The identity of this Duncan is not made clear; he could be Duncan son of Sir Cailein Mor, he could be that Duncan's nephew who was son of Sir Neil, or he could be one of the Duncans who are respectively sons of Sir Donald or Sir Thomas. Such are the problems of identification of similar names on insufficient evidence; what may be interesting in this case is the location of the lands in question at the head of Glenfeochan, the area later in the possession of the Stronchormaig or Glenfeochan Campbells who formed part of the Clan Dhonnachie Campbells whose chieftain was Campbell of Inverawe with the patronymic 'MacConnochie', or 'Son of Duncan'. The favoured candidate for the source of their patronymic is one Duncan *Crosta* who is some two generations later, but the earlier connection of a Duncan Campbell with the lands at the head of Glenfeochan may justify further consideration on the matter.

There is a great temptation to think that, after Bannockburn, peace ensued; but such was far from the case. It was to be a further fourteen years before the Treaty of Northampton at last brought hostilities to a close and it was then only a momentary peace. Raiding against the northern counties of England

resumed almost straight away after Bannockburn and there was spasmodic
English retaliation, although during this period it was the Scots who held the
initiative – as ever, the north was far away from the English heartland, and the
Border Scots rode blithely to harry their neighbours, burning and slaying
and driving the cattle where they could.

And the year following the Battle saw the King's brother Edward, as the
duly inaugurated King of Ireland, lead a force of Scots into Ulster with the
intent of conquering the whole country and setting up a Celtic kingdom
which might, had it been successful, have also included the Isles. The reasons
for this invasion are intriguing; Scots and Irish still thought of themselves as
being of common stock, and a firmer grip on the Irish Sea and the consequent
opportunity to divert the English from operations against Scotland may not
have been the only attraction.[19] But in particular, John of Argyll, the forfeited
former (MacDougall) Lord of Lorne, now Admiral of the English Fleet, was
causing considerable trouble; in February 1315 he had succeeded in recap-
turing the Isle of Man for King Edward and in installing a garrison there
and the King's Justiciar in Ireland had received orders to assemble a force of
10,000 troops under command of John of Argyll that April with a fleet of
sixty ships to invade Scotland.[20] In any case, it would appear that this was
prevented or diverted by Edward Bruce's landing in Ireland late in May.
His force included many mercenaries from the Western Highlands and Isles
and, while we do not know whether Colin Og was among this original force,
we do know that he was with them when, in early 1317, Edward had been
joined by his brother King Robert.

Once more the Scottish force set off on the road south, taking every precaution against ambush. According to Barbour, contact was made on one
occasion when the English were clearly trying to entice the Scots to break
ranks in order to lure them into attack. King Robert gave stern orders to his
troops to stay in line, but the sight of the enemy was to much for Sir Colin
who, no doubt anxious to emulate the deeds of his father in front of the
King, set spurs to his steed and dashed at the enemy. He rode at the English
archers and overtook two of them, killing the first man with his spear. The
second, however, turned and brought down Sir Colin's horse. Things might
have gone badly for him had not the King himself arrived at this point, in a
towering rage.

> With a trounsoun intill his new
> To Schyr Colyne sic dusche he geve
> That he dynnyt on his arsoun.[21]

In other words, the King gave such a blow with the truncheon he was carrying that his victim slumped across his saddle-bow. The luckless Sir Colin was given the dressing-down he so richly deserved for imperilling the Scottish army. It is in fact impossible to pinpoint the actual occasion on which this incident took place, but there would seem little doubt that the story is founded on something which actually happened.

Edward Bruce was in Ireland until 1318. His expedition met with mixed fortunes which included, as well as actual fighting, the ravages of disease and famine. But it came to an end in October 1318 when, with his characteristic impetuosity, Edward made an immediate attack on the forces waiting to receive him at Fochart outside Dundalk, where he allowed the English to deal piecemeal with his columns as they came up. Edward himself was killed, his body subsequently decapitated and the four quarters sent for display the length of Ireland. The great slaughter of the Scots included both a leading MacRuari of Garmoran and a leading MacDonald of Islay. Unlike his brother, it would seem that Edward Bruce was not loved; as the *Annals of Connacht* have it,

> Edward Bruce, he who was the common ruin of the Galls and Gaels of Ireland, was by the Galls of Ireland killed at Dundalk by dint of fierce fighting. MacRuaidri, king of the Hebrides, and MacDomnail, king of Argyle, and their Scots were killed with him; and never was there a better deed done for the Irish than this, since the beginning of the world and the banishing of the Formorians from Ireland. For in this Bruce's time, for three years and a half, falsehood and famine and homicide filled the country, and undoubtedly men ate each other in Ireland.[22]

The references to MacRuari as 'king of the Isles' and of MacDonald as 'king of Argyle' are interesting, although the term 'King' was used commonly for an important chief in the Norse-influenced Isles at this time. But it underlines yet again the extent to which the (MacDougall) Argyll family had been eclipsed as holders of land in the area and the extent to which MacDonald, more than any other, had benefited with grants of land including Mull, Coll, Tiree, Ardnamurchan, Duror, Glencoe and Lochaber as well as further grants in Kintyre. John (MacDougall) of Argyll himself died in 1316 or 1317 while on pilgrimage to Canterbury. Thus was laid the foundations of what was to become the Lordship of the Isles. In fact, by doing this, King Robert was building up a problem for his successors, since, by the time the MacDonald Chiefs had acquired the MacRuari territory through marriage and had successfully laid claim to the Earldom of Ross, their over-mighty ambition was to pose a threat both to the Crown and to Scotland itself.

The King was not unaware of the threat posed by the Western Highlands and Isles. While his brother Edward was setting off for Ireland, King Robert with a strong force had returned to the west. It was on this occasion that he followed ancient tradition in having himself dragged across the narrow stretch of land at Tarbert, sitting at the helm of his galley with its mast stepped, following the example of Magnus Barelegs, the tradition being that any would-be conqueror of the Isles who did this would succeed in his purpose. And here some years later, he commenced the rebuilding of the Castle of Tarbert, on a hill overlooking the East Loch and dominating the narrow strip of land which was used frequently to drag boats across, thus avoiding the dangerous waters off the Mull of Kintyre.

We have at this time the accounts of the Constable of Tarbert, Sir John de Lany, dated 1326, which include payment to Sir Arthur Campbell for the use of his ship. The sums required for the work that year were in part funded by the money paid over by Dougall Campbell, younger brother of Sir Neil, in his capacity as Sheriff of Argyll and Baillie of Atholl.[23] But it was peace with the English that failed to materialise, the struggle continuing both through the continuation of active hostilities and by the attempts by the English to prevent the recognition of Robert Bruce as King of Scots, notably by the Pope.

It was this that caused the writing of the letter in 1320, now known to us as 'The Declaration of Arbroath'. Addressed to the Pope by some forty Earls and leading men of Scotland representing the whole country, it ranges from the pathetic to the proud: 'we beseech . . . that you will deign to admonish and exhort the king of the English, who ought to be satisfied with what he has, since England used to be enough for seven kings or more, to leave in peace us Scots, who live in this poor little Scotland, beyond which there is no dwelling-place at all, and who desire nothing but our own' to the resounding 'For as long as a hundred of us remain alive, we will never on any conditions be subjected to the lordship of the English. For we fight not for glory nor riches nor honours, but for freedom alone, which no good man gives up except with his life'.[24] Among the names mentioned in the document as one of the originators was that of Donald Campbell, almost certainly that Donald who was Colin Oig's uncle and the progenitor of the later Campbells of Loudoun. He is the only West Highlander involved. Again, while comment has been made on the inclusion of his name and not that of Colin Oig's, it can only be repeated that at this time there seems little evidence for the Lochawe branch of the family to be the chief among the Clan Campbell. But peace was to come at last – if only for a short time. In March 1328, a treaty was eventually concluded between the two countries; among the provisions of the treaty was the recognition that King Robert and his heirs should rule Scotland completely freely without any form of homage to the English King.[25]

The King's days were sadly now numbered. Among his last acts was the grant in 1329 to Sir Arthur Campbell of the lands of Kinlochlyon, Glenstandil, Killargie and Auhingewell and others in Appin, all for the service of a birlinn of twenty oars. He also granted to Sir Duncan Campbell the lands in Benderloch granted and now resigned by his father Sir Donald:

> the haill lands of Benderloch and pertinents with the tenandry of Gillecallum MacGillivan (except the lands which Arthur the father had there from the crown) which lands were resigned by Donald before the nobles of the King's Council and the barons of Argyll for infeftment to himself and his heirs to be held by the said Duncan for the service of a birlinn of twenty-six oars. . .[26]

Much later, these lands were claimed by the Campbells of Loudoun, and it is possible to identify them as follows:

> 3dl Torrinturk, 1 dl Strontoiler, 2 dl Lochnell, 6 dl Glencruitten(?), 3dl Barachaltine(?), 2 dl Kilmore, 2 dl of Pennyfuir, 1 dl Dunolly, 3dl Ardstaffnage (Dunstaffnage), 3dl Inverawe, 5 dl Achnaba, 5dl Ferlochan (in Benderloch), 5 dl Achnacree together with the lands of Blarenaerchennach, 4 dl Altanakelich and Achinrachich and the 5dl of Archendekath, all in free barony.[27]

On 27 June that year, the King died at the age of 55 at his manor of Cardross on the Clyde near Dumbarton. His successor was his son by Elisabeth de Burgh, David, born in 1324, who was therefore hardly five years old when he ascended the throne. By the Treaty of Northampton, he had already married King Edward II's daughter Joanna in a vain move to bring a lasting peace between the two countries. She was to prove equally ineffectual in producing a son and heir to the Scottish throne. The arrival of a vulnerable minor on the throne opened up the situation to the defeated followers of Balliol and the English cause, and once more Scotland was plunged into the turmoil and uncertainty of civil war. This of course was of particular moment to those who, like so many of the Campbells, had profited by the late King's disposal of lands. All, now, was once more in the melting pot.

In June 1331, Henri Beaumont and David de Strathbogie went to see the exiled Balliol in Picardy to plan his seizing the Scottish throne. That December, Balliol moved to Yorkshire, where he took up temporary abode in the Manor of Standal, Yorkshire, belonging to Beaumont's sister, Lady de Vesci. The following year, 1332, Randolph, the Guardian of Scotland, died, allegedly poisoned by an English monk. In his place, the Scots Parliament appointed Donald, Earl of Mar, nephew of King Robert, although his ultimate loyalty was somewhat in question. There was considerable support in Scotland for Balliol among those who had lost out at the hands of King Robert. This was not anglophilia so much as dislike of Bruce and his adherents, fury at the loss of lands and a feeling that the true claim had been that of Balliol and not Bruce. The names of Balliol's followers included Henri Beaumont, one-time Earl of Buchan, David de Strathbogie, claimant Earl of Atholl (grandson of the Red Comyn), Gilbert de Umfraville, claimant to the Earldom of Angus, Henry Ferrers, Walter Comyn, son of William Comyn of Kilbride in Lanarkshire, Geoffrey, John and Alexander Mowbray, sons of Roger Mowbray, Murray of Tullibardine, William Sinclair, Bishop of Dunkeld and the Abbots of Coupar, Inchaffray, Scone, Arbroath and Dunfermline.

Balliol had been gathering a fleet in the Yorkshire ports, said to number some eighty-eight ships. His army was said to be some 500 men-at-arms and 1,000 foot soldiers in strength, to which were added a party of English knights and German mercenaries. On learning of Randolph's death in July, the fleet set sail and headed north. Mar had split his army, taking command north of the Forth while Patrick of Dunbar was in command to the south. At first the invasion prospered. Landing in Fife, at Kinghorn, it captured Scottish stores left at Dunfermline and moved north towards Perth. Mar confronted Balliol at Forteviot, barring his route with an army greatly superior in numbers, while Dunbar marched to take him in flank from the south. Beaumont mounted a night advance, being shown the fords across the Earn by Murray of Tullibardine, and at dawn King David's supporters found themselves confronted by a well-marshalled enemy against whose position they squandered their strength in a series of ill-controlled attacks. The Battle of Dupplin was a clear victory for Balliol and among the many Scottish slain lay the Guardian, Donald Earl of Mar. Dunbar meanwhile had been diverted by the rising in Galloway, home of Bruce's inveterate foes the MacDowalls and the MacCanns of the pro-Balliol faction there under Eustace de Maxwell.

So it was that Balliol came to Scone, where he was crowned upon the Moot Hill observing all the old ceremonial for the inauguration of the King of Scots. The crown was placed on his head by the Earl of Fife, whose allegiance was a repeatedly changing one but whose participation added greatly to the visible legitimacy of Balliol's coronation. But his grip on the country was far from uncontested. He had already sworn fealty to King Edward III of England and in March 1333 Balliol rode with a great English host to the siege of Berwick, being joined there in May by King Edward himself. The defenders were eventually so hard-pressed that they agreed to a truce by which they would surrender the walls if not relieved by 20 July. This caused Sir Archibald Douglas, youngest brother of the Good Sir James and now Guardian of Scotland, to abandon his invasion of Northumberland and march rapidly northwards; he and his army arrived the day before the truce was due to expire and the town to surrender, to find the English well positioned on Halidon Hill. There was no alternative to an immediate attack if Berwick was not to capitulate. The men-at-arms dismounted and, wading through a bog, started to climb the hill towards the English. Here they came under a hail of arrows, and those who reached the English lines were easily disposed of. There was great slaughter; again the Guardian of Scotland was among those killed, and with him fell no fewer than five Scottish earls, among them John Campbell, Earl of Atholl.

Balliol was now able to reign as King, and in February 1334 he held a Parliament at Perth. His followers 'the disinherited' were restored to their former holdings, which were in many cases extended. The earldom of Atholl reverted to David of Strathbogie, to whom was also granted the Stewardship of Scotland, Robert the former Steward making a hasty escape from Rothesay Castle by rowing-boat. He joined the young King and his wife in Dumbarton Castle, one of the few which still held out for the Bruce cause. Dunoon Castle had also fallen, but the Steward managed to retake it with Campbell help under the leadership of Colin Og, according to *Ane Accompt*, which does however admit that Boece says it was Archibald, no doubt that one who was Colin's son, while Holinshed's *Chronicles* have it as being a Dougall Campbell. All may easily have been there. In any case, it is said that it is from this occasion that the Chief of the Campbells holds the Keepership of the Castle of Dunoon which has remained in the family ever since.[28]

Robert the Steward, grandson of King Robert, who was himself to succeed as King Robert II, also succeeded in taking Rosneath and as a reward granted all the lands not already granted to others together with the castle and office of Bailie to *Eugenius*, son of Sir Arthur Campbell. *Eugenius* is usually taken to be the Latin form of Ewen, and Sir Arthur's son and heir was Yvar; this may either have been confusion on the part of the clerk making out the charter, or Sir Arthur had another son called Ewen whose name does not occur elsewhere.[29] An undated charter of Robert the Steward's, thought to be from this time, grants Sir Gillespic Campbell the lands of Kinlochstriven at the head of Loch Striven in Cowal.[30] – again, it would seem clear, for services rendered in difficult times.

Meanwhile, a message arrived from France offering sanctuary to King

David and his queen; they arrived there in May. But all was far from over. The realisation of French support gave heart to the Bruce faction, and warfare broke out across the kingdom. Bruce's adherents scored several notable successes, and by the time Edward had managed to muster an army in the closing months of 1334 they were in a strong position. The English King was not able to accomplish anything of note by the time his force disbanded in February 1335. Increasing French diplomatic pressure brought about a truce that was to last from Easter to midsummer 1335. In July the English mounted a two-pronged attack, Balliol from Berwick and Edward from Carlisle. They met in Perth, where peace was offered to all those who hitherto had held out against Balliol. This proved hard to resist, and many former foes of Balliol now came into his peace. Among those who joined him was David de Strathbogie, who had given short-term allegiance to King David. An expedition mounted from Ireland against the former Steward in his lands of Bute and Arran proved a success, and Robert the Steward, too, submitted.

In spite of all this, resistance continued, and, after the defeat and death of David of Strathbogie at Culblean near Kildrummy at the hands of King Robert's son-in-law, Sir Andrew Moray, the tide began to flow once more in King David's favour. The English King was back in Scotland again in summer 1336, harrying the north-east and destroying Aberdeen. But the supporters of King David mounted strong attacks across the land, and by the following year, 1337, most of the castles which had been set up as garrisons had fallen into the Bruce party's hands. But by now the English King's eyes were firmly fixed on a target that offered more in the way of personal glory and gain than Scotland which had proved so contrary and difficult to bring under submission. His objective now was nothing less than France and the war that ensued was to last for 100 years. Scotland as far as England was concerned was now a backwater and Balliol suffered accordingly. There was still fighting to be done, but, by the spring of 1341, after the capture of Edinburgh Castle by William Douglas, the Knight of Liddesdale, the Balliol faction was once more in final decline and the young King David could safely be invited back from France.

Once more a Bruce was on the throne and the balance of power shifted again. Old scores were to be paid off. And around this time – the exact date is uncertain – Sir Colin Campbell of Lochawe died. These events had an effect on the emerging Clan Campbell which is not to be underestimated. Had John Campbell not fallen under the English arrows at Halidon Hill and had he married and established a line of his own, it is difficult to see how they would not have emerged as the Chiefs of the Clan. The Earldom was a title which was rare in Scotland at the time and placed its holder among the very highest in the land. It would be another century and more before the Chief of the Campbells would be so honoured. And the lands of Atholl far outstripped in extent and richness those held by John's brother Sir Colin Campbell of Lochawe. Sir Colin had been married to Helena about whom *Ane Accompt* gets confused, saying she was a daughter of a son of the Earl of Lennox; in fact, she was almost certainly the daughter of Sir John Menteith, Robert Bruce's former enemy and then loyal supporter, who had briefly been granted the Earldom of Lennox by Edward I of England in 1306. This connection was to have important results for the Campbells. Their eldest son was Archibald or Gillespic, who succeeded his father. Other sons of whom we know are Dougal and John.

There were clearly some Campbells who supported not King David Bruce but King Edward Balliol and who found themselves in trouble when King David was firmly established. In 1342, King David grants to Gillespic Cambell, son of Sir Colin Cambel, the forfeited lands of the late Dougall Cambell, his brother, who has died 'against our faith and peace'.[31] The same year, Gillespic is given the lands and barony of Melfort for his loyalty and faithful service, the said lands having fallen into the King's hands by reason of the forfeiture of its heirs.[32] Who had been the previous possessor of Melfort is unknown, but Archibald appears to have passed it on to his illegitimate brother Neil, son of Sir Colin by a girl of the McIldhuie family. From him descended the later Campbells of Kenmore and Melfort.[33]

The Campbells were by no means alone in feeling the effects of what appears to have been almost another civil war. John (MacDonald) of Islay had flirted with Balliol and had in 1336 received a grant from him which increased his former territory by the addition of more lands in Kintyre and Knapdale together with the Isle of Skye. Out of favour on King David's return, he had, in 1343, concluded 'a final concord' with him which confirmed him in his possession of Islay, Gigha, Jura, Colonsay, Mull, Tiree, Coll and Lewis with the lands of Morvern, Lochaber, Duror and Glencoe, together with the custody of the royal castles of Cairnaburg More, Cairnaburg Beg and Dunchonnell.[34] This confirmation, it will be noted, did not include the lands granted by Balliol, which reverted to their Stewart and Menteith owners in the case of Kintyre and Knapdale. The MacRuaris, who had also changed sides more than once, were also once more brought back into favour with the confirmation to Ranald MacRuari of Garmoran of his ancestral lands of Uist, Barra, Eigg, Rhum and lands in Garmoran, namely Moidart, Morar, Arisaig and Knoydart.[35]

The same year saw a Royal Charter to Alexander McNaughton of all lands belonging to the late John son of Duncan son of Alexander of Islay and all lands belonging to the late John son of Dungall the parson, in the King's hands by forfeiture since the two Johns 'died as enemies and rebels against His faith and peace'.[36] John son of Duncan is a MacDonald grandson of Alexander of Islay who supported Balliol and who was supplanted by his brother Angus Og; what his lands were we do not know. Dungall, or Dougal, the Parson may well be a Campbell; we have met him before in the guise of 'Dugald the Parson', reputed son of Sir Cailean Mor.

In 1346, Gilbert of Glassary had a charter of the lands of Ederline and others in Glassary belonging to the heirs of John son of Ewen which were in the King's hands due to the said John having been forfeited. The lands were listed as Ederline, Garvalt and Craigneur, which are identifiable, and Cambyseneu, the two Carvenys, the two Oywoldys and Calkylkest which are not.[37] Gilbert of Glassary was a cousin of John, descended like him from Gilchrist, great-grandson of Anrothan, the Ui Neill Prince who had married the Dalriadic heiress of Glassary, Cowal and Knapdale. Gilchrist was the nephew of the great *Suibhne* or Sween whose castle in Knapdale, named after him, was the earliest in Scotland. Gilchrist had three sons among whom he divided his patrimony of Glassary: Gilpatrick from whom descended the later MacLachlans, Gillespic from whom came Gilbert through a marriage of Gillespie's heiress to Master Ralf of Dundee, and Ewan, whose lands reverted on forfeiture to Gilbert. It was the marriage of Gilbert's daughter Agnes to Sir Alexander Scrymgeour, the Royal Banner-bearer and Constable of Dundee, that brought the Scrymgeour family, later Earls of Dundee, to this part of Argyll.

In 1346, disaster struck Scotland again. Seeing an opportunity with the English concentrated on the campaign in France where they had just soundly beaten the French at the Battle of Crecy, King David led an army into England. The list of those taking part reveals the absence of John of the Isles, but there must initially at least have been a Hebridean contingent under Ranald MacRuari. He however had fallen out with the Earl of Ross, at whose instigation he was murdered at Elcho, near Perth, on his way to join the King's army.[38] The Scottish army was met by an English force under the Archbishop of York outside Durham at Neville's Cross. Claimed later to have been grossly outnumbered, the Scots made an ineffectual assault; two of their three divisions were defeated, while the third, under the Earl of March and Robert the Steward, beat a retreat. The second division had been under the King, who, after a desperate hand-to-hand struggle, was taken prisoner.

We do not know if there were any Campbells from Argyll in the Scots army, but we have on record that Sir Andrew Campbell of Loudoun, Sheriff of Ayr, was taken prisoner there. He had subsequently been lodged at the Tower of London by command of the King before being sent off to Nottingham Castle, where he was in the custody of William de Vaux.[39] There are fifty-five Scots prisoners-of-war listed, and, apart from Andrew, there are two Duncan McDonnells in the list. He was eventually released with the King, who later granted him half the lands of Redcastle,[40] which Sir Andrew then resigned in 1368.[41] The effect on Scotland was little short of calamitous. With the exception of the castles of Edinburgh, Stirling and Dunbar, Scotland south of the Forth and Clyde was once more in English hands, and it would take the best part of a century before the Scots would win back what they had lost.[42] King David himself was not to return to Scotland until 1357. If this was not enough, shortly afterwards Scotland was hit by the Black Death, an onslaught of bubonic and pneumonic plague that swept across Europe. The actual statistics of the damage it caused are unknown; it was not the only outbreak of pestilence to hit Scotland by any means, but it was the worst and, even in a relatively sparsely populated area by today's standards, its effect was severe.

In 1355, the Barons of Argyll met at Inverleckan south of Inveraray, where they held an inquest to decide on the gift of lands made by John, father of Gilbert of Glassary, to his brother-in-law Dougall Campbell. John had later been declared insane.[43] The lands consisted of a third of John's lands of Glassary, and the barons found in favour of Dougall Campbell, this being obviously less than popular with Gilbert. This may be borne out by an undated charter from John Campbell, Lord of Ardscotnish, to his 'dear cousin' Gilbert of certain lands in Glassary in life rent (i.e. to Gilbert for his life only), the lands listed by name being those of Cross Gillespie, Derybelach, Glacnagobal and Kilmichael (Kilmichael Glassary). This may have been meant as a means of defusing the situation, but it would appear to have been only partly successful. That December, Gilbert of Glassary made a pact of mutual defence with his kinsman John Lord of Lorne, who obliges himself to protect Gilbert against all men excepting the King and Gillespic Lord of Lochawe, with whom he has previously made an agreement.

It has been suggested[44] that this inquest was another result of the upset of 1343 by which Dougall, brother of Gillespic Campbell of Lochawe, had been forfeited. The question was not whether John of Glassary had been insane at the time of the grant but whether or not the lands granted had been merely for life, in which case they would have reverted to the Glassary family on Dougal's death, or whether the gift had been made to Dougal and his heirs, in which case they would have been included in the lands forfeited and later regranted by the King to Dougall's brother, Gillespic Campbell of

Lochawe. As it happens, the charter is quite clear on the point: the gift being made is to Dougall and Margaret and their heirs lawfully procreated between them, and so the inquest duly found.

The composition of the inquest is interesting, as it names a number of the most important people in this part of Argyll at the time. The list with probable identifications is as follows: Sir Arthur Campbell (of the Strachur line, grandson of Sir Arthur Campbell, Bruce's Constable of Dunstaffnage), Lachlan juvenis (MacLachlan of MacLachlan's son), Duncan MacTavish (a descendant of Sir Thomas Campbell, Chief of Clan Tavish), John MacEwan (one of the descendants of Anrothan, probably a McEwan of Otter), Alexander MacSorley (another descendant of Anrothan, this time probably one of the MacSorleys of Moneydrain), Donald MacPherson (one of the Campbell sept of Macphersons who had strong Glassary links) and Christinus MacSween ('Huasuibne' in the text, again one of the descendants of Anrothan; most of the MacSweens by now were carving out fearsome reputations as gallowglasses in Ireland). The meeting was held in the presence of Alexander MacNaughton, Sheriff of Argyll.[45]

The mention of John Lord of Lorne above is also worthy of note; the MacDougall chiefs, too, were once more back in Argyll. John was the grandson, it would seem, of John of Argyll, Admiral of the English fleet, his father being Alan, on record as a member of the English royal household. Quite how the family had returned to Argyll is unclear. According to a document said to be at Taymouth, Ewen, another son of John of Argyll, is described as being Lord of Lorne – not, be it noted, Lord of Argyll – in 1334 when he makes a grant of lands in Lismore to the Bishop of Argyll. He also held the lands of Duror from the Lord of the Isles until resigning them in 1354.[46] This was presumably under the aegis of Edward Balliol. In 1346 John of Lorne, Ewen's nephew, was restored by King David to all the lands of Alexander of Lorne – his great-grandfather – within Lorne.[47]

These lands were but a fraction of the former MacDougall holding. John was not restored to the lands which had been granted to the MacDonalds, where John (MacDonald) of the Isles, in spite of having quite clearly backed both sides, was left in possession by King David, who needed his support. Something of the flavour of the somewhat uneasy relationship between the Lord of Lorne and the newly styled Lord of the Isles at this period may be gathered from the following agreement concluded on the Isle of Seil on 8 September 1354 by which John of Lorne resigned his claim to Mull, the fortresses of Cairnaburgh and Dunchonnell, the upper part of Jura and Tiree except three unciates of Tiree nearest to Coll and the churchlands of Duror and Glencoe, which John of the Isles regrants to John of Lorne.

They will act as brothers, with John of Lorne having the right to build eight ships of twelve or sixteen oars. Three MacDougall hostages will be given to the Lord of the Isles until such time as Cairnaburgh More is handed over. John of the Isles will not accept any gift from the King of Scots of any of the said lands granted to John of Lorne, and the two will not rise against each other unless on the side of the King of Scots. Any man-slayer will be exiled by either party, and no criminal may switch from the following of one to the other without answering for his crimes. No member of the Clan Fingon – the MacKinnons – is to be given the custody of Cairnaburgh More.[48]

The restoration of a MacDougall chief was due no doubt in large part to his marriage to Joanna Isaac. She was a granddaughter of King Robert the Bruce, her mother Mathilda, the King's daughter, having married the mysterious Thomas Isaac, described as 'a Squire'. Meanwhile, the power of the MacDonald Chief had been greatly increased by his marriage to Amy MacRuari, through whom he took possession of the large MacRuari territories in the north. He was by now lord of a vast area and in a position to accept the clientship of lesser chiefs who became the servants and supporters of the new Lordship of the Isles. In view of this, he continued to be seen as a potential ally by the English King who, in 1356, was sending envoys to negotiate with him.[49]

The question remains of the very different treatment at this stage of the Campbells. If the Crown appears deliberately to have concentrated power in the hands of one man in the case of the Chief of Clan Donald, such was clearly not so with the Campbells, where a number of leading men of the name at that time received preferential treatment without any one being pre-eminent. There are two deductions as to the reasons why this happened which may, I think, be made. One is the historical precedent that existed for the Isles being controlled by a single power, whether Norse or that of Somerled. Although for much of the time an ideal rather than an actuality, the idea and the precedent were there, even if constantly disputed by competing factions. The idea of a necessary counterweight, based on the mainland of Argyll, had not yet become evident. The other deduction concerns the nature of clans at this time, or rather their absence; the idea of a power bloc based on family relationship under the leadership of one particular dynasty was still to evolve. Thus it was that, given the disgrace of the MacDougalls, there was as yet no obvious contender to act as the Crown's agent to curb the growing power of the Lords of the Isles.

Indeed in the case of the Campbells, the Crown almost seems to have gone out of its way deliberately to avoid favouring one family among them over another. Two charters listed of King David II, one to Arthur Campbell, the other to Dougal of Craignish, specify that the recipient *nulli viventi subi-ciatur pro terris suis nisi regi* – 'is subject to none living for his lands except the King' – a formula which does not appear elsewhere and which might seem a deliberate move to avoid the emergence of any particular chiefly line.[50]

This brings up the question of the 'Barons of Argyll', a term which appears again in the Inverleckan Inquest of 1355. There seems to be some differentiation in the term which sets the Barons of Argyll apart from others of the same description. This difference has been made a legal term by the Lord Lyon who, in cases where the feudal *chapeau* of a baron is shown in a grant of arms, denotes a Baron of Argyll in possession of his barony with a chapeau turned back with *contre-ermine* instead of the normal *ermine*. This distinction is extended to all barons within the bounds of ancient earldoms, the implication being, presumably, that they predate the establishment of the Kingdom of Scotland.

The term 'baron' has had various meanings at various times, and it may well be that the term as used here has little meaning beyond denoting that those thus designated held their lands direct from the Crown and not through any intermediary. While this might have had some attraction as conferring social pre-eminence, it was often not as attractive as it appeared, and holding from some nearer power than a distant Crown could become a safer and more attractive option – hence, as we will see, the resignation of lands held from the Crown into the hands of a local magnate for regrant to the former possessor.

The granting of lands *in liberam baroniam* – 'in free barony' – as in the case of the lands of Loch Awe became a preferred method by which the King in making the grant made the recipient responsible for good order within his bounds, the various legal powers involved extending even to the ultimate penalty whether *cum furca et fossa* – 'with pit and gallows' – was specified or not. The holding of baron courts during the year was part of the obligation laid on the possessor at which justice was dispensed either by the baron himself or by his appointed deputy or bailie, whose emblem of office was a white wand – still carried today on state occasions by certain high officials within the royal household. This position can be an interesting one, since it can on occasion be found to be held by the family who were previous possessors of the land before being displaced.

Latterly the term 'baron' was used merely to denote a freeholder who thereby was one of the few people entitled to vote. The description was in use well into the eighteenth century, usually for the heads of small but ancient houses. Size had little to do with it; the Baron of the Bachuil, hereditary Keeper of the Staff of Saint Moluag, once again possesses his family lands on the Isle of Lismore which were granted in payment for the office held by the head of the family. Even before the depredations of Sir Donald Campbell of Ardnamurchan, of which more below, the lands were very small but their owner was and is still 'the Baron'. This usage seems to have been particularly prevalent in Cowal, for what reason one can only speculate, but the widespread powers of the various barons may be discerned still today with the number of place names in Argyll which may be translated as 'Hangman's Hill' or 'Hill of the Gallows', which denote the site where the ultimate penalty was exacted.

Even now, half way through the fourteenth century and beyond, there is no clear leader among the Campbells. As far as can be judged, the main branches in existence at the time were the Craignish family, the Clan Iver and the Clan Tavish Campbells, all of whom appear established on their lands without making any dynamic expansion. Sir Donald Campbell's descendants, the Campbells of Loudoun, although still holding lands in Argyll, were clearly turning their attention to affairs in Ayrshire. The two branches which appear to have been vying for the leadership at this time were those of Lochawe and Strachur. It would appear that the latter's lands in Lorne and Benderloch, which had included the castle and lands of Dunstaffnage, had once more reverted to the MacDougall family. Whether or not the King had felt it necessary to make any compensation to them for this loss is unknown, but at this period we find the family now based on Loch Fyne with increasing interests in Cowal and the castle and bailiary of Rosneath.

In 1349, Yver Campbell of Strachur had a grant from his nephew Alexander, son and heir of Alexander Menzies, Lord of Glendochart, of twenty merklands in Glendochart, stretching from Loch Dochart, to the east of what is now Crianlarich, up the glen to the march with the head of Loch Lomond, an important new area of Campbell development, while the family appear to have been claiming the lands of Garmoran in north Argyll, based on Christine MacRuari's charter to Arthur Campbell. The Campbells of Loch Awe, meanwhile, as well as the lands of Loch Awe and Ardscotnish, the latter approximating to the present parish of Kilmartin, seem also to have held the barony of Kilmelford as well as the lands of Dunoon in Cowal.

One other branch was of major importance within the Campbell hierarchy: that of Sir Dougall, younger son of Sir Cailein Mor, who was the possessor of significant lands in Argyll and who had held the positions of Sheriff of Argyll and Bailie of Atholl. It was he who had come to an agreement with his nephew – also Dougall – over Ardscotnish. In 1324, it was Sir Dougall to whom King Robert gave a charter of Menstrie, the lands above the Forth which had been granted to Dougall's grandfather Sir Gillespie back in

1263 – long the Campbell family's most important holding. It is difficult not to see Sir Dougall as having been during his lifetime at least on a par with his brother Sir Neil. Of him, more shortly. Having survived a period of political turbulence, with the successful establishment of a springboard for expansion, the story of the growth of Campbell power and the emergence of the Lochawe line as Chiefs now accelerates.

CHAPTER FIVE

Laying the Foundation

During the period of King David's captivity, Scotland was ruled by the Steward, nephew of the King. There seems to have been little love lost between them, David being much taken with the English way of life, while the Steward remained strongly Scottish in his attitude. At least, the situation was somewhat simplified when, in 1356, Edward Balliol renounced his claim to the Scottish throne in favour of King Edward III in return for a life pension. There is little evidence of Campbell participation in national affairs during this time but a number of significant events took place nearer to home where the local magnates were jockeying for position after the upsets of preceding years.

It was at this period that the Campbells of Lochawe seem to have benefited to a considerable degree through the relinquishment in their favour of lands held in Argyll by members of the Stewart family and by their cousins the Menteiths who were Stewarts under a different name. These families seem very early to have pushed into Argyll from their base across the Clyde in Renfrew, with the island of Bute eventually becoming a strong Stewart base with its fortress of Rothesay Castle.

The existence of mottes has already been mentioned, possibly the vestige of this Stewart/Menteith attempt to dominate the area. There does seem to be a logical progression in their siting if they were indeed used for this purpose. From Dunoon, across the Clyde from the Stewart homelands, where there is one behind the present town, the entry route to Argyll follows Loch Eck to Strachur, where there are no fewer than three motte sites. Another at Ballimore covers the crossing of Loch Fyne at Otter Ferry, while the route up Glen Fyne at the very head of Loch Fyne is covered by another. The route from Bute via Loch Riddon up Glendaruel is also protected in similar fashion, while there is another possible motte at Machrie in Kintyre. It seems not impossible that these sites, which are far from frequent in this part of the world, are relics of early Stewart/Menteith inroads into the wilds of Argyll where the Menteith family emerge as Lords of Arran and Knapdale while the Stewarts have much of Cowal and Kintyre. But the interest of both families in Argyll seems to have faded at this time, the Menteith family being without male heirs and the Stewarts with their eyes now on altogether richer prizes. From these circumstances, the chief beneficiaries seem to have been the Campbells of Lochawe.

An undated charter of around 1350 from John, Lord of Menteith and Knapdale, grants Gillespic Campbell, Lord of Loch Awe, the one-pennylands of Clachelan, Kilbryde, Beachmore, Kenlochorednesay with the castle and the Isle of Saint Molasse, lands which are not immediately identifiable.[1] This is followed in 1353 with a further grant by the same to the same of lands in Knapdale listed as Ardnanno, Ervergy, Ariluig, Arienrioch, Bercorari, Leachenaban, Drumlynd, Craglyne, Obinhan, Bealalah, Tonardri, Danna, Glencagiduburguill, Arigeargage, Lagan, Kyllmychel, Cragnanyach, Lergna-hunsend, Drumnaherisage, Metnach, Achagnadarach, Achagnagarthe, Brackwerneill, Kyllaldubursealan, Atichuan and Inwerneill, most of which are alike impossible to identify from today's map.[2]

Kyllmychel is, however, Kilmichael of Inverlussa on Loch Sween. Lergana-hunsend is Lergnahension, at that time the name for what is now Ashfield near Kilmichael of Inverlussa, while Danna is on the opposite shore of Loch Sween. Tonardri is Dunardry, later the holding of MacTavish on the present Crinan Canal, while Achagnadarach (Auchendarroch), Brackwerneill (Brackley), Kyllaldubursealan (Kilduskland), Atichuan and Inverneill are all on the Loch Fyne side of the peninsula near Ardrishaig and Lochgilphead. Another undated charter covers much of the same ground. Again by John Lord of Menteith to Gillespic Campbell, it gives the lands as those of Castle Sween, Apenad, Barmore in Danna, Ulva, Dallicheliche, Strondour and Drissaig, all in Knapdale. The reddendo was a pair of white gloves at Martinmas if required.[3]

The most significant grant in this example is of course that of Castle Sween, the extremely powerful fortress at the mouth of Loch Sween which not only dominated the surrounding area and covered the inner seaway between the mainland and Islay and Jura. It also covered the ancient route from Ireland that came via Islay and the land journey up Jura to Lagg and across the Sound to Keills on the mainland, whence it proceeded up the spine of the land past modern Tayvallich, the route still marked by standing stones, and through the tangle of hills to Crinan and on to Dunadd. In early days this had been an important trade route with the Kingdom of Dalriada, and it was to become so again with the export of black cattle which came from Islay and Jura by the old way before being driven up the valley of the Add and over the hill to Inveraray on their way to the markets in the east.

This Sir John de Menteith was the grandson of the betrayer of Wallace who went by the same name. His grandfather, who later became one of Bruce's most loyal supporters, had been the younger son of Walter, the first Stewart Earl of Menteith. His elder brother Alexander had inherited the title which was now in the hands of Sir John's second cousin, Mary, Countess of Menteith in her own right. Sir John had no children, and Mary, who had married Sir John Graham, found her interests were moving to concentrate further eastwards. The disposal of her lands in Argyll now allowed her to play the peacemaker in a quarrel which seems to have erupted around this time and in which she found herself heavily involved since her daughter and heir, Margaret, had married firstly John Moray, Earl of Bothwell, and thirdly Sir John Drummond of Concraig. She found herself somewhat uncomfortably in the middle when serious trouble broke out between the Drummonds and the Morays on one side and the Menteiths on the other. On Sunday 17 May 1360, under the supervision of Sir Robert Erskine and Sir Hugh Eglinton, Justiciars of Scotland, an agreement was signed on the banks of the Forth near Stirling between John Drummond of Concraig, husband of the future Countess Margaret, his brother Maurice and Walter Moray on one side and John and Alexander Menteith on the other, following the murder of their brothers Walter, Malcolm and William Menteith.

John Drummond granted to Sir Alexander Menteith his lands of Rosneath which had previously been granted to him by the Countess Mary, his mother-in-law. A further undertaking by John Drummond promised to leave in peace *Gillespic* and *Kessan McGhillecharrick, Douenaldus fil Gilberti* and *Duncanus fil Negelli* who had killed Bricius the Procurator, probably the original cause of the quarrel. He also promised not to harm 'Finlay son of Ay'. The Menteiths could not promise the good behaviour of Gillespic and his son Colin Campbell, but swore to defend John Drummond against them and their men if necessary.[4] In order to guarantee Campbell cooperation in settling the quarrel, it is thought that the Countess granted Gillespic Campbell of Lochawe further lands in the Kilmun/Loch Eck area of Cowal. An undated charter lists the lands, which are those she held of the Steward, as being those of Kinlochkilmun, Correrkmore, Stronlonag, Correnlie, Bernicemore and Stronnachun, for which the rent is a silver penny yearly.[5] This charter was duly confirmed by King David.[6] It will be noticed that the lands mentioned include those of Kinlochkilmun, the lands at the head of the loch of Kilmun, or the Holy Loch as it is now called. We shall hear of them again.

King David's ransom was for the sum – enormous by Scottish standards – of 100,000 merks, to be paid over a ten-year period. This burden was increased by general unhappiness over the King's performance after his return to the throne. A Parliament was called in 1365 at which John of Lorne and Gillespic Campbell are present while there is no mention of John, Lord of the Isles, who does not appear to have turned up. This was almost certainly deliberate since, to pay fairly for the King's ransom, it had been ordained that the whole of Scotland should be valued; the response from Argyll was adjudged both out-of-date and very understated, and, at a later Parliament the same year at which three out of the five absentees summoned were John, Lord of the Isles, John Lord of Lorne and Gillespic Campbell of Lochawe, it was decided that the rebels in Argyll should be arrested.[7]

John MacDougall, Lord of Lorne, in particular might have felt gratitude to the King, since in 1363 he had received a charter confirming him in all his lands in Lorne that had belonged to his forebear Alexander.[8] It is not clear whether this meant a complete return of all the former MacDougall possessions or of only those which had not been granted to others, notably the Campbells. It is of course possible that the latter might have been left in possession but holding now of the Lord of Lorne and not of the King. There is no reason to think otherwise, since there is no evidence of any trouble breaking out between the two families at this time.

The March 1368 Parliament, while adjudging John of Lorne and Gillespie Campbell to be loyal to the King, nevertheless included them in the agreement made between John, Lord of the Isles, and his father-in-law the Steward, which required them all to come into the King's presence and there declare that they and their adherents would trouble the whole community of the realm no more and that they would bear their fair share of the tax for the King's ransom.[9]

Gillespie was again absent from Parliament in 1369, but the same year he received a charter of confirmation from the King of all grants made to him of Craignish, Melfort, Strachur, Cowal, Kyldachanane and other lands and rents in Argyll to be held as freely as his ancestor Duncan MacDowne had held his lands in the barony of Lochawe and elsewhere.[10] This charter has already been remarked upon. It is of particular interest since it would seem to authenticate the existence of Duncan MacDuibhne, who appears in the traditional pedigrees before the existence of verification offered by contemporary written record, and it suggests that Duncan was the actual possessor of his lands of Lochawe and not solely acting for the King. But the Lord of the Isles was not so well regarded, and in November 1369 he appeared before the King and made formal submission, admitting past misdeeds and promising to pay contributions due and to expel the King's enemies from his lands. He left in the King's hands three hostages, two of his sons and a grandson. For the moment, the Lord of the Isles appeared in humbled and obedient guise. It was not to last long.

In 1371 King David died suddenly, leaving no legitimate issue. His successor was his nephew, Robert the Steward, son of King David's sister Marjory and her husband Walter the Steward. By the time he came to the throne, he was aged 55, well into middle age by the standards of the day, with the fire of his youth much quenched and with the desire for a quiet life the guiding spirit of his philosophy. Himself no stranger to making his dissatisfaction with the Crown felt (in 1363, along with the Earls of Douglas and March, he had openly protested against the King's shortcomings to the extent of armed rebellion) he now adopted a policy of appeasing those who opposed him and seeking support by the payment of what were virtually bribes to ensure cooperation. At the same time, he made quite sure that the fortunes of his own paternal family prospered, and during his reign the Stewarts fairly blossomed, to the point where no fewer than six of the then sixteen earldoms of Scotland, those of Carrick, Menteith, Fife, Atholl, Strathearn and Caithness, belonged to Stewarts. Nor was this all, for the King's sons-in-law included the existing or future Earls of Douglas, Crawford and Moray, the Constable, the Marshal and the Lord of the Isles.

The last was now in a strong position. In 1372 he received a charter of the former MacRuari lands, and by 1376 the Lordship covered Moidart, Arisaig, Morar, Knoydart, Sunart, Letter Lochletter, Ardnamurchan, Duror of Appin, Glencoe, the Lordship of Lochaber, Kintyre and much of Knapdale on the mainland and the islands of Islay, Jura, Scarba, Gigha, Colonsay, Tiree, Rum, Eigg, Canna, North and South Uist, Barra, Lewis, Harris and Benbecula. Under his wing were now grouping the subordinate chieftains of the Lordship, who held these lands from him and supported him in peace as well as war. These were made up both by the heads of the branches of his own kin and by other subordinate clans such as the Macleans, the MacLeods, the MacKinnons, the MacQuarries, the MacEachrans, the MacNeils, the MacNicols and a host of others. It was now that the Lordship of the Isles became a great power centre, focusing the loyalties of the Western Isles on what was, increasingly, to be seen as a threat to the Scottish Crown itself.

It is at this time that the Campbells of Lochawe perhaps show early signs of the increasing momentum that was eventually to push them to the very top of the tree in the Highlands if not, indeed, in all Scotland. In 1373, as Sheriff of Argyll, Gillespic Campbell had rendered his account for £56.[11] This position was now followed, in 1382, by the appointment by King Robert with the consent of his eldest son, John Earl of Carrick, Steward of Scotland, of Gillespie Campbell and Colin his son and heir as King's Lieutenants and Special Commissioners from Carndrome to Polgilb and from Polmelfirth to Loch Long in the Sheriffdom of Argyll. The post was to be a hereditary one. The Lieutenants were to have full plenary powers over all the inhabitants of the area, for which their recompense was to be one half of all wards, reliefs, marriages, escheats, fines, amerciaments and all other emoluments arising from the office.[12]

The area was a large one. Carndrome is just where the main road crosses the District border between Argyll and Bute and Stirling, just to the west of Tyndrum, the -*drome* or -drum in each case referring to the great ridge that stretches north/south virtually the whole length of Scotland north of the Forth and which marks the watershed between east and west. Polgilp is Loch Gilp, at the head of which is now Lochgilphead, and Polmelfirth is Kilmelfort. It can thus be seen that the area over which the Campbells of Lochawe were to be given complete power in the King's name comprised the districts of Loch Awe, Kilmelford, Glassary, Mid Argyll, as we know it today, and Upper Cowal, in which areas there was now a major Campbell presence.

This strength had been further advanced in 1373, when Gillespic received a grant of Stronewhillen and Finnart from Paul Glenn (*Paul filius Glaii*), and again in 1375 when Gillespic's son Colin had been given a charter of the Island of Inishail, on Loch Awe, by John of Prestwych, son and heir of the late Mariota Garrechal together with the lands of *Iesikhedyh, Selechan and Dalyen* in which Duncan MacNaughton had died vested and seised, to be held of John for due service to the King.[13]

But the position of King's Lieutenant was in a new category. It was the first of many, increasingly important such appointments which were to raise the Campbells of Lochawe to hitherto undreamed-of heights. For the moment, though, the leadership of the Lochawe branch over the whole Clan Campbell still does not seem to be firmly and clearly established. Their closest rivals remained the Campbells of Strachur, who seem to have adopted – or been adopted by – the Earls of Lennox, from whom Arthur Campbell some time between 1333 and 1364 had received a charter for a third part of Gillespic Macmartin's lands, a third part of Benderloch, a third part of Lorne and a third part of Rosneath. This was the return of lands already held by the Strachur Campbells but which, as part of some deal, had been temporarily passed to the Earl of Lennox. In the charter, Arthur is described as 'our dear and special cousin', the exact nature of the link being unknown.[14]

It was not unknown by any means for lesser lordlings to resign their lands into the hands of a neighbouring potentate. Holding direct of the King, as the Strachur family had once done for all their lands, might be all very well for prestige, but in practical terms possession was more strongly guaranteed by a neighbouring overlord who was of friendly disposition and who could provide immediate protection. It has to be noted that Campbell of Lochawe did not, as yet, appear to have the power to be considered an attractive overlord. Only for their lands of Strachur, and by inference Cowal, did the family still hold of the King; in 1374, on Yver's resignation, Arthur received a charter of confirmation for Strachur.[15]

By now, as noted in the previous chapter, the family appear to have relinquished Dunstaffnage and the lands that went with it to the MacDougall Lord of Lorne. A later charter of this period by Yvar Campbell of Strachur to his dearest cousin Duncan Earl of Lennox confirms the grant to the latter of all *Jus et clameum quod habemus, habuimus aut habere poterimus in futurum* – 'right and claim which we have, have had or could have in future' and then lists all the lands in Lorne which had previously been granted to Sir Arthur, including Dunstaffnage and Dunolly.[16] But the family had extended their holding in Cowal, where Strachur was now their chief base, which now included the lands of Kinlochlong, Glencroe (at the head of which is the famous Rest-and-be-Thankful, the point at which the old road succeeded in climbing out of the depths of Glen Croe, where many a radiator has boiled over in more modern times) and Gannan, which is also near Glencroe.[17] A mysterious clause in the charter thought to date from around 1375–80, by which Yvar Campbell, Lord of Strachur, confirms his son Arthur in these lands which border the head of Loch Long, requires that any criminal who is sentenced to be hung for murder or theft should be hung on the gallows belonging to the heirs of Malcolm Campbell.[18]

Who this Malcolm may be, why his gallows had to be used and where they were is unclear. Malcolm, here described as the 'son of Dougall', appears again in another Royal Charter of 1371 confirming his grant of the lands of Gannay, the surrounds of the loch called 'Lochanressaliche' and the lands of 'Glenhifernemor' to his brother Dougall. Gannay is Gannan, as we have seen on Loch Long, and Lochanressaliche is almost certainly Loch Restill close to the aforementioned Rest-and-be-Thankful. This would seem to be the earlier of the two charters, since Malcolm is still alive in 1371, and from the other it would seem that the same lands were now in Strachur's possession. It may be that Malcolm and the two Dougalls were a younger branch of the Strachur family who had clearly been sufficiently important to have exercised baronial rights of pit and gallows which they were anxious to keep in use.

Another mysterious Campbell family, clearly of considerable importance, appears in this period. Identification, as far as it exists, depends on a later document, a Royal confirmation of 1431 which confirms a 1385 charter of

Robert, Earl of Fife and Menteith, who grants to William de Spensa, burgess of Perth and to Isabella Campbell his wife, daughter and heiress of the late Duncan Campbell, the lands of Achaland, Ketidy and Craigsanquhar in Fife in exchange for the lands of Drummond, to be held by either Isabella or William while either of them is living or by their heirs or, whom failing, by the heirs of Isabella.[19] This last clause shows that the lands of Drummond had originally belonged to Isabella rather than to William since her heirs are given precedence over his, should their joint line fail. Douglas's *Baronage* then provides identification for Isabella:

> William Spens, the undoubted ancestor of the later family of Lathallan, married toward the end of the fourteenth century Isabel, daughter and heiress of Duncan Campbell of Glen-Douglas with whom he got a considerable fortune, particularly the lands and barony of Glen-Douglas, Tarbit etc., in Dunbartonshire and several others in Fifeshire.[20]

Glen Douglas is on the west bank of Loch Lomond, well down in Lennox territory, while Tarbet is further north where today's main road crosses the isthmus to Loch Long. The mention of Tarbet is something of a surprise since it is usually recognised as being within Macfarlane territory, but that this is no mistake is shown by a 1392 Indenture between Duncan Earl of Lennox and *William of the Spens, burgess of Perth and Issabel hys spouse* concerning the lands of Tarbet and Glendouglas, with Tarbet Isle within the *pluchlands of Macgylcrist.* This is a reinfeftment, the Earl or his father having already recognised their ownership. 'The ploughland of MacGilchrist' refers to the former surname used by the Macfarlanes until, according to legend, their chieftain's son, Parlan, led a particularly successful attack on the Norse detachment that had ravaged the shores of Loch Lomond during Haakon's 1263 invasion, and his people then took his name as their own.

This is recorded in Fraser's *Lennox*, as is another obligation concerning the above transaction. Isabel's surname is not given but seals are attached, including one showing the Campbell gyronny with the addition of a label of three points and one with a lion's head erased within a border engrailed.[21] These arms appear combined as those of Spens of Lathallan in Sir David Lindsay of the Mount's 1542 Armorial: *a gyronny of eight argent and azure; overall on an escutcheon a lion's head sable langued gules within a border gules.* The Campbell gyronny is included in later Spens matriculations of arms, and the present practice is to quarter the Campbell gyronny with, however, two gyrons in blue and silver with the remaining six in the more normal black and gold.

The actual date of the exchange of lands of Drummond appears to have been 1385 as mentioned above, at which point Isabella and her husband appear still to have been in possession of Glendouglas and Tarbet. These lands are thought by some to have given their name to the Drummond family, the first on record of whom was Malcolm Beg *de Dromod* who was Steward to Maoldomhnaich, Earl of Lennox, and who was alive in 1225 and 1250. But there are other lands of the same name in Strathearn, and it may be they that are the origin, since Fraser says the lands of Drummond in the Lennox were royal until 1489 when they were first granted on lease to John, Lord Drummond, and later granted to him in feu.[22] There is potential confusion in that the Strathearn lands were granted in 1362 to Maurice Drummond of Drommane and Tulychchram, by Robert Steward of Scotland, Earl of Strathearn.

It would appear that, prior to 1364, *Yvarus Cambell de Stratchur* – Yvar Campbell of Strachur – granted an undated charter to his 'most revered and dearest cousin', Duncan (8th) Earl of Lennox, of all claims he had to Torrintuirks and other lands for the Earl's acquittance of £40 sterling, in which Ywar stood to the Earl and his heirs for the ward and marriage of the lands of Drummode (Drummond), and of £20 daily due to him from Ywar as long as the same rested unpaid to him or his heirs, to be held of the Earl of the Kings of Scotland as freely as Arthur Cambell, father of the said Ywar, held them of the same Kings.[23] In other words, Yvar would be able to control the marriage of the heiress to the lands of Drummond and, by choosing a member of his own family to be her husband, bring the lands into the hands of his own close relative. It seems 'not unreasonable', to quote David Sellar, to suppose that the husband, Campbell of Glen Douglas, is also a member of the Strachur family, although the exact identity of Isabella's father Duncan remains a mystery in spite of his considerable importance.[24]

The advancing age and infirmity of King Robert had been giving cause for unease for some time, and in 1384 the General Council appointed the King's eldest son, John, Earl of Carrick, to rule the kingdom as Guardian. There now appears on the scene one of the more remarkable of the early Campbells who was largely responsible both for the acceptance of himself and his line as Chiefs of the Clan and for a marked advance in the fortunes and standing of the line of Lochawe. Colin appears to have been the son of Gillespic Campbell of Lochawe by his wife Isabella, daughter of Sir John Lamont of that Ilk, a neighbouring lord. This is the only marriage of which we can be sure; a suggestion that Gillespic may also have been married to a daughter of Sir John of Menteith is an obvious confusion with his mother, whose true identity was concealed by her being described as daughter of the Earl of Lennox, a title briefly held from King Edward of England by the said Sir John de Menteith.

Apart from Colin, if *Ane Accompt* is to be believed, Gillespic and Isabella had had a son, *Duncan Skeodnish*, so called from his being fostered in Ardscotnish by a family of MacCallums there, probably the ancestors of the Malcolms of Poltalloch. From him are said to descend the *MacDhonnachie* or MacConnochie Campbells – the sons of Duncan – of Inverawe, Stronchormaig and Glenfeochan, of whom more below.[25] They are also said to have had a daughter Helena married first to John MacDonald, passed-over eldest son of John, Lord of the Isles and Amy MacRuari of Garmoran, the marriage by which the MacDonald dynasty finally established itself as the dominant power in the Western Isles. The Lord of the Isles' second wife was Margaret, daughter of King Robert II and it was from this politically advantageous marriage that the later Lords of the Isles descend. John MacDonald and Helena Campbell had one son, Angus, who appears briefly but of whom there is no known issue, while it was to John's younger brother that the former MacRuari lands were granted and the future line of Clanranald established.[26] Helena went on to marry Duncan, 8th Earl of Lennox, as his second wife.[27] He was to be even less fortunate, as the story will shortly reveal.

Colin's soubriquet of *Iongantach* is translated as 'wonderful, surprising, strange, extraordinary or droll'.[28] It would appear that he justified all of these descriptions, and of him several legends are told. One concerns his throwing his treasure into Loch Fyne shortly before he died in order to prevent his sons quarrelling over its division; another tells of his having burnt down his own house deliberately. This was due to his having met the O'Neills in Ireland and having invited them to visit him in Scotland when he made some unwise boasts as to the grandeur of his dwelling. Rather than be shown up, he apparently resorted to this drastic expedient which gave him the excuse of having to receive them with satisfactory pomp and ceremony in tents in the open air.[29] The event is commemorated, so local legend has it, by the place name Ardachuple (Gaelic, *pubull*, a tent) – 'Point of the tent' – at the foot of Glendaruel on the eastern shore of Loch Riddon, on the river estuary where the present farmhouse of that name is said to be built on the site. According to the story, the Irish were not only greatly impressed by the sumptuosity of their *al fresco* accommodation but also so sorry for their host that they gave him the rich furnishings they had brought with them to help refurnish his house.

In his youth, he had apparently been lucky to escape death at the hands of the Clan Callum, who wanted their foster-son to succeed to Lochawe. They are said to have set fire to the house in which Colin was situated, where he waited for so long that his coat of mail or *lureach* became agonisingly hot.

Being unable to bear it any longer, he burst from the house through the ring of men that surrounded it and plunged into the waters of the Kilmartin Burn, where a pool was long known as 'The Pool of the Lureach'. Colin Iongantach was also much admired for his bravery and skill as a spy, notably on the occasion when he went right through the army of the Lord of the Isles dressed as a beggar. Indeed, says *Ane Accompt*, 'His great work was the bringing down of the Lord of the Isles and these sorts of men who were disobedient to the Crown whose wings were never more clipped by any man'.[30] He appears to have been married twice, firstly to Margaret, second daughter of Sir John Drummond of Stobhall and sister to the future King Robert III's Queen, Annabella. There do not appear to have been any children of this marriage, and his sons all appear to have come from his second marriage. This was to his second cousin Mariota Campbell, daughter of John Campbell, who, *Ane Accompt* says, was the son of Sir Dougall. Although *The Scots Peerage* follows this, I believe both to have missed out a generation, a not unlikely happening due to what I believe to be the repetition of the names John and Mariota.

Colin Iongantach was able to hand over the lands of Glenorchy to his son Colin, as we will see in due course. These lands appear to have come into Campbell hands with the marriage of Mariota of Glenorchy to a John Campbell; she in due course inherited, and in 1358 the couple had a charter of Glenorchy, by which time they were at least middle-aged.[31] The family of Glenorchy were the ancestors of the later Clan MacGregor who so mismanaged things as to allow their lands around the head of Loch Awe to pass into alien hands through this fateful marriage, with the result that subsequent Chiefs of the Clan Gregor were virtually landless and unable to provide holdings for their people – the resultant friction leading to the subsequent bloody history of that unhappy race. I believe that the couple also had a daughter named Mariota who is the subject of the 1366 Papal Indult for 'Mariota, daughter of John Campbell' to marry 'John Campbell, son of Colin Campbell', although related in the fourth degree.[32] This second John I believe to have been the brother of Gillespic of Loch Awe and son of Sir Colin Oig. Niall, Duke of Argyll, has suggested that he is also the John Lord of Ardscotnish who we saw earlier granting various lands to Gilbert of Glassary. It is not impossible, since he could have inherited this position through his wife's paternal line, Sir Dougall having come to an agreement over Ardscotnish with his nephew, also Dougall. But the undated charter to Gilbert of Glassary could, it seems to me, have been to this Mariota's father, husband of Mariota of Glenorchy, who could equally well have been the holder of the title Lord of Ardscotnish.

In any case, I believe this second John and Mariota to have had a daughter, yet again a Mariota, who married Colin Iongantach as his second wife and bore him a large family. Not only was she a fertile mate, but she also brought with her the lands of Glenorchy and of Ardscotnish. Her great-grandfather Dougall had also been Lord of Menstrie, and in 1364 Colin Iongantach has a gift from Robert Erskine of the ward and marriage of the lands of Menstrie belonging to the son and heir of John Campbell of Menstrie. This unnamed heir was clearly the son of John Campbell and Mariota of Glenorchy and therefore uncle of Colin Iongantach's wife Mariota. There is an element of theory in this, but I believe it to be entirely supportable. The important thing is that by this marriage and his dealings, Colin Iongantach brought back to his line the important Campbell lands of lands of Ardscotnish and of Menstrie to which were added the lands of Glenorchy. It is possible that the first two might have been due to the main line anyway if they had been regarded as younger sons' portions which, according to long-held custom, were leased out and then required to revert to the main line after three generations for redistribution to more recent younger sons, the previous possessors being left with whatever they had managed to add to their original patrimony. But even if this was the case, the marriage was a highly convenient one and it shows every sign of having been a happy one as well.

Colin was, in 1361, while his father was still alive, the recipient of a grant from his 'cousin' Christina, daughter and heir of the late Dougall of Craignish, now a widow, of her part of her late husband Alexander MacNaughton's barony, in return for a sum of money and cows already handed over.[33] This was the 'notorious' Christian or Christina, 'the eldest and unhappy daughter' as *The Manuscript History of Craignish* has it,[34] who was married very young to MacDougall of Lorne by whom she had a single son in a twenty-year marriage. When her first husband died, she married Alexander McNaughton of that Ilk but was widowed again a year or so later. Although her rights in the lands of Craignish had reverted to her uncle Malcolm, her MacDougall son considered himself the rightful possessor and used to dispute the lifting of rents with his great-uncle Malcolm and Malcolm's son, *Ranald Mor na h-Ordaig* – 'Big Ranald of the Thumb'. Meanwhile, it appears, his mother was kept under house arrest at Dunolly until the night she broke out and escaped across the hills to Loch Awe and Innischonnell. Arriving on the bank of the loch and knowing her son was close behind, she shouted loudly for the boat which came just in time for her to escape her pursuers. She was still within range when young MacDougall, infuriated by his mother's mocking taunts, drew bow at a venture and in a fury sent an arrow winging in the direction of the boat. By good luck or bad, it is said to have nailed his mother's hip to the gunwale, whereupon she let fly a torrent of invective including the vituperative couplet that may be translated

> You with the white bow that frisk upon yonder shore,
> pray God I may hear the noise of the Fowls of the air feeding,
>   or picking on your face.

In due course her less than maternal wish was granted, her son being killed by the men of Craignish while attempting to extract a rent from them.[35]

This was not the last tale told of this lady, described by the author of *The Manuscript History of Craignish* as 'this vile creature'. A widow once more, she fell violently in love with young MacIver of Asknish who was servitor to Colin Iongantach and, insisting that he be her only companion on a journey from Innischonnell to Craignish, she managed to seduce him in a wood known thereafter as 'The Lady's Wood'. Finding herself pregnant, she wanted to marry the young man but for this had to gain the permission of Colin. Although the author of the tale goes so far as to suggest that he too may have been a recipient of her favours, the Knight of Lochawe drove a hard bargain. Christina was forced to renounce any right she may have had as her father's daughter and heiress to the barony and lands of Craignish to Colin Iongantach, who now became their possessor. This took place only a few months after the transaction above by which Christina had done a deal with Colin over her share in the MacNaughton lands, which was in August 1361, while the deal over Craignish is dated November of the same year. This grant was confirmed to Gillespic, Colin Iongantach's father, by King David II along with those of his other lands some years later, in 1369. It was this document, already mentioned, which confirmed that Gillespic should hold them as freely as had his progenitor, Duncan MacDuine.

The acquisition of Chrisitina's share in the MacNaughton lands seems to have opened the door on another field for Campbell expansion. Some time later, in 1403, by which time Colin Iongantach was in his mid-sixties, he had a resignation from *Margaret McGilliecreist MacGilligeachin* with the consent of her son and heir *Fynlay Macawaran* ('Son of the Baron') to Sir Colin Campbell of Lochawe of a sixth part of lands formerly belonging to *Alexander Macneacden*.[36] These are listed as Cruachan, Letterawe ('Letterben upon Lochow'), Glenshira and Achany.

The process continued, when, in 1375, Colin had a charter from John of Prestwych, son and heir of the late Mariota Garrechal, of fifteen pennylands, including half the Isle of Inishail and half of the lands of Terivadich, Selechan and Dalyen.[37] These are to be held of John of Prestwych in return for due service to the King. Quite who John of Prestwych and his mother were is not known, but presumably the latter was a MacNaughton widow or daughter. It would seem, anyway, that it must have been at this period that the Castle of Fraoch Eilean at the north end of Loch Awe would have passed into Campbell hands and that the MacNaughton chief place of strength had then passed from there first to the castle at the end of the Dubh Loch, at the very foot of Glen Shira, and then to their later base at Dunderave on the seashore further up Loch Fyne. Legend has it that it was the plague that drove them out of the castle on the Dubh Loch, of which but a trace now remains, while the location of the burial place of the plague victims on a nearby bank is still well known. But the acquisition of Fraoch Eilean was a not unimportant one for the Campbells, dominating as it does the Loch Awe end of the Pass of Brander and still further strengthening the Campbell hold on the top end of Loch Awe, while the mention of Glenshira signals the Campbells moving into an area which was to become particularly important to them during the following century, as we shall see.

By 1387 Sir Colin was clearly married to his second wife, Mariota, since that year the Order of Carmelites granted them and their offspring a share in the masses and good works performed by the Order throughout Scotland, stating that their deaths and anniversaries would thereafter be celebrated with the same solemnity as had they been members of the Order. Mariota appears to have been the mother of his several children who were, according to *Ane Accompt*, Duncan, John, Colin, *Dugald* or Dougall, and another Duncan. Neil, Dean of Argyll, was the offspring of Colin and the daughter of the Abbot MacAlister, while a charter of 1403 is witnessed by Celestine and Patrick, sons of the Lord of Lochawe.[38] Nothing more is known of these last two, who only occur as a passing reference. The Lord of Lochawe, their father, may be Colin Iongantach, or, perhaps more likely, they are brothers of his. They need not, of course, be legitimate. It was usual for high-spirited young men to sow their wild oats, with no lack of willing partners among the local girls when the young man was one of rank. These children from the wrong side of the blanket were well regarded and their father usually looked after their later welfare. Some of them rose to a high place in society and there is little doubt that today's looser morals as regards marriage have their forerunner in history over a long period. In early days, the offspring of such irregular couplings were cheerfully accepted in society and readily acknowledged for what they were.

The second son, John, has the by-name *Annam* or 'the weak', as opposed to Duncan, his elder brother, who goes by the name of *na Adh* or 'the Fortunate'. John, *Ane Accompt* admits, was reckoned by some to be the eldest legitimate son who was passed over in favour of his brother. He was given instead, as his portion, the lands of Barbreck at the foot of the Strath of Craignish, or Glen Domhain as we have it today.[39] There is further uncertainty in the account in the *Scots Peerage*, where John Annam is confused with the previous John, Colin Iongantach's uncle. In both cases, he is said to have been ancestor to the later family of Campbell of Succoth, one statement for which there is absolutely no evidence and which we can be pretty sure is incorrect. It does seem highly possible that he was the elder son and that this was a case of a deliberate reversion to the older, Celtic system of succession in order to produce the best result. It will be noted in due course that the Campbell chiefs went to considerable lengths to ensure that when John Annam's male line came to an end, Barbreck was still kept in the family.

Sir Duncan's brother, also Duncan, who in a charter of 1422 is described as 'senior', is clearly illegitimate and the product of a liaison prior to the marriage of Colin and Mariota. In this charter, he is granted a number of lands in Ardscotnish: Ayridechaistol (except the pennyland of Kilchoan), Achadrchoim, Poltalloch, Bennan, Balgarissa, Peulcair, Culachmie, Crinan Mor and Crinan Beg and half the fishing of the Add.[40] Among the list, such names as Poltalloch, Bennan, Crinanmore and Crinanbeg may be readily discerned, and half the fishing of Add poses no problems. The exclusion of Kilchoan is an interesting one, as this small property seems to have been long in the hands of a professional family of Dewars or keepers of holy relics. They were MacLucases or alternatively Mackernehows – the name is spelt in various forms – and used all three names as surnames on occasion. They were to produce a goodly number of priests and professional servitors and the like in Argyll, and several of them are later found to have moved to Lochfyneside. Kilchoan, a name which also appears in Argyll on Loch Melfort and in Ardnamurchan as well as in other parts of Scotland, may derive from the Church or cell of Saint Comhghain, uncle of Saint Fillan, but what or whose relic was guarded by the MacLucases for which they received these lands is now unknown.[41]

There is no mention of Duncan as being 'of Duntroon', nor does the appellation appear for some time. *Ane Accompt* describes him as 'Duncan More of Glenshiro' or Glenshira, lands which had been resigned to Colin of Lochawe by MacNaughton's widow and says that his descendants were known as *Slioch donocheemore* (sic). The first name in the list of lands granted to him as above would indicate, however, that the castle site of Duntroon was included in the grant. This possibly was an older, less sophisticated fortification, since the Royal Commission on the Ancient and Historical Monuments of Scotland dates the earliest part of the present castle to 1400–50, judging it to be of similar design to such castles as Breacachadh on

Coll. If this is so, then the present important castle would probably have been the work of Duncan or his immediate successors, whose possession was later confirmed for the provision of a twelve-oared galley and who also held the post of Seneschals or Stewards of Ardscotnish for the Campbells of Lochawe.[42]

From Dougall, says *Ane Accompt*, are descended the Campbells of Dunstaffnage. *Dougal and Donald Cambel*, brothers german, appear on a charter to Duncan Campbell of Lochawe in January 1414/15.[43] The 10th Duke takes them to be brothers of Sir Duncan Campbell of Lochawe, although there appears to be no indication in the charter of their being anything other than brothers german to each other. Another Donald appears in the 1442 charter of Kilmun (see below) where his name is preceded by a Duncan Campbell, Knight, who is taken to be the Duncan *a quo* Duntroon. Neither the *Scots Peerage* nor *Ane Accompt*, however, makes any mention of him.

Dougall's identity, however, is not in doubt, although, as Dunstaffnage was not to pass into Campbell hands until 1470, there is no question of his being 'the 1st Captain of Dunstaffnage' as he is described in some genealogies. Another brother was Neill, the Dean of Argyll, said by *Ane Accompt* to have been the forebear of the Parson of Kilmartin and the Campbells of Auchinellan, a remarkable family of churchmen of whom more below. The other, legitimate, full brother of Sir Duncan was Colin, sire of the important Campbell branch who were to become the Campbells of Ardkinglas. Colin is so described in a charter of 1428 where his son Iain is granted lands in north Cowal, on the banks of Loch Long, by his uncle Sir Duncan in an area which they were increasingly to dominate.[44] Any fear of the neighbouring chief, MacFarlane of Arrochar, may have been allayed by his marriage to Sir Duncan's daughter, Christiana, which had taken place by 1395.[45]

Ardkinglas occupies an important strategic position at the head of Loch Fyne. Although fronting the loch shore, it is rather unusual for this part of the world in that its prime task must have been landward-facing, covering the route into Argyll from the Lennox via Glen Fyne. It also dominates routes leading through the glens to the head of Glen Croe and to the head of Loch Long, close to the lands of Achnagaunan which Iain was to be granted. Perhaps there were too many Colins, but it is from Iain, not his father Colin, that subsequent Chieftains of the Ardkinglas branch were to take their Gaelic patronymic *MacIain Riabhaich* – 'Son of John the Freckled'.

There does not appear to be any record of the involvement of the Campbells at this time in the major affairs of the kingdom, which were far from happy. There was general dissatisfaction with the conduct of King Robert III, and in 1399 his son David, Duke of Rothesay, was appointed to act as King's Lieutenant, aided by a council of twenty-one. David was however only 21 at the time, and the real power in the land lay with his uncle, the King's brother, also Robert, Duke of Albany and Earl of Fife and Menteith. Albany clearly had ambitions for himself and his own branch of the family. In 1402, his nephew David, the heir to the throne, having asserted his new powers with youthful over-enthusiasm, laid himself open to the charge of 'frivolity' and was, by order of his father the King, placed in the keeping of his uncle at Albany's castle of Falkland. Whether by mischance or worse, he died there in March. Malicious tongues had it that he had been starved to death, but dysentery is more commonly held to have been the cause. Next in line was David's younger brother, James.

In 1404, King Robert sought to strengthen the position of the 10-year-old James, by granting him a new regality composed of all the lands of the Stewartry, that is the baronies of Renfrew, Cunningham, Kyle-Stewart and the islands of Bute, Arran and the two Cumbraes, along with Cowal, Knapdale, the lands and earldom of Carrick and the baronies of Ratho and Innerwick in Lothian. This at least gave him a firm base composed of his family's ancient lands from which to operate in an increasingly uncertain future.[46] In 1406, for James's longer-term welfare, his father had him sent over to France to be brought up at the French court. But the plan misfired in disastrous fashion when James's ship was captured off Flamborough Head by the Norfolk pirate *Hugh atte Fen*. This was in March, and the blow was a fatal one to King Robert, who died, a broken man, the following month. The young king was to spend some eighteen years in English hands. He was well treated for the most part, and he was by no means alone. The intermittent fighting with the English had culminated in 1402 at the defeat of Homildon Hill at which both Douglas, the Scottish commander, and Murdac, the King's cousin, son and heir of the Duke of Albany, had been taken prisoner.

Albany was now made Governor of Scotland, He was, however, only first among equals among the great nobles, particularly in the south of Scotland where it was Douglas who was the predominant power. His authority was by no means unquestioned, and in 1411 he was faced with a new danger. Donald, Lord of the Isles, had claimed the earldom of Ross through his marriage to Mariota, sister of Alexander Leslie, Earl of Ross. She was heir presumptive to her brother's daughter, Euphemia, a nun, whose mother Isabella was the daughter of the Regent Albany.[47] His claim was not allowed, no doubt because of Albany's interest in the earldom for his own family, and Donald collected the full array of the Isles to take over by force the disputed territory whose lands stretched right across the north of Scotland from the Atlantic shore to well to the east of Inverness. At first his expedition prospered; Inverness was taken and the Islesmen moved east towards Aberdeen.

But an army had been assembled to meet them. Formed from the local families of the lowland east of Scotland, under the command of the Earl of Mar, it was inferior in numbers but very much better armed. The struggle that followed when they clashed at Harlaw, in Aberdeenshire, was a bloody one and a battle remembered to this day in song and story. Both sides claimed victory, but in fact it was the Lord of the Isles who, realising that the whole of lowland Scotland at least was in opposition to him and his claim, drew back off to the west in the hope of a better day dawning. The Campbells do not appear to have been involved in the actual struggle, although they had links with both sides. As it was, the Campbell interests lay very much with the Stewarts, Colin Iongantach's son and heir, Duncan, being married to the daughter of the Regent Albany, Marjory Stewart.

In 1407, Colin Iongantach had a regrant from Albany which confirmed him in his possessions, which were listed as the baronies of Lochow, Glenorchy and Over Cowal together with a list of individual lands in Cowal: Ardenslait, Dallongford, Glenkenich, Glenlethane and Lochstrivenhead. This list by no means comprehends the total landholdings of Campbell of Lochawe at the time, and either it is very incomplete or Campbell of Lochawe had not yet established his feudal superiority over lands held by lesser members of his clan, some of whom, as in the case of Sir Arthur Campbell which we have already seen, were subordinate to no man for their lands except the King. Both are probably the case.

If not involved in the campaigning of 1411, the Campbells, probably under Sir Duncan of Lochawe since his father, Colin Iongantach, was by now a very old man, must surely have been involved in Albany's expedition against the Lord of the Isles of 1412. Little is known of the details of what happened, and the MacDonald historians prefer to claim that it never took place. Bower, however, is perfectly clear: he says that Albany led three forces against the Lord of the Isles, who was forced to submit and came to Lochgilphead where he signed a peace treaty.[48] The spot where this took place is known to this day in the shape of three boulders standing on the seashore just below the entrance to Kilmory Castle, site of today's local government headquarters for Argyll and Bute.

The same year, a transaction of some significance took place when Colin Iongantach granted various lands to Ronald, son of Malcolm of Craignish, and his heirs male. These were the lands of Corranmore, Gartcharran, Ardcraignish, Barrackan and Soroba, all on the Craignish peninsula, and the islands of Reisa Mhic Phaidean and of MacNiven (sic) together with the lands of Lochavich, which appear to have included the keeping of the Caisteal na Nighinn Ruaidhe.[49] This charter has two points of particular interest. This is the first occasion on surviving record when lands are granted by Campbell of Lochawe to anyone outside his immediate family of son or nephew. The charter would appear to be handing back most if not all of the old lands of Craignish to the present head of that family, who now holds from Campbell of Lochawe rather than directly from the King, as opposed to his father who was, as we have seen, specifically listed as being subordinate to no-one except the King for his lands. The inclusion of the lands of Lochavich which a later charter states to accompany the Keepership of the castle is also interesting in that the Craignish family, as we have already seen, are said to have earlier married the heiress of these lands and to have them in their possession already.

It is also worthy of note that yet again there is no mention of Ronald or his father as being Campbells; he is merely referred to as Ronald, the son of Malcolm of Craignish. His by-name in the Gaelic was *Ranald Mor na h-Ordaig* – 'Big Ronald of the Thumb' – so called because of the extraordinary size of the thumb on his left hand. He is a colourful character of whom several tales are told. One concerned the time when the area was being ravaged by a band of robbers under the leadership of a brigand known as the *Ceannaiche fada* – 'The Long Merchant' – so christened in irony since he merely took whatever caught his eye without paying for it. Ronald went after him and his band with a force that included his six MacIsaac foster-brothers. Their encounter was a bloody one and at the end of it the Long Merchant lay dead as did four out of the six MacIsaac brothers. Ronald himself was wounded and one of the remaining MacIsaacs stayed with him while the other ran home with the news which, as seems to be the not infrequent case with survivors, he made out to be worse than it actually was, reporting to his old and blind father that he was the sole survivor, both Craignish and all his brothers being among the slain. The old man lamented his loss, that of his foster-son the most, and invited the survivor to come to him for comfort; but his old mother, spotting the father's drawn dagger, gave a shriek of warning at which the young man recoiled as the old man, cheated of his design, hurled his dagger at the point where he judged his apparent coward of a son to be, shouting out through his tears: 'You coward, who are the good wife's son and none of mine, when my *dalt* (foster-son) was killed, why did you not dare to die bravely with him, than dare to come home to me, and what you deserved to have gotten there, I had a good mind to have given you here!'[50]

Some time after, Ronald made one of the brothers his *Marty* or Chief Officer for his estates, for which service he was given the lands of Corranbeg. It is from this MacIsaac that the later MacCallums or Malcolms of Poltalloch spring. The tale is a good one and typical of the legends that are frequent in

Highland history. It is in all probability true in outline, particularly as the author of *The Manuscript History of Craignish* claims to know the site of the Long Merchant's grave, or 'Bed' as it was locally known, between Ormaig and Kilmartin.

Colin Iongantach's return of the Craignish lands to Ronald was made in June 1412.[51] In January 1413, Duncan Campbell of Lochawe is granted relief of the dues payable on the death of his late father, Colin, by Robert, Duke of Albany, Regent of Scotland. Sometime during those six months, Colin Iongantach had passed away. His achievements for his own family and his clan had been considerable. Among them may be listed the acquisition or regaining of a considerable extent of territory which included many of the former MacNaughton lands, Glenorchy, Menstrie and Ardscotnish. He had gained the superiority of Craignish and had established Duntroon and Ardkinglas as important branch houses of the Clan. He had been the King's brother-in-law and, most significant of all, had been appointed with his son to be the King's Lieutenant over a large part of Argyll.

By now, the Campbells of Lochawe, in his person, were clearly established as the leading kindred of the Campbells, and if his quaintness and droll 'lateral thinking' as we might now describe it gained him the title 'Iongantach', it was not least due to his achievements that his son and successor Duncan justified his by-name 'The Fortunate' and was successful in advancing the fortunes of his family to new heights.

CHAPTER SIX

The Arrival

The new Campbell of Lochawe went by the name of *na Adh* – 'The Fortunate'. His life was to justify this epithet, thanks to his father, to two important marriages and to his own efforts which were to see the emergence of the line of Lochawe now not only as the undisputed leaders of the Clan Campbell but also as great Gaelic Chiefs and the leading power in all mainland Argyll.

In 1415, Duncan of Lochawe received a charter from Duke Robert of Albany, his father-in-law, of the lands of Menstrie, previously in the hands of Charles Campbell, their hereditary possessor. These lands, as we have seen, had been granted to Colin Iongantach fifty years before. They had subsequently been granted to Charles's father Arthur Campbell of Strachur by King Robert III[1] some time before 1398, when he is addressed by Colin Iongantach as 'Lord of Menstrie'.[2] Why, having been secured to the Lochawe line, these important lands should have passed to the rival line of Strachur for a time is unclear. Also in 1415, Murdac, Albany's son and heir, was released from captivity in England in exchange for Henry, Earl of Northumberland. Five years later, his father died at the age of 80 and Murdac succeeded him as the Governor of Scotland. The significance of this position becoming hereditary would not have been lost on the young King James for whose release negotiations were dragging on.

In 1423, Duncan was listed as one of the hostages to be sent to England in return for the King's release. An indenture the following year, between King James and the English ambassadors delivering the hostages, includes Duncan as well as David, son and heir of the Earl of Atholl, Thomas Earl of Moray and Alexander Earl of Crawford. There are two points of interest in this document: the income of each hostage is quoted, and, while Crawford and Moray are listed as having 1,000 merks and Atholl 1,200, the income of Duncan is given as 1,500 merks, the largest of all of them.[3] He has been sometimes described as 'the richest man in Scotland' on this basis, which would seem optimistic. The second point is his designation as 'Lord of Argile'. The increasing status of the Campbell of Lochawe family is clearly underlined by this designation. Hitherto 'Lords of Lochawe', we now see them acknowledged as the leading family of Argyll. Previously, the only family to aspire to this title with its ancient connotations was that of the MacDougalls, Lords of Lorne, who had used the designation latinised as *de Ergadia* – 'of Argyll' – as a family surname.

It would appear that Sir Duncan was kept in a number of locations. In May 1424, Sir Thomas Burton, Constable of Fotheringay, was to deliver him to the Lieutenant of Dover Castle who was to be his custodian. At the same time, King Henry VI gave safe conduct to various Scots to come to their hostage compatriots. In July, Sir Duncan asked by name for Archibald Campbell, Walter Clerk and Morys Neilson. Among his fellow hostages was George Campbell, son and heir to Loudoun; but, apart from the two Campbells, one of whom had for several generations been firmly ensconced in Ayrshire, there is a conspicuous lack of Highland names among those who were called to render service to the King in this way. The full list of their names is given in 1425 when King Henry gave orders that all fifteen Scottish hostages be delivered to Sir John Langeton, sheriff of York and Warden of the castle there.[4] Again, this is of some significance as underlining the dual identity of the Campbell chiefs – great Lords in the *Gaeltacht* while at the same time part of the Lowland 'civilised' Establishment that attended the King, the centre of power.

But the long captivity of King James I was at last at an end, and, in April 1424, accompanied by a great concourse of both English and Scottish nobles, he returned to his Kingdom. A young man full of vigour, he took early steps to establish his domination. A major target was the Stewarts of Albany whom he regarded, not without cause, as would-be rivals for the Crown and who he felt had not tried as hard as they could have to obtain his release from the English. First to fall into his hands was Walter Stewart, powerful son and heir to Murdac, Duke of Albany. On 13 May, Walter came to Edinburgh where he was immediately arrested, along with his two companions, by order of the King. A further move followed the death of John Stewart, Earl of Buchan, at Verneuil when his younger brother, Robert Stewart, the heir of entail, was prevented by the King from inheriting the Earldoms of Buchan and Ross and his brothers from taking over various Aberdeenshire lordships.[5] Around October 1424, Duncan, Earl of Lennox, Murdac Stewart of Albany's father-in-law, was also arrested. The noose was tightening around the Albany family.

'It's an ill wind that blows nobody any good', as the old saying has it and major beneficiaries from the fall of the Albany Stewarts in the north were the

MacDonalds. The dispute over the inheritance of the Leslies' claim to the earldom of Ross, which had culminated in the Battle of Harlaw a decade and more before, was eventually settled in favour of Alexander, Lord of the Isles, who now found himself in the King's good books while the Earl of Mar, leader of the Royal Army at Harlaw, now found himself in a distinctly difficult position.[6] It was now that the Lordship of the Isles reached its pinnacle, with lands that stretched from the Irish coast across to Nairn and the borders of Aberdeen in the east. Its triumph led to a style which was little if anything short of kingly and an actual belief in its own Royal status that was to lead, inexorably, to an over-mighty posture that brought the antagonism of the Scottish Crown down upon it. In the events that were to follow, the Campbells were to play a major part.

The final blow to the Albany Stewarts came at the Parliament of March 1425 when, on the ninth day, the King gave orders for the arrest of Duke Murdac and his son Alexander. Various of their followers were also taken and the two major Albany strongholds, the castles of Doune and Falkland, captured. Murdac's wife Isabella was also seized, and she and her husband were eventually immured in Tantallon and Caerlaverock respectively, far from their adherents and safely in the hands of the King's nephews, the Earl of Angus and the Earl of Douglas. The only member of the family to escape was Duke Murdac's son James Stewart, who went by the less than flattering by-name of *Grossus* or 'the Fat'. He fled to his mother's family lands in the Lennox where he provided a focus for the discontented followers of his grandfather, Duncan, Earl of Lennox. Here, he also received the help of the Bishop of Argyll, Finlay of Albany, a long-time supporter of the family. On 4 May, as a pre-emptive strike before the crucial Parliament at Stirling which was imminent, the town of Dumbarton was attacked by the men of Lennox. Stewart of Dundonald, the King's leader in the area, was killed along with thirty-two of his men, but the castle, under the command of John Colquhoun, held out and indeed managed to pick up some of James the Fat's followers, who met a speedy end on the gibbet at Stirling. James the Fat himself, Bishop Finlay and various of Earl Duncan's illegitimate offspring and followers were all forfeited. The attempt to strengthen the Albany position had failed.

It provided the King with the final excuse, if such were needed, and on 24 May a jury which included the somewhat unlikely figure of the Lord of the Isles[7] found Walter Stewart guilty and he was taken out and beheaded – probably on the heading hill just beside Stirling Castle itself. The following day, his father, Duke Murdac and his brother Alexander also met the same fate. James the Fat shortly afterwards fled from the Lennox to neighbouring Argyll and thence to Ireland, from where he continued to pose a threat to his cousin and namesake. History is silent as to his actual route, but it would seem highly likely that he sought help in his adversity from the Campbells of Lochawe. His grandmother Helen or Elena was the daughter of Gillespic Campbell of Lochawe and had, previous to her marriage to Earl Duncan of Lennox, been the wife of John of the Isles, while his aunt Marjory Stewart was the first wife of Sir Duncan Campbell of Lochawe. Sir Duncan presumably had been released some time after the King, in 1425. With such close links with the Campbells of Lochawe, it seems hard to believe that he did not seek succour from them in his flight overseas.

The King was now intent in bringing the whole of Scotland to heel. In 1428, after the destruction of the Albany branch of his family, he turned his attention to the Highlands and Isles. He went to Inverness, where on his arrival he first of all had the castle repaired, and summoned the Lord of the Isles and the Highland chiefs to meet him there. Again, there were wholesale arrests which included Alexander of the Isles and his mother and most of the notable men of the north, described as 'other outlawed caterans [of gentle status] and some captains who were by their standards great men'. They were invited to the tower where the King was holding court, one by one, and there arrested. 'In the meantime while all this was taking place, the king composed a verse, saying to those standing around: Let us take the chance to conduct this company to the tower with care, for, by Christ's death, these men deserve death'.[8] Mentioned in particular among their number was Angus Dubh Mackay, the chief of 4,000 men of Strathnaver; Kenneth Mor, a chief of 2,000 men with his offspring; John Ross, William Leslie, Angus de Moray of Culbin and MacMachan, who were chiefs of 2,000 men. Kenneth Mor was surely the chief of the MacKenzies, and MacMachan chief of the Mathiesons. 'After conviction Alexander Macruarie of Garmoran chief of 1,000 men and John MacArthur a great prince among his followers and chief of 1,000 men were condemned to death. These two were beheaded.'[9]

It was, I believe, the historian Gregory who was the first among more recent historians to spot the identity of John MacArthur, a subject which continues to confuse some clan historians to this day. It is the connection of his name with that of Alexander MacRuari that identifies him. As we have already seen, it was early in the previous century that Christina, the heiress of Garmoran, is thought to have been betrothed to Arthur, son of Sir Arthur Campbell, Constable of Dunstaffnage and progenitor of the Campbell of Strachur family. The marriage does not seem to have come off, but the charter still exists by which Christina grants to her prospective

THE ARMS OF THE DUKE OF ARGYLL, MAC CAILEIN MOR

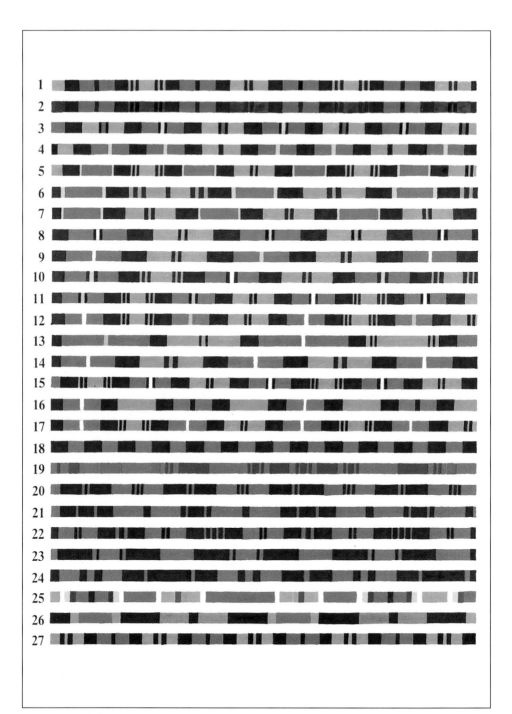

THE TARTANS ASSOCIATED WITH CLAN CAMPBELL

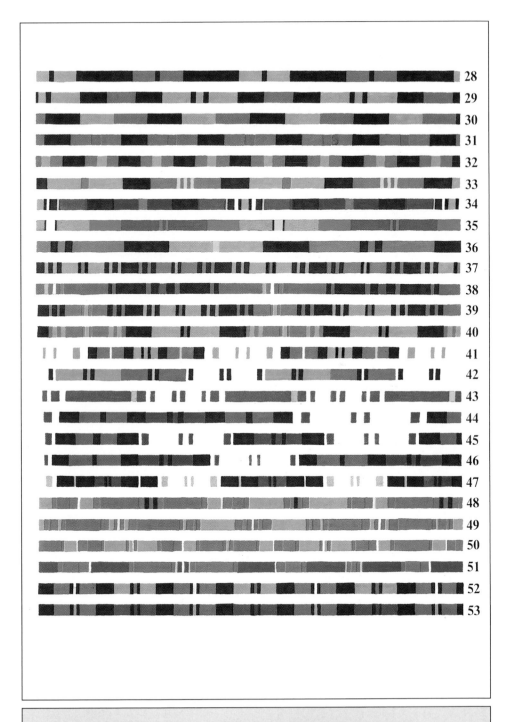

28
29
30
31
32
33
34
35
36
37
38
39
40
41
42
43
44
45
46
47
48
49
50
51
52
53

THE TARTANS ASSOCIATED WITH CLAN CAMPBELL

CAMPBELL (Darker Version)

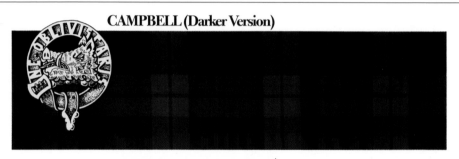

CAMPBELL OF CAWDOR

CAMPBELL OF BREADALBANE

CAMPBELL OF LOUDOUN

THE CAP BADGES AND TARTANS OF CLAN CAMPBELL

husband her lands of Garmoran. Although the MacRuari lands were now in the possession of the Lords of the Isles, there were clearly still male-line MacRuaris in contention with Arthur Campbell's descendant who was using the old Highland fashion of identification by patronymic and who, so Gregory suggests, was claiming the lands by virtue of his ancestor's charter to them. In typically aggressive and ruthless fashion, King James now sought to end the quarrel and the lawlessness it no doubt involved, at a stroke – or two, to be more accurate.

But there has been considerable confusion over John's identity, and even Sir Thomas Innes of Learney, the late Lord Lyon, makes him a member of the Clan Arthur of Terivadich, whose head was apparently known as *Mac-ic-Artair*, 'Son of the Son of Arthur', stating that he received much MacDougall land from King Robert the Bruce. No such grants are on record, and Sir Thomas is clearly confusing *Mac-ic-Artair*, who much later, as we shall see, received the lands of Terivadich for his services to the Earl of Argyll, with the aforesaid Sir Arthur Campbell whose descendants commemorated their descent by identifying themselves as the MacArthur Campbells of Strachur with the arms of the head of the family officially carrying the senior title of *MacArtair Strachuirr*.

If Gregory is right, and I have come across no modern serious historians who doubt him, then we have another important Campbell, head of a branch of the House of Strachur, of whose previous existence nothing is known. He is described by Bower, the only source for this story, as *magnus princeps apud suos et dux mille hominum* – 'a great prince among his own people and leader of 1,000 men'. It would seem likely that this figure is a flight of literary fancy – the whole of Clan Campbell at the time of the 1745 rebellion was estimated as being some 5,000 men by Lord President Duncan Forbes of Culloden, a figure far in excess of any other clan, most of whose fighting strength he put at a few hundred. For the same reason, it seems unlikely that the Mackay Chief could field as many as 4,000 men or that any others of the Chiefs listed had anything like the number of followers ascribed to them. The truth, most likely, is that the actual numbers were far smaller, and it may be by no means unduly fanciful to suggest removing the final nought from each of them.

If an untraced body of 1,000 men in Argyll is discarded, deductions may still be drawn from the relative size of the numbers quoted, the disputants' followers being a quarter in number of those of the Chief of Clan Mackay, and half that of the leaders of the Rosses, the Leslies, the Murrays of Culbin and the Mathesons. It is of course possible that the followers themselves came from Garmoran and the area in dispute rather than all from Argyll, and

that the existence of a potential male heir to Garmoran being of equal embarrassment to the leading family of the MacDonalds as the power of a rival line
to the Campbells of Lochawe, the whole episode has conveniently been written
out of history by the official historians of both Clans. Another solution to the
identity of Alexander, which is also far from clear, has been put forward that
he was a MacGodfrey or MacGorrie, son or grandson of Godfrey, son of
John of Islay, who had been granted the lands of Garmoran by the Lord of
the Isles.[10]

Be that as it may, this episode would seem to have removed any lingering
threat to the unquestioned chiefship of Clan Campbell by the Lochawe line
in a dynastic sense – by now, their actual position was clearly far ahead of any
rival – and two years later, in 1430, George Campbell of Loudoun, 'for the
friendship shown towards him by his kinsman Duncan Cambell, Lord of
Lochaw and to be shown by the same Duncan *as chief to all his Kin and
surname*' (author's italics), resigns all rights he possessed in lands in
Lochgoil Parish.[11] Although in actual fact a position no doubt held by the
Campbells of Lochawe for some time now, this would appear to be the first
mention of them in contemporary record as being the acknowledged chiefs
of the clan.

But the King had not finished with Clan Campbell and the last victim of
his summary justice was one James Campbell who was charged and con-
victed of the killing of John MacDonald of Islay – *Iain Mor* – released not
long before by the King.[12] There is no record of who this James Campbell
may be and the exact circumstances in which the killing took place are
equally mysterious. The MacDonald historians have it that the King was
intent on reducing the power of Alexander Lord of the Isles and was plan-
ning to make him transfer some of his territory to his uncle Iain Mor. Iain
Mor had not agreed and Campbell had been sent by the King to arrest him.
Equally, Iain Mor was apparently acting as protector of James the Fat, of whom
King James was still aware as a major threat. The MacDonald historians
make no bones about blaming the King, but continue: 'In Campbell he found
a willing instrument ready to his hand and it is to be noted that now for the
first time there fell athwart the path of the Family of the Isles the shadow of
that ill-omened house which was to be its evil genius in times to come'. If
they are right, and even if James Campbell exceeded his orders, which he
may or may not have done, this casts an even uglier light on the incident as
far as the King is concerned.[13] Having exiled or imprisoned many of the
other chiefs who attended the Inverness Parliament, the King departed for
the south. Decisive as it may have appeared, his attempt to awe the Highlands
and Isles and bring them to heel was soon to be proved a fiasco. Among

those imprisoned for a while and then released were the Lord of the Isles and the MacKenzie and Matheson Chiefs.

Intent on revenge, in 1429, the former summoned his men to rise, and with a force of some 10,000 men burnt the town of Inverness. With the intention of installing him on the Scottish throne, a fleet had gone to Ireland to collect James the Fat, but he died on its arrival.[14] In turn, the King raised an army from the Lowlands with which he came north, catching up with the Lord of the Isles in Lochaber. The sight of the unfurled Royal Banner of Scotland, the Lion Rampant, was too much for two of the principal clans in the rebel army and both the Camerons and the Mackintoshes went over to the King. In face of this, the Lord of the Isles had no option but to withdraw. Protracted resistance being useless, he was at length forced to throw himself on the King's mercy and to that end he appeared at Holyrood to beg for his life. Whether he was clad only in his shirt and underpants as it has been averred – it is quite possible that he was clad in his war-shirt, a garment probably unfamiliar to a Lowland writer – is unknown, but his abject posture had the desired result and his life was spared.

With their Chief imprisoned in Tantallon Castle, the Clan Donald mustered behind Donald Balloch, the young son of the assassinated Iain Mor. Once again the Clan Donald galleys sailed up Loch Linnhe to land at Inverlochy where the King's army were to meet them for the second time. On this occasion, the outcome was very different. The Royal army was decisively defeated and its commander, the Earl of Mar, victor both at the previous encounter and at Harlaw itself, was forced to take to the heather for his life. Donald with his men took their revenge on their former allies, the Camerons and the Mackintoshes and then returned to their island fastnesses, laden with booty. The King was furious, but his expeditions to the north had both been less than successful and any further action would require replenishment of the Royal coffers. Donald Balloch, however, had fled to Antrim where he took refuge in his lands of the glens, inherited from his Bisset mother. The King's demand to Hugh Buy O'Neill for Donald Balloch's head was answered by the delivery of that of some unfortunate substitute.

But a settlement with the Lord of the Isles was becoming a more attractive solution as problems built up elsewhere and the birth of the future King James II in October 1431 gave an excuse for his release from Tantallon. One edict agreed in Parliament dated 1430 is worthy of note. As it is of some interest, its content is given here as follows:

At Perth. 6 March. – ITEM it is statute and ordained that the barons and lords having lands and lordships near the sea in the west and on the north parts and namely fornent the Isles that they have galleys that is to say of each four marks worth of land one oar. And that is to understand of they that are not feft of galleys before for they that are infeft of before shall keep and uphold the galleys that they are infeft of and holden to sustain by their old infeftment. And that the said galleys be made and refitted by May each 12 month under the pain of half a merk to be raised to the King's use of each oar. And the lands and lordships what-ever they be stretching along the coast and inwards in the land six miles shall contribute to the repair and upkeep of the said galleys.[15]

In other words, all landholders within six miles of the sea, a description which covers a very large part of mainland Argyll, were to contribute to the supplying and upkeep of galleys on a scale of one oar of a galley for each four merklands of land they held. This underlines the military importance of the galley in the west, where it played the part of today's main battle tank – or perhaps, more aptly in view of the mobility it conferred, a fully armed and armoured helicopter would be a better simile.

We are so inured today to the motorcar and the roads it runs on that we see geography from a landward perspective. Our forefathers saw it very dif-ferently, and even the shortest of crossings in one of Caledonian MacBrayne's ferries serves to remodel our perception of our surroundings. In spite of all its dangers – and they are many in the Western Highlands and Isles, tides, currents, storms and rocks all taking their toll – the galley with its comple-ment of armed men could range the area, penetrating far inland up the fiords of the indented coast, speeding to the outermost isles and indeed to the Isle of Man and to Ireland, whose coast was only a good summer day's sail from as far north as modern Oban. Our forefathers' view of the sea had also changed with the arrival of the Norsemen with their longships. No-one knows for sure when exactly or for what reason these greyhounds of the sea were first built, but they quickly proved their worth. No longer did the people of the area confine their sea journeys to the shortest possible route, a wise precaution in view of their wicker-framed, hide-covered craft. The new ships were eminently seaworthy, taking their owners into the Mediterranean and across the Atlantic long before Christopher Columbus. The Hebridean galley was a direct descendant, and, although only discernible from contem-porary gravestones since, unlike its Viking predecessors, no original has yet been discovered, we have a good idea of what it looked like and what it could do, not least thanks to the efforts of an intrepid band who have recreated and sailed one in the stormiest of seas.[16] For long voyages, the sail was the main means of propulsion, but there were also oars, one each side for each thwart, and when wind or tide or danger threatened the crew could turn to rowing. The boats could be brought ashore and beached, provided they were not too large and heavy. The crew were used to manoeuvring them over quite long stretches of land in order to gain the next navigable water, and they penetrated far into what is now Russia up the rivers. They had their limitations, however, and were usually employed for summer sailing; in winter they were brought home and pulled out of the water for maintenance. We also tend to forget the extent to which they were subject to weather and that in winter they were seldom if ever used.

From early times, when the holding of land under feudal law required a rent to be paid in military service, lands held in the West Highlands and Isles were frequently held in return for the service of a galley which was to be ready fully equipped, provisioned and manned for the usual period of forty days' service if the King so demanded. This was most likely to be in early autumn with the consequent minimum disruption to the harvest. To what extent this edict was obeyed we do not know; certainly the ownership of galleys with the troops to man them was the expression of power in the region and no doubt galleys were kept by the most important people in excess of the number required by the Crown. The size varied widely and, in times of war, no doubt even domestic small boats would be pressed into service. The Norse themselves built great battleships of seventy oars and more; these provided a magnificent fighting platform but were of little use in the open sea. The grant to Sir Neil Campbell in 1315 of the Lordships of Lochawe and Ardscotnish was in return for the service of a galley of forty oars, that is to say twenty a side and it is the largest vessel mentioned in such documents as far as I know. Some grants were made in return for the service of a boat of eight oars, hardly more than a large rowing-boat. The famous Gokstad ship of around AD 900, preserved in a museum in Oslo, is a ship of thirty-two oars; it is an impressive size which is seldom revealed in its photographs and fully manned it would no doubt be capable of carrying a total of over 100 men for relatively short voyages. On voyages of any length within sight of land, the ships might be beached and an encampment set up; sometimes a semi-permanent base was constructed – traces of which may be used in the suffix –*longart* in place names – also used for the base made for long hunting expeditions, of which a number of examples exist in Argyll.

The tradition of sea-service goes back long before the arrival of the Norsemen on this West Highland seaboard, to the days of the early Dalriadic settlement. The use of galleys continued right down to the seventeenth century, when this type of vessel finally yielded to the high sides and gun-power of the modern warship of the day. Every castle or stronghold by the sea has its boat noost or hollow carved out of the shoreline, where a boat could be kept alongside a rock pier or drawn up out of the water. Most are large enough to contain one decent galley; other and smaller boats would no doubt have been drawn up on the shore. A fleet in being, however, would often require a safe haven for anchoring; these are relatively infrequent and the best, like that at Dunstaffnage, assumed major strategic importance. The long stretch of coast, for instance, down the length of Kintyre on the Atlantic side has no such refuge between Gigha and the Isle of Sanda, the intervening stretch of water involving the hazardous turning of the Mull of Kintyre itself with dangerous tide rips and rocky cliffs and no shelter from the Atlantic gales. The great number of small channels between the many islands produce many a strong tidal rip and sail- or oar-driven boats would have to wait for slack water to proceed.

But it was the sea that mattered, both locally and on the grander scale, with the coast of Argyll providing relatively sheltered passage for much of its length on the sea highway that stretched from 'Norroway over the Foam' via the Northern Isles into the Minch and round Ardnamurchan Point through the Sound of Mull and away south through the Sound of Jura round the Mull of Kintyre to the Isle of Man and to Dublin. From 1315 when the grant of Ardscotnish brought the Campbell landholdings down to the open sea, right down to the 1600s, the Campbells were no strangers to seafaring and many were the lands held in return for the services of a fully provided ship.

But King James had plenty of preoccupations elsewhere both inside his Kingdom and on its borders. In 1436, following his daughter Margaret's marriage with the Dauphin of France, James moved against the common foe with the intention of capturing Roxburgh Castle, still in English hands. On 1 August, a powerful force, strong both in archers and in artillery, invested the garrison. But the siege was another fiasco, and, after two weeks, rent by internal dissension and jealousies and with the news of strong English rein-forcements approaching, the Scots army broke up in disorder and melted away. We do not have the details, but we know that Sir Duncan must have been with the King since he was later to receive a Royal grant of lands for his services there.

But the reign of James I was now drawing to a dramatic close. Never loved by his subjects, his attempts to raise money for yet another campaign against the English were met in Parliament by downright hostility, one Robert Graham going so far as to attempt to arrest the King himself. This failed, and Graham was arrested in turn before being sent into exile. The train, however, was set. Chief of the King's enemies was his own uncle, Walter Stewart, Earl of Atholl, whose relationship with the King had long been a difficult one. Over it hung the ghosts of the executed Albany Stewarts as well as a long history of the Earl being thwarted by his Royal nephew. In February 1437, the Parliament met again in Perth. It appears that Graham had been sought out by Atholl and that he found ready accomplices in the burgh.

The end came on the night of 20 February when Robert Stewart, grandson of Walter, Earl of Atholl, left the doors unbarred, thus allowing the rush of assassins into the King's Lodging at the Dominican Friars in Perth. There was just time for the wretched King to take refuge under the floorboards; he was discovered as he attempted to extricate himself and was despatched by Robert Graham.[17] We do not know for certain what if any part was played by Sir Duncan in these affairs; he was to be thanked, as we have seen, for his services to King James I at the end of the latter's career and he was closely allied to the house of Stewart by marriage, both his wives being of that clan. His first marriage had been to Marjory Stewart, daughter of Robert, Duke of Albany, who had borne him a son and heir, Celestine, otherwise Gillespic or Archibald. She appears to have died and he remarried, this time to Margaret, daughter of Sir John Stewart of Ardgowan, Blackhall and Auchingoun, a natural son of King Robert III. (There is note of a grant of lands in Cowal – Ardenslate, Dallingford, Innerdavegan and Glenlean – resigned by Sir John to Sir Colin for a sum of 200 merks to be paid to the King in June 1404, which may well coincide with the wedding.) By her he had Colin, later of Glenorchy, said by the *Scots Peerage* to have been born around 1406, Neil, later of Ormidale, Duncan, later of Auchinbreck and Archibald, ancestor of the Campbells of Otter. A later entail of 1481, however, puts the younger sons in the order Glenorchy, Auchinbreck, Otter and Ormidale and this may in fact have been the order in which they were born.[18]

There is note of a Papal dispensation for Celestine, the eldest son, to marry Mariota, daughter of Donald Lord of the Isles (such an early age for a marriage being perfectly normal for the times) but the marriage does not appear to have come off. Celestine is said to have been married to Elisabeth, daughter of John, 3rd Lord Somerville of Carnwath, by whom he had a son and heir, Colin. There is no proof of his having married a daughter of Duke Murdac of Albany as some accounts would have it.[19] The possessions Celestine was due to inherit were by now large enough to allow for them to be divided, with portions being allocated to his brothers. His father Sir Duncan had, as well as all else, been steadily increasing the extent of his family possessions. He was also making arrangements for the future. In 1432, in a somewhat strange agreement, *Suffne M'Ewyn* – Sween, son of John,

Lord of Otter on the east bank of Loch Fyne – resigned the Barony of Otterinverane into the hands of the King for a regrant with remainder to Celestine, the son and heir of Sir Duncan Campbell of Lochawe.

The deal was a somewhat complicated one. It would appear that Sween had no male heir of his own; should this change, in recompense for his no longer inheriting the Barony on Sween's death, the latter would either pay Celestine sixty merks Scots and give him twenty-five cattle or, if Celestine preferred, would give him the lands of the two Lerags and of Killalla for a yearly rent of half a merk. It is only possible to guess at the considerations which led Sween to make this remarkably generous arrangement; perhaps there were no near male heirs to a line, mentioned in the person of Gilbert MacEwan among the Barons of Argyll in 1292, whose antecedents stretched back to the marriage of Anrothan Prince of the O'Neills with the local Dalriadic heiress. The site still stands of 'MacEwan's Castle', a prehistoric *Dun* on Kilfinan Bay, just south of Otter itself, which shows signs of use well into medieval times, but of the MacEwans of Otter and their Chief there is no trace. The Barony itself fell into Campbell hands, and in 1540 we find it among a list of the Campbell Chief's Baronies which are then incorporated anew into the Barony of Lochawe.[20]

Then, some time around 1440, Celestine, his father's son and heir, died. He was alive as late as 1437 when, on 10 May, a Royal Charter appointed him and his son Colin as King's Lieutenants from Carndrome to Lochgilp and from Loch Melfort to Loch Long under the same terms as already existed, on the resignation of Sir Duncan. A grant of an annual gift of half a merk from his lands of Ardenslate to the church at Dunoon was made on 12 March 1440 for the safety of the souls of Sir Duncan's grandparents, Celestine Campbell and Isabella Lamont, his father Colin and mother Mariota, daughter of MacDougall Campbell and of his late wife Marcellina Stewart, his wife Margaret Stewart *and for his late son and heir Celestine*.

This would seem to have been the germ of an idea – the establishment of a more permanent memorial on a much grander scale: in August 1441 Sir Duncan petitioned the Pope for leave to set up a Collegiate Church at Kilmun, incorporating the benefices of Saint Conan's Kirk there with the Kirk of the Three Holy Brethren at Lochgoilhead. Permission was granted, and the new Church was dedicated by Sir Duncan to the late King James, the reigning King, James II and his wives and to his late, first-born son Celestine, in honour of God, Saint Mund the Abbot and all the Saints. The new establishment was to be funded by Sir Duncan from his lands of Finnart and Blairmore, which would produce forty shillings of rent to which would be added the two merks' rent from his merkland of Ardentinny. There were to be five perpetual chaplains, of whom one would be appointed Provost, with an extra chaplain as well. He also added the rents which belonged to him of the churches of St Conan's and of the Three Brethren for the premises at Kilmun and for the lighting of candles and lamps and for the ringing of bells.[21]

So it was that Kilmun became the chief ecclesiastical foundation for the Campbell Chiefs and the place where, for generations, they were to bury their dead, having previously, so it has been claimed, used the Holy Island of Inishail in Loch Awe for this purpose. A church was built with a tower, which stands to this day and a vault included which was used by the Campbells of Lochawe. The vault was improved in 1794–5 and is still to be seen today but no longer as part of the original church which was replaced by today's separate building in 1841.[22]

A popular legend exists by which Campbell of Lochawe's heir died as a student in Glasgow and the body on its way back to Lochawe was held up by a fearsome snowstorm which made further progress impossible. Thereupon the Chief of the Lamonts took pity on the sorrowing chief and granted him a place in which to bury his son in the words 'I, Great Lamont of all Cowal, do give unto thee, Black Knight of Lochawe, a grave of flags, wherein to bury thy son, in thy distress'. The original inscription, in Gaelic, was said to have been inscribed over the burial vault until, presumably, its rebuilding at the close of the eighteenth century. The story is a good one but, as so often happens, does not stand examination in detail. Celestine was born prior to the birth of Colin of Glenorchy, thought to be around 1406, and would thus be in his late thirties at least – an advanced age for his being at Glasgow University where, perhaps not surprisingly, there is no record of him. 'Great Lamont of all Cowal' would seem to be an overstatement for the Lamont chief, who was merely one of several lairds who divided the peninsula. Most, however, if not all were descended from the marriage of the O'Neill Prince Anrothan with the dynastic heiress of the whole area. It may just be that at one time one of the line of Lamont was the chief among this cousin-hood, but of his existence as such no record survives. Further complications exist in the title 'Black Knight of Lochawe', a soubriquet for Sir Duncan which exists nowhere else, and, above all, in the fact that Kilmun itself had long ago been gifted to Paisley Abbey without any conditions affecting a burial there, while the Campbells were already major landholders in the surrounding area.[23] But there is no doubt that Sir Duncan is buried there and there would seem no more pressing reason for this rather odd geographical choice for his interment than the previous burial there of a beloved son and heir. The Lamont story would seem much more likely to be a later flight of romantic fancy added on to the tale.

There is also considerable interest in the origins of the name Kilmun, thought to be the church or cell of Saint Mund, claimed to be the patron saint of the Campbells by Niall the 10th Duke. Apparently he had already come to this conclusion before coming across a note to the same effect by one James Campbell, of Craignure, who was according to Duke Niall a noted sennachie. The name Kilmun was located at the head of the Holy Loch long prior to Celestine's death – in 1262 the church was gifted to Paisley Abbey by a Lamont forebear, but it will be noted that the name of the nearest church at that time was apparently Saint Conan's and that Sir Duncan took for his new Collegiate Church the alternative nearby name of Kilmun. This name – possibly by mere coincidence, but, if so, it is a remarkable one – is found close by to all the likely previous strongholds of the Campbell chiefs, a few hundred yards away from the Castle of the Red-Haired Maiden on Loch Avich, and on the other bank of Loch Awe opposite Innischonnell and up Glen Aray near the present Stronmagachan House, which was said to be the site first occupied by the Campbells in Glen Aray before they moved down to the sea at Inveraray. This is an intriguing coincidence since there is only one other site with a similar name in Argyll, the Eilean a Munde burial site in Loch Linnhe, where the MacDonalds of Glencoe buried their dead. But, as with many if not the majority of early Celtic holy men, there are a number sharing the same name, and it has been suggested that the site in Loch Linnhe may commemorate another saint.[24]

The Saint Mund with whom the Campbells are associated is thought to be Saint Fintan Munnu, an O'Neill cousin of Saint Columba's who came to Iona but was rejected by the recently dead Columba's successor Baithene on the grounds that he was of too great a stature to be any Abbot's monk but should be an Abbot himself. He therefore returned to Ireland where he founded the Monastry of Taghmon or Teachmunnu. He long suffered from a form of leprosy, an inexact term for those days which could be applied to any form of skin disease.

While the prefix Kil- could on occasion signal the actual if temporary habitation of a saint, it could also be an early church dedicated to his name. In the case of Kilmun on the Holy Loch, there was for long a real connection with the saint in the form of his *baculus* or staff, long cared for by a family of dewars or guardians who went by the name of MacMunn, more correctly *Mac-Gille-Munn* or 'Son of the Servant of Saint Mund', who were granted the lands of Pordewry – 'The Dewar's Portion' – near Inverchapple for the maintenance of this task (see Appendix 3 on Septs). There were several such families in the area, the most famous probably being those who took the name of their profession, Dewar, as their surname. They lived between

Tyndrum and Killin, guarding the relics of Saint Fillan. These relics were several in number, and several families were involved. They were not necessarily related, although all used the same surname. The most important was the Dewar responsible for Saint Fillan's staff, the *Dewar Coigerach* or *Quigrich* as the staff was named. He possessed the lands of Ewich between Tyndrum and Crianlarich in Strathfillan. His ancestor is described as Donald M'Sobrell in a confirmation of these lands by Alexander Menzies of that Ilk in 1336. Bruce commanded the Quigerich to be brought to join the Scots army before Bannockburn, where it was borne into battle to encourage the troops. The possessor of the Quigrich also had the task of following any *creach* or cattle-raid, sometimes right across Scotland, and with the authority of this holy relic repossessing the stolen beasts and restoring them to their rightful owners. The Dewars *na Bernan – Bearnane* or 'Little Gapped One' – looked after St Fillan's Bell while the Dewars *na Main*, it is thought, looked after St Fillan's arm-bone; this when he was alive was said to have given out a miraculous light to illuminate his reading in the dark. It, too, was summoned to Bannockburn by Bruce, but its keeper, rather than risk it, took the empty case instead.

Another well-known family of dewars is that of the Livingstones of Bachuil on the island of Lismore. Their lands were granted to them in return for the keeping of the staff of Saint Moluag after which it was named. The family is there once more after travelling around the world, and they still have the staff, now worn down to a twisted and gnarled baton, having reclaimed it from the Dukes of Argyll in whose care it had remained for some time. The MacKessocks at Luss, on Loch Lomond, were more properly *Mac-Gille-Kessog*, 'Sons of the Servant of Saint Kessock' whose relics they guarded, while at Kilchoan near Poltalloch, as we have already seen, there lived a family whose surname alternated between MacLucas, Mackernehow and Macindeor, the last of course being 'Son of the Dewar'.

There was also a family of Campbells engaged in this profession. They lived at Balindore, outside Taynuilt, 'Balindore' being 'The township of the Dewar'. According to legend, they kept the staff of Saint Maolrubha of Applecross and acted as almoners to the Priory of Ardchattan across Loch Etive; the head of the family was apparently known as *An-deora-mor* – 'The Great Dewar'.[25] It would seem likely that the *Karistina nein a Dowra, Mora nein a Doura* and *Joannis Glas Macgillemore vic indowra* listed among the inhabitants of Taynuilt in 1541 were of the same family, of whom we shall hear more in due course (see Appendix 3, under 'Burns'). But the propinquity of the name to the Campbell Chiefs' base remains a mystery, since in all cases the name Kilmun would seem older than either the base concerned or the establishment of the burial place and collegiate Church on the Holy Loch.

Another family who were given land for their services appear in written record at this time. In 1439, Sir Duncan granted to Dominic MacPhedran the lands of Sonachan and the office of porter and ferryman over Loch Awe between Portsonachan and Taychreggan. The post was a hereditary one in the MacPhedran family and one which would have provided a good living. There are two legends as to its origin, which, although quite different, need not be incompatible. One has it that the original grant was made by King Robert – no doubt during his foray into Argyll – in gratitude to the MacPhedran of the day who had been one of the rowers who brought the King back to the mainland from Rathlin Island. The other states that the grant was made by the Chief of the Campbells in gratitude for his son having been saved from a sinking galley on Loch Awe by a MacPhedran.

Sir Duncan contracted another long-drawn-out land deal at this time with final settlement over the lands of Glassary, immediately to the south of the two original Campbell holdings of Loch Awe and Ardscotnish. In March 1427, 'Lorde Kambal' and Sir John Scrymgeour were summoned to appear before the Parliament to settle their quarrel over the third part of Glassary together with the lands of Ederline at the south end of Loch Awe, which were claimed by MacCorquodale of Phantilands. Summoned to appear at the next Parliament in Edinburgh in June, Sir Duncan failed to do so, and in December he was cited to appear, Sir John Colquhoun of Luss, Sheriff of Dumbarton, stating that he had already delivered the summons to Sir Duncan *apud le Carryk* – at Carrick Castle on Loch Goil.[26] By June the next year, Sir Duncan had still not appeared, and his absence and that of MacCorquodale was described as 'contumacious'. In March 1430, the Sheriff of Perth was appointed to carry out an inquest or inquiry on the quarrel over the disputed lands. In May that year, Ewan MacCorquodale had still not appeared in spite of a rather smug endorsement by Sir Duncan as sheriff of Argyll that he had personally summoned him to do so.[27]

In 1431, a fresh aspect appeared with an agreement between Sir Duncan and his son Gillespie with Sir John Scrymgeour for the exchange of the lands of Glassary with those of Menstrie. Under its terms, Sir John Scrymgeour was to grant Sir Duncan two parts of Glassary with the church of the same and all rights to superiority over the third part together with the superiority of a third part of the lands of Kilmun and all his rights to Ederline and Camusnewe to be held of the King in free barony, the Barony of Glassary.[28]

There was still an amount of tidying-up to do before the deal could be finalised, however. In 1434, John Makane – 'John Son of John' – gave Sir John

Scrymgeour a discharge or receipt for the forty merks paid by Sir John for his lands of Kilmun, presumably previously held by the MacIans or Makanes, whoever they may have been; Scrymgeour already held lands in this part of the world which had come to him through his MacGilchrist inheritance.[29] In 1443, nearly a decade later, an indenture for the exchange of the lands was at last issued in which it was agreed that because the lands of Menstrie had once been exchanged for the lands of Strachur with Arthur Campbell, father of the present Charles Campbell of Strachur,

> the said Sr Duncan sal gar the said Charles gif his lettris of qwytcleme for hym and for his ayris of the landis of Menstry to the said Sr John Skrymgeour and his ayris in als fast and sikir fourme as can be made that the said Charlis na his ayris sal nevyr mak clayme in na to the landis of Menstry in tyme to cum.[30]

In return for ensuring that there was no argument from Strachur over the ownership of Menstrie, Sir Duncan and his heirs were required to give a rather remarkable undertaking:

> Item it is acordit that the said Sr Duncan na his ayris sal nevir mak clayme na lettyng in tyme to cum to the said Sr John Skrymgeour or his ayris in the beryng of the lioun in their armys bot at the said Sr John Skrymgeour and his ayris sal oyse and bere the lioun in thair armys frele as thair eldris did befor [sic].[31]

From a heraldic point of view this is an interesting condition. The arms of the Constable of Dundee are a lion rampant carrying a scimitar for difference; it would appear that these had been adopted in recognition of the Scrymgeour inheritance of the lands of Glassary which they were now relinquishing, ultimately from the MacGilchrist/Anrothan connection. If, indeed as is probable, the lion rampant is the heraldic device of the royal line of Dalriada, Scrymgeour's anxiety not to lose it is understandable.[32]

It was another five years before, in 1448, the matter was brought to a close with the final charter by Sir John to Sir Duncan of the lands in question, the charter including a magnificent series of feudal rights including that of *cum furca et fossa* – the right of pit and gallows which empowered the baron to hang or drown offenders. There are a number of interesting questions about this transaction. Why did it take so long, and what was so important about the lands of Glassary as to justify the swapping of such an important and historic holding as Menstrie for them? It does look as if Sir Duncan's original case was not as as strong as it might have been. Glassary had been part of Anrothan's territory, thought to have been obtained by his marriage to the Dalriadic heiress of Cowal, Glassary and Knapdale. Glassary in due course became the holding of Anrothan's great-grandson Gilchrist, younger brother of the more famous Suibhne or Sween.

Gilchrist had three sons, it would appear, among whom he shared Glassary. One was Gilpatrick, ancestor of the MacLachlans, who also held land on the far shore of Loch Fyne; another was Gillespic and the third was Ewan. Gillespic's line went with the marriage of a daughter to one Master Ralf of Dundee, who held lands in Argyll in 1292 and whose descendants took the name *de Glassereth* or 'of Glassary'. Their holding was increased by the forfeiture, around 1346, of Ewan's descendant John MacEwan, whose lands were granted to Gilbert de Glassereth. Gilbert's daughter then brought them to her husband Sir Alexander Scrymgeour, Constable of Dundee. The lands, however, were not at the original extent since, in about 1315, *John de Glassereth*, Gilbert's father, had granted certain of them to his sister Margaret and her husband, Sir Dougall Campbell of Lochawe. So the lands in question were by no means the whole of Glassary but only those which were in the possession of the Constable of Dundee. It may well have been that Sir Duncan's case and that of his neighbour the Baron MacCorquodale could have been stronger and their reluctance to appear in Parliament reflected this; the King was also in the full flush of his intent to impose discipline on the Highlands at the time and they may have decided that it was as well to keep out of his way.

As regards Menstrie, we have already come across the rather mysterious transaction by which the lands, once more in the hands of the main line, had in the 1390s been granted to Strachur and then, in 1415, been regranted to Sir Duncan Campbell of Lochawe by his father-in-law the Regent Albany and again by James I in 1434. This appears to have further delayed settlement while the ownership of Menstrie was clarified. But the introduction of Menstrie into the equation strongly suggests that without its inclusion Sir Duncan would not have obtained what he wanted even though Menstrie would appear to be a disproportionately valuable item of exchange. Why then was Sir Duncan so determined to possess the lands of Glassary and prepared to give so much for them?

The answer would appear to be geographical. The early Campbell heart-lands had been added to, both around the fringes of the lands of Lochawe and Ardscotnish, while they had also gained a considerable foothold in the district of Cowal on the other side of Loch Fyne. The acquisition of Glassary, which stretched from the south shore of Loch Awe to the north side of Loch Fyne, bridged that gap and made the Campbell landholding much more of a comprehensive one. The inclusion of the lands of Ederline and of Camusknewe would also make sense, since Ederline lies at the south end of Lochawe in the glen which leads out to the south, down to Kilmartin; the location of Camisnewe is unknown but one may hazard the guess that it is nearby, since one of the meanings is 'Channel'. There is the site of a strong early stone fort on a hill on the north bank just where the loch narrows to its end, with nearby the site of a much later tower; both have clearly been placed there at different times in what is obviously a strategic location dominating the route from the south end of the loch, and it seems probable that the obtaining of these two properties would give the Campbells domination over the southern end of the loch while their transactions at the north end with the MacNaughtons, which we have already seen, would have the same effect there.

With the death of King James I in 1437, Scotland once more found itself with a child monarch; James II was only six when he succeeded to the throne, and the affairs of the Kingdom were once again in the hands of an older relative, this time Archibald, Earl of Douglas and French Duke of Touraine, who was the late King's nephew and a cousin to the new one. James's mother had been appointed Regent, but the real power lay in the hands of Douglas as Lieutenant-General. Meanwhile, the King himself was in the hands of Sir William Crichton and Sir Alexander Livingstone of Callendar. Then, in June 1439, Douglas died and no new Lieutenant-General was appointed. One who sought to take advantage of the situation was the Queen's new husband, Sir James Stewart, 'The Black Knight of Lorne', whose designation derived from his uncle having married the heiress of the MacDougall Lordship of Lorne which now resided in this branch of the Stewart family.

It was to be years before the King managed to extricate himself from the toils of those who sought to control him for their own ends. The period was a troubled one, although Argyll seems to have escaped the worst of it. There was trouble, however, in neighbouring Lennox over Stewart of Darnley's claim to the earldom through his mother; and Alexander, Lord of the Isles and Justiciar of Scotland North of Forth, was involved. Shortly after he appeared in Parliament in 1439, a party of Islesmen descended on Loch Lomond and killed Colquhoun of Luss. But the Livingstones and the Crichtons managed to remove the Douglas threat with the notorious 'Black Dinner', held in Edinburgh Castle, at which the new young Earl of Douglas together with his brother were confronted at the end of the meal by a great black bull's head placed on the table as a sign of their fate. The two boys were forthwith arrested and, after a mockery of a trial, ostensibly for treason, were executed on the Castle Hill. By October 1444 the 14-year-old King was held to have come of age and from that point progressively took matters into his own hands.

It was not easy as the great magnates competed for power. In the west, Arran came under attack once more in 1443, this time at the hands of the Lord of the Isles' men from Knapdale and Kintyre, described in the Exchequer Rolls as *maledictos invasores* – 'cursed invaders'. Then, in 1445, the Earls of Crawford and Douglas came together with the Lord of the Isles in a fatal combination which, after rocking the throne to its foundations, was to prove deadly to all three participants and particularly to the last-named. But it was not Alexander of the Isles but his son John who was to reap the whirlwind. In 1449, Alexander died and was succeeded by his 18-year-old heir. That year, too, the King descended on the house of Livingstone; one of the survivors, Sir James Livingstone, was to escape from confinement the next year, 1450, when he took refuge with the MacDonald Chief. Douglas was by now on the Continent, carrying out what was described as virtually a Royal Progress in order 'to advance his mightiness'. He was apparently accompanied by a Campbell Knight whose exact identity is unknown, but Sir Hugh Campbell of Loudoun is a possibility.[33]

In 1451, reflecting hostile moves against King James from the English King Henry VI from south of the Border, the three conspirators raised the standard of rebellion. Apparently John of the Isles was further incensed by the failure of the King to grant him various lands promised him on his wedding to Elizabeth Livingstone – a marriage no doubt encouraged by the King in the hope that a douce Lowland girl might bring the MacDonald chief to heel. Her husband now moved with his forces northwards along the Great Glen. Urquhart and Inverness Castles were seized and garrisoned, while the castle of Ruthven was razed.[34] On the east Coast, however, Huntly defeated Crawford at Brechin the following year and advanced as far as Moray before the defensive posture of the Lord of the Isles, who realised he was now next to be dealt with, caused Huntly to draw back. Douglas was now summonsed to Stirling, where the King failing, to make the agreement with him that he had hoped for, was overcome by fury and stabbed his unwilling guest to death.

The mention of a Campbell knight in Douglas's train is somewhat misleading. Sir Duncan Campbell of Lochawe himself was in good odour at Court and seems to have escaped the attentions of his fearsome neighbours for the main part. He was advanced to the rank of Lord of Parliament in 1445 when he officially became Lord Campbell. In fact this had been a gradual process; as early as 1425, as we have seen, the Campbell Chief had been referred to as 'Lord of Argyll', while from 1427 he was intermittently referred to as 'Lord Campbell'. This now became official with the establishment of the new rank. The original great lords or *mormaers* were little short of provincial kings and ruled – at least notionally – over great stretches of territory. They are reckoned to have evolved into the earls to whom in due course were added the dukes. They, together with the old, great Lordships were all connected with the holding and administration of territory. But their number was small and the number of titles became extremely concentrated in the hands of a few families – by 1390, indeed, the number of earldoms and great lordships had shrunk to thirty-one, shared among fifteen people who came from only ten families, the families of Douglas, Stewart and Dunbar accounting for no fewer than twenty-two of them.[35] Sir Duncan now joined their number.

The other aspect of the new rank was a totally pragmatic one; the effective government of the kingdom required the presence at Parliament of what in today's parlance might be termed 'the real movers and shakers'. Theoretically, all who held land were required to attend in Parliament, held several times a year at various locations. This was obviously inconvenient and the system of representation grew up by which shires and burghs appointed a set number from their ranks to attend. But there were those whose position was really essential by reason of their station and power and so it was that the new rank of Lord of Parliament was introduced. This separated the Lords from the Lairds – the latter of course being the title 'Lord' as pronounced in the Doric – the latter title designating the members of the lesser aristocracy who were no longer required to attend Parliament.

If the governance of Scotland was being organised, so too Sir Duncan was giving thought to the organisation of his own possessions. In 1447, *Ronald Mor na h-Ordaig* – Big Ronald of the Thumb – son of Malcolm of Craignish, Laird of Corvarron, was given the post of Steward, Toscheador and Marty of Craignish.[36] In 1450, Sir Duncan appointed his cousin Iain, son of Alexander Campbell, as Toscheador of Melfort, from Poll Melfort to the burn of Squegadill near Craignish and Melfort, together with a fourth part of the *Toseachdeorship* of the whole Lordship of Argyll[37] while, in 1452, the Knight of Lochow as he is described gave a charter to his 'cousin' John Campbell of Ardkinglas of the office of *Stewartrie* within the lands of Lochgoyle.[38] The term 'cousin' rather than nephew may suggest that in spite of the date it was Colin rather than his grandfather Sir Duncan who was the granter. The office of Steward or Seneschal was a well-known one, never less so than in Scotland, where the very line of Kings took their family name from this office. That of *Toscheador* was an ancient Celtic position which has very much the same connotation, although the latter would seem to involve the maintenance of law and order as well.[39] Here we may discern the start of the great system of delegated administration that was, in time to come, to maintain law and order, administer justice and collect the revenues over the huge sweep of Mac Cailein Mor's possessions.

A further mark of the King's approval came in June 1452 when he granted Sir Duncan, as we shall continue to call him, for services rendered to him and to his father, notably to the latter at the siege of Roxburgh, twenty merklands at the foot of Glendaruel in Cowal, all to be united into the free Barony of Kinlochruel – the Barony later to be known as Glendaruel. Three weeks later, Sir Duncan granted the lands concerned to Colin, son of Neil Campbell of Ormidale.[40]

But these were among the last acts of a long and successful life; in 1453, Sir Duncan 'the Fortunate' died. He was laid to rest in the Church of Kilmun alongside the tomb of his beloved eldest son, where his effigy may still be seen today. While the tombs of the Lords of the Isles and their dependent Chiefs display effigies clad in the West Highland form of armour – pleated and quilted war coat, spear and great sword – Sir Duncan is shown in a suit of the latest plate armour as worn across Europe. Not only had he added greatly to his family's possessions and established himself as a great Highland Chief, but also the Chief of Clan Campbell was now to be reckoned with as an important personage on the wider stage of Scotland as a whole.

CHAPTER SEVEN

The Greatest Power in the West Highlands and Isles

Colin, 2nd Lord Campbell, must have been aged around 20 at least when he succeeded his grandfather. *The Black Book of Taymouth*, that chronicle compiled by Master William Bowie, family notary and teacher of the 7th Laird of Glenorchy's grandsons in 1598, says that his uncle Colin of Glenorchy acted as Tutor or Guardian to the young Lord. But the latter must have been of age by the time he took over from his grandfather, so if the statement is true it must apply to the later years of Sir Duncan's life. In any case, a large part was played in young Colin's life by his uncle, who clearly saw himself in the role of the boy's dead father.

It is now time to introduce the family of Campbell of Glenorchy, who play a part in the story of Clan Campbell second only to that of the Campbells of Lochawe themselves. It is a strange story, a mixture of love and hate, of support and opposition, of emulation and indeed, on occasion, of outright hostility by a family whose achievements were allied to a display of ruthless ferocity and great cunning which has undoubtedly been responsible for much of the obloquy levelled at Clan Campbell as a whole. The elder Colin would seem to have been born around 1406,[1] the elder son of the second marriage of Sir Duncan to Margaret Stewart of Ardgowan. In 1432, his father granted him the eighty merklands of Glenorchy and twenty-seven merklands around Inverinan further down Loch Awe. This gift included several islands, among them Island Kilchurn at the north end of Loch Awe and Eilean an Stalcair, an island in Loch Tulla away to the north-east at the very head of Glen Orchy. The Lochaweside lands included those of Upper Sonachan on the other side of the loch from Inverinan, while it may well be significant that just south of Achahenna, on a hillock overlooking the loch, is the site of a gallows, indication of the dispensation of final justice and of someone with the power to wield it.[2]

Sir Colin, as he became, was married several times. He was a lusty blade, it would appear, and the number of his marriages is not easy to chart. His first wife is said by *The Black Book of Taymouth* to have been Mariota, daughter of Walter Stewart, a son of Isabella, Countess of Lennox, and one of the unfortunate Albany family so summarily despatched by the vengeful King James I in 1425. The *Scots Peerage* is unconvinced by this and refers to Mariota as 'whoever she may be', which seems unnecessary since a charter of 1440 from Isabella Duchess of Albany and Countess of Lennox to her dear relation Colin Campbell Lord of Glenorchy grants him a list of lands around the head of the Gareloch in Dunbartonshire, north of Helensburgh, because of his marriage to 'Mariota Stewart, daughter of the late Walter Stewart of good memory'.[3] He does not appear to have had any children by this marriage, his son and heir Sir Duncan being the offspring of his marriage to Janet Stewart, eldest daughter to Walter Stewart of Innermeath and Lorne and one of three sisters of whom we shall hear more shortly.

Although most authorities give this as Sir Colin's second marriage, this does not appear to be the case. On 7 May 1449, at the Blackfriars, Stirling, Sir Colin gained a disputed divorce from Dame Janet Borthwick, Lady of Dalkeith, due to his previous relationship with Alicia Lindsay, being of the fourth and fourth degree of consanguinity with the said Dame Janet which rendered the said marriage null and void![4] It is obvious Sir Colin had espied the chance of a bigger fish to net, since, according to a charter from John of Lorne of various lands around Loch Awe and in the Braes of Lorne dated at Kilchurn on 15 March that year, he had already married Janet Stewart! Janet's dowry included further lands around Loch Awe and on the Braes of Lorne, the north shore of Loch Tralaig west of Sir Cailein Mor's Cairn. The names are in several cases unrecognisable, but among them are Corrielorne, Pollanduich at the head of Glen Nant, the Isle of Inchconan on Loch Awe and the Loch and Isle of Stryng, which would seem to be the String of Lorne on which there is an island which shows the remains of a fortification. All were to be held for one penny in the coinage of the realm at the feast of Pentecost at the church of Kilmore in Lorne, if asked for.[5] By Janet Stewart, Sir Colin had a son and heir, Duncan and a daughter Geillis who the *Black Book* claims to have married the MacDougall chief.

His next wife was said to be 'ane woman off the Clandonoquhie', according to *The Black Book*, identified by the *Scots Peerage* as Margaret or Mary Robertson, daughter to Robert Robertson of Struan, whose family also used that patronymic.[6] By her he had John, later Bishop of the Isles and a daughter Katherine, who married Walter Stewart, Baillie of Balquhidder.

The last wife, as far as we know, was Margaret Stirling, daughter of the Laird of Keir, by whom Sir Colin had two more sons, John, later 1st Laird of Lawers and George who died young. They also had a daughter, Helen, married firstly to MacIan of Ardnamurchan and secondly to the future MacGregor Chief.

To one of these wives – or was it another one? – is attributed the supervision of the building of Kilchurn Castle during Sir Colin's absence, reputedly for seven years soldiering in the east. During this time and as the castle neared completion, nothing was heard of the absent husband and the wife, reluctantly accepting that she was now a widow, eventually gave in to the importunings of one of the local lairds who were competing for her hand and agreed to marry him. According to the splendidly dramatic tale, Sir Colin was at last on his way home and indeed reached the hill above the castle just as the wedding festivities were about to start. Joining in the throng, he sought and received a cup of wine from the hand of the bride, in which he pledged her before handing it back. At the bottom of the cup lay a ring which she had given him on his departure. Shock, horror, delight, depending from which point of view you see the situation; the would-be husband is sent packing and the wedding feast becomes a welcome-home party!

It would appear that Sir Colin did indeed see overseas service in the Mediterranean against the infidel. His by-name was *Cailein Dubh na Roimh* – 'Black Colin of Rome' – where he had been three times and according to *The Black Book* he had been made a Knight of Rhodes, then the headquarters of the Hospitaller Knights of Saint John who later moved to Malta. As it happens, there is no mention of his name in the records of the Order of Saint John as being a Member; there were, however a good number of Scots who fought with the knights against Islam and he may very well have been among them although there is no written record of his service. The fact that he was married would have anyway prevented him from joining this celibate order as a full member.[7]

An intriguing piece of circumstantial evidence lies in the existence of the Glenorchy Charm Stone, which may be the *stone of the quantitie of half a hen's eg sett in silver* mentioned in a 1640 inventory of the late Laird of Glenorchy's possessions,[8] where it is stated that Sir Colin had worn it in battle against the Turks as one of the Knights of Rhodes. The Charm Stone today is in the hands of the Royal Museum of Scotland; it is one of a number of these mysterious crystal balls which seem to have been possessed by various Highland families of which a sufficient number are Campbells to make them the subject of a special appendix (5). It is probably from the same service overseas that Sir Duncan Campbell, a younger brother of *Iain Riabhaich* of

Ardkinglas and first cousin of Colin of Glenorchy, is regularly referred to as 'Knight of Malta', but the whole question of Highland participation in the Christian campaigns against the infidel remains tantalisingly unclear.

Sir Colin is also credited with the establishment of the new seat for the Campbell Chiefs over the hill at Inveraray on Loch Fyne which is thought to have taken place around the middle of the fifteenth century. A new castle was built above the mouth of the River Aray whose entry into the Loch was shielded by the projecting point on which the present town of Inveraray stands. There is no clear-cut account of how, why and when the move took place. According to some accounts, it took place in stages, with the first foothold of the Campbells being further up the glen at Stronmagachan near which, needless to say, is an ancient Celtic church dedicated to Saint Mund. Following a well-used tradition recounted of several incoming Highland clans, the former owner was tricked into giving much more than the cow's hide of land he had offered, the said hide being used to produce thread of a quite prodigious length which enclosed a sizeable acreage. The former owners are said to have been MacVicars; the boundary of their lands with those of the MacIvers is claimed to be marked by the standing stone on the edge of the field in which the local shinty team play their matches and the Inveraray Games are held.

It is often said that Inveraray was chosen as a site which gave access to salt water as opposed to the enclosed inland waters of Loch Awe. If so, it may seem a rather odd choice, right up at the head of Loch Fyne as opposed to lands further south which were in Campbell hands and which might have seemed to give better access to the open sea. If the Campbells were confident they could contain the MacLachlans and the Lamonts who possessed much of the littoral of Loch Fyne, then it might be argued that Inveraray at the head of the loch provided a base safe from sea-borne invasion; if not, then they had landed themselves in a position where they might have serious difficulties before they reached open water. And the open sea in question was not that of the Hebrides or of the main western sea-routes. To reach them, a long voyage round the perilous Mull of Kintyre was necessary. It was more the Firth of Clyde with its easy access to the Lowland coasts of Ayrshire and Renfrewshire that was opened to the voyager from Inveraray.

It would seem that communication was the deciding factor, both by land and sea. The Campbell Chief was now playing a part both as a West Highland magnate and as a meaningful player of power politics in Scotland as a whole, dominated as it was by the relatively rich Lowlands. A network of cross-country routes and ferries gave relatively easy access to the centres of power; Loch Fyne itself could either be crossed by ferry or circumvented on foot via the lands of Ardkinglas, whence the long trail over the Rest-and-be- Thankful down to Loch Long and the pass through to Loch Lomond from Arrochar gave access to the centre of Scotland; the ferry to Saint Catherine's and the narrow waters of Loch Eck brought the traveller to Dunoon, with the waters of the Clyde then giving another route into the Scottish heartland via the mighty stronghold of Dumbarton.

But Inveraray offered even more. To the land-bound traveller, such as the drover of cattle from a large area of Argyll and its islands, nearly all roads led through the new stronghold of Mac Cailein Mor. Whether he came up the long spine of Kintyre, from Knapdale, from Mid Argyll, from Islay via Jura over the short sea-crossing to Keills at the mouth of Loch Sween and then over Crinan Moss to Kilmichael in Glassary and away up the glen of the River Add over the Leckan Muir, whether he came from Mull or from Lorne, to the traveller all roads led through Inveraray. Only the route round the very head of Loch Awe and away up past Dalmally through the long, wild glens to Tyndrum offered a northern alternative, but by far the most popular route was across Loch Awe by one of the ferries and over the hill to Loch Fyne and Inveraray. So it was that the Campbell headquarters shifted from the great stronghold of Innischonnell on its island down to the foot of the Aray's glen, to a new fortress. Round it clustered a number of lesser buildings, of followers and in time, of traders, craftsmen and artisans who clustered in the shadow of the chief of Clan Campbell.

Colin of Glenorchy rapidly built up his landholding. He had tacks of the lands of Auchmore and Ardtalnaig on Loch Tay, a further forty merk-lands. He acquired heritable possession of Inverneill in Knapdale, which he later exchanged for Balloch and the ten merklands of the Port and Isle of Loch Tay. He built or extended the fortifications of the latter as well as building a tower in Strathfillan (between the modern Tyndrum and Crianlarich). As a reward for his help in arresting Chalmers, one of the assassins of King James I, he was later given Chalmers' lands of Lawers, again on Loch Tay. These he gave in turn to his son John, from whom descended the important branch of the Campbells of Lawers. In 1467, he acquired the lands of Auchreoch above what is now Crianlarich.[9]

By the time he died, at Strathfillan, in 1480, he had in a remarkably short space of time established his family as a major power within the clan and had extended the borders of Campbell influence well to the east. But before he died, much else of importance had happened. In 1457, King James II created Colin of Lochawe, Lord Campbell, Earl of Argyll, one of five earls so created during his reign. The other Lords so advanced were Lord Hay who became the Earl of Errol, Lord Douglas who became Earl of Morton, Lord

Leslie, the Earl of Rothes, and Lord Keith the Earl Marischal. They joined the Earls who were members of the Royal family and the further five earls whose positions descended from that of the old provincial *mormaor* whose origins were lost in the mists of time. The Lord of the Isles was among them by virtue of his possession of the earldom of Ross, but the Campbell Chief now equalled him in rank and was to further strengthen his position by his acquisition of the Lordship of Lorne.

This had by now passed to the Stewarts with the marriage of Robert Stewart of Rosyth, younger son of Sir Robert Stewart of Innermeath, to Janet, daughter and heiress of John (MacDougall) Lord of Lorne, who brought the Lordship with her. Robert later exchanged the Lordship with his elder brother Sir John Stewart of Innermeath. Sir John's grandson, John, Lord of Lorne, had three daughters all of whom married Campbells. Janet married Sir Colin of Glenorchy, Isabel married Colin of Lochawe, Lord Campbell, and Marion, of whom little is subsequently heard, married Arthur Campbell of Otter. John Stewart also had a son out of wedlock, Dougal, from whom the Stewarts of Appin descend.

Relationships at this time between the Stewarts of Lorne and the Campbells of Lochawe seem to have been entirely friendly. The Earl of Argyll came to the aid of his future father-in-law in 1460 when John Stewart, Lord of Lorne, had been seized by one of the MacDougalls – described as 'Alan of Lorne of the Wood' – with the intention of making away with him in order to facilitate his own claim to the Lordship of Lorne. He now held Stewart captive in the Isle of Kerrera, guarded by a force of 100 men. Argyll descended on the island in a swift move that gave no warning and which gave Alan no chance to escape in his ships. The entire force were killed apart from four or five survivors with whom Alan made his escape. The rest of Alan's ships were burnt and John Stewart released.[10]

The Earl of Argyll seems to have been married as early as December 1462, when we find an indenture signed at Inistrynich by him and Walter Stewart, next brother to John, Lord Lorne. In this agreement, the Earl undertakes to help and defend Walter against anyone who attempts to interfere with or alter the tailzie made by John Lord Lorne in favour of Walter as his heir to the Lordship. In return for this support, Walter agrees to grant the Earl 100 merklands of land in Lorne, including all the land between the waters of Awe and Etive with half the fishing of both rivers, and lands commencing with Ardmaddy and Auchnasaul and including lands in Benderloch if necessary to make up the tally together with twenty merklands of the lands of Kildonyng in Perthshire all for the rent of a penny. A charter of the above 120 merks' worth of land is to be granted within forty days of Walter's becoming

Lord Lorne or, in case of failure, a payment to the Earl of 4,000 merks. Meanwhile the Earl, with consent of his wife, renounces all claim to the lands in Lorne due to fall to her through the tailzie made out by her father.[11]

But violence was to intervene. Late in his life, in 1463, John of Lorne was persuaded to marry the mother of his illegitimate son Dougall. By Scots law, subsequent marriage of the parents confers legitimacy on any child or children previously born out of wedlock. Had this marriage taken place, Dougall's position would have been transformed and he would have had a strong claim to inherit his father's lands and titles which by the tailzie were due to pass to his uncle Walter. But it was not to be. As the couple stood at the very altar, a figure burst into the chapel at Dunstaffnage and rushed up to John, who was stabbed to death. Hardly surprisingly, Dougall's descendants the Stewarts of Appin claim to this day that the actual marriage had taken place and that their now legitimate ancestor was the rightful Lord Lorne. They also claim that the whole affair was a villainous plot of the Campbells.

On this occasion, there is some doubt. One intriguing charter does exist, dated 20 June 1471 at Inverawe, by which the Earl of Argyll grants to Alan, son of Somerled son of John, otherwise *Alan Sorleson McCoul*, the eight pennylands of the two Lerags and the four pennylands of *Dernaach* (Dunach) in Lorne to be held in tenendry and for a ship of eight oars.[12] Could this be the Allan MacDougall named as the assassin at Dunstaffnage? Be that as it may, there seems to have been no general opinion at the time that Dougall had in fact been cheated, and his uncle was accepted as the next Lord Lorne without apparent demur. It is not impossible of course that a plot had been executed, but there is no evidence to lay it at the Earl's door, while if in fact such a plan did exist it has to be pointed out that Walter Stewart had at least as much reason as the Earl to be at the bottom of it.

Walter does not seem to have stood by his agreement over the transfer of lands; there was trouble over the Perthshire ones included in the former agreement. In 1465, the King found in favour of the Earl of Argyll acting on behalf of his wife and her sisters over the lands of Kildonyng and Innerdonyng. Argyll had produced all the necessary documents while Walter, Lord Lorne, had not bothered to put in an appearance. The following year, in April 1466, Marion or Mariota, the third Stewart sister, resigned her third of the lands of Kildonyng, Baldonyng, Innerdonyng in Perth, of the lands of Culdrane and le Maw in Fife, and Rothibrisbane in Aberdeen to the King, who regranted them to Colin Earl of Argyll and his wife Isabella.[13] That same month, Walter granted the Earl, in gratitude for his help, the lands of Kippen and of the Muirtoun and Myretoun in Perth. On the same date, however, the Earl redelivered the lands to Walter for a payment of £433 sterling.

Then, late in 1469, an agreement was struck between the two over the Lordship of Lorne itself which Walter would resign for regrant to Colin, provided Colin should ensure the King's agreement that Walter should continue to rank as a Lord of Parliament under the title of Lord Innermeath or whatever honourable name should please him. Colin in turn would resign for regrant to Walter all the lands furth of Argyll, the lands of Baldonyng, Kildonyng and Innerdonyng in Perth, the lands of Culdrane and the Maw in Fife, and the lands of Culcarny in Kinross together with the lands of Balnagoune and Laidboith in Perth which were held by the Earl on a wadset. Should the reversion of the lands be less than 300 merks, Colin shall make up the sum; if in excess Walter shall keep the whole sum. Also included in the deal were the lands of Latheris and Rothibrisbane in Aberdeen. In addition, Colin would resign the coronership of all the shire of Perth and would ensure the agreement of his wife's sisters and their husbands.

The Earl moved swiftly to obtain this. Mariota seems to have been no problem, but the Earl granted his uncle of Glenorchy the stewardship of his own lands in Glenorchy and that of MacLachlan's lands there, a third of the lands of Upper, Middle and Nether Lorne, one third of the advowsons and benefices of the churches in Lorne and a third of the income derived from the Barony Court held there. In addition, Glenorchy was to receive one third each of the lands of Auchincheych, Soroba and Ardoran Easter, Barnacarry and Kilbride. Glenorchy also gave a bond of 6,000 merks to be forfeit should he ever oppose the grant of the lands of Kildoning (and by inference the other Perthshire lands) to Walter. Walter formally resigned the Lordship to the King on 14 April 1470, and, three days later, on the 17th, the Earl of Argyll received a Royal Charter of the whole lands and Lordship of Lorne with all that pertained to it to be held from the King for payment of a mantle at Whitsunday if asked for.[14]

The symbolic importance of his possession of the Lordship of Lorne was more significant to the Earl than the lands and income it brought with it. While his elevation to the ranks of the relatively few Scottish earls was proof enough of his status in Scotland as a whole, in the world of the Gael he was now able to claim one of the oldest and most prestigious of all titles and descents. This gave him and his heirs recognition as being among the successors of Somerled with a lineage which was every bit as good as, if not better in its time, than that of the Lord of the Isles. If there had been a feeling that the Campbells were incomers to the *Gaeltacht*, this was now set aside with their ownership of a title and, for the Earl's children, of a bloodline which, albeit on the distaff side, led them back to the eldest son of Somerled himself. Little wonder that the Campbell Chiefs from now on were to quarter Somerled's galley with the gyronny of eight in their arms and that the title of the eldest son and heir was to be that of Lorne.

But it is now necessary to go back in time in order to pick up the thread of the story. The capture of the English King Henry VI by his Yorkist opponents in 1460 was an immediate invitation to King James II to raise an army and invade. His chosen route led first of all to Roxburgh and its castle garrisoned by the English. The Scots mounted a siege, which was in the end successful, but not before the bursting of a gun had killed the King. He was succeeded by his young son, aged eight, who ascended the throne as King James III. Scotland was once more faced by an infant King, and for the next seven years no Lieutenant was appointed. It was in 1462 that the Lord of the Isles again overstepped the mark with consequences that were in due course to prove fatal to the Lordship and to his Clan. The relationship of the Lordship with the Crown had long been an equivocal one. By now, it would seem that self-aggrandisement had led the Chiefs of Clan Donald to consider themselves as equally Royal by blood to the King of Scots by virtue of their descent from Somerled. This appears to have led to an inflated sense of their importance, paying scant regard to the number of other chiefs in the west who could make equal claims of blood and to the multiple use of the title 'king' in earlier times. By now, they had established a Council to assist in the rule of their domain. It was made up of a number of the various ranks of chief men in their empire, of whom the most important were four of the leaders of Clan Donald itself. While a charge of over-inflated self-importance might well be justified for what follows, one of downright treachery might be naive in view of the overwhelming priority given to self-interest over mere loyalty by so many of the Scottish leaders over the centuries.

Be that as it may, dated from London in February 1462 we find an indenture between the English King Edward IV and John Earl of Ross and Lord of the Isles, his cousin Donald Balloch and Donald's son, John, by which they agree to take over Scotland and divide it between themselves and the Earl of Douglas as vassals of King Edward. By the terms of the indenture, from the following Whitsunday, the MacDonalds named above, together with all their people, were to become liegemen and subjects to King Edward. From that date, they were to hold themselves ready to come out in arms as directed by him. The Lord of the Isles and the others would also be paid from that date, a different rate according to whether they were on active service or not, until such time as the Kingdom of Scotland with their help be brought under English control. As a reward, the Lord of the Isles and Douglas would be granted all Scotland north of the Forth/Clyde line to be divided equally between them, while Douglas would also receive all his former lands to the south.[15] Somewhat grandly styled by later historians 'The Treaty of Westminster–Ardtornish', the existence of this remarkable agreement remained a secret which only became known some thirteen years later. It was however the final straw which was to prove fatal to the Lordship, which from now on was existing on borrowed time; its final forfeiture and fall was to prove of major importance to the Clan Campbell.

Argyll himself continued to flourish. The same year, 1462, saw him appointed Justiciar of Scotland south of the Forth along with Lord Boyd. With the latter's fall from favour, he continued to exercise the office on his own. In 1463, he was one of the Commissioners appointed to negotiate for a truce with the English, and in 1464 he was appointed Master of the Royal Household, a post which was to become vested as a hereditary one in the family of Argyll and which is still carried by the Duke of Argyll today. His advancement on the Scottish stage brought more reward at home; in January 1473 he became Keeper of the Royal castle of Dunoon. The following month, he was given a charter of the offices of Justiciar, Chamberlain, Sheriff and Baillie within the King's Lordship of King's Cowal.[16] In 1474, Inveraray was erected into a Burgh of Barony, a status which brought important privileges and which encouraged settlement and trade under the walls of the castle as well as providing a most useful source of income for the earl's coffers.[17] That year, the Earl was again appointed one of the Scottish Commissioners to England, this time to treat over the marriage of Prince James of Scotland with the Princess Cecilia, youngest daughter of the English King.

If the star of Clan Campbell was in the ascendant, that of Clan Donald was very much in decline. Seldom out of trouble for long, John, Earl of Ross and Lord of the Isles, was charged with treason. Unicorn Pursuivant was sent north and, at the castle of Dingwall and at the Cross there and at the Cross of Inverness, summoned the MacDonald Chief to appear before the forthcoming Parliament. By now the details of the Treaty of Westminster–Ardtornish had belatedly become known, and the charges against him included making agreements with Edward IV of England and assisting the forfeited Earl of Douglas. He had usurped the King's authority in appointing his own illegitimate son as his Lieutenant and had himself besieged Rothesay and wasted the Isle of Bute.

MacDonald failed to appear and was duly forfeited. Three days later, the Earl of Argyll was given a Commission of Lieutenancy by the King within the bounds of Argyll and Lorne to be carried out along with Lord Oliphant, John Drummond of Stobhall, William Stirling of Keir and Argyll's tenants in Strathearn. He was also given the right to raise the men of Lennox, Menteith, Strathgartney and Balquhidder, Discher, Toyer, Glenfalloch and

Glendochart and with all of them, aged from 16 to 60, to invade the territories of the Lord of the Isles with fire and sword, pursuing him until his very death.[18]

By July 1476, the Lord of the Isles had had enough. He came to Edinburgh and submitted himself to Parliament, where he was stripped of his earldom of Ross, which was taken into the hands of the Crown. He was also divested of the Sheriffdom of Inverness together with the custody of its castle and that of Dingwall. The lands of Kintyre and Knapdale were taken from him and forfeited to the King. On the intercession of Queen Margaret, it is thought, he was, however, made a Lord of Parliament with the title of 'Lord of the Isles'.[19] Needless to say, the MacDonald historians are not slow to see the hand of Argyll in all this; the record of treason and troublemaking is not enough cause for all the Lord of the Isles' fate, lucky though he undoubtedly was not to lose his head.

> The historian of Sleat connects the loss of these lands (Kintyre and Knapdale) with certain dealings which John had with Colin, earl of Argyle, and while the details of his story do not seem very probable, there is every likelihood that this wily and unscrupulous nobleman and courtier may have had something to do with that unfortunate occurrence.[20]

In 1478, MacDonald was again in trouble, summoned to Parliament on a charge of treason for giving aid and counsel to traitors based on Castle Sween, which he had 'stuffed' with victuals, men and arms, and for supporting Donald Gorm and Neil MacNeil with their men who had been the cause of trouble in the area.[21] By the end of that year, however, he was once more restored with a regrant of his Lordship of Parliament and of his lands in the Isles. The truth of the matter is that the loss of his earldom had deprived the MacDonald Chief of a major source of his power; an ageing man, he found it difficult if not impossible to combine command of the loyalty of his own people with obedient subservience to Royal authority. Among his own clan and neighbours, it was increasingly his bastard son, Angus of Islay, who commanded respect. Clan Donald lost its cohesion and began to break up, with those who blamed the Lord of the Isles for the loss of his once great territories of the earldom of Ross and for the loss of Knapdale and Kintyre, made all the more significant by the grants of territory he had made to the subordinate clans of the Isles, turning away from the old chief to his son. It was Argyll who now emerged as the greatest power in the Western Highlands and Isles.[22]

So much of his time was now spent in affairs of state at court that Argyll continued the process of appointing deputies to carry out his duties for him and protect his interests. In February 1476, he appointed his well-loved cousin Sir Duncan Campbell of Glenorchy to act as his Deputy in Discher, Toyer (the north and south banks of Loch Tay) in Glenfalloch, Glendochart and Glenorchy.[23] In 1477, he gave a bond of maintenance to John Scrymgeour of Glassary, thereby binding that magnate to his side.[24] In September 1478, he gave a charter of various lands to Gilbert, son and heir of Alexander MacNaughton of that Ilk, including the lands of Dunderave, now the seat of the MacNaughton Chief.[25] He appointed Sir John Lamont as his Deputy and Bailie of Cowal.

In 1480, the death took place of that doughty old warrior Sir Colin Campbell of Glenorchy, who was succeeded by his son, Sir Duncan, also a staunch ally of the Earl. In 1481, the Keepership of Castle Sween was given to the Earl together with surrounding lands; the Campbell chief, as well as the major fortresses of Innischonnel, Inveraray and Carrick, now had in his possession the even greater power centres of Lorne (Dunstaffnage) and Knapdale.

In 1482, there took place 'The Raid of Lauder' in which the King's allegedly base-born favourites, Cochrane, Roger and Preston, were killed by the jealous nobles who now took the King into their own hands. Argyll may or may not have been there – accounts differ – but he was thereafter definitely out of favour as Master of the Household. Seeing their opportunity, an English army under the Duke of Gloucester with Albany, the Scottish King's brother, invaded Scotland. There was no popular enthusiasm for the latter in Scotland and he anyway concentrated his main ambition on regaining his lands and offices rather than claiming the throne. By the end of his troops' required duty of a month's service, Gloucester was getting little further. The Scots were keen to get rid of their unwelcome visitors and Gloucester was equally keen to come to an accommodation. The English withdrew and Argyll was one of the Scottish Commissioners appointed to negotiate the peace. He was soon back in favour. The following year, he and Sir Duncan Campbell of Glenorchy were pardoned for their part in the Lauder killing – not so much for having taken part in it but for lack of any effective help to the King.[26] When Parliament sat again, they elected a Committee of the Articles – an inner Committee of Parliament which set its business – among them Argyll. That August when Bishop Livingston died, Argyll was appointed in his place as Lord Chancellor.

The Clan Donald continued to cause trouble. Efforts to reconcile Angus Og with his father having failed, their enmity came to a head with a sea-battle off Mull between the two factions, known as the 'Battle of Bloody Bay', in which Angus came off the better. Atholl, who was playing a leading part, then crossed to Islay and took captive Angus's young son, Donald Dubh, whom he handed over to Argyll for incarceration in Innischonnel. Angus had been married to Argyll's daughter Mary according to the *Scots Peerage* which says, however, that they had no issue; Donald Dubh, like his father before him, was illegitimate and the earl was not his grandfather.[27] There is certainly doubt on the matter, but the MacDonald historians do not agree and castigate Argyll for an act 'of unspeakable meanness', one which 'not only consigned an innocent grandchild to a living death but one which cast an unfounded suspicion on the fair fame of his own daughter'.[28] Atholl, they claim, was acting as the Earl of Argyll's catspaw.

Angus Og himself does not seem to have seen things quite like this, since it was into Atholl that he now led a revenge raid. The Earl was taken by surprise, and he and his Countess took refuge in the sanctuary of Saint Bride's Chapel, but the Islesmen ignored the sanctity of the place and carried them both off captive. On the way back to Islay, Angus and his ships were overtaken by a violent storm which sank several of the galleys. In a superstitious dread, Angus thereupon released the Atholls and returned to Saint Bride's, where he made penance in a bid to avert further disaster. This was not long in coming. The exact date is not certain, but it was some time in 1490 that Angus, on his way to attack his foes the Mackenzies, was assassinated by his harper. The Lord of the Isles' other son, John, having died without issue, the leadership of Angus's party now passed to Alexander MacDonald of Lochalsh, son of his brother Celestine alias Gillespic.[29]

But if Argyll was carrying out the Crown's policy in the Western Highlands and Isles, his personal relationship with the King was again deteriorating along with those of many of the other nobles. In 1488, matters came to a head with the King's son and heir, the 15-year-old Duke of Rothesay, leaving Stirling Castle to join with the disaffected among whom was Argyll, by now removed from the Chancellorship. He was one of seven ambassadors sent to England, presumably to seek the aid of the English King at least as far as to obtain permission to raise troops on the English side of the Border. He may therefore have missed – accounts differ – the ensuing Battle of Sauchieburn, near Stirling, where the unfortunate King James III met his end. The story is better known than historically authenticated of how he fell from his horse while fleeing from the battlefield, how he was carried into the mill of Bannockburn where he asked for a priest to shrive him, and how a mysterious man, claiming to be a priest, approached him and stabbed him to death. The Earl of Argyll was swiftly returned to the post of Chancellor by the new King over whom he exercised a strong influence, along with the Lords Bothwell, Gray and Drummond.

The year 1489 saw mounting crisis in the west. At Easter, Argyll, as Chancellor, was summoned to attend at Court. The King's hand was a weak one and there was considerable resistance to the taxes which he needed to raise. An embassy to France in order to boost recognition of his regime was to cost £5,000. Plans were laid in order to overcome the malcontents who were led by the Earl of Lennox, Matthew Stewart and Lord Lyle. The first stage of operations was to be the capture of Glasgow by the King. Once there, Argyll and his men, raised from the Lennox, Menteith and Strathearn, as well as from Argyll, were to move along the north bank of the Clyde and take the rebel base of Dumbarton. After twenty days, with the term of his troops' employment running out, he was to be relieved. Argyll's heart may not have been fully in it; his son and heir Archibald was married to the Earl of Lennox's daughter Elizabeth, but for whatever reason Dumbarton did not fall. That October, Lennox and his troops moved out from Dumbarton and set off for Stirling. The Royal troops met them and, in a series of skirmishes across the marshy pools of the Carse, defeated the rebels. The main engagement, known as the Battle of the Moss, was apparently near Touch at Kippen, where Lennox's men bore the bloody shirt of King James III into battle as a talisman which, however, availed them little.

In 1490, Argyll successfully petitioned for the Castle of Gloom to be retitled Castle Campbell. On a spur of the Ochil Hills, between the ravines of the Burn of Care and the Burn of Sorrow, overlooking Dollar and the winding bends of the River Forth, the castle had been exchanged with Walter Stewart of Innermeath as part of the transactions over the Lordship of Lorne. The castle had been in Campbell hands since April 1465. Held from the Bishops of Dunkeld, it provided a convenient place of safety within easy reach of Stirling, Perth or Edinburgh. It was a magnificent symbol of power and strength, and its closer identification with the Campbells would worthily reflect the growing importance of *Mac Cailein Mor*.

In 1491, it was the turn of the Western Isles to cause trouble once more. Clan Donald as ever was at the heart of it, this time under the leadership of Alexander of Lochalsh who was now, following the murder of Angus Og, in opposition to the ageing and increasingly ineffectual John Lord of the Isles. Joined by Clanranald, Keppoch, Lochiel, Rose of Kilravock and by Clan Chattan, the rebels took Inverness and garrisoned it. They plundered the lands of Sir Alexander Urquhart, Sheriff of Cromarty. Part of their forces then moved against the MacKenzies, who were, however, waiting for them and who defeated the invaders at the Battle of Park. The MacDonald leader was wounded and driven from Ross.[30]

Such disturbances do not seem to have involved the Clan Campbell directly, but the existence of such an armed force on foot in the Highlands would have allowed little sleep to Mac Cailein's men, who would have kept their weapons close by at such an anxious time. But the long and remarkable life of their chief was drawing to a close and on 10 May 1493 Colin, 1st Earl of Argyll, died.

CHAPTER EIGHT

Triumph and Disaster

Colin was followed by his eldest son, Archibald (the English equivalent of Gillespic), who now became the 2nd Earl of Argyll. We do not know the exact date of his birth, but, since his sister Margaret, who *The Scots Peerage* says married George, Lord Seton 'after 1469',[1] was apparently aged around 12 at her wedding, she must have been born some time after 1457. She is also said to have been the eldest girl in the family, and, as there was only one other boy who might also have been born before her, it would seem logical to suppose a birthdate for Earl Archibald some time after 1455 or thereabouts. If this were the case, he would have been approaching 40 when he succeeded his father.

His wife was Elizabeth, daughter of John Stewart, the first of the Stewart Earls of Lennox. By her, he had four sons: Colin, who in due course succeeded him as 3rd Earl of Argyll; Archibald, first of the earlier line of Skipness; John, later Sir John Campbell of Cawdor and Donald, who went into the Church and became the Abbot of Coupar. Among their daughters were Catherine, married first to Maclean of Duart, and Jean, married to the Lamont Chief. Another daughter, Marion, in pursuance of the custom of using marriages for political ends, was married to Sir Robert Menzies, who found himself on the eastern flank of Campbell expansion. Mention in the Irish *Annals of the Four Masters* of a *Dowell* or Dougall and a *Donough* as sons of a Gillespic Campbell may indicate further, probably illegitimate, offspring of the Earl.[2]

Earl Archibald succeeded at a difficult period. For some time now, relationships with the Crown, which had been so good for most of the previous King's time, had been less cordial – partly since the arrival of yet another minor on the throne had left Scotland in the hands of competing councillors and so vulnerable to the shifts in political power. Earl Archibald was not appointed to his father's post of Chancellor, which instead went to the Earl of Angus. His role in the rebellion of 1489 may have been questioned; at any rate, when he attended the Scottish Parliament of 1493, while he was elected one of the Lord Auditors, appointment as a member of the Privy Councillor or as one of the Officers of State eluded him. He had to be content with the powers and offices over in Argyll and its neighbourhood which he had inherited from his father. The situation was to remain the same for the next two years. The Douglas star of the Earl of Angus was now in the ascendant.

The year 1493 saw the final forfeiture of the Lordship of the Isles and its annexation to the Crown. John, Lord of the Isles, as we have seen, had been forfeited in 1476, being, however, partially restored to some of his lands, with the new Parliamentary title of Lord of the Isles. From then on, Clan Donald and the Lordship started to come apart, with John's illegitimate son Angus, designated as his official successor, attempting to take the reins of power from his hostile father. While the subordinate clans of the Lordship who had been kindly treated and advanced by John still followed him, the core of the Clan Donald followed Angus, who led expeditions into Ross and Inverness. Following his assassination in 1490, it was Donald Gorm of Sleat and Alexander of Lochalsh who took over leadership of most of the Clan Donald, their rival John, last MacDonald Lord of the Isles, losing what face he retained by his new and final forfeiture.

This left a power vacuum in the Western Isles, since there was no one single, obvious successor to fill the gap. There was no real opportunity to impose Royal authority over the area, since Argyll was never going to be acceptable to the Clan Donald and there are, anyway, indications that at this time his position was somewhat ambiguous. Argyll had not been unfriendly to John, and there was of course the situation of his alleged grandson, Donald Dubh, John's grandson, held safe at Innischonnel, who might serve as a useful tool with which to re-establish the Lordship under suitable influence. But in any case the Isles were in turmoil, and the same year as the forfeiture saw a Royal expedition assembling at Dunstaffnage, without apparent participation by Argyll although the Campbell Captains of the castle would no doubt have been fully occupied in accommodating Chancellor Angus and the Royal army. The expedition was only a brief one, but it would seem that several of the local chiefs did attend to make their peace. Maclaine of Lochbuie, who a year later appears as baillie of Southern Tiree, and Ian MacIan (MacDonald) of Ardnamurchan appointed Baillie of Islay in June 1494 for his good services,[3] may well have come in at this time, while John MacDonald of Dunyveg and Alexander MacDonald of Lochalsh, both knighted, may also have submitted at Dunstaffnage.

But by now it was MacIan of Ardnamurchan, himself a Clan Donald chieftain, who was identified as the most effective agent of the Crown against his kindred. The MacDonald historians are not slack in their condemnation of this wayward member of their Clan, whose black deeds are put down, they aver, to his having been married to a daughter of the Earl of Argyll. No trace of this lady would appear to exist in Campbell records.[4] It may well have been MacIan's appointment in Islay that caused the revolt of MacDonald of Dunyveg in protest at this encroachment on his territory by a rival.

The King was briefly in the Isles in May 1494 in response. By July he was at Tarbert with a large part of his host which had been summoned to meet him there. From Tarbert, it is said, he moved to secure Dunaverty, where he came to an arrangement with MacDonald, installing a Royal governor of the castle. Satisfied for the moment, he set sail once more for the Clyde, but, as the Royal fleet sailed past on its return from Islay, the King was greeted by the sight of his governor's corpse suspended from the battlements.[5] Little had been achieved at any rate. The King was back at Stirling by August. Early in September, MacDonald of Dunyveg was summoned for treason, the execution of the summons proving hard to put into effect. Again, it was MacIan of Ardnamurchan who proved to be the answer. Some time during the same year of 1494, he had sucessfully dealt with Alexander of Lochalsh, cornering him on the island of Oronsay, where he killed him. Sometime later, in 1499, he led an expedition against the ancient capital of the Lordship of the Isles at Finlaggan on Islay, where he captured Sir John and his three sons. They were brought to Edinburgh and all hanged on the Boroughmuir.

Recent excavation of Finlaggan, the historic centre of the Lordship of the Isles, suggests that it was systematically destroyed at this time; indeed, it may have been symbolically razed. The old stone Council Table which apparently stood on the Council Isle has disappeared, as has the stone with the carved footprint used by the Lords of the Isles in a re-enactment of the ritual observed on Dunadd at the inauguration of the early Scottish Kings. On more than one occasion, I have been asked by members of the Clan Donald if either of these stones was to be found at Inveraray. I have been able to assure them that no such trophy exists there, nor is it likely to, since it was one of their own who committed the damage and, since he may well have included such powerful symbols in the scheme of destruction, I would be more inclined to look for them in the nearest stretch of deep water!

The following year, 1495, the King mounted yet another expedition to the Isles. Shortly before it set out at Easter, Earl Archibald was appointed to the office held by his father as Master of the Royal Household. In charge of Cowal for the King, he was much involved in the organisation of the force of ships now ready to sail from Dumbarton. The King himself was in the *Flower*, commanded by Sir Andrew Wood. Argyll was with the expedition and no doubt took with him many of his clan. The force sailed via Bute and round the Mull of Kintyre to its forward base of Mingary Castle, seat of the Royal henchman MacIan of Ardnamurchan. Here they once more took the submission of the local chiefs. Maclean of Duart was confirmed as Keeper of the castle of Cairnaburgh, the important island fortress to the north-west of Mull; Alan Cameron, Captain of the Camerons, was confirmed as Keeper of the castle of Strome, while McNeill of Barra was given a charter of confirmation for the whole of Barra.[6] Nor had Earl Archibald been idle nearer home; there is a list of charters reflecting a steady increase in his territory.

In June 1494, Elisabeth Menteith, Lady Rusky, widow of John Napier of Merchiston, sold to Earl Archibald half of her lands in Argyll, or, to be more precise, in Cowal. They totalled seventeen and a half merklands and ranged from Ardmarnock to Glenmassan and Craigtarsan and further confirmed the Campbell takeover of the former Stewart/Menteith dominance of Cowal. This expansion was by no means all in Argyll; during the years 1493–4, the Earl obtained considerable lands in Perthshire and in Fife. He was also able to regularise the position at the Castle of Gloom when, in February 1494, he took sasine of the lands of Dollar or Gloom, previously resigned to the Bishop of Dunkeld, who regranted them as a whole to the Earl. They had originally been part of the deal which involved the acquisition of the Lordship of Lorne, and, at the time of the resignation, one third was held by Earl Colin, the 1st Earl, one third by his wife Isabella Stewart and one third by Sir Duncan Campbell of Glenorchy. The destination of the lands was carefully set out: should the male line of the earls die out, the lands were to go to Sir Duncan of Glenorchy; should his male line die then to Archibald Campbell of Kilmichael (Auchinbreck) and so on through the male lines in turn of Archibald Campbell of Otter, Colin Campbell of Ormidale, Ian Campbell of Ardquhonzie, Iain Campbell of Lawers and, lastly, that of Robert Campbell, Constable of Carrick, a younger son of Campbell of Ardkinglas. And by desire of the the Bishop, if any closer female were to be excluded by reason of male heirs, they should be given reasonable recompense in lands or goods and a tocher on their marriage.[7] This is a very interesting charter, since it would appear to give the 'pecking order' within Clan Campbell at that date, in a fashion which would not be the normal order of succession today but which no doubt reflects the most important leaders of the clan at that time. It demonstrates very clearly a recurring insistence in Campbell charters which explicitly guarded against the loss of any territory through an heiress marrying outwith the Clan. Should such a situation arise, a Campbell husband was swiftly found and possession maintained. Other clans were not so careful – a fact of which the Clan Campbell were able to take advantage on several occasions.

There is also evidence of what today might be termed 'wheeling and dealing' in the acquisition of land by the Earl; in 1495 he has a charter from Ewen MacCorquodale of Ederline for the lands of Ederline, Camisayen and Carren in exchange for the lands of Phanans, Shelechan, Craigenterive and Corvoran, thus gaining full control of the southern exit to Loch Awe.[8] In 1497, he gave over to his cousin, Humphrey Colquhoun of Luss, the lands of Bordland of Sauling in return for the lands of Inverchapel, and others which included Blairbeg, Strone and Stuck.[9] That year, he also entered into a rather strange agreement with Gilchrist M'Lamont of Inverneilbeg, who had just made over to him the lands of Conchra in Glendaruel. Now Gilchrist, having no male heirs, resigned the lands of Inverneilbeg, Glack, Kildalvan and Inveregan together with the Coronership of Cowal into the King's hands for regrant to him, and after him to the Earl and his heirs on payment of 100 merks. Should Gilchrist produce a male heir, then the Earl would give Gilchrist reversion of the said sum and would be infeft in the lands and office in blench ferme. The next year, in March 1498, he resigned the whole lot into the King's hands for a straightforward regrant to the Earl of Argyll. The extent of the coronership was given in detail as extending 'from Togall from the water of Altnapscoon (aliter Altneskynny) to the point of Tolbard and from the point of Tollard (Toward) to the point of Ardlawmoind and from thence to the water of Lynsaig and from the water of Lynsaig to the well which is commonly called Tybberoyr'. Among the list of witnesses is one *Ewen Oig Archipoeta* – 'Young Ewen the Arch-poet', an interesting name which probably denotes a member of the bardic family of the MacEwens of Otter.[10]

A straightforward purchase the same year was made from David Lindsay of Beaufort 'in his urgent necessity' of a quarter of the castle and fortalice and of many nearby lands together with a quarter of the seller's superiority of the Lordship of Beaufort.[11] Had this purchase allowed the Campbell chief a foothold which he could have exploited, the subsequent history of the Frasers of Lovat would have been very different. But marks of the King's favour were plentiful at this time: in January 1498, Earl Archibald received a grant from the King of the lands of Lochnell in Lorne which were resigned by Ranald, son of Ian son of Alan Dubh of Lochnell, with his brothers german Dougall and Ian – the lands having previously belonged to Alan Dubh. It is hard not to feel sorry for the poor youngsters, who were obviously leant on to make them give up their patrimony – sixty-four merklands, no less. The Lochnell in question, which was shortly to give its name to an important new branch of Clan Campbell, is the inland loch of that name which lies south of Oban. There is an islet at the north end of the loch on which are the remains of a fortification – an occupied site which long predates the unfortunate young MacDougalls and which was now taken over by the Campbells together with much rich land around the loch including the properties of Strontoiller, Cabrachan and Torrinturks.[12]

On 22 April 1498, the King granted Earl Archibald the forty-shilling land of Easter Toward in Cowal, resigned by Robert Fleming. On 8 May, he was given sasine of all the lands of Glassary. Nor was the Earl the only beneficiary; in August 1498, for his service to the King in the Isles and otherwise, a charter was given to *Colin Campbell Knychtsone* – 'Colin Campbell the Knight's son', or Colin son of Neil Campbell of Ormidale – of Clynder on the Gareloch and of Boroman in Rosneath, for his life.[13] This last charter was written at the New Castle of Kintyre. Having restored both Dunaverty and Tarbert, the King now had another stronghold constructed at what is now Campbeltown. This was probably in response to the need for a pro-tected and secure fleet anchorage on the eastern coast of Kintyre near to the Mull, whose passing involves perilous seas and very little shelter apart from that offered by the island of Sanda on one side and the distant Isles of Gigha and Cara on the other.

As shown by the charter's place of writing, the King was once more on expedition to the west. The policy of the Crown towards the recalcitrant Isles had hardened. In 1497, it was ordained that henceforward each chief in the former Lordship was to be personally responsible for the execution of any summons against any of his people. While its intention was obvious, the implementation of this new degree was far from simple; Earl Archibald is seen as one of its main architects, but its unforeseen pressure which set chief against clansman militated against its success.

So it was that in 1498 King James appears to have visited Kilkerran – the later Campbeltown – no fewer than three times, in March, May and June. The first two visits were short ones of no more than a week, but in June he came again and stayed in the area until August, the forty days for which his lieges were normally required to do military service each year, if required. His reception was distinctly chilly; in March, an Act had been passed revok-ing all past charters to lands in the Lordship which were to be regranted – at a price. The King waited in vain for the procession of galleys bringing the Chiefs to him. Only three turned up, among them Torquil MacLeod of Lewis, Argyll's brother-in-law, who was granted the bailiary of Trotternish in Skye, a post which only a fortnight before had been granted in Stirling to Alexander MacLeod of Dunvegan. This confusion, it has been suggested, was at the behest of Argyll, who might profit by the resultant rivalry between the two MacLeod Chiefs. Once again, any evidence for this is lacking.[14]

Earl Archibald was certainly a major beneficiary of the changed situation. King James had by now lost interest in the Western Highlands and Isles. This time, as he left Kilkerran, it was never to return. From now on, he was to delegate Royal authority in the area and Earl Archibald was clearly now the chief power in the land. In 1499, he was made the Keeper of the Royal Castle of Tarbert and Baillie of the Royal lands in Knapdale with all the profits therefrom;[15] the following spring, 1500, he was first of all, together with five others including Sir Duncan Campbell of Glenorchy, given the power to set all lands within the Lordship for three years with the exception of Islay and Kintyre. A few days later, he was made King's Lieutenant-General over the same area – again for three years. For this period, he was invested with full powers by his Commission to govern those dwelling in the designated area; to execute statutes for their restraint; to capture and punish transgressors and disobedient persons and rebels; to assemble the lieges to arms against any rebels; to raise the royal standard as often as necessary and bear it against such rebels; to besiege castles, appoint officers and generally to do all things pertaining by law or custom to the office of Lieutenant.[16]

It is perhaps now, for the first time, and perhaps later than one might have thought, that the Earl of Argyll is clearly identified as the main tool of the King's authority in the area and the effective successor of the erstwhile Lord of the Isles, although his succession was by no means an effortless one in this latter capacity. But the date 1500 must be seen as another important milestone in the Campbell rise to power in the West Highlands and the ascendancy of the Clan Campbell over the Clan Donald. As we have seen, King James had recently made every effort to favour Argyll. One of the most significant boons which he gained at this time came about in the following way. In 1498, John, the Thane of Cawdor, died, leaving two small daughters as his heiresses. Earl Archibald immediately asked the King for their ward and marriage, which was granted him.[17] The grant, if he could arrange their marriages to members of his own family, would represent a rich accumulation of fertile territory to the Campbells. It was far from popular with the girls' family on both sides – the Cawdors, or Calders as they spelt their name – who saw their ancestral lands about to pass to strangers and to their mother's people, the neighbouring Roses of Kilravock. One of the girls was Muriel, for whom her uncle, Hugh Rose of Kilravock, had hoped to arrange a suitable marriage to his grandson; but Argyll's position as Justiciar and a little local difficulty over the laying waste of the lands of Urquhart of Cromarty by the Roses ensured his compliance.[18] The situation was further complicated by the fact that her old grandfather, William, Thane of Cawdor, was still alive, having, however, handed over the Thanedom to his eldest son, John, the father of the two small girls, some years previously.

Although Muriel of Cawdor is famous, the existence of her sister Janet is not generally so well known and she remains a shadowy figure – to the extent that it is unknown for certain whether she was older or younger than her sister (there are indications she may have been the elder – see below) or what exactly happened to her. There was bad blood between old William and his daughter-in-law, and the former signed an instrument to the effect that the younger of the two, whichever one that was, was not in fact John's child. John, according to his father, had sworn on his deathbed that he had not been sleeping with his wife during the period of the child's conception.[19]

Earl Archibald and Hugh Rose of Kilravock were declared tutors or guardians to both Muriel and Janet Cawdor on 16 January 1499, and Janet was alive as late as the 27th of the month, her last appearance on record.[20] Thereafter no more is heard of her, and there is no record of the manner of her death. While there is no particular reason to think it was other than natural, if her end was a violent one it might well have influenced what then followed. In early February, the two tutors, Argyll and Kilravock, signed a Bond of Friendship. Later in the year, at harvest time, Earl Archibald sent a party of sixty of his men from Argyll to Cawdor under Campbell of Inverliever, a scion of the Barbreck family, to bring the child back with them for safe-keeping. Until the time she was safely married off, Muriel was a vulnerable asset. At the time, she was being looked after by her mother's family, the Roses, who were fond of the child and reluctant to give her up as well as being highly conscious of the change of circumstances that would attend her untimely death.

Someone is reputed to have taunted Inverliever with the fact that Muriel was not yet married and might never be so if she failed to survive, to which his answer was 'Muriel can never die while there is a red-haired lassie on the shores of Loch Awe . . . !' Obviously the Campbells would produce a suitable girl of the right age and colouring when the time came, and nor would her old nurse's action in biting off the top joint of the child's little finger and branding her with a red-hot key to ensure her identification have presented any major obstacle should a double have to be produced. Inverliever and his party then set off home with the child. They were, however, followed up and intercepted by a superior party led by Muriel's Calder uncles, appar-ently near Daltulich. It was this moment that produced the saying *'S fhada glaodh o Lochow! 'S fhada cobhair o chlann dhaoine!* – 'It's a far cry to Loch Awe! It's far the help to the Campbells!' Inverliever left his men in a circle around an upturned basket which was duly taken to contain the child while, with a few companions, he slipped away across the hills, leaving eight of his sons with the beleaguered party. They never came home, but Muriel was brought safe to Inveraray, and, in 1502, after the failure the previous year of an attempt by her half-uncle Andrew to have her declared illegitimate, she was finally served heir to her father, John.[21]

Muriel's grandfather, old Thane William, died some time in 1503. In 1510, now aged 13, Muriel was married to John Campbell, Earl Archibald's third son. The marriage is commemorated at Cawdor Castle by a splendid carved stone fireplace inscribed with the couple's initials. Although of later date, it is a fittingly solid memento of what was clearly a long and very happy marriage which was in due course to leave Muriel as a formidable matriarch of her ancestral lands. These she had resigned not long after her marriage for a regrant to herself and her husband, on which they had sasine dated 21 April 1512. The lands included were those of the Thanage of Cawdor; the lands and baronies of Clunes and Boith; the lands of Balmaklaith; half the township of Rait; the lands of Moy and those of Dunmaglas, the two Kinkells, Kyndeis, Innermarky, Mulquhaich, and Drumwornye, all regranted in one free barony and thanage to both of them.[22]

Trouble continued, however, in Cawdor, where Muriel's uncles continued their protest at the loss of the ownership of the family's lands. Chief among them was her illegitimate half-uncle Andrew, whose exploits led to his being outlawed and a reward being offered for his capture, dead or alive. The final scene in this drama was apparently played out when Andrew was shot dead near the Castle of Rait at a spot known as 'Calder's Stone' to this day. After his death, the young couple were able to enjoy their possession without hindrance and a new and important branch of Clan Campbell was born.

Not all such marriages turned out so well. It was around this time that the marriage of Earl Archibald's daughter with Maclean of Duart broke up. Apparently he found her less than satisfactory in bed and determined to get rid of her. This he attempted to achieve by leaving her at low water on the rock which rises from the turbulent waters just off the end of the Island of Lismore, today marked by a beacon and the name of 'The Lady's Rock'. At her husband's pitiless command, the lady in question was here abandoned and left to the mercy of the rising tide – a terrifying fate which even today from the safety and comfort of the deck of one of Caledonian MacBrayne's ferries requires little imagination to send a shiver of horror down the spine. A passing crew of fishermen, however, heard her screams for help and pulled her aboard, delivering her to the mainland, according to traditional accounts, further down the coast to the south of Crinan whence she made her way overland to her father's house of Inveraray. Here it was, goes the tale, her long-faced husband arrived a few days later, bewailing the loss of his beloved wife, while all the time his intended victim was safe upstairs. It will always be a puzzle why Maclean was not dealt with on the spot – perhaps the unfortunate Catherine's family were enjoying the situation so much they did not want to spoil it by bloodshed – but it was to be some years before, as we will shortly see, the Maclean chief met his deserts.

Meanwhile, the Earl of Argyll's attempts to impose Royal authority on the area under his command had met with no success. This and his links by marriage to several of the main troublemakers – as well as Maclean of Duart being a brother-in-law, MacLeod of Lewis was his uncle by marriage – may not have helped his reputation. In any case, he was more or less superseded in 1501, when Alexander Gordon, now Earl of Huntly, was given the right to collect all monies due to the Crown from north of the Mounth and to apply force if he was opposed. This covered a great area of the Earldom of Ross and the Lordship of the Isles and from now on it was Huntly who took over the leading role as agent of the Crown in these parts.[23]

Who was therefore the leading spirit or whether it was entirely by mutual agreement is unknown, but that same year an indenture was signed between the two Chiefs. By its terms, Huntly's heir, his grandson George, was to have the choice of Katherine or Elisabeth Campbell, daughters of Earl Archibald, while Archibald's son and heir Colin should have the choice for wife of either Janet or Margaret Gordon. The marriage in each case was to be solemnised within forty days of the attainment of the 'perfect age' of marriage for either party – that is to say, explains the document, fourteen years for the boy and twelve years for the girl. If George Gordon should die, his place in the agreement would be taken by his brother John or whoever was the next heir, taking for wife whichever of Earl Archibald's daughters 'of lawfull bed' should be the most suitable in age. If on the other hand Colin should die, then his brother John should take his place, followed if the necessity arose by the next heir and so on. Each of the son's fathers was to give him and his wife £100 of land of old extent in Badenoch and in Lorne and Argyll respectively, while a penalty clause and security were also included in the deal.[24]

In the event, the only marriage which clearly took place was that of the future Earl Colin to Janet Gordon. George Gordon, who was to become 4th Earl of Huntly, appears to have married Elisabeth, daughter of the Earl Marischal. At this time, Earl Archibald also made provision for his second son, Archibald, granting him the keeping of the castle of Skipness, south of Tarbert and therefore geographically in Kintyre, although for administrative purposes it was always held to be part of Knapdale. This was another historic property, the original castle having been built by Dougall, son of the great Sween, early in the thirteenth century. It sits on the green machair, looking out to Arran where the Castle of Lochranza faces it – also thought to have been built by Dougall MacSween. Between them, the castles dominate Kilbrannan Sound.

In September 1502, King James had granted the castle and its keeping together with thirty-six merklands of land in Knapdale to Earl Archibald on the resignation of the then owner, Sir Duncan Forrester, the grant being to the Earl and his heirs male, whom failing Sir Duncan of Glenorchy and his heirs, whom failing Earl Archibald's nearest heirs bearing the name and arms of Campbell. At the same time, the whole estate was erected into the barony of Skipinch, or Skipness as we now have it.[25] This was no doubt the confirmation of an earlier agreement, since Earl Archibald had already passed on the castle and the new barony to his son in July 1501. With additional land, the estate now totalled ninety-two merklands, creating another major Campbell branch and making Archibald of Skipness the greatest power in Knapdale.

The same year, 1502, the Earl granted his 'dear relation' Alexander Campbell Ciar the custody of the castle of Dunstaffnage with the surrounding lands and a further eighteen merklands extending to and including Glencruitten, which is just above today's town of Oban. Alexander Ciar had to maintain a garrison of at least six well-armed men and sufficient hostlers to a total of eight persons in time of peace while guaranteeing hospitality to the Earl and a base for operations in time of war. His office was described as being, in the vulgar tongue, that of 'Marnichty' – *officium quod in vulgari vocatur Mernychti*, and neither Alexander nor his heirs were to marry without their Chief's permission.[26]

There are a number of interesting points raised by this charter. The first is that it is some thirty years – a whole generation – since the castle had come into the hands of the Argyll family, who clearly regarded it as being of sufficient importance to want to keep it directly under their personal control. It would very much look as if the Earl now felt himself under some considerable pressure which again impelled him to delegate responsibility to another trusted lieutenant. Most of these were close relatives, brothers or first cousins, but in this case the relationship was a more distant one, Alexander being a second cousin once removed of Earl Archibald. Both shared a common descent from Colin Iongantach, Alexander Ciar's being from Colin's son Dougall. It is of course possible that this grant was a regularisation of an existing position, but earlier reference is made to Alexander as 'Bailie of Glenaray' a good distance from Dunstaffnage, which would make the two responsibilities somewhat difficult to combine. What the intervening generations had been doing is also unclear. Whatever the way of it, the appointment marked the placing of another lieutenant in a strategic position and the establishment of yet another highly distinguished branch of Clan Campbell, whose chieftain today still goes under the name of 'The Captain of Dunstaffnage'.

As it happens, the family themselves have displayed considerable confusion over their origins. The appointment of Sir Arthur Campbell, from whom the Strachur branch descends, has, as already pointed out, confused MacArthur historians; it also led the later Campbells of Dunstaffnage to believe they must be descended from the earlier Campbell Constable of the castle appointed by Robert the Bruce. So it is that, for some years now, the family have displayed relics which are claimed to have belonged to that King. In fact they are demonstrably of a much later period, and their display was obviously first occasioned by the family's feeling that they needed proof for their appointment at a date much earlier than the one at which it had actually taken place.

These moves seem to be part of a pattern which had been going on for some time now. As the Campbell Chief's territory extended, so did its governance become more of a problem. The answer was initially to appoint members of the family to act as deputies over the lands, in the guise of seneschals, stewards, toiseachdeors, bailies and the like. But there was now a move to place these relatives in the position of heritable possessors of the lands of which they had hitherto been in charge. Such possession was very much under the superiority of the Chief of the day, who was recompensed not only by such rents and continuing rights as he saw fit to exact but also by the pledge of military service, not only as required by the original Royal grant of the lands to the chief but also by 'Special Retinue', to the Chief as well whenever and for as long as required. This last clause was often accompanied by a specific requirement to provide a fully manned boat of a specific size, Archibald Campbell holding Skipness on the undertaking to provide two galleys for the earl, one of sixteen and one of fourteen oars.[27]

As well as the inclusion of the clause involving the provision of boats, the Campbell Chiefs' charters are distinguished by insistence that all inheritance of the lands should be by male heirs only. The various branches of the family concerned were carefully laid out in the charter so that, if one descent should fail in the male line, the next senior is specified and, should that fail, the next one and so on, always ending with the proviso that should the family fail altogether then the lands are to return to the Chief of the Clan.

Another family of note which seems to have become established at around this time is that of the MacConnochie Campbells of Inverawe. A charter of 1485 is said to make mention of Campbell *of* Inverawe; but, as the original is now lost, it is impossible to confirm that that is the exact wording used. But sometime during this period, they appear to have moved their base from the tower house of Fraoch Eilean, the island at the north end of Loch Awe, to the other end of the pass of Brander, the short, narrow defile under the slopes of Ben Cruachan where Loch Awe empties into the sea. Here, at the river's mouth, stands a motte, a natural mound in this case much improved by human labour, on which stood the *Dunan of Inverawe*, a wooden-palisaded fortification well placed to dominate the crossings of the river at its mouth and also that across Loch Etive. But it cannot exactly have been a place of much comfort, and before long the chieftain had built a towerhouse in a more commodious setting a mile upstream which was to develop into the mansionhouse of Inverawe.

Another two branches of the same stem seem to have been established at this time around the head of Loch Feochan, where now appear the Campbells of Lerags and the family of Stronchormaig from whom, in due course, were to evolve the Campbells of Glenfeochan. But things otherwise had not gone well. In 1501, a party of MacDonalds from Glencoe had succeeded in rescuing Donald Dubh from incarceration in Innischonnel – whether with the connivance of the garrison commander or not, we do not know. He was spirited away to Torquil MacLeod of Lewis. The Isles rose in revolt, and both MacLeod and the young Donald failed to appear when summoned to do so in front of the King.

The following years were spent in subduing this new outbreak of violence which engulfed the west. The newly renovated castles of Kilkerran and Tarbert were ineffectual in protecting the island of Bute, which was devastated by the Islesmen so badly that its inhabitants were let off any payment of rent for three years.[28] During the winter of 1503, Lachlan Maclean of Duart and Torquil MacLeod of Lewis invaded Badenoch. That year also saw the passing of John, last MacDonald Lord of the Isles, a once-great figure who for years now had been eking out his life on Royal charity – a pathetic figure whose passing left no more than a ripple. He had served the Crown as a symbol, no more, but his death now opened the way for his grandson to be seen as the rightful Lord of the Isles despite repeated counter-arguments on the grounds that both he and his father were illegitimate.

In 1504, King James decided on a new beginning. At a meeting of Parliament, the King declared all previous charters to be revoked – again. All the West Highland chiefs in rebellion were forfeited, while eight of their number were to be sent letters encouraging them to attack the rebels. Huntly was to rebuild the castle at Inverlochy, covering entry into the Great Glen and into Badenoch. Argyll was to strengthen both Dunaverty and Kilkerran.[29] Throughout the country, owners of ships were to prepare their vessels to sail; the royal artillery was to be assembled and made ready. Earl Archibald's performance – or, rather, the lack of it – meanwhile led to his being placed very much 'on probation'. An early clause of the 1504 Parliament – later erased – laid down that, as Hereditary Sheriff of Argyll and Lorne, Argyll was to hold his Justice Ayres or Courts in Argyll only *als lang as the said lord kepis gude Reule and dois Justice.*[30] Failing this, the Ayres would be transferred to Perth so that the King could ensure matters were correctly carried out. Argyll protested and the insulting edict was replaced by one pronouncing that the Ayres would be held at Perth only if the King so desired.

The whole kingdom north of the Forth and the Clyde was called out and on 20 April the Royal fleet under that famous sailor Sir Andrew Wood sailed from Dumbarton. Duart, Lochbuie and Locheil were declared traitors; in their confusion, Parliament called on several of the leading chiefs engaged in rebellion to harry and capture those thus forfeited. Torquil MacLeod's role as leader of the revolt was still not realised and it was not until the Parliament of February 1506 that he was finally declared a traitor. The fleet called first at Ayr and then headed west for Kilkerran before rounding the Mull of Kintyre and setting course for the island fortress of Cairnaburgh, which they proceeded to besiege – a far from easy task. The Earl of Arran was appointed to the command of this part of the expedition. Huntly commanded in the north, where he took the castles of Strome and Eilean Donan.[31] Little of real worth, however, was accomplished, although Cairnaburgh was eventually taken and its safe-keeping entrusted to the Earl of Argyll.

Earl Archibald was lucky in that, as it became clearer that the Crown had little or no alternative to controlling the west through the use of loyal subordinates, his position as the only real contender became manifest. In August, he was appointed King's Lieutenant within the bounds of Argyll, Lorne, Knapdale, Kintyre, Discher and Toyer, Glenlyon and Balquhidder. His powers were extensive. He was also involved at the same time in the reorganisation of the judicial system of the west. According to the new plan, there was to be a Sheriff for the North Isles holding courts at Inverness or Dingwall. The earldom of Ross was also under another Sheriff whose courts would be at Tain or Dingwall. Further south, Mamore and Lochaber would be under the jurisdiction of Inverness; Duror, Glencoe and Argyll proper under the Court at Perth. Cowal, outside the Earl of Argyll' s heritable jurisdiction, would come under Dumbarton and Bute, while Kintyre and Knapdale, Arran and the Cumbraes would come under Rothesay or Ayr. And a Sheriff for the South Isles would be appointed holding court at Tarbert or Kilkerran.[32]

Early the next year, in February 1505, Earl Archibald was accordingly appointed to the offices of Justiciar, Sheriff, Coroner and Chamberlain of Knapdale and Kintyre and also Captain of the House and Fortalice of Tarbert (when completed) together with a number of lands in the south half of Knapdale. The whole was to be united into the free barony of Tarbert and was to be a hereditary possession of the Earl of Argyll, which would bring him half the fines and fees of the said courts.[33] The Royal expedition against the Isles was renewed that year which saw the eventual submission of all the chiefs except MacLeod of Lewis. Matters were eventually settled – for the time being – in 1506, when Huntly was sent to finalise matters. The castle of Stornoway was taken by siege; MacLeod of Lewis fled into exile while his lands in Assynt and Coigeach were given to the loyal Mackay of Strathnaver. Donald Dubh was once more taken prisoner and this time incarcerated in Edinburgh Castle; he was to spend most of the remainder of his life as a prisoner, a period of nearly forty years.[34]

In 1505 Earl Archibald had gone to collect the rents of Kintyre along with the other Royal Commissioners for the Highlands and Isles. Their number included the Earls of Huntly and Lennox, the Bishops of Aberdeen, of Argyll and of the Isles and a number of other magnates, including Sir Duncan Campbell of Glenorchy. It was given to any three of them acting together to apply the full weight of their powers, or only two of them if one was the Comptroller.[35] In 1506, however, the formula was somewhat altered. Argyll, accompanied by seven Commissioners but quite clearly in charge as King's Lieutenant for the area, appears to have issued a summons for a gathering at Dunadd. The significance of the location is not to be underestimated. The Lordship of the Isles was no more, and it was *Mac Cailein Mor*, acting for His Royal Majesty, who was henceforth to rule in the Western Highlands and Isles. What clearer way to underline the new order than to hold a new form of the Council of the Isles at the place which had of old been the capital of the ancient Scottish Kings of Dalriada? For three days at least, from 8–10 June, Argyll held court, collecting rents and issuing regulations. No-one was to interfere with Church lands or teinds; Bailie Courts were to be held at due intervals and were to be properly and fully staffed, and each was to establish a committee in order to identify sorners and other evildoers, who were to be forced to work or be expelled. Finally, no gathering was to be held unless it was in the King's service *and nocht uthirwayis, as ye will ansuer to the kingis hienes apoun the execution of your office herupoun.*

On the same occasion, MacIan of Ardnamurchan solemnly promised not to harm Lachlan Maclean of Duart at least until 1 May the following year, the like guarantee being also made to Maclaine of Lochbuie. All three bound themselves to appear before the King and the Council on 15 October following, bringing all the necessary writs and charters to enable their quarrel to be settled. It has been suggested that this was an official meeting of that rather nebulous body, the Barons of Argyll, whose precise identity and indeed existence remains a fascinating mystery. It is not helped by the various meanings of the word Baron, which has changed dramatically through the ages from its early use for a mere follower to a leading magnate holding land *in liberam baroniam* with powers which included the ultimate sanction of pit and gallows – a power which was by no means left unused, as attested by the frequency with which the landscape is graced by the names 'Hanging' or 'Hangman's Hill' – *Tom a Chrochaire* and *Tom a Chrocadaire*. It has also been used to denote those who held direct from the King rather than from a great Lord Superior and latterly those whose status as freeholders gave them a vote in Parliamentary elections. It has nothing to do with the English rank of Baron, the lowest in the peerage.

The term 'Barons of Argyll' does occur in official documents – we met them at Inverleckan in 1355 – but the qualification for being so described is unclear. It is of course just possible that the term merely denotes those of baronial status *in* Argyll; but if so, why does the specific description occur as it does? The Lord Lyon accepts the difference, and a Baron of Argyll – actually a Baron located in Argyll – displays a Baronial *chapeau* in his arms which is of a special pattern. Those at Dunadd in 1506 were not mere rent-payers; they were clearly those in authority, as the injunction to hold proper courts would indicate, and Lochbuie, Duart and MacIan of Ardnamurchan are unlikely to have been the only chiefs and chieftains present. But while accepting the importance of the occasion and its location, both symbolical and actual, it still seems unclear whether this was an official meeting of the Barons of Argyll.

Although his main efforts were devoted to settling the affairs of the Western Highlands and Isles, Earl Archibald was not slow to advance his interests elsewhere, whenever possible. In 1503, Walter Buchanan of that Ilk, unable to pay a debt owed to the Earl, substituted lands in Balquhidder to the same value of £242 with the provision that they could be bought back at any time within the next seven years. In 1505, the Earl actually disposed of land when he granted Meikle and Little Pinkerton to the Edinburgh merchant, Thomas Inglis. What the other half of the deal was, we do not know, but it seems unlikely to have been to the Earl's disadvantage. Then in 1506 the Collegiate Church of St Salvator, St Andrews, added Balconquhar to the lands the Earl already held in Sawling, Fife, for his counsel and help. All these scattered grants added to the Earl's wealth.[36]

Also prospering was the Earl's boon companion Sir Duncan Campbell of Glenorchy, whose record in advancing his family's fortunes was as outstanding as his father's had been. He was twice married, first to Margaret Douglas, daughter of the Earl of Angus, and secondly to the Laird of Moncreiffe's daughter. By his first wife he had three sons, Sir Colin, who was to succeed him, Archibald, and Patrick who died young; by his second wife he had a son, John, who was to become Bishop of the Isles. He obtained a tack of all the King's lands in Breadalbane and also of the lands belonging to the Charterhouse of Perth in the same district. He also took a tack of the twelve merklands of Cranduich which were later granted to him by charter.[37] The balance of power in his home area was being upset by the King's preference for Robert Menzies over the sitting tenant of much land, Stewart of Fortingall. The latter's failure to pay rent owed to the King for several years opened up the chance of his replacement by a richer and more complacent tenant. Menzies was accordingly given a charter for the lands of Apnadull.[38]

In order to ensure his acceptance of the new moves, in 1502, Sir Duncan was given the sixty merklands of Glenlyon by the King. These were lands over which he had been given the Bailiary some four years previously and which were now erected into the barony of Glenlyon. Sir Duncan in due course transferred these lands to his second son, Archibald, together with his third of the lands of Lorne, thereby founding a powerful family whose name was to weigh heavily in the subsequent history of their clan – the Campbells of Glenlyon.[39] In fact, the King's attempt to placate Sir Duncan was unsuccessful. Shortly afterwards, Sir Duncan and Stewart of Fortingall together with Robertson of Struan and with the support of the Earl of Atholl attacked Menzies in his castle of Weem, capturing him and putting him in prison. The King was furious and ordered his immediate release. When this produced no result, the malefactors were summoned to appear at a powerful Justice Ayre held by the King in Perth the following June; none of them did so and they were all duly declared traitors at the Parliament. Eventually the Lords of Council succeeded in calming the situation down, and Menzies was restored.[40]

Even when in difficulties with the Crown, he continued to increase his estates; in April 1503 he obtained a charter from John Lord Drummond of the lands and barony of Finlarig. This must have been the superiority, since he purchased ownership of the lands themselves from James Muschet of Tolgarth in early 1506, a transaction which was duly confirmed by Royal Charter in 1508.[41] This particular gain secured his holding of both ends of

Loch Tay and strengthened his line of communication back to Argyll. He also, so the *Black Book of Taymouth* tells us, built the great hall and chapel on the isle of Loch Tay where he had his eastern base. He also is said to have built 'the Laigh Hall of Glenorchy' by the *Black Book*, but where this was located we do not know for certain. Having obtained the lands of Glenquoich, he gave them to his brother Lawers.

Nor did he forget his family roots in Argyll. He swapped his share in the lands of Dollar, inherited through his mother, for the lands of Kilbride on Loch Fyne. In 1508, he had a charter from John Stewart of Ardgowan of the lands of Shian, Balloch and Acharn. In 1511, he had a charter from Sir Robert Menzies of the lands of Crannich, and in early 1513 he resigned all these lands for a regrant which combined them all into an enlarged barony of Finlarig.[42] This was a remarkable effort by a family which already had established itself as second in importance in Clan Campbell only to that of the Chiefs themselves. But greater things were afoot as King James once more turned his eyes south of the Border.

In July 1513, King James IV summoned the Scottish host to meet him at Ellem in Berwickshire, the same rendezvous that had been used in 1496. The result was one of the largest and best-equipped Scottish armies ever to invade England[43] with at least seventeen guns, the largest of which were capable of firing a ball weighing 60 lbs. Earl Archibald summoned his clan, and the Campbells turned out in full force – Glenorchy, Inverawe, Ardkinglas, Otter, Ormidale. All the Campbell chieftains mustered their men to follow the banner of Mac Cailein Mor.

They were encouraged by the words of the *Brosnachadh Catha* – the incitement to battle – penned by an anonymous bard, of which fragments remain. Following the famous Ode to Clan Donald penned before the Battle of Harlaw a century previously, it reminds the Chief of his heritage and the deeds of the heroes and calls on him to emulate them:

> Who now, in that man's wise, will succour Gael from Saxons, in our
>   time, as once Lugh aided his race against reproach?
> Known to me, were such his will, is one who could do likewise, even
>   as Lugh did, throughout the land of Banbha; it is fitting to compare
>   him to thee.
> Thou Archibald, who refusedst no man, thou art the Lugh of this
>   latter time; thou Earl of Argyll, be thou a champion triumphant.
> Send thy summons east and west for the Gael from the field of
>   Leinster; drive the Saxons westward over the high sea, that Alba
>   may suffer no division . . .

Attack the Saxons in their own land; awake thee, thou Mac Cailein:
    for a man of war, thou with hair like gold, not good is too long sleep.[44]

By boat and on foot they came, out of the far west, over the hills and down into the valley of the Tweed, far from home. There they met with the ranks of the Scottish host who, on 22 August, with the King at their head, once more crossed the Border into England.

In spite of the size of the Army, the objective was a limited one, the reduction and capture of the castle of Norham on the English bank of the Tweed. The King had failed in his effort to take the castle in 1497; this time he planned a short campaign in overwhelming strength. The strategy was successful. Five days later, under cover of a stormy night, the Scots assaulted and took the castle, destroying part of it immediately. The Bishop of Durham, whose castle it was, was shattered at its loss and wrote to Cardinal Wolsey that he would never forget nor recover from grief.[45] With time remaining out of the forty days' service the host was required to perform, the King moved south following the line of the Till and early in September took up a defensive position on Flodden Hill, where he and the army awaited the arrival of the vengeful English.

They did not have long to wait. Thomas Earl of Surrey had hurried north from his base at Pontefract; by the end of August he had reached Lord Dacre at Newcastle, and shortly thereafter at Alnwick they were joined by Surrey's son, Lord Thomas Howard, Admiral of England, who arrived from France with 1,000 men. Further encouraged by the Banner of Saint Cuthbert loaned them by the Bishop of Durham, the English pressed on towards the Scots on Flodden Hill. Surrey manoeuvred his army past the Scots, who watched in some astonishment, debating whether they should attempt to take him in flank as he moved on north. But they did nothing, and Surrey turned again and this time approached the Scottish position from the opposite direction, blocking any retreat towards Scotland. Branxton Hill lay between the armies, and there was just time for the Scots to pack up and move out in order to take the hill's summit before the English got there. There they formed up in five large phalanxes and, so organised, began the advance down the hill towards the English.

It was not a good idea. The Scots were heavily reliant on their long, fifteen-foot pikes which were employed much as they had been at Bannockburn, two centuries previously, to produce a thick wall of points against which cavalry could only hurl themselves in vain. But the ground was heavy and broken, the phalanxes lost cohesion and, once at the bottom in muddy ground which slowed manoeuvre, they came up against a new weapon, the eight-foot halberd or bill, an axe shaped with a spear point which, although shorter, was quite capable of dealing with the Scottish weapon. It was an infantry battle, the cavalry took little part and the artillery no more.

The Scots were badly mauled. Only the division commanded by the Earl of Home defeated its opponents, the Cheshire men under Surrey's younger son Edmund Howard. It was not enough. Particularly badly cut up was the division commanded by the Earls of Lennox and Argyll. Restive under the storm of English arrows, they broke ranks and were taken in flank and rear on the summit of Branxton Hill by Sir Edward Stanley and his men, who inflicted fearful casualties on the Highlanders, driving them pell-mell across the battlefield over the ground on which already the Scottish King lay stiff and stark.

The Scottish losses were horrendous. Of the twelve Earls of Scotland in the host, most were killed, as were a great number of lords and lesser gentry. Among the men of ordinary rank, the English bills had reaped a terrible harvest and swathes of bodies lay out, white-faced, in the rain, awaiting the attentions of birds or the victorious plunderers. It has been said that hardly a hamlet the length and breadth of Scotland did not suffer tragedy that day. Some 10,000 Scots, a third of the greatest hosting that Scotland had ever seen, did not return.

Clan Campbell was hard hit, even in comparison with the slaughter all around. The men from Argyll had been with their Chief in the division that had been broken and comprehensively destroyed. It is not easy to give a detailed account – even the identities of the chieftains of the clan at this time are not easy to discern, and the list of those who held lands of their own and who would have brought their men to follow Mac Cailein Mor when the summons came will not be complete. And not only Campbells from Argyll were among the fallen – Campbell of Loudoun was among the dead, as were his relations, George Campbell of Cessnock and Matthew Campbell also from Ayrshire. George Campbell, known for being the chief gardener of the King's great garden under the walls of Stirling Castle, is another name that has come down to us as being killed at the battle.

As regards the Argyllshire contingent, it is mainly a question of studying the surviving charters and noting those whose names cease to appear after the fatal date of 1513. Archibald Campbell of Lerags is thought to have been a survivor; his cross dated 1516 now stands by the narrow roadside leading down to the old Church of Kilbride, south of Oban – said to be built as an offering of thanks for his safe escape. His cousin John Campbell of Stronchormaig also seems to have come through,[46] as does his kinsman young Archibald Campbell of Inverawe.[47] Of most of the Campbell lairds of the day – they were still few in number – we do not know beyond doubt; what happened to Otter and Ormidale, to Barbreck, Inverliver, Ardkinglas, Ardentinny, Pennymore, Carnasserie or Torbhlaren remains uncertain and we may never know.

Campbell 'in' the Knap – still only a tenant rather than an owner, which would have qualified him for the title 'of' Knap – came through, as did MacIver Campbell of Lergahonzie. Campbell of Inverliver is a possible victim, and Dougall Campbell of Inverawe, father of Archibald, a probable one. But the Earl's brother, Thomas Campbell of Lundy, was certainly among the fallen, as were the Lairds of Duntroon[48] and, it is said, MacTavish of Dunardry. Other brothers fell in the fight together, John Campbell of Lawers, another son of Sir Colin Campbell of Glenorchy, and half-brother to the redoubtable Sir Duncan who was also killed. And as Sir Duncan Campbell of Glenorchy had followed his cousin and chief, Argyll, throughout his life, so he accompanied him in death, since, most grievous of all, Archibald Campbell, 2nd Earl of Argyll, *Mac Cailein Mor*, was among the slain, killed fighting at the head of his clan. The grieving survivors brought his body back to Argyll, and he and Glenorchy were both interred in the chapel at Kilmun.

CHAPTER NINE

The Clan: an Overall Survey

The end of the first volume of this History affords an opportunity to look at Clan Campbell overall, its composition and organisation and the progress it has made so far since its earliest appearance. In order to place this in context, an indication is also given of the heights to which in due course it was to rise.

The whole question of a Clan is one which is less clear than is desirable. For a start, the word *clann* in Gaelic has three meanings – children or offspring; descendants; clan or tribe.[1] It is the last meaning of a social/political/ military grouping that occupies most people's understanding today. In fact, the use of *clann* merely to denote a kindred was common in early society and meant no more than that, just as today the media are wont to describe the immediate family of the late President of the USA as 'the Kennedy Clan'. All 'clans' originally existed in the first two senses, while not all evolved into the third.

The problem has perhaps not been improved by the recognition over the years by the Lord Lyon of the day of Chiefs – either of 'Names' or of 'Clans' – who are so qualified for technical, armorial reasons, but whose name is one which was never that either of a single body or of one which operated as a clan on its own. The widespread use of patronymics in Scotland, whether in the Gaelic form of *Mac-* or the English *-son*, produced a host of surnames with totally different origins. To group all with a name of this type into a single 'Clan' makes historical nonsense.

Happily, the system is both flexible and remarkably sensible. It was possible to defuse the situation when Nicolson of Scorrybreac, chief of an ancient Hebridean clan of Norse origin, found himself placed under the banner of Lord Carnock as Chief of all the Nicolsons. Nicol is anyway far too popular a name for all users of the name to be of one blood, but Scorrybreac and his clan had nothing to do with the myriad other users of the name. Lyon recognised Scorrybreac as a separate Chief, and all is well, but the example does point up the potential for confusion.

169

Then there is the popular view of the Clan, which, nursed by romantic Victorianism and modern misconception, can often be extremely inaccurate. Some years ago, I was required to spend a whole morning in front of an audience at an historical seminar. I took for my subject 'The Clan' and gave three hour-long lectures, dealing with the subject from the actual, historical reality, from the official view of the Lord Lyon and from the general, popular view, with all its misconceptions. It was interesting that each of the three lectures overlapped the other two hardly at all.

The process that brought the Highland clans (there were others, south of the Highland line, notably in Dumfries and Galloway) into being is one which is far from clear. There were certainly power groupings in existence in very early times, and we know the tribal divisions of the early Scottish immigrants into Argyll not long after the major immigration of AD 500. The later evolution of tribes is shrouded in mystery until they begin to emerge in the later thirteenth and the fourteenth century. There are earlier mentions of clans – in the *Book of Deer* – a century and more earlier, but it may well be that the use of the word there denoted a kindred rather than an organised body. The Gaelic kindred or *Fine* was based on the head of the family, whose descendants formed a kindred until the end of the fourth generation when the kindred broke up and the process began again. There were different forms of succession to the Chiefship, which, instead of being confined to the eldest son of the eldest son, could go to anyone within the requisite degree of closeness to the main stem, being appointed by the reigning chief according to a system still in force in Lyon Court today known as tanistry. Failing this, a new chief could be appointed by a *derbhfine* of relatives who elected one of their number. The word is still used, in rather different form, today, for the duly qualified body within a chiefless clan who put forward a candidate to Lord Lyon for recognition as the temporary Commander of the Clan concerned, to act in place of the rightful Chief. Meanwhile, the Pictish succession seems to have been through the female line. These different systems were soon taken over by the feudal one which was virtually universal in Europe, but every now and then, in exceptional circumstances, it is possible to find a reversion to an older method of appointing a more suitable chief when the feudal system would have produced an incompetent successor.

In Argyll, the situation is confused. The old order was no doubt upset and changed by the invasion of the Norsemen and the setting-up of their kingdom or kingdoms along the western seaboard. It may be that the move by Kenneth MacAlpine to the east took much of the local nobility with him, leaving something of a vacuum behind. It is with the death of Somerled in 1164 and the splitting-up among his descendants of the rival kingdom he had managed to carve out of the Norse one that we see the first emergence of distinct clans as we know them today, the MacDougalls, the MacDonalds and the MacRuaris.

There must surely have been continuity from earlier times, although we lack exact information. Perhaps it is the old Celtic system of succession with its endless break and renewal, and perhaps it is the large number of incomers who came into the area and took over, that have made the picture so hard to discern. But continuity there must be; there is always a need for a fortified place to exert power, and its location remains the right one through the generations. Even if it is taken over by a newcomer lord, the people who lived there and worked there are still largely the same. A new owner, whether he took over by marriage, by parchment or by the sword, still needed people to run the place, and the old inhabitants remained. Only at the top of the table might the faces be different. Even there, the former rulers might still be seen, now acting as agents or managers for the new owners. So it is that we find the MacEachrans of Killellan and the Mackays of Ugadale acting as Mairs of Fee or Serjeants of South and North Kintyre respectively for the MacDonalds, and Fergusson of Glensellich as Officer of Strachur for the Campbells.

A possible analogy is that of drops of rain on a window-pane. Some run into each other to make a larger entity; smaller drops are swallowed and drained by larger ones, some grow to the extent they flow off the pane while others just wither and dry on their original spot. It could just be that a somewhat similar process saw the transformation of some small kindreds into the larger 'clans' that became prominent with an importance to which other family groups never aspired. The other conglomeration of power lay inland, in Cowal, Knapdale and Glassary where the descendants of the eleventh-century probable marriage of the O'Neill Prince Anrothan to the dynastic heiress of these districts gave rise in time to such clans as the MacLachlans and the Lamonts and the MacGilchrists of Glassary that straddled Loch Fyne.

From at least the early thirteenth century, the Campbells were inserted between these power groups along the north or west bank of Loch Awe. Whether as lords or as king's bailies, they were of little account and size. They seemed to get on well enough with their immediate neighbours, the MacNaughtons around the head of Loch Awe, the MacCorquodales, the clan that owned Glenorchy, later to become known as the Clan Gregor and the host of small kindreds that inhabited Argyll. During the period of which this volume treats, the major influence on the Campbells in their earliest days and their intermittent foes were the MacDougall Lords of Argyll; later, as Campbell power grew and they became the principal arm of Royal authority in the Western Highlands and Isles, it was the Lordship of the Isles and in particular the Clan Donald who became identified as their chief rivals and enemies. Rather as young plants struggle to compete for growing space, a clan could be restrained and even stifled to extinction by its neighbours. To succeed, there is bound to be pressure to survive, and there is little doubt the Campbells would have made uncomfortable neighbours. There is, however, little or no evidence at this early stage for the reputation for ruthless and devious behaviour by the Campbells so readily placed at their door by later popular mythology. It seems entirely fair to suggest that the Clan Campbell were neither nicer nor nastier than their neighbours – only perhaps more efficient!

For the transformation in size and power and wealth they were to achieve in a short 200 years, there have to be a number of factors. The first, it scarcely needs saying, is that of a line of chiefs equal to the task, backed by a sufficiently powerful clan. To achieve the second, the acquisition of land is vital; land not only could produce wealth in the form of surplus but it also produced the men necessary to exert military power. Among the many other factors required is political *nous*. Here the Campbells were well served, both by chiefs and by such leading chieftains as the Glenorchy Campbells. They did not allow their remote power base to cut themselves off from the centre of power in Scotland, and, to an extent unequalled by any of their actual or potential rivals, they managed to combine the roles of Gaelic potentates with those of major political figures at the Scottish Court. That is not to say that they always got it right or that they were always in favour – far from it – but they and their chiefs were always conscious that there was a world beyond the west coast, and they maintained a firm foothold in it. Largely through marriage, their chiefs also maintained close links with the most important families in Scotland, links which were of great advantage to them in a number of ways.

It is perhaps this maintained connection with the Lowland power centre that has sometimes given a somewhat equivocal aspect to the Campbells rather than their racial origins as Britons instead of Dalriadic Scots – the suggestion that they were not quite the genuine article. Many if not most of the Highland Clans, after all, were based upon incomers, including Somerled and his descendants whose claimed male descent was from an Irish line quite distinct from the old, Royal line of Scottish Dalriada. Even the clans of Cowal and Glassary who claimed to be of that blood could only do so in the female line; their male progenitor, although of impeccable lineage, was a comparatively late incomer to Argyll.

Outside events, politics and war, and the ability to shape them to advantage were other major factors. The impact of the Norse on the area, the Wars of

Independence and the later wars with the English, the over-mighty ambition of the Lords of the Isles – all offered both threat and opportunity, triumph for some and disaster for others. The early small size of the Campbells as a clan meant that their main objective was survival against overwhelming neighbours; as they grew, it was a question of finding themselves on the winning side and exploiting that fact, chiefly in the acquisition of forfeited lands and, in due course, by the appointment to offices that brought both power and wealth. Here lies one of the chief charges laid against the Clan, that they constantly turned their coats to ensure success. There is in fact remarkably little sign of this – and certainly no more than was prevalent among their competitors. The Campbell loyalty to the earlier Stewarts and then to the Reformed religion was steady, although there were of course individual exceptions. Nor is there any suggestion, in the years here under review, that the Campbells behaved in any way which was not matched by their neighbours. But their success was in due course to bring them much unpopularity, a notable trait in a nation which today is still intensely envious of the achiever, namely anyone who manages to raise themselves above the ruck by their own efforts.

The key figure in the success of a Clan is the Chief or, rather, the succession of Chiefs. Equally, no line of chiefs can hope to build a power base without a strong and devoted clan to follow them. Each depended on the other. The Chief was the father of his people; he was their leader in war, their provider of justice, and, perhaps, most importantly for their success as a body, the provider of land. It is clear that the eventual line of Campbell Chiefs did not emerge for some time. There were other contenders, it would seem, apart from the line of Lochawe. The 'official' genealogy *Ane Accompt* makes the Lochawe line one of chiefs from the earliest times, a necessary political claim with the feudal system of succession from father to eldest son, but one which did not obtain before the arrival of that system. While the line of Lochawe was no doubt close to the stem, it would not have been able to produce an unbroken line of chiefs or heads of the kindred as *Ane Accompt* has it. There seems nothing unusual in this, since other chiefly lines in other clans display exactly the same pattern with the chiefly line extending back well before the actual appearance of the clan on the stage of history.

From what information it is possible to obtain during the period of the Wars of Independence, there would seem to have been a number of contenders for leadership of the Clan both from outside and from within the line of Lochawe. Campbell of Strachur at one time seems a clear rival while, from within the Lochawe family, Sir Cailean Mor's son Neil was rivalled by his brother Sir Dougall. When a weak link was identified, there seems to have been little hesitation in replacing it in such cases as John Annam of Barbreck, reputedly the elder son of Colin Iongantach, who was rejected in favour of his brother Sir Duncan, as was Sir Duncan's other brother distinguished as 'Duncan the elder', from whom sprang the Campbells of Duntroon. The same fate befell Lord Ormelie, the eldest son and heir of the 1st Earl of Breadalbane, who was also passed over in view of his perceived inadequacy.

Quite what made Sir Cailean Mor 'Great Colin' is not entirely clear, and it is tempting to suspect that 'Mor' was merely a description of a robust physique – but then why have generations of Chiefs commemorated their descent from him as they have? Their record is a remarkable one – from a local figure in the wilds of Argyll to great magnates of state whose thoughts and actions were not only to sway the whole of Scotland but also in due course to have influence throughout the worldwide British Empire. It is difficult to pick out the essential characteristics that produced such a remarkable family record: it was not mere bravery or skill in military leadership, as the record of the family in these areas was by no means uninterruptedly brilliant; it was not intellectual power in every generation, nor was it the cohesion of their increasingly powerful clan, which on occasion came near to such disastrous dissension such as had rent the Clan Donald apart. While they displayed political sensitivity, they were by no means always on the winning side, and it is worthwhile reminding ourselves and others that two successive chiefs went to the scaffold in defence of their religious views. Already by the end of this volume, it is possible to see the devotion and affection felt by the clan for their chief together with great respect, not unmixed, even at this early stage, one suspects, with some fear. It is by no means inappropriate, given the extremes of veneration and hatred aroused by this remarkable family, that the two entries referring to the Chiefs of Clan Campbell in the index to *The Oxford Book of Quotations* under 'Argyll' should read

Argyll, the State's whole thunder born to wield
And shake alike the senate and the field

and, quite simply

The master-fiend Argyll.[2]

Next to the Chief were his immediate family. From an early stage, they were his closest companions and supporters. Once the estates were large enough, the chief provided for many of his closest siblings who were made into great magnates in turn, holding lands of their own and providing in due course for their own offspring. Not all younger sons were provided for in this way, and among the earliest branches were several where more than one generation had elapsed before the grant of lands seem to have been made. Whether, during the intervening period, the head of the house had been on the actual lands granted later to his descendants is impossible to say; he and his family may have acted as agents for the chief before they themselves became the owners of the lands concerned. If not, then it seems likely that they rendered service to the chiefs in other ways – military leadership seems a probable option. And then there was the Church, which always served as another alternative career for younger sons.

Some of the younger sons founded great houses of their own. Loudoun was an early example and one with which it has been difficult if not impossible to deal. The Campbells of Loudoun obviously thought of themselves as Campbells, and, when their main line came to an end with an heiress, she was very quickly married to another Campbell, a cadet of the Glenorchy branch, who was the first of the family to be ennobled as Earl of Loudoun. Even though Loudoun is not far from Ayr where successive Campbells of Loudoun held the position of Sheriff inherited from the original marriage of Donald Campbell and his Crawford wife, and although the Ayrshire coast is just across the water from Cowal and Kintyre, there seems always to have been a clear distinction between the Campbells in Argyll and those of Loudoun. The latter prospered and their landholdings grew in their own particular area of Scotland; their chieftains attained great positions in the state, but somehow their history is not that of a clan so much as that of a Lowland family, influenced by different neighbours, by a very much richer terrain and by the quarrels and alliances of an area far removed from the situation faced by their distant cousins further north.

The greatest branch after that of Lochawe was the family of Campbell of Glenorchy, later to be ennobled as Breadalbane. During the period covered by this volume, their support of the Lochawe family was total. At this stage, there is no sign of the antagonism that was to develop as their power and wealth grew. Founded no doubt on envy, this rivalry was still in evidence in the early years of the twentieth century; it very nearly brought down the whole of Clan Campbell, with the Glenorchy of the day prepared to go as far as murder in his desire for the chiefship. But this was still in the future. The other great branch, that of Cawdor, has only just emerged as this volume comes to a close. It, too, was to attain considerable importance, but, although like Loudoun it was based on an area far from Argyll, the family always kept a strong link with its earlier homeland.

It is difficult sometimes to place these great branches of the Clan in proper perspective since they eclipse so many well-known other clans in actual size and importance. It is hard to equate Breadalbane, for instance, as

a mere 'Chieftain' as opposed to the chiefs of the many small clans that
proliferate; perhaps an answer might be the recognition of Mac Cailein Mor
as a 'High Chief', as is the case with Lord MacDonald. Certainly, if many a
chief met with one of the greater Campbell lairds in a narrow city street, it
would not have been the Campbell who stepped off the pavement.

The question of chiefs and chieftains, of minor importance from a historical
point of view which would have been entirely pragmatic, assumes a different
aspect from the standpoint of Lyon Office and from the frantic world of
modern clannery. It also concerns those earlier branches off the main stem
which have long formed a *de facto* part of Clan Campbell. Whatever the true
origin of the Campbells of Craignish may have been, and it probably was a
Campbell one, they never show any sign of ever having considered themselves
or wanted to be anything other than members of the Clan.

The position with three other kindreds is less clear, with the recognition
by Lyon of the MacArthurs and the MacTavishes as Clans who at the
moment seem determined to claim a totally separate identity. They, along
with the MacIvers, possess patronymic surnames which are used by people
of completely different origins to each other. To pretend that all users of
any of these names ever formed a single clan is manifestly false; as far as
the MacIver Campbells, the Lochaweside MacArthurs and the Argyllshire
MacTavishes are concerned, it is clear that in earlier days they had no doubt
of their Campbell identity even if the details of their origins as set out in *Ane
Accompt* may owe more to political expediency than genealogical actuality.[3]
All three have displayed Campbell heraldry, and MacTavish of Dunardry's
use of the boar's head as crest and the motto 'NON OBLITUS' (*Not
Forgetful*) in answer to Mac Cailein Mor's injunction 'NE OBLIVISCARIS'
(*Do Not Forget*) shows an intention both on his part and that of the Lord
Lyon which is surely quite clear in defining his position.

Much is made of the contemporary use of the word 'Clan' in assessing the
status of these groups while apparently ignoring the use prevailing at the
time to denote no more than a related kindred. Such genealogies as we have
also include names of younger sons who appear fleetingly and tantalisingly,
sometimes in no more than a single entry. They are not necessarily
insignificant – one of the great mysteries is that of the Arthur Campbell who
might, had he managed to implement the terms of his charter, have found
himself chief over the large territory that was the portion of Somerled's
descendants the MacRuaris. Another mysterious figure is that of Duncan
Campbell of Glendouglas, whose importance in the Lennox was clearly
considerable. Had John, Earl of Atholl, son of Sir Neil of Lochawe, survived
Halidon Hill, the whole course of Campbell history would have been altered.

But it is those whose names we know and no more who present a problem. In some cases they were ancestors of the great Campbell branches, but of them themselves we know little or nothing.

Descent from an important line would certainly be a help in obtaining what in modern terms might be styled the management if not the ownership of lands, or a post in command of men for hosting or war, but it was not a guaranteed position; social mobility worked in both directions, and before long Campbells of blood as well as by name could find themselves in subordinate positions. It seems fair to suggest, however, that prior to the end of this volume in 1513 there was probably a dearth of Campbells of the blood to fill all the positions of command offered by the rate of expansion in territory and power obtained by successive chiefs and their immediate subordinates. The actual line of descent of the Lochawe family itself is a narrow one. From the time of the 3rd Earl onwards, it would appear that no lasting junior line was ever established and that, with one possible but unproven exception, should the present line fail for any reason, the succession to the chiefship and to the Earldom of Argyll would probably go all the way back to the Lochnell line, descended from the 3rd Earl in the early sixteenth century.

In all of this, land was of absolutely overwhelming importance. The geographic Highlands are very different from the Lowlands in the quality and amount of good land they contain; so much of the former is covered by unproductive rock and bog which even a plentiful supply of manpower could do nothing to make worthwhile. Not that manpower was at all plentiful until the eighteenth century, when such factors as the introduction of the potato as a plentiful food crop and the eradication of smallpox produced a population explosion. But for much of the period there was a limit on numbers further tightened by pestilence and by war. The Black Death swept through the Highlands as through the rest of Europe, and it was followed by other outbreaks. At various periods, townships are shown to be 'waste' where, for one or other of these factors, they were no longer viable. Within these limits, however, life was good enough. But the land and what it could bear was always a limitation on population and the standard of living it could enjoy. This underlines the essential importance of land not only as the provider of rents and the wealth that might be derived from them but even more importantly as the provider of subsistence for men who would act as followers and provide vital armed strength.

Rents might be paid in the form of corn or of bestial or in the form of cheese – one of the relatively long-lasting forms of agricultural produce. Much of this rental would be recycled back to the producers by the Chief or

Lord, in the form of feasting that was such a traditional expression of status in Gaelic culture, as was the provision of hospitality on a grand scale. Much of the remainder would be used to support the Chief's immediate tail of retainers, another expression of his status. It was not a money economy, but it did export the surplus of cattle on the hoof, hides, salt fish and the like. With the beginnings and growth of the great cities, indeed, the cattle trade grew to major importance in the life of the Highlands; already it was a significant factor.

It is often suggested that Clan Campbell achieved its expansion of territory by less than honourable means. In fact there is no discernible trace of that in the story so far, although attempts are made to invest the murder of John Stewart, Lord of Lorne, with sinister overtones. To this writer they are hardly convincing. The Crown was the main source of grants of land, usually as a reward for loyalty and for services rendered. King James II gave the lands of Lawers to Campbell of Glenorchy for the arrest of one of his father's murderers and Glenorchy passed it to a younger son of his, thus establishing yet another important branch of the Clan. Many of the grants were from relatives or connections; this particularly applied to lands in the district of Cowal, where marriage connections with the Stewarts and their descendants the Menteiths led to the transfer of much land to the Campbells. This was at a time when the interests of the two other families were diverted elsewhere and the Campbells of Lochawe were seen as the successors best able to maintain tranquility in the area.

Marriage was also a very important factor in bringing fresh possessions to the Clan. Loudoun came by Campbell marriage to an heiress, as did Glenorchy and Cawdor. Untimely death removed the earldom and lands of Atholl which had come by marriage to the King's sister; and, had fortune proved kinder, the lands of Clan Ruari in Garmoran and, later, the lands of the Dunvegan Macleods would also have come into Campbell possession. The Lordship of Lorne did not come by marriage as is so often thought, but its acquisition may certainly have been eased by it. Purchase or mutually beneficial financial arrangements were not ruled out, while the Church also played a part, even before the Reformation, when such a well-placed cleric as Donald, Abbot of Coupar, son of the 2nd Earl of Argyll, was able to provide for a clutch of unofficial offspring out of the Church lands over which he was in charge. The Campbell lands were spread right across Scotland and lay far beyond the contiguous counties of Argyll, Perthshire and Dunbartonshire. At this early stage, there do not seem to have been any in England, a source of so much conflict of loyalty for many Scottish magnates during the Wars of Independence.

So much for the Chiefs and their immediate family and the steadily expanding gentry of the Clan. But the Clan as a whole was never confined to those of the name or blood of Campbells. The modern sept system, designed as much to maximise customers for the various clan tartans and Clan Societies as for any resemblance to historical truth, does, however, confuse what actually did happen. As already described, the bulk of a clan was made up of the *nativi*, the Native Men who had long inhabited the area and who continued on there under a new Lord if the previous one was dispossessed. MacIlvernock of Oib was given the grandiloquent style of 'Hereditary Trumpeter to Campbell of Auchinbreck' and held one half of the property of Oib at the head of Loch Sween – *Oib-MacIlvernock* – the other half being called by then *Oib-Campbell* to differentiate it. His trumpet did apparently exist down to the nineteenth century, but it and MacIlvernock's duties of blowing it to summon the people of the area to attend Auchinbreck's Baron Courts held in the field below the church at Kilmichael-of-Inverlussa surely hid the fact that his predecessors had themselves been the possessors of the lands and responsible for the good behaviour and well-being of all those inhabiting them.

So too, lower down the social scale, the clan lands presented a very different truth from that encouraged by the limitations of 'clan maps' and by popular modern clannery. The point may be made by a closer look, taking as random example a 1592 rental of Craignish. This lists the individual farms and the occupants of each. It will be noted that where there are Campbells – not always immediately identifiable as such due to the use of patronymics – they are at the head of the list and were obviously the chief tenants.

Craignish
Angus M'Ean Roy Beg (Campbell)
Donald M'Ean Roy
Donald Bane M'Grassich
Dougall M'Ewair VcKarin
John M'Kynych
Ewin M'Gillespie Ure
Ewine Dow M'Kaik
John VcGilmernock

Pennycastell
Ranald Campbell of Barrichbeyan
Gillechallum M'Agowne
John M'Chairlich VcEan VcGilchallum

Donald M'Olchallum VcDonell
Allestar M'Cleriche

Ardcraignish
George M'Barroune ('Son of the Baron') – a Campbell
Duncan M'Donnell VcDonchie
Donald M'Donchie VcDonill
Donald Ger M'Donill Dannay
Dougall M'Donill VcDonchie
John M'Gilchallum VcDonnill

Corvoranmore
Molcallum M'Feroquhair
Ewir M'Donchie VcFeroquhair
Gillespic M'Gilmartin
John M'Sennykessage

No doubt the list above hides a number of Campbells who were not using their surname, but it serves to make the point very clearly as to the actual composition of the Clan. Clansmen showed their allegiance by the payment of the *Calp* to their Chief, usually the best beast in the family's possession when the head of the family died. Sometimes the recipient was also their landlord, but not always, and they might pay *Calp* to one and rents to the other. If it came to divided loyalties during a campaign, whether local or national, it would have been very difficult to do other than to follow the local lord whatever the name one was born with – that is, if you wished to go on living in the same place. This explains the apparently odd appearance of Campbells in strange hostile company, as it does for odd surnames in the ranks of the Campbells.

Mention of the social scale points up the fact that, contrary to much modern popular opinion, Highland society was clearly structured with a defined hierarchy. While shared descent and kinship was of great importance and while good manners acknowledged all such links, there was nevertheless a distinct consciousness of rank. This structure can be traced back to early Gaelic society in Ireland as revealed by various surviving Old Irish law texts. These include the *honour price*, a system which assigned to much of society a value for the position they occupied which can thus be compared with those in other walks of life. The standard measure of value was the *set* which equated with one half the value of a milch cow or ounce of silver, while six *sets* equalled one *cumal* which had the value of one female slave.

There were four grades of King and four grades of Lord. The High King of Ireland was beyond pricing, but a provincial King was rated at eighty-four *sets* while the fourth grade of King, of whom there were some 150, was rated at forty-two *sets*. Very roughly, these last might be equated with the smaller clan chiefs in the Highlands. Below them, the four grades of Lord, or *Laird* as we might prefer, ranged from honour prices of thirty to ten *sets*. Ranked alongside the landholding classes were the dignitaries of the Church. An Archbishop, indeed, or the Abbot of one of the great monasteries, was rated at eighty-four *sets*, the same price as that of a provincial King, while a Bishop at forty-two *sets* equalled the lowest grade of King. A Deacon at thirty *sets* was rated the same as the top-ranking Laird, while a sub-Deacon at twenty *sets* and an ordinary Priest at nineteen and a half were on a par with the second rank. Below them came the intriguingly named Exorcist on fifteen *sets*. Even a lowly Usher was ranked at ten *sets*, the same as the smallest class of Lord, and a mere Lector, the lowest rank given in the church hierarchy, rated seven *sets*.

Thereafter come the learned professions. It is most interesting to see which are rated and how they compared with each other. The only one to be compared with the first two categories is that of the *Fili* or Poets, whose original role and status was far greater than it became with the arrival of Christianity. The composition of satire was held to be near-magic and could even kill its victim; poets were also historians and soothsayers; their powers were uncanny and were neither to be wielded lightly or ignored. A Master Poet or *Ollam* was rated at forty-two *sets*, the same as a provincial King or a Bishop, while below him were seven grades, down to the merest beginner who still qualified for one *set*. Bards were reckoned to be of lighter weight; they were the providers of pop music as opposed to the classical compositions of the Poets; they lacked the element of fear and mystery wielded by the latter and were accordingly rated at half the value of their fellow composers. After them, the highest-rated profession would seem to be that of Wright; four basic skills are given them – construction of a church, of a mill and of a boat, and the art of working in yew wood. The possession of one of these skills gave an honour price of seven *sets*; of all four, fifteen *sets*, while one graded as a Master Wright was rated at twenty *sets*. Thus it is hardly surprising that the craft gave its name to an entire clan – the Macintyres or *Sons of the Wright*.

The legal profession came next. There were also three grades here; the top one, for a 'Judge of three languages', demanded expertise in traditional law, canon law and poetry, receiving a rating of fifteen *sets*. Canon law was not required for the second grade, rated at ten *sets*, while the junior grade, given seven *sets*, was for judges dealing with matters for craftsmen. Other professions were also rated. Possibly because of a limited rate of success, all physicians were given a rating of seven *sets* whatever their seniority, the same rating being awarded to Black-, Copper- and Silver-smiths. Harpers were rated at five *sets*, but there was at this time no ranking for pipers.

This system in earlier Ireland has been given in some detail, for it seems in large measure to have been brought to Scottish Dalriada; the categories it deals with are still very much in evidence in the West Highlands and Isles at the period with which we are dealing.[4] It reveals a whole hierarchical system of status detached from the parallel qualifications of landowning and leadership in war. The skills for such classification were varied, and, as in Ireland, so in Scotland they led to much interchange; once professional standing was achieved by a family, members of that family might well change their calling in order to keep their learned status. Some skills were very close: writing skills at the early stages were almost exclusively in the hands of those trained for the church, so in time the church led to the secretarial and to the emerging legal profession. The position of poet became merged with that of bard and sennachie. The church in fact was wont to recruit its members from all sorts of professions. There was also a strong connection between Ireland and Scotland, with many of the great professional families only recently having crossed the North Channel.

The skills themselves were handed on largely verbally within the family, some of whom, however, might also hold collections of learned manuscripts. These skills were treated, it appears, as a precious family inheritance which was not broadcast to outsiders. Some of the greatest families had skills that allowed them independence from the patronage of a great Lord – the medical skills of the Beatons were so great that they were able to establish more than a dozen branches of the family spread from Ulster to Sutherland to Angus, all practising the art of medicine. Most skilled practitioners, however, were more locally confined and relied on the patronage of a Chief who would reward them for their services by the grant of land, which would provide for their subsistence. In turn, the fame and the number of his dependent learned kindreds would redound to the credit of the Chief concerned and enhance his status.

Most of the learned professions listed as having an honour price can be identified in Argyll. While, for instance, the Lords of the Isles had their great family of poets and sennachies, the MacVurichs, most famous of all, the Campbells of Argyll had their MacEwans. This family has on occasion had a MacDougall origin ascribed to it, but its repeated use of the name Arne – *Athairne* – echoes the practice of the Irish bardic family O'Hosey, and it seems most likely that in the same way as the MacVurichs were an offshoot of the Irish O'Dalys and the Morrisons, poets to the Maclean Chiefs, of the

Irish O'Muirgeasains, the MacEwans had arrived in Argyll from the other side of the North Channel. This family has nothing to do with the MacEwans of Otter on Loch Fyne. They first appear on record when, in 1558, Colin Campbell of Glenorchy granted the two merklands of Barmolloch, in Lorne, to *Eugenius M'Duncan M'Arne* and his son *Arnaldus M'Ewin M'Duncan VcArne – jocularites vulgariter rymours* – 'commonly known as poets'. They were only required to pay a penny as rent, but this was to be increased to four merks should they fail to carry out their hereditary duties as bards, sennachies and genealogists to the Earls of Argyll.[5]

Then in 1567, the six merklands of Kilchoan, also in Lorne, were granted by Dougall MacDougall of Dunollie to *Ewine makdonichie vcArne poet* and *Arne MacEwine* his son.[6] *Duncan M'Ewin V'Neill V'Arn*, witness at Dunstaffnage in 1597, must have been a member of the same family.[7] In 1626, Archibald MacLachlan of Craigenterive enters a contract with *Neil Makewine Makdonichie VcArne* in Nether Lorne, who by the following year had inherited Kilchoan; but around 1630 he had to dispose of the lands to MacLachlan of Craigenterive, himself a hereditary servant of the House of Argyll. Neil died around 1650 and, according to Duke Niall, he was the last of his family.[8] This was the family whose version of the pedigree formed the base for *Ane Accompt of the Genealogie of the Campbells. The Book of the Dean of Lismore* contains a poem lamenting the MacDougall Chiefs by *Eoghan Mac Eoin Mheic Eichthighearna*, who may have been one of them.[9]

Another probably related kindred was that of the MacEwan harpers, who must have diversified into this other, lesser, profession. As we have seen, this movement between the different skills was by no means uncommon, a path followed by two other musical families connected with the Campbell Chiefs – the MacVicars and the MacKellars, who alternated music with more robust skills. According to a letter written in 1802 by Patrick MacVicar to James Ferrier, the Duke's Chamberlain, asking for land or jobs for his MacKellar nephews, 'Even before the Reformation as well as since, the MacKellars of Glen Shira on the one hand and the MacVicars in Glenaray on the other were looked on by the Noble Family of Argyll as a kind of Life Guard almost within cry'.[10]

The MacKellars had long been hereditary harpers and musicians to the Chief, while *Brayne MacVicar Cytharista* (Harper) appears in 1549.[11] The MacVicars, as their name suggests, were also, perhaps more often, employed as churchmen, writers and notaries in the service of the Argyll family. It may have been one of the former who appears at the King's court in 1506, where as *the Erle of Ergile's clarsha* (from *clarsach*, the Gaelic for the Highland harp) he is paid the sum of fourteen shillings; this was repeated early the next year. On the latter occasion, 'Duncan Campbell's bard' was paid the sum of five shillings. Both the Earl of Argyll's piper and his harper were among the captives taken at the Battle of Glenlivet in 1594.

Probably the most famous holder of the post is 'The Little Harper' – the ghost of a boy killed either by Montrose's men or possibly by the Athollmen a generation later when they occupied the castle at Inveraray. No-one seems quite sure, and the actual castle of today is some distance away from the site of the old one, a detail which does not seem to worry the young instrumentalist, the strains of whose playing are still heard from time to time. My grandfather heard him while staying as a guest at the castle; on a wet day, he was writing letters in the library when he heard, far away, a sweet sound of music, hard to define but soft to the ear, which went on and on. He thought it might have been the wind spattering the drops from the eaves, but, when he mentioned it at lunch, Duke Niall exclaimed 'Oh, but that's the Little Harper!' Other great harper families in Argyll were the O'Shennogs, *MacilShenaich* or Shannons, who held lands in Kintyre for their services in this capacity to the Lords of the Isles. The MacBhreatnichs – 'Sons of the Briton' – or Galbraiths, who had come from Loch Lomondside, were also players. So too were the family of MacEwans, already mentioned, who worked for the Lamont chief and who went with a daughter of that house to Lude in Atholl; the Lude Harp exists to this day.

There do not seem to be any families of hereditary pipers in Mac Cailein Mor's service, although there have been plenty of notable piping families in the area. One of them, 'the Campbells of Nether Lorne', came into prominence in later piping circles with their system of recording pipe music in *can-ntaireachd* – by which different vocal syllables are used for the various notes. Their first known ancestor, Donald, had been MacDonald of Glenalladale's piper at Culloden and had carried his employer from the field; he later took service under Campbell of Carwhin – later to succeed as Breadalbane – at Ardmaddy, who sent him for instruction by Patrick Oig MacCrimmon. It was Donald's son Colin who was the writer of the canntaireachd manuscript, while his grandson, John, who won the Highland Society of London's Gold Medal at the great piping competition at Falkirk in 1819, was employed by Walter Frederick Campbell of Islay as his piper and later taught J. F. Campbell of Islay to speak Gaelic. In 1816, the family offered their manuscript books to the Highland Society of London, who could not understand its import and refused. As luck would have it, the books surfaced again in 1909 and this time found their way to the Piobaireachd Society, who have used the pibrochs the books contain, eighty-three in one and eighty-six in the other, in their magisterial series of publications. A third volume has gone missing.[12]

While the Beatons were the most famous family of physicians in the Highlands, the Campbells had as their particular medical family the MacLachlans of Craigenterive. Again, their origin is somewhat mysterious; they are thought not to be MacLachlans from Loch Fyne, although the head of the cadet branch of Innischonnel was to follow the Jacobite MacLachlan of MacLachlan to the '45, where he was killed at Culloden (he was a Roman Catholic). The family are first on record in the later 1400s and were granted the lands of Craigenterive between Ford and Kilmartin by 1512. It is probably a member of the family who witnesses a charter of the 1st Earl 'at our manor of Inneraora' in 1470 as *Angus Medicus*. The family used the work-name *Leich* – 'Leech', now Leitch – as physicians were often referred to, and the name MacLachlan does not seem to appear until after *Lauchlan leyche Makane vcAngus of Craigyntyrf*, who flourished in the 1530s.

Duke Niall was of the opinion that they were of Campbell origin, basing the theory on the existence of Campbells who were doctors, such as 'Archibald Leche alias Campbell' who appears at Cairnbaan in 1568, and 'Colin Campbell Leiche of Duntraffie or Dunteraffe' who witnesses a charter of the 6th Earl's in 1582. The key point is whether 'Dunteraffe' is a scribe's botched attempt at 'Craigenterive'. Certainly, Dunderave was in MacNaughton hands by this date, and I know of no Campbell who ever possessed it nor of any place name which resembles either of the two versions above. Duke Niall suggested that the surname MacLachlan derived from the above-mentioned Lachlan who, with his wife, had a charter in 1529 from the Earl of a house and garden in Inveraray to them and their heirs being skilled in the medical art whom failing their nearest heir whomsoever who was so skilled.[13] Obviously, however rudimentary their art, it was even then comforting to have a doctor close at hand.

This possible Campbell connection may be a long shot, particularly as the family themselves never made any claim to being such even when it would have been of undoubted use to them, and they used arms based on those of MacLachlan of MacLachlan.[14] It is, however, worth noting that when the MacArthurs were sacked as Keepers of the old Campbell stronghold of Innischonnell for theft in 1613, it was a cadet branch of the MacLachlans of Craigenterive who took their place, combining it with the undoubtedly profitable office of malt-making for Over and Middle Loch Awe *and Brousterie of Ail and Acquavity within the bounds*. The MacArthurs were anciently of the same blood as the Campbells, and it can be queried whether a post of such symbolic importance as the custody of Innischonnell would ever be given to one who was not of Campbell stock.

The other famous branch of the MacLachlans of Craigenterive was that of the MacLachlans of Kilbride, in Lorne, a famous family of churchmen and antiquaries whose collection of manuscripts, several of them early medical treatises, is now in the National Library of Scotland, having come, according to an intriguing legend, from the great library at Iona which was broken up and destroyed at the Reformation. Their contribution to the Church was exceptional for a single family to the extent that in the mid-1600s they were providing ministers for no fewer than six of the parishes in Argyll.[15]

Another medical family who operated under Campbell patronage was that of the O'Connachars, who were again probably of Irish origin as their name suggests. They held the property of Ardeoran for their services for several generations from the mid-1500s onwards. They seem to have been attached to the MacDougalls of Dunollie as well as to the Earls of Argyll. When John Campbell, younger of Cawdor, had to be adjudged insane in 1639, it was *Duncan O'Conchobair* who attended him. The family were still at Ardeoran in the eighteenth century, although by that time there is no sign of their still being engaged in medicine.[16]

Yet another learned family was that of the MacPhails in Muckairn, who may also have been there for some time since their patrons were the MacDougalls of Dunollie and the later Campbells of Cawdor. *Dubhghall Albannach mac mhic Phail* – 'Dougall MacPhail the Scot' – contributed a number of West Highland families to the famous Irish collection of genealogies known from its believed date as 'MS 1467'. From him descended a family of clerics and a doctor, in Eoghan Og MacPhail, *mediciner and servitor* to Sir Donald Campbell of Ardnamurchan in 1632.[17] The family was particularly attached to the MacDougalls of Dunollie and then to the Campbells of Barbreck.[18]

This connection between the Church and other learned professions was very marked at a time when reading and writing was largely confined to those trained by the church; this led to diversification into the field of what was eventually to become the legal profession. In particular, there is frequent mention of the post of 'servitor', which should really be translated in modern terms as 'personal assistant' and which was of considerably greater importance and status than its title might at first suggest, combining the role of 'right-hand man', lawyer, secretary and general aide. These posts could be of considerable importance to the holder; both MacArthur of Terivadich and MacUghtre of Kildalvan were granted their estates in the early 1500s for their services to the Earls of Argyll as men of business; both came of families long associated with the Church. MacArthur, indeed, was transmogrified not only into a Laird of some substance but into a Clan Chief as well (see Appendix 3, 'Septs'). Something of the kind can also be seen at the end of the same century, when Mr Donald Campbell, an illegitimate son of Campbell of Cawdor who had been put to the Church, found himself in charge of clearing up the situation which followed his father's assassination in 1592. This brought him into close contact with the young Earl, whom he thereafter followed as his tireless supporter both in the field and in the council chamber. He ended up as Sir Donald Campbell of Ardnamurchan and founder, through his granddaughter's marriage to his nephew, of a family, the Campbells of Airds, who in 1751 were rated among the twenty-five most wealthy in Argyll.

As can be seen, the Campbells took over a number of hereditary professionals from their previous patrons, particularly from the MacDougall Lords of Lorne. Another such example is that of the Livingstones, Barons of the *Bachuil*, or Crozier, of Saint Moluag, contemporary of Saint Columba. This is still in their possession, as are the lands on the island of Lismore which they held as recompense for their hereditary task. The Baron of the Bachuil is said to have been the Earl of Argyll's Standard-bearer, and in 1544 a *John M'Mollemore vic Evir* appears in a charter of the Earl's as *Signifero nostro*.[19] In the Latin of the schoolroom, 'signifer' was always 'standard-bearer', the officer who carried the Eagle, but in later usage it was also used for the junior rank of Herald, the Pursuivant. The late Sir Thomas Innes of Learney, a great Lord Lyon, claimed that the term was used in this sense and that the Baron of the Bachuil was the private Officer of Arms to the Chief of Clan Campbell just as some other great lords had and still have their own heraldic officers – the Earl of Erroll's Slains Pursuivant, the Countess of Mar's Garioch Pursuivant and the Earl of Crawford's Endure Pursuivant.[20]

The only possible reference I have come across to such a figure in the Earl of Argyll's retinue occurs in 1548, when, in a letter of 7 March, Palmer writes to Somerset:[21] 'Also on Saturday last, the Governor's and Rothes' pursuivants were with him (Argyll) at St. Johnstone, whence he despatched them *with one of his own*, to the Governor next day . . .' (author's italics). But it seems far more likely that the Livingstones were standard-bearers, the standard being the precious relic of Saint Moluag which they guarded, and that, in the same way that Bruce had ordered the *Quigrich*, the Crozier of Saint Fillan, to be brought to the Scots army before Bannockburn in order to raise the morale of the troops, so the *Bachuil* was on great occasions borne into battle to encourage the MacDougalls and then, when they took over, the ranks of Clan Campbell.

Lesser chieftains and Lairds within Clan Campbell also had their hereditary retainers; *Mac-a-Chrosgraich* was hereditary standard-bearer to Campbell of Ardkinglas. He was really a MacArthur, one of several brothers who had had to flee after a fight in which a man was killed.[22] The MacIsaacs were armour-bearers to the Campbells of Craignish. Perhaps most remarkable is the family of MacKillops who were hereditary standard-bearers to the Campbells of Dunstaffnage. They were for centuries right-hand men to the Captain of the day and were proud of their right to carry the head of the coffin at the funeral of each Dunstaffnage. When Michael, Captain of Dunstaffnage, was laid to rest some years ago in a colourful ceremony, there was no MacKillop present since the present holder of the post, much to his chagrin, was himself too ill to attend.[23]

Then there were a host of other appointments which performed necessary services and which were rewarded by a living; the great forest of Stratheck between Glendaruel and Dunoon provided much sport and venison for the Chief and his family. At Conchra in Glendaruel lived a family of MacLachlans who held the lands in recompense for their task as the Kennel-keepers in charge of the hounds for the chase. A family of Campbells held the lands of Torrans at the south end of Loch Awe, where they acted as Fishers at that end of the loch, providing salmon and trout for Mac Cailein Mor. The MacPhederans were for centuries in possession of the lands of Sonachan, further up the loch where they were the hereditary ferrymen, a post which brought a lucrative income. Legend has it that they had ferried King Robert the Bruce back from Rathlin Island and he had rewarded them for this service; another story is that the gift had been from the Campbell Chief whose son they had saved from drowning when a sudden storm blew up on the loch. The two tales are not necessarily incompatible. In any case, as early as 1439, Domenicus M'Federan had a charter of confirmation of the one merkland of Sonachan and the rights of the ferry from Sir Duncan Campbell of Lochawe.

The family continued on until the seventeenth century, when after a considerable fight with their Campbell neighbours they sold up and Sonachan became a property belonging to the Campbells of Cawdor. They too, it would appear, were a skilled family who diversified, being related to the MacPhederans who were noted smiths and armourers in Benderloch. Their forge was near the present Barcaldine House, at Ferlochan, and their swords were particularly prized.[24] The *Cormacus MacPhaterin* who is commemorated on a stone of fourteenth- or fifteenth-century date at Keills on Loch Sween in Knapdale may well be of this race; under the patronage of the powerful Lords of Castle Sween the area became a gathering place for craftsmen.[25]

Another, less important family of ferrymen were the MacInturners or Turners who held the post at the mouth of the River Awe, where they had long been employed by the Campbells of Inverawe. In fact they had been there before the Campbells arrived in 1485, according to the old saying *Bha*

Tamhus Tuairneir air fhichead naim fir aiseag aig rudha thiriagach agus bha fichead MacDhonachaidh nan tighearna air Inbhir-Atha – 'There was twenty-one Tavus Turners, ferrymen and there was twenty MacDonachies, Lairds of Inverawe'.[26] According to the Rev. John MacInnes, the Earls of Argyll had two hereditary families of boatbuilders under their patronage, the MacGilleChonnails on Loch Awe and the MacLucases on Loch Fyne.[27] The MacLucas connection is one I have been unable to make, but research into the MacGillechonnels led to correspondence with Dr Donald MacWhannell (the modern spelling of the name) and the gradual uncovering of a fascinating story. The MacGillechonnels may well have built galleys for the Campbell Chiefs on Loch Awe; a tombstone on the Isle of Inishail shows a boat together with a joiner's adze, as does a tombstone in Craignish where the name is also early on record. But by the seventeenth century, the family's boatbuilding efforts were concentrated at Dunstaffnage, and their bills are preserved in the Argyll Archives. Some of them went east with Campbell of Glenorchy, and the family prospered in the central Highlands. But it appears that their earliest origins may lie in Galloway, where there are very early traces of them, and it may be that they are one of the families who used the great sea-route from Dublin right up the west coast, for there is a Ballimacilchonell just by the location of today's lighthouse on the Mull of Kintyre, where seventeenth-century M'Ilchonnels are to be found. And there were M'Ilchonnels among the victims of the Massacre of Dunaverty in 1646.[28]

Then there were the Macnabs of Barachastlain, by Dalmally, descended from a younger son of the Macnab chief, who were famed for their skills as jewellers and armourers, important because of the status their artefacts conferred. According to the family tradition, Duncan, younger son of Macnab of Macnab, set off for the Holy Land with Sir Colin Campbell of Glenorchy, to whom his brother was standard-bearer, stopping off in northern Italy where he learnt the craft of making swords. On his return, he was given the task of supervising the building of Kilchurn Castle. This version may or may not be true; others have it that the Macnabs had been smiths and jewellers long before Sir Colin's time, but there is no doubt that they long served both the Macnab Chiefs and the Campbells of Glenorchy.[29] But all these are people of some status in the Clan, providing services to their patrons and, by doing so, emphasising the importance and standing of the magnates who were able to support them.

In a different category were the Broken Men – men from Broken Clans who had become detached from their ancestral leaders or who had never had a Chief of their own. They roamed the land, stopping off where there was opportunity for profit in whatever form. When the Crown clamped down on the prevalent state of lawlessness, they made the magnates, Chiefs, Chieftains, landlords or Bailies responsible for all the men on their lands and at the same time made the rootless wanderers find themselves a Chief. The lot of the Broken Man outside his own people or without his own Chief to take care of him was not easy. The prime example is that of the MacGregors, whose chief did not have the lands with which to support his people; they as a result would attach themselves where they could, but always at the end of the queue and with the obvious attraction of unlawful ways of improving their lot – a vicious circle that was to cost them dear. Nor were the Campbells totally immune; there is the tale of the Campbell family away up in Uist, where they were known locally as *Sgriob a Chabair*, a reference to the furrow made by their roof-tree, their only personal possession – a valued one in areas where good timber was scarce – which they were allowed to keep as their former house was given to someone else and they dragged it off to a new site, still further on the edge of the community.[30]

But if Broken Men were a potential cause of nuisance, they were also an addition to the numbers who followed the leader to whom they attached themselves. It is interesting to see that, when in 1587 the government were making strenuous efforts to improve the state of law and order in the Highlands and they published 'The Roll of the Names of the Landlordis and Baillies of landis in the Hielandis quhair Broken men hes duelt and presentlie duellis', the list includes the Campbell Lairds of Glenorchy, Lawers, Ardbeiche, Glenlyon, Lochnell, Cawdor, Inverawe, Auchinbreck, Ardkinglas, Barbreck, Duntroon, Ellangreig and Otter besides the Earl of Argyll himself. This comprises over 15 per cent of the total number of names included on the list, which covers the whole Highland mainland; it is a remarkable proportion for a single clan. On the other hand, it has to be admitted that the Campbells are listed among the clans providing Broken Men elsewhere in a similar Act of Parliament of 1594.[31]

So much for the constituent parts of the Clan which ranged from the Chiefs themselves through the heads of the great houses, several of whom were to all intents and purposes Chiefs themselves, through the lesser lairds who descended from younger sons and younger sons of younger sons to those of good blood who had to earn a living in less exalted ways. As time went on, those of the blood spread right through society and mingled with those of other names who had, perhaps, been on the land long before the arrival of the Campbells. As with all centres of power, craftsmen and professionals attached themselves to the Chief and his most important followers, who became their patrons, as did lesser kindreds who found themselves under the shadow of the Campbells. Lastly, as we have seen, were the Broken Men.

One classification which this work tends to avoid is that of 'Chieftain', a rank which has assumed great importance in today's Clan 'system'. This is applied to the heads of the great houses which go to make up the branches of the clan. It has never been satisfactorily defined and within different clans appears to have different meanings in the modern sense. In earlier times, the word seems to have been interchanged on occasion with the title of chief; nowadays, while the heads of great houses may be easily enough recognised, the usage differs – Maclean of Duart, for instance, having proclaimed a number of Maclean chieftains who include, for instance, a distinguished younger son of a younger son of one branch, rather than the head of that branch itself. Lyon, on occasion, has suggested that the holding of a territorial designation for three generations is sufficient requirement for the rank of chieftain. While that may be the case in smaller clans, the Campbells became so powerful and extended over so much territory that over 200 Campbell Lairds could, on that basis, claim to be chieftains. That recalls the Gilbert and Sullivan ditty 'When everybody's somebody, then nobody's anybody'! Our present Chief has declined to be drawn into the question and does not 'recognise' any Chieftains, but it is quite certain that the heads of such great Campbell Houses as Breadalbane, Cawdor, Loudoun, Inverawe and at least half a dozen others equalled, if they did not surpass in actual power and importance, many of the Chiefs in the rest of Scotland. From a historical point of view the question is unimportant, but it has assumed great weight in the modern world of largely overseas Clan ceremonial where, for instance, the wearing of feathers in the bonnet to denote 'rank' has become a major issue.

Another rank, if that is what it is, which is often written about is that of 'tacksman'. A 'tack' was a lease by which land was rented out, with preference being given to the gentlemen of the Clan. It has been claimed that the officers of the clan regiment were drawn from this class. This may have been true in smaller clans where the supply of land at the Chief's disposal was limited, but in Clan Campbell there would appear from an early stage to have been enough land for cadet branches to become heritable possessors or 'Lairds' in their own right. Tacks certainly did exist, but they seem in most cases to have gone to a lower stratum of society, and certainly a mere tacksman would have been unlikely to have been given a company to command in any turnout of the Clan Campbell for war.

A good deal is known of the Council of the Isles who helped the Chief of Clan Donald maintain control over his wide dominions. Efforts have been made to identify a similar body operating in the case of the Clan Campbell. It is not easy to judge how succesful they have been; from the mid-1500s at least, there is mention of 'The Friends of Argyll' or 'The Friends', who are consulted on occasion by the Earl. There does not seem to be much evidence for the formal setting-up of such a body which seems as often as not to be consulted on what appears to be a rather *ad hoc* basis when there is need for money to be raised. One such example is the occasion when, in February 1559, a bond was entered into by the 'Lords, barons and gentlemen, special friends of Archibald, earl of Argyll, to aid him in the journey laid to his charge by the Queen towards the parts of France and to pay 20 shillings from each merkland'. There are nineteen signatures, among them

> John Campbell, Bishop Elect of the Isles; John Campbell, Commendator of Ardchattan; Colin Campbell of Ardkinglas; John Campbell of Cyprus; John Campbell; John Stewart (of Appin?) Lamont of that Ilk, MacLachlan of MacLachlan; John MacLachlan of —; MacDougall of Dunollie.[32]

Another list of signatures appended to 'Heads and Articles to be sent to theLord Regent's Grace for advice of kin and friends convened in Inveraray, with Lairds of Glenorchy and Ardkinglas', a document also endorsed 'Article by 6th Earl of Argyll in prescence of his Barons, anent the Crown Jewels', would suggest some more formal kind of summons to attend, but the lists of signatories seem to vary somewhat; another example, an agreement in 1564 between the Earl of Argyll and Campbell of Boquhan, Campbell of Glenorchy and others to support action against MacGregor of Glenstrae, is signed among others by the chief protagonists and the Lairds of Auchinbreck, Ardkinglas, Lochnell, Ardgartney, Barbreck and Inverliver.[33] On other occasions when there is mention of 'The Friends', those signing include Stewart of Appin, Lamont of Inneryne, MacDougall of Raray and John MacNaughton, fiar of Dunderave in addition to those non-Campbells already mentioned.[34]

It is certainly tempting to consider the existence of some form of equivalent to the Council of the Isles, and the subject matter of the meetings which seems on several occasions to concern the raising of money for the Earl himself suggests that this is an internal Campbell rather than a government body, paradoxically although it contains non-Campbell members. But the constituent signatures as far as I can decipher them do not include all the undoubted leaders of the clan; indeed, some of the signatories appear to be relatively unimportant, and they change from occasion to occasion. This does not seem to argue for the existence of a formal body of the sort set up by the Lords of the Isles. As the estates developed, so too did the management system develop, and by the seventeenth century the Earl's lands were covered by a network of Chamberlains, Officiars, Commissars, Martys, Collectors and the like, together with a host of lesser officials all devoted to the good governance of the area and the collection of due rents for the Earl.

Even though their main lands might be far away, the great Campbell chieftains recognised their link and allegiance to Mac Cailein Mor. Somewhat ironically, since he was perhaps the furthest removed if not in miles then in the role he played, as a lowland magnate rather than a Highland chieftain, it was George Campbell of Loudoun who, as we have seen, in 1430 resigned his lands of Lochgoyle to Duncan Campbell of Lochawe 'for friendship and as Chief of his kin'.[35] The link that had become somewhat tenuous was strengthened by the marriage of Campbell of Lawers to the Loudoun heiress, which not only kept the connection but considerably strengthened it; but a series of eighteenth- and nineteenth-century marriages in due course moved the Loudoun family far from Loch Awe. This did not happen with the Breadalbane branch, nor with that of Cawdor, helped by the fact that both held large stretches of territory in Argyll; even Donald, Abbot of Coupar's descendants, included two who moved back to their ancestral home and took over the lairdships of Otter and of Ormidale.

If Campbell prowess in exploiting the power of the pen to manipulate the legal system in their favour excited unfavourable comment from their rivals, few would fail to agree that it was balanced by both considerable military strength and individual intrepidity. Bravery in battle was of course one of the chief attributes of the hero and the warrior was held in high regard. Few men, one suspects, would not, at one point in their lives at least, have taken up the sword, either in a major campaign or in a local tulzie, since cattle-raiding was a major part of Gaelic culture. It played a part in training the young for war and allowing a future leader to establish his reputation; it gave opportunity for the acquisition of wealth, although this was unlikely to last very long since cattle-raiding was a two-way game; and, a mixture of excitement with a spice of danger, it was no doubt great fun for high-spirited young men.

But there was obviously a more serious side to the profession of arms, both in the furtherance of Royal authority and in the exercise of power by the Chief. The importance placed on this by successive Chiefs of Clan Campbell is underlined by the number of important early land grants whose provisions include a mention of 'special retinue' – a military obligation over and above that owed by all men of military age to the Crown.[36] Right down to the seventeenth century, land grants which bordered the sea were very often tied to the provision of a boat or boats whose number of oars was specified and which had to be on call when required for forty days, fully manned, armed and provisioned. The biggest galley so specified – forty oars – was one of the conditions of the grant of the Lordship of Lochawe and Ardscotnish to Colin, son of Sir Neil Campbell, in 1315. In the 100 years between 1410 and 1510, clauses requiring special retinue and the provision of boats were inserted in land grants of the following: Duntroon, Glenorchy, Dunach and Lerags, Barrichbeyan, Otter, Ardkinglas and Skipness, while the provision of boats was also a condition for grants of Benderloch and Kenmore and for the custody of Craignish and Lochavich castles. Over the years there were many such. A later charter of 1576 spells out one such transaction in detail, when the 6th Earl regranted the Keeping of the Castle of Dunoon and the Bailliary and Seneschalship to Ian Campbell, son and heir of the Captain of Dunoon, the terms of the reddendo for the last were set out as follows:

> the said Earl Colin and his successors will give to the said Ian and his heirs a galley of ten oars sufficiently adorned in singular necessities, which galley the said Ian and his heirs shall thereafter upkeep and arm in victuals, men-at-arms and other fitting things of the said galleys in the wars of our Supreme Lord the King and in our private wars as often as need shall be and when they shall be so required to do, And our heirs shall give a new galley to the said Ian's heirs of the above quality which they themselves shall upkeep . . .[37]

The professional warrior was long a feature of the social make-up of the clan, although little mention is made of him. Leadership in war has a long history in this country of being a gentleman's profession; the professional warrior – Professor Allan MacInnes refers to them as *Buannachan* – was billeted out among the clan and was not expected to labour for his keep. Surplus in rents would also contribute to the upkeep of a force of armed men in the Chief's retinue, and it may be that this occupation was filled by many of the younger sons of the house who make such fleeting appearances unless, as in some cases, they or their descendants were called forward to be given the lands which enabled them to found territorial branches of their own. Many of the typical tombstones of the area and the period display either an armed figure or a sword, either on its own or sometimes accompanied by a galley. It is hard not to believe that these symbols denote those who had performed armed service afloat and/or on shore. To have such a tombstone denotes some status, and again it seems probable that they served as leaders and may even have been the owners of the galleys shown.

Their services could be hired out for gain or be offered, for instance, as part of a daughter's tocher. When, in 1569, Argyll's sister, Lady Agnes Campbell, was married, for the third time, to Turlough O'Neill, Chief of the O'Neills, her brother arranged a strong force of warrior 'redshanks' to accompany her to Ireland as dowry, 1,000 strong. The same month, her daughter Finola was married to Hugh O'Donnell, and again she brought men to increase her husband's armed strength. Ireland in particular had for long been a customer for armed men from the western coast and Isles. The once-great family of the MacSweens, having lost their power in Argyll, were able to re-establish it by making a tremendous and richly rewarded reputation for themselves in Ireland as the leading family of *galloglaich* – heavily armed professional mercenaries who settled in Ireland. They were accompanied in early days by such families as the MacCabes, the MacDowells, the MacRuaris, the MacSheehys and above all by the MacDonalds who in due course established the earldom of Antrim.

Nor was this all. Boatloads of warriors arrived each year from the Isles, returning home when the campaign season was over. When the Lordship was forfeited, the way was left open for other clans to participate in the lucrative demand for trained warriors or redshanks offered both by internal strife in Ireland and by the continuing English/Irish conflict. This last had considerable political attraction for Scotland until the combination of both the Scottish and English Crowns in the person of King James VI made Scottish intervention unacceptable. By that time, the Campbells, whose early intervention in Ireland with Edward Bruce in 1315 had been perhaps rather less than glorious, were playing a major part, notably in the person of successive Earls who were by now able to influence and play a leading role in the international political scene and such figures as the Tutor of Inverawe, the leading redshank commander at the end of the 1500s. During this period, a considerable number of the Clan actually settled in Ireland. They tend to appear in what records exist of their exploits not as Campbells but as MacConnochies, as regards the Campbells of Inverawe, or as some form of Mac Cailein which often comes out as Mac Allen or Mac Ailein or the like. One such name was MacCallion, which has now returned to Scotland in some number.

It seems highly likely that families devoted to the profession of arms must have been in existence, but there is remarkably little direct reference to them. Could this be, just possibly, to the later embarrassment they caused to their chiefs and leaders when the Crown was trying hard to suppress them? One exception to the rule is the family of Campbell of Auchinbreck, who are often referred to as 'Hereditary Colonels of Argyll' and who may have undertaken formal military training on the continent to fit them for this role which lasted for several generations at least. Their record was an unfortunate one; having led Argyll's forces at Inverlochy and after the 1685 Rebellion, they changed sides, being converted to Roman Catholics in time to take part in the 1715 and 1745 Rebellions, again on the losing side. They do appear to have served as standard-bearers to Mac Cailein Mor, but whether the post of commander of Argyll's forces in fact ever existed as a formal, hereditary appointment seems somewhat unlikely – what, for instance would happen if the incumbent died without a son of sufficient of age and experience to take over?[38]

It is not easy to assess the full strength of Clan Campbell as opposed to their rivals. Numbers by themselves give little idea – in early days they tended to be greatly exaggerated while in fact they were remarkably low by today's standards. There is no contemporary account which mentions by name the Campbell contribution in battle, not even at Flodden where, from the casualties sustained, the Clan clearly took part in strength. Argyll of course was often able to magnify his power by the influence he could exert over other clans. Successive Earls were also very modern-minded; they had proper ships of their own while the rest of their neighbours were still operating exclusively in galleys which, mobile as they undoubtedly were, were no match for gun-carrying ships. They also owned their own artillery, and at one time the 5th Earl of Argyll had at his disposal an armed force made up of an army some 5,000 strong, a fleet of galleys and a train of artillery which was unmatched by any private individual in England, Scotland or Ireland.[39]

By the time of Culloden in 1746, the strength of Clan Campbell was far ahead of that of any other clan. According to Duncan Forbes of Culloden's report to government, they numbered well over 5,000 men while the various branches of the fractured Clan Donald even if added together totalled some 2,200. The Athollmen he reckoned at 3,000 in strength, the MacKenzies at 2,000. All the other clans were under 1,000, the Grants at 850, the Camerons and the Mackintoshes at 800 coming nearest to that figure. Other close neighbours of the Campbells in Argyll included the Macleans at 500, the Stewarts of Appin at 300 and the MacLachlans and MacDougalls both at 200.[40] In the event, some 2,500 men of different names made up the Argyll Militia which took an active part in the campaign, the Duke of Cumberland on one occasion addressing them as 'My Brave Campbells'!

With the struggle for the succession finally settled in favour of the House of Hanover, the Highlands were transformed into a source of manpower that produced some of the finest troops in the British army. The expansion of the Empire gave abundant opportunities for service and the younger sons and lesser lairds whose predecessors had earlier filled the ranks of the clan's professional soldiers and of the mercenary redshanks in Ireland now took a large part in the leading of the country's armed forces, both on sea and on land. By the end of the eighteenth century, there was scarcely a regiment which did not include a number of Highland officers and often as not a

Campbell at that. Nor was this all; by the end of the Napoleonic wars, no fewer than sixteen regiments of the British army, line, militia, fencibles and volunteers had been raised by Campbells, a record in no way approached by any other clan.

The Campbells also produced a remarkable number of senior officers, both admirals and generals – the family memorial to the Campbells of Melfort is a remarkable example of the ranks attained by a single family – but the very highest command came to them but rarely. One of the two exceptions was the 2nd Duke of Argyll, the other being Sir Colin Campbell of Crimea and Indian Mutiny fame. He was actually only half a Campbell, his real name being MacLiver; but, when his Campbell uncle took him to the Horse Guards to be entered for a commission, the clerk, who knew Colonel Campbell, thought his nephew must be of the same name and entered him so. We can take legitimate pride in the fact that it was considered that the name Campbell would help the young man's career in the Army and so it was left.

The 2nd Duke, *Iain Ruadh nan Cath* – 'Red John of the Battles' – was a notable commander; he was unlucky that the political party he backed was out of favour at the time that the chief command to lead our army on the continent was to be made. It went to the future Duke of Marlborough, a lesser soldier, some have said, than the Duke of Argyll. Be that as it may, he went on to become one of the first two officers of the British army to hold the rank of field marshal, and he commanded the government forces at Sheriffmuir which spelt an end to the Jacobite Rebellion of 1715. His family was to have a remarkable record. The 5th Duke, 'Colonel Jack' of the '45 was also a field marshal, while the 4th Duke attained the rank of four-star general.

This military tradition has continued to the present day, and it is by no means an undistinguished one. It was the late Sir Iain Moncreiffe of that Ilk who drew attention to the record in the last two World Wars of the Campbells of Cawdor, around fifty of whom were of military age, who alone had managed to amass no fewer than three Victoria Crosses, fifteen DSOs, two MCs and a DFC together with a host of lesser decorations during that period, a record which completely defies statistical expectation.[41] Well may it have been said of the Campbells:

> Gur guineach na Duimhnich
> Nam rusgadh nam lann
> Bidh naimhdan ga'n ruagadh
> L'en cruadal nach fann . . .

'Fierce are the Campbells when swords are drawn from their sheaths; enemies will be scattered by their hardiness and might . . .'[42]

Their military prowess was by no means the only factor which contributed to the Campbell rise to power; we have already seen the high regard in which ancient Celtic society held the Church. The Campbell links to the Church were strong, both from the inside as churchmen and from the outside as laity. Next to the profession of arms, entry into the Church was a favoured occupation for younger sons. As we have seen, the MacArthurs were a clerical kindred before they became lairds; another kindred with Campbell affiliations was that of the Argyllshire MacPhersons who are thought to have derived their name from Dugald the Parson, a son of Sir Cailean Mor. The family grew and at various times held a number of small properties, the chief being that of Dubhpenyg or Duppine, in Glassary. Donald MacPherson was one of the Barons of Argyll who served on the 1355 inquest at Inverleckan. The MacPhersons spread all over the area taken over by the Campbells – into Breadalbane, Kintyre, Cowal and Bute. One family which also claims descent from an early scion of the chiefly line is that of the Campbells of Auchinellan, a famous family of churchmen known as 'The Race of Bishops' from the number of senior churchmen that they produced. Their progenitor was Mr Neil, Dean of Argyll, a son of Colin Iongantach, who was flourishing in 1400.

If the Campbells were benefactors of the Church, and such establishments as the Collegiate Chapel of Kilmun were the result of their benevolence, then they themselves benefited as much and more from the church in turn. The lands of Gloom on which sat Castle Campbell were originally Church lands transferred to the Chief as Ardchattan was obtained by Campbell of Cawdor. Much other land came from the same source, while Donald, son of the 2nd Earl of Argyll and himself Abbot of Coupar, managed to provide for a numerous unofficial progeny out of the rich lands that had belonged to his former charge. Many a younger son both of the chiefly family and of lesser Campbell houses entered the Church, including such unlikely figures as Sir Donald Campbell of Ardnamurchan, castigated by James Turner in his memoirs as 'ane terrible old man, steeped in blood from his verie infancie . . .',[43] who carried out a successful career as 'hit-man' for both the 7th Earl and the Marquess of Argyll, having started his career as a churchman. While not all their clan always followed them, and with the exception of the 7th Earl who changed to Rome in later life, once the Chiefs of Clan Campbell had embraced the Reformed Church they remained staunch to the Kirk.

It always seems strange to me that academic historians do not pay more attention to genealogy and that many of them profess to despise it along with its attendant science of heraldry. Both give rich clues as to family connections which in the past, as now, are so important a factor in success. The Campbell

Chiefs were aware of this at an early stage; the flexible system of Celtic marriage customs allowed a number of types of liaison, and the substitution of a current wife if a better opportunity came along was relatively common. This may be of some comfort to genealogists faced by apparently conflicting marriages – they are probably all true! Certainly the Campbell Chiefs made full use of the marriage bond and managed to establish important and useful connections by marriage both as links with important houses, including the Royal one, and as a means of taking over land. On the other side, they were clearly determined to avoid the loss of land with an heiress's marriage and, once the parcelling-out of estates to junior branches commenced, it is noteworthy how the destination was always to heirs male, whom eventually failing, the lands were to revert to the chiefly line.

It was the Emperor Napoleon who apparently said 'Give me generals that are lucky' and how right he was, for luck is an indispensable part of success. Equally, it has also been claimed that people make their own luck. Both statements are true in the case of the Clan Campbell and its rise to power. In spite of their abilities – and they were not lacking – without luck, little would have been achieved. Clan Campbell's progress was far from uniform; as we have seen, there were periods when they and their Chief were out of Royal favour and matters went against them.

The Clan Donald were both the architects of their own downfall and the major cause of the Campbell rise; the story is nothing less than that of the struggle for *Ceannas nan Gaidheal* – The Headship of the Gael – between the mainland Scottish Crown which, 'civilised' or 'Anglicised' as it might have become, was nonetheless of the line of Dalriada, and the Lordship of the Isles, whose Gaelic blood was also heavily influenced both actually and politically by the Norse Kingdom of the Isles and by Somerled. With the Clan Donald the main protagonists on one side, a counterweight had to emerge on the other. As has been said, 'if the Campbells had not existed we should have to invent them'.[44] But the Campbells did exist, and, if the present volume is a remarkable tale of a rise from a small, insignificant lordship by Loch Awe to a dominant position in Argyll and a major power in Scotland as a whole within the short space of a mere two centuries, it is nothing compared to what is to follow.

The Structure of Clan Campbell

Clan Campbell is unique in the number of lairds it has produced – that is to say, heritable proprietors of land rather than those who held on short-term leases or tacks. Nearly 250 are listed here although the list may not be complete, particularly in the case of lairdships which only lasted for a generation. The number is worthy of comment; it is far larger than any other clan and may be compared with a small clan which might not produce more than seven or eight such cadet families.

Following Highland custom, these lairds were known by the name of their property, as 'Campbell of Inverawe' and sometimes (as with peers) just by the name of the property alone, hence 'Inverawe' or 'Glenfeochan', although this form as a signature is only allowed to peers, lesser lairds signing as 'Duncan Campbell of Inverawe' or whatever. The form 'of' denotes ownership, as opposed to a tenant or tacksman, when the form 'in' replaces 'of'. This territorial designation, once recognised officially, remains with the original family to use, regardless of whether or not they still actually own the property. Hence 'Campbell of Inverawe' is still so styled although the family no longer owns the estate. The new owner should not be styled 'of Inverawe' even though he may own the place. Even if now a nicety, correct usage is to insert a comma replacing 'of' – hence 'Mr Robert Campbell-Preston, Inverawe' is the correct form of description of the present owner. In Scotland, a territorial designation is legally part of a surname and corresponds to the French 'de' and the German 'von'.

While on the subject of correct social usage, once a matter of considerable importance, it is still the formal practice to refer to the eldest son as the 'Younger of' whatever the designation; hence, for instance, 'David Campbell, Younger of Strachur' or 'David Campbell of Strachur, Younger' is correct formal address. 'Younger' may be shortened to 'Yr'. The territorial designation is not used by younger sons, although all daughters may do so; the eldest daughter is known by her surname alone as 'Miss Campbell of Succoth', while her younger sister would be 'Miss Candia Campbell of Succoth'. While somewhat archaic, the use of territorial designations can be particularly helpful, apart from being formally correct, in a clan so large as the Campbells where the choice of Christian names such as Colin, Archibald, Duncan and John/Ian is so often repeated. The author for long thought himself virtually unique but in recent years has been joined by such kenspeckle figures as a famous Scottish rugby forward, the commanding officer of one of the battalions of Highland Volunteers, the opening bat for the Rhodesian cricket XI and the prime minister of Great Britain's press secretary.

The first part of this section places the various lairdships in alphabetical order and shows to which major branch of Clan Campbell they belong.

Aberuchill	Glenorchy
Achalader	Glenorchy
Achanduin and Barbreck	Lochnell
Acharn	Lochnell
Achavorran	Inverawe
Achnaba	Glenorchy
Achteny	Lochnell
Airds	Cawdor
Airds Bay	Cawdor
Altries	Kenmore and Melfort
Ardachy	Cawdor
Ardchattan	Cawdor
Ardentallen	Lochnell
Ardentinny	Ardkinglas
Ardeonaig and Lochend	Glenorchy
Ardlarach	MacIver
Ardmarnoch	Donald, Abbot of Coupar
Ardnamurchan	Cawdor
Ardpatrick	Ardkinglas
Ardslignish	Lochnell
Arduaine	Inverawe
Arthurstone	Donald, Abbot of Coupar
Ashfield/Lergnahension	Duntroon
Asknish	MacIver
Askomel	Craignish
Auch	Glenorchy
Auchawillan	Ardkinglas

Auchendarroch (now Inverawe)	Inverawe
Auchinbreck	Lochawe
Auchlyne	Glenorchy
Auchmannoch and Avisyard	Loudoun
Avisyard	Loudoun
Balgirsho	Donald, Abbot of Coupar
Ballachlavan	Craignish
Ballimore	Lochnell
Ballinaby	Cawdor
Balliveolan	Glenorchy
Ballochyle	MacIver
Bangeston	Cawdor
Barbreck (Old Line)	Lochawe
Barbreck (New Line)	Lochnell
Barcaldine	Glenorchy
Barlea	Dunstaffnage
Barmolloch	MacIver
Barnacarry	Lochnell
Barquharrie and Mayfield	Loudoun
Barrichbeyan	Craignish
Blackhouse and Finlaystone	Inverawe
Blackriver	Auchinbreck
Blarcherin	Cawdor
Blythswood	Ardkinglas
Boat of Islay	Donald, Abbot of Coupar
Boith	Cawdor
Bragleen	Lochnell
Brounsyde	Loudoun
Cabrachan	Lochnell
Cammo	–
Carrick	Ardkinglas
Carrickbuoy	–
Catrine	Loudoun
Cawdor	Lochawe
Cessnock	Loudoun
Clachan	Ardkinglas
Claonary	Ardkinglas
Clathick	Glenorchy

Clenamacrie	Dunstaffnage
Clenary	MacIver
Clochombie	Dunstaffnage
Clunes	Cawdor
Colgrain	Glenorchy
Corries	Glenorchy
Crackaig	Dunstaffnage
Craigends	Glenorchy
Craigie	–
Croonan	Donald, Abbot of Coupar
Croy	–
Culgatro	Auchinbreck
Culraith	–
Cultoun	Cawdor
Danna	Auchinbreck
Denhead	Donald, Abbot of Coupar
Denoon	–
Dergachy	Ardkinglas
Douglas Support	Ardkinglas
Drimsynie	Ardkinglas
Drumnamuckloch	Duntroon
Duchernan	MacIver
Dudhope	Auchinbreck
Dunardry	MacTavish
Duneaves	Glenorchy
Dunmore	Cawdor
Dunoon	Ardkinglas
Dunstaffnage	Lochawe
Duntroon	Lochawe
Easter Shian	Glenorchy
Edenwood	Donald, Abbot of Coupar
Ederline	Dunstaffnage
Edinample	Glenorchy
Ellanrie	Duntroon
Eriskay	Cawdor
Eskan	Glenorchy
Fairfield	Loudoun

Finlaystone	Inverawe
Fraochyllan	Inverawe
Gargunnock	–
Gartbeg	MacTavish
Gartsford	Glenorchy
Glassnock	Loudoun
Glasvar	MacIver
Glenavey	–
Glencarradale	Auchinbreck
Glencharran	Duntroon
Glendaruel (Old Line)	Glenorchy
Glendaruel (New Line)	Lochnell
Glendouglas	–
Glenfalloch	Glenorchy
Glenfeochan (Old Line)	Inverawe
Glenfeochan (New Line)	Lochnell
Glenlyon	Glenorchy
Glennan	Auchinbreck
Glenorchy	Lochawe
Glensaddell	Auchinbreck
Glensalloch	Cawdor
Glenure	Glenorchy
Grandvale	–
Hallyards	–
Ichterachyn	Cawdor
Inchanoch	Kenmore and Melfort
Innellan	Ardkinglas
Innerzeldies	Glenorchy
Innistore	Dunstaffnage
Inverawe	Lochawe
Inveresragan	Cawdor
Inverhae	Auchinbreck
Inverinan	Glenorchy
Inverliver (on Loch Awe)	Barbreck (Old Line)
Inverliver (on Loch Etive)	Glenorchy
Inverneill	Craignish
Islay	Ardkinglas

Keithock	Donald, Abbot of Coupar
Kenmore	Lochawe
Kilberry	Auchinbreck
Kilbrandon	Cawdor
Kildalloig	Auchinbreck
Kilduskland	Auchinbreck
Killermont	Glenorchy
Killoch	Loudoun
Kilmartin	Inverawe
Kilmichael	Auchinbreck
Kilmory	Auchinbreck
Kinloch	Glenorchy
Kinnabus	Cawdor
Kinnochtree	Donald, Abbot of Coupar
Kirktoun	Cawdor
Kirnan	MacIver
Knock	Lochnell
Knockamellie (Old Line)	Ardkinglas
Knockamellie (New Line)	Auchinbreck
Knockbuy	Auchinbreck
Kolmkill	Lochnell
Lagg	MacIver
Lagg	Auchinbreck
Lagganlochan	Craignish
Lagvinsheoch	Glenorchy
Lawers	Glenorchy
Leckguary	MacIver
Leix	Ardkinglas
Lerags (Old Line)	Inverawe
Lerags (New Line)	Lochnell
Lergachonzie	MacIver
Lergnahension (Ashfield)	Duntroon
Lochdochart	Glenorchy
Lochend and Ardeonaig	Glenorchy
Lochend and Thurso	MacIver
Lochlane	Glenorchy
Lochnell	Lochawe
Lossit	Cawdor
Loudoun	Lochawe

Lundie (Old Line)	Lochawe
Lundie (New Line)	Donald, Abbot of Coupar
Mains	Ardkinglas
Mayfield	Loudoun
Melfort	Lochawe
Mochaster	Glenorchy
Monzie	Glenorchy
Morpeth	Auchinbreck
Mossley	–
Moy	Cawdor
Murthlie	Glenorchy
Nether Largie	Duntroon
Netherplace	Loudoun
New Inverawe	Inverawe
Octomore	Cawdor
Oib	Duntroon
Orchard	Ardkinglas
Ormidale (Old Line)	Lochawe
Ormidale (New Line)	Donald, Abbot of Coupar
Ormsary	Auchinbreck
Orrobolls	Ardkinglas
Otter (Old Line)	Lochawe
Otter (New Line)	Donald, Abbot of Coupar
Park	Glenorchy
Peatoun	Ardkinglas
Pennymore	MacIver
Possil	Glenorchy
Quoycrook	MacIver
Rachean	Ardkinglas
Raray	Glenorchy
Raschoille	Duntroon
Rudill	Duntroon
Scamadale	Dunstaffnage

Shankeston	Loudoun
Shawfield	Ardkinglas
Shirvan	Inverawe
Skeldon	Loudoun
Skerrington	Loudoun
Skipness (Old Line)	Lochawe
Skipness (New Line)	Ardkinglas
Smiddygreen	Donald, Abbot of Coupar
Sonachan	Cawdor
Soutarhouses	Donald, Abbot of Coupar
South Hall	Inverawe
Springfield	Ardkinglas
Stonefield	Lochnell
Stracathro	Kenmore and Melfort
Stratheden and Campbell	Donald, Abbot of Coupar
Stronchormaig	Inverawe
Strondour	Auchinbreck
Strones	Duntroon
Stuck	Auchinbreck
Succoth	–
Sunderland/Shinderlin	Cawdor
Thames Ditton	Glenorchy
Thurso	MacIver
Torbhlaren	Auchinbreck
Torrie	Dunstaffnage
Torrobolls	Duntroon
Torrobolls	Cawdor
Treesbank	Loudoun
Tullichewan	Kenmore and Melfort
Whitehaughs	Loudoun
Wideford	MacIver
Woodhall	Ardkinglas
Woodside	Ardkinglas

This section shows how each family is connected with the main stem. This is done through showing families in descending order of relationship; the main stem families are shown thus:

LOCHAWE;	those immediately descending from them thus:
AUCHINBRECK;	those immediately descending from them thus:
Danna;	those immediately descending from them thus:
Kilberry;	those immediately descending from them thus:
Glencarradale;	those immediately descending from them thus:
Drumnamuckloch.	

To establish the ramifications of the family tree, take each name back to the last name of higher category. Hence the entry for Kilmory

Kilmory;	Stuck; *Kilduskland*; *Glensaddell*; *Torbhlaren*; *Blackriver*; *Knockbuy*; Kilmichael; Kildalloig; *Danna*; Morpeth.

shows, for instance, that Danna comes from Kildalloig which comes from Kilmory, while Blackriver comes from Stuck which comes from Kilmory.

In some instances, there has been more than one owner of a property at differing times. It should be noted that there is no significance as to relative importance of the various lairdships shown below in the typesize by which they are listed.

LOCHAWE
    LOCHNELL
    Cabrachan;
    Bragleen; Knock.
    Kolmkill;
    Stonefield;
    Lerags (new line);
    Jura; Glendaruel (new line); Glenfeochan (new line).
    Barnacarry;
    Ardentallen;
    Achanduin and Barbreck;
    Ardslignish;
    Acharn;
    Achteny; Ballimore; Barbreck (new line).

    CAWDOR
    Ichterachyn; Ballinaby; *Dunmore*. Kirktoun; *Lossit*.

Boith;
Moy;
Inveresragan and Ardachy;
Eriskay;
Ardchattan; Sunderland; Glensalloch.
Sonachan;
Geddes and Torrobolls;
Ardnamurchan;
Airds; Octomore; Kinnabus; Cultoun; Airds Bay.
Kilbrandon;
Urchany and Boghole;
Clunes;
Bangeston.

SKIPNESS (Old Line)

DONALD, ABBOT OF COUPAR
Croonan; Carsgownie; *Lundie* (*New Line*); Balgirsho; *Croonan and Balgirsho*.
Arthurstone;
Boat of Islay; Soutarhouses; *Kinnochtree*; Smiddygreen;
    Otter (*new line*); *Ardmarnoch*; *Ormidale* (*new line*).
Keithock; Edenwood; *Stratheden and Campbell*.
Denhead.

LUNDIE (Old Line)

GLENORCHY
Lawers; Murthlie then Kinloch; *Park*; *Possil*; *Craigends*; *Colgrain*;
    Eskan; *Colgrain*. Easter Shian; Aberuchill; *Thames Ditton*;
    Clathick; *Ardeonaig and Lochend*; *Killermont and Garscadden*.
Glenlyon; Duneaves.
Achalader; Gartsford.
Lagvinsheoch then Monzie; Fornocht; Finab; *Finab and Monzie*;
    Lochlane.
Edinample;
Innerzeldies then Barcaldine; Blarcherin; Achnaba; Inverinan;
    Auchrioch; Auch; Inverliver; Balliveolan; Corries; Raray;
    Glenure.
Lochdochart;

Auchlyne;
Mochaster;
Glenfalloch.

ORMIDALE (Old Line)

AUCHINBRECK
Kilmory; Stuck; *Kilduskland; Glensaddell; Torbhlaren; Blackriver;*
    Knockbuy; Kilmichael; Kildalloig; *Danna*; Morpeth.
Strondour;
Danna; Kilberry; *Lagg; Ormsary; Inverhae; Glennan; Glencarradale;*
    Drumnamuckloch.Culgatro; Dudhope.
Knockamellie.

OTTER (Old Line)

BARBRECK (Old Line)
Inverliver.

ARDKINGLAS
Auchawillan; Springfield; Claonary; Innellan and Dunoon; *Orrobolls*.
Ardentinny; Skipness (New Line); *Shawfield; Shawfield and Skipness;*
    Skipness; Woodhall and Islay; Ardpatrick. Blythswood;
    Woodside; Mains; Douglas Support.
Clachan;
Carrick;
Dergachy; Drumsynie; Leix; Knockamellie.
Rachean; Peatoun.
Orchard.

DUNTROON
Oib; Ellanrie; Torrobolls; Duntroon and Oib.
Rudill;
Knap;
Lergnahension (Ashfield);
Nether Largie;
Ulva;
Glencharran;
Strones and Drumnamuckloch;
Raschoille.

DUNSTAFFNAGE
Barlea;
Clenamacrie; Cloichombie; Ederline.
Scamadale;
Innistore;
Torrie;
Crackaig.

INVERAWE
Stronchormaig; Glenfeochan.
Lerags;
Achavorran;
Kilmartin;
Shirvan;
South Hall;
Fraochyllan;
Blackhouse and Finlaystone; Auchendarroch (now Inverawe);
    Arduaine. New Inverawe.

KENMORE AND MELFORT
Inchanoch; Tullichewan; *Altries*. Stracathro.

LOUDOUN
Treesbank and Cessnock; Glassnock; Barquharrie and Mayfield;
    Sornbeg.
Skerrington;
Brounsyde; Netherplace.
Shankeston;
Skeldon;
Auchmannoch and Avisyard; Avisyard; Killoch, later Whitehaughs.
    Fairfield; Catrine.

STRACHUR

CRAIGNISH
INVERNEIL.
BARRICHBEYAN. **Ballachlavan**; Askomel. **Lagganlochan**; Baron
    Campbell von Laurentz of Saxe Coburg Gotha; Baron Craignish
    of Saxe Coburg Gotha.

MACTAVISH OF DUNARDRY
    GARTBEG.

MACIVER CAMPBELL OF LERGAHONZIE AND STRONSHIRA
then ASKNISH
    KIRNAN then GLASVAR; **Stroneskar; Leckguary; Barmolloch;**
        Lagg.
    BALLOCHYLE.
    PENNYMORE; **Clenary.**
    ARDLARACH.
    QUOYCROOK; **(Iverach of) Wideford; Thurso and Lochend;**
        Duchernan.

The connection of the following Campbell houses is unknown: **Alloway;
Cammo; Carrickbuoy; Craigie; Croy; Culraith; Denoon; Gargunnock;
Glenavey; Glendouglas; Grandvale; Hallyards; Mossley; Succoth.**

The 1751 Valuation:
Proprietors of Argyllshire

It is claimed by many people that the end of the '45 Rebellion spelt the end of the old Clan system. Therefore, 1751 is not a bad time at which to look at the relative position attained by the various families who held land in Argyll.

The valuation below gives the rateable value of the lands rather than their actual market value. It shows relative rather than actual values. It has been compiled from a document in the archives at Inveraray which lists each property in the county, parish by parish, together with its value and its owner. It should be remembered that such magnates as Campbell of Breadalbane and Cameron of Lochiel had most of their property outwith the county, while such important figures as Campbell of Cawdor and Campbell of Loudoun do not figure here at all. Breadalbane, in particular, was little or no distance behind his Chief in extent of acres and wealth, and several of his House's cadets would be among the leaders of those shown here.

But the roll does show the position within the Campbell heartland of Argyll and the quite extraordinary dominance achieved there by the Chief and his Clan.

1	Duke of Argyll	£ 2,210.	11.	11
2	Breadalbane, John Campbell, Earl of	£ 594.	7.	1
3	Campbell of Shawfield, Daniel	£ 558.	9.	4
4	Campbell of Ardkinglas, Bt, Sir James	£ 371.	10.	8
5	Campbell of Lochnell, Sir Duncan	£ 356.	7.	2
6	Campbell of Auchinbreck, Sir James	£ 290.	17.	8
7	MacMillan of Dunmore, —	£ 246.	10.	0
8	Lamont of Lamont, Archibald	£ 208.	10.	12
9	Murray of Ardnamurchan, Charles	£ 194.	5.	8
10	Campbell of Inverawe, Captain Duncan	£ 155.	14.	11

11	Campbell of Craignish, James	£	144.	18. 3
12	Campbell of Otter, John	£	141.	5. 7
13	Maclaine of Lochbuie, John	£	141.	3. 3
14	Campbell of Knockbuy, Archibald	£	139.	3. 0
15	Campbell of Ederline, Colin	£	135.	12. 4
16	Campbell of Glensaddell, John	£	132.	4. 4
17	McNeill of Taynish, Rodger	£	130.	4. 8
18	Maclean of Coll, Hector	£	129.	1. 10
19	Stewart of Appin, Dugald,	£	128.	13. 10
20	Campbell of Stonefield, Archibald	£	128.	5. 5
21	[omitted – error in original document]			
22	Campbell of Airds, Donald	£	123.	4. 0
23	Campbell of Jura, Archibald	£	122.	18. 7
24	Macalister of Loup, Angus	£	118.	17. 1
25	Campbell of Barcaldine, John	£	117.	16. 0
26	Campbell of Skipness, Colin	£	110.	16. 2
27	McNeill of Colonsay, Donald	£	103.	17. 4
28	Campbell of Strachur, Capt. John and wife	£	103.	6. 0
29	MacNeal of Ugadale	£	98.	13. 1
30	MacDougall of Dunollie, Alexander	£	98.	5. 6
31	Campbell of Glencarradale, Dugald	£	95.	11. 3
32	Campbell of Shirvan, Alexander	£	95.	9. 8
33	Campbell of Southhall, Duncan	£	93.	17. 9
34	Cameron of Dungallon, Alexander	£	87.	8. 5
35	Campbell of Dunstaffnage, Neil	£	86.	16. 1
36	Campbell of Duntroon, Neil	£	86.	16. 1
37	MacLachlan of MacLachlan, Robert	£	83.	8. 7
38	Campbell of Inverliver, Archibald	£	81.	0. 2
39	Maclean of Ardgour, Hugh	£	78.	11. 1
40	Campbell of Glendaruel, Duncan	£	75.	3. 3
41	MacDonald of Sanda, John	£	75.	2. 7
42	Cameron of Locheil, Donald	£	75.	0. 0
43	Campbell of Glenure, Colin	£	62.	6. 7
44	Cameron of Glendessary, John	£	62.	3. 5
45	Maclean of Torloisk, Hector	£	55.	18. 10
46	Campbell of Melford, Archibald	£	55.	10. 6
47	Campbell of Barnacarry, John	£	55.	6. 1
48	Campbell of Lagganlochan, Ferquhard	£	53.	11. 10
49	MacTavish of Dunardry, Dugald	£	52.	13. 9
50	Campbell of Finab, Captain Robert	£	52.	3. 3

51	Maclean of Kingairloch, Lachlan	£	49.	4.	11
52	McNeill of Macrihanish, Neil	£	48.	12.	8
53	Macalister of Tarbert, Archibald	£	47.	12.	9
54	Campbell of Kildalloig, John	£	47.	8.	0
55	Wishart of Greenhall, Mr George	£	46.	16.	8
56	Campbell of Kilmartin, Dugald	£	46.	15.	5
57	Campbell of Dunoon, Archibald	£	46.	15.	1
58	Campbell of Ardchattan, Charles	£	44.	17.	11
59	Campbell of Danna, John	£	44.	13.	0
60	Melville of Kilmichael, Robert	£	44.	11.	2
61	Campbell of Balleveolan, Charles	£	44.	5.	8
62	Campbell of Knap, Duncan	£	43.	2.	11
63	Campbell of Cloichombie, John	£	41.	2.	4
64	Campbell of Glenfeochan, John	£	39.	8.	0
65	MacKinnon of MacKinnon, John	£	39.	4.	3
66	Campbell of Kirnan, Duncan	£	37.	1.	0
67	Campbell of Sunderland, Duncan	£	36.	12.	11
68	Campbell of Kilberry, Colin	£	36.	11.	1
69	MacDonald of Clanranald, Ronald	£	35.	19.	10
70	Campbell of Ballinaby, James	£	33.	9.	2
71	Duncanson of Keills, Alexander	£	33.	7.	11
72	Stewart of Ardsheal, Charles	£	33.	6.	8
73	Lamont of Knockdow, Colin	£	32.	14.	10
74	MacLachlan of Craigenterive, Colin	£	32.	14.	1
75	MacArthur of Inistrynich, Duncan	£	30.	14.	1
76	Clerk of Braleckan, Dugald	£	30.	13.	7
77	McNeill of Gallochellie, Hector	£	30.	10.	8
78	Stewart of Ballachulish, John	£	28.	18.	0
79	McNeill of Ardnacross, Neil	£	28.	13.	1
80	Campbell of Ballimore, Archibald	£	28.	8.	5
81	Campbell of Lossit, Donald	£	28.	2.	11
82	Campbell of Oib, James	£	27.	15.	5
83	Campbell of Auchawillan, Neil	£	27.	7.	2
84	Fraser of Askomilbeg, Thomas	£	26.	3.	10
85	Maclean of Ellenamuck, Hector	£	25.	15.	6
86	Campbell of Ormsary, William	£	26.	5.	6
87	MacDougall of Ardencaple, John	£	25.	5.	8
88	Campbell of Ballochyle, Alexander	£	25.	2.	2
89	Campbell of Auchnaba, Patrick	£	25.	2.	2
90	McNeill of Arichonan, Neil	£	24.	16.	9

91	Campbell of Knockamillie, Mr John	£	24.	15.	8
92	Campbell of Orchard, John	£	24.	7.	7
93	Campbell of Ulva, Donald	£	24.	4.	11
94	Campbell of Lix, Hugh	£	24.	4.	9
95	McNeill of Kilchrist, Lachlan	£	24.	2.	10
96	Campbell of Dergachy, Duncan	£	23.	16.	0
97	McNeill of Tirefergus, Torquil	£	23.	13.	5
98	Campbell of Barbreck, James	£	23.	13.	0
99	MacKellar of Drumfin, Patrick	£	23.	9.	5
100	MacQuarry of Ulva, Lachlan	£	23.	8.	11
101	MacLachlan of Ardelay, John	£	22.	9.	5
102	Fisher of Durren, Angus	£	22.	8.	3
103	MacDougall of Creganish, Coll	£	22.	2.	2
104	MacLachlan of Dunadd, Duncan	£	21.	16.	6
105	Stewart of Invernahyle, Alexander	£	21.	14.	6
106	Talmash of Kilkivan, —	£	21.	4.	7
107	Campbell of Cruachan, Dougald	£	20.	19.	4
108	McNeill of Ardeglammy, Lachlan	£	20.	19.	2
109	MacCallum of Poltalloch, Archibald	£	20.	18.	4
110	Campbell of Killenallen, Donald	£	20.	14.	6
111	Campbell of Inveresragan, James	£	20.	9.	1
112	Campbell of Glenshellich, Archibald	£	19.	14.	4
113	Campbell of Lerags, John	£	19.	10.	8
114	Maclean of Kennachtrie, —	£	19.	0.	0
115	MacGillespie of Ballie, Colin	£	18.	19.	8
116	MacDonald of Glencoe, John	£	18.	17.	7
117	Fletcher of Dunans, Archibald	£	18.	16.	8
118	Campbell of Octomore, Donald	£	18.	16.	4
119	Campbell of Dell, Colin	£	18.	9.	8
120	MacQuarrie of Ormaig, Donald	£	18.	7.	9
121	Campbell of Kintraw, Robert	£	18.	3.	1
122	Campbell of Askomelmore, John	£	18.	1.	2
123	Stewart of Fasnacloich, James	£	17.	19.	11
124	Campbell of Scamadale, Donald	£	17.	18.	3
125	Campbell of Ellary, Angus	£	17.	17.	0
126	Campbell of Ardlarach, Angus	£	17.	16.	10
127	Drummond of Ardentinny, Alexander	£	17.	10.	4
128	Campbell of Asknish, Robert	£	17.	8.	7
129	Cowan of Kenararoch, John	£	16.	13.	4
130	Maclea of Lindsaig, Alexander	£	16.	12.	0

131	Lamont of Strone, —	£	16.	2.	6
132	Campbell of Ashfield, John	£	15.	13.	11
133	Campbell of Ellister, George	£	15.	13.	1
134	McNeill of Chancerioch, Lachlan	£	15.	12.	0
135	Maclean of Drimnin, Allan	£	15.	9.	6
136	MacColls of Glasdrum	£	14.	16.	4
137	Campbell of Frackersaig, Archibald	£	14.	12.	2
138	Campbell of Achalader, Archibald	£	14.	9.	11
139	Elder of Belloch, Robert	£	13.	15.	9
140	MacLachlan of Innischonnell, Angus	£	13.	14.	5
141	Campbell of Linegartan, Patrick	£	13.	10.	0
142	Campbell of Stroneskar, Donald	£	13.	5.	10
143	Ferguson/Duncanson of Glenshellich	£	13.	5.	10
144	Lamont of Achagoyle, James	£	13.	1.	10
145	Lamont of Monydrain, Coll	£	13.	0.	10
146	Campbell of Achachrossan, Robert	£	12.	18.	0
147	MacDougall of Gallanach, John	£	12.	17.	2
148	Murray of Blackbarony, John	£	12.	16.	4
149	MacDonald of Auchiltrichattan, Angus	£	12.	16.	2
150	MacDougal of Knipoch, Duncan	£	12.	13.	10
151	Campbell of Ellanrie, Angus	£	12.	12.	2
152	MacKellar of Dell, Alexander	£	12.	8.	11
153	Campbell of Duchernan, Duncan	£	12.	6.	0
154	Campbell of Glasvar, James	£	12.	5.	6
155	McNeill of Ardmenish, Neil	£	12.	5.	0
156	MacGilvray of Pennyghael, Alexander	£	12.	4.	2
157	Campbell of Carsaig, Daniel	£	12.	2.	5
158	Campbell of Barmolloch, Mr Charles	£	12.	2.	0
159	Campbell of Blairintibbert, Archibald	£	12.	1.	4
160	Campbell of Sonachan, Duncan	£	12.	1.	1
161	Campbell of Achaworran, Dugald	£	12.	0.	0
162	MacLachlan of Lephinmore, Archibald	£	11.	19.	4
163	Elder of Achachoirk, John	£	11.	15.	9
164	Campbell of Evanachan, Alexander	£	11.	9.	11
165	Campbell of Raschoille, James	£	11.	8.	3
166	MacIlvernock of Oib, Duncan	£	11.	5.	4
167	MacLachlan of Kilbride, John	£	11.	3.	10
168	Cameron of Inverscaddell, John	£	11.	2.	2
169	MacIntyre of Glenoe, Donald	£	11.	0.	0
170	Campbell of Ballachlavan, John	£	10.	18.	3

171	Campbell of Downie, Robert	£	10.	12.	9
172	Campbell of Rudil, James	£	10.	12.	8
173	McNeill of Carskey, Archibald	£	10.	10.	0
174	Campbell of Kilmory, John	£	10.	6.	4
175	Campbell of Ardnablaich, John	£	10.	0.	2
176	MacLachlan of Kilnochanoch, Kenneth	£	10.	0.	0
177	Campbell of Clenamacrie, Dugald	£	9.	16.	7
178	Lamont of Achinshelloch, Duncan	£	9.	15.	9
179	MacLachlan of Achigerran, Colin	£	9.	15.	6
180	O'Conochir of Ardeoran, John	£	9.	12.	0
181	Stewart of Auchenskioch, James	£	9.	1.	0
182	Campbell of Tirefour, Archibald	£	8.	15.	6
183	Lindsay of Terivadich, John	£	8.	15.	3
184	MacCalman of Terivadich, Archibald (wadset)	£	8.	13.	2
185	Omey of Kilcolmkill, Duncan	£	8.	12.	3
186	MacFarlane of Glenralloch, John	£	8.	11.	9
187	Campbell of Achinellan, Patrick	£	8.	11.	0
188	Campbell of Ardnahow, Colin	£	8.	9.	3
189	Stewart of Achnacone, Donald	£	8.	8.	0
190	Stewart of Achnacone, Duncan	£	8.	6.	8
191	McNicholl, portioner of Elrigmore, —	£	8.	6.	1
192	Bannatyne of Kames, James	£	8.	0.	6
193	MacLachlan of Kilchoan, Mr John	£	7.	18.	11
194	MacPhun of Drip, John	£	7.	14.	2
195	MacIntyre of Lettirs, John	£	7.	13.	3
196	MacDougall of Soroba, Alexander	£	7.	10.	0
197	Maclean of Inins, Colin	£	7.	9.	1
198	MacLachlan of Barnagad, Angus	£	7.	7.	2
199	Campbell of Leckuary, Malcolm	£	7.	5.	8
200	MacIlvernock of Ardnakaig, John	£	7.	3.	2
201	McOshennog of Lephinstraw, Hugh	£	6.	19.	9
202	Malcolm of Glenan, Alexander	£	6.	17.	3
203	Stewart of Leckantuim, Alexander	£	6.	13.	4
204	Campbell of Cultoun, John	£	6.	5.	8
205	Campbell of Achanna, John	£	6.	2.	9
206	Campbell of Kildalvane, Colin	£	6.	2.	5
207	Campbell of Bragleenmore, Archibald	£	6.	1.	1
208	Campbell of Blarcherine, Alexander	£	5.	18.	7
209	Maclean of Kilmorie, —	£	5.	17.	9
210	Maclean of Gruline, Lachlan	£	5.	13.	10

211	MacIntyre of Grunachy, Donald	£	5.	8. 0
212	Munro of Stuckagoy, Archibald	£	5.	7. 5
213	MacInturner of Drumlie, —	£	5.	5. 0
214	MacLachlan of Conachraw, William	£	5.	1. 4
215	MacArthur of Ardbrecknish, John	£	5.	0. 0
216	MacKay of Kilmahumaig, —	£	5.	0. 0
217	Campbell of Bragleenbeg, Donald	£	4.	19. 8
218	MacIndeor of Kilchoan, John	£	4.	12. 6
219	MacCannanich of Achadachiranbeg, Duncan	£	4.	11. 8
220	MacLachlan of Craigquhurelan, Duncan	£	4.	8. 10
221	Maclean of Killean, John	£	4.	3. 4
222	Maclean of Lunga, Allan	£	4.	3. 4
223	MacKellar of Kenchregan, Malcolm	£	4.	0. 11
224	MacQuarrie of Culinish, Allan	£	3.	18. 10
225	MacKinnies, portioner of Stuck	£	3.	18 7
226	Maclean of Pennycross, John	£	3.	16. 8
227	Campbell of Mellachy, Alexander	£	3.	13. 8
228	Campbell of Corries, John	£	3.	1. 1
229	MacQuarrie of Balligartan, John	£	3.	0. 0
230	Mrs Jean Cameron	£	2.	19. 3
231	Campbell of Barmaddy, Hugh	£	2.	18. 4
232	Campbell of Garrocharon, James	£	2.	15. 3
233	Campbell of Leachy, Angus	£	2.	13. 9
234	Campbell of Corrichaive, Robert	£	2.	13. 1
235	Ferguson of Upper Craighole, Mr John	£	2.	11. 11
236	MacFarlane of Erines, Alexander	£	2.	10. 0
237	MacMillan of Bailie, Neil	£	2.	6. 1
238	Campbell of Laggandarroch, John	£	2.	0. 0
239	MacQuilkan of Culdrynich, Allan	£	2.	0. 0
240	MacInturner of Nether Craighole, Colin	£	1.	13. 4
241	Mackendrick of Cluanie, Hugh	£	1.	13. 4
242	MacOlchynich of Chapelverna, John	£	1.	7. 9
243	Carmichael of Annat, John	£	1.	6. 0
244	Stevenson of Belnahua, Robert	£	1.	0. 0
245	Campbell of Rudil, Donald	£	0.	13. 9
246	MacKellar in Kilmichael, John	£	0.	11. 6
247	MacInlea of Bachuil, Duncan	£	0	8. 4
248	Clerk in Kilmichael, Archibald	£	0.	6. 3

Septs

The name 'sept' is given to members of a branch of a clan who do not share its name, although they may or may not be of the same blood. Within a clan, following the Highland fashion of designating people by the names of their fathers, grandfathers and sometimes more remote ancestors, other names could be used for certain family groups. Hence in Clan Campbell we have the MacTavish ('Son of Thomas', in Gaelic) sept, descended from a Thomas Campbell, the MacConnochie ('Son of Duncan', in Gaelic) sept, descended from a Duncan Campbell, and early offshoots like the MacArthurs and the MacIvers who descend from the chiefly stock before the adoption of the name Campbell. Other family kindreds who had no blood connection but who might be *nativi* or 'native men', former inhabitants of lands taken over by a new chief, might also choose to follow him and to become septs of his clan.

The word *clann* in Gaelic need signify no more than 'family' or 'children', and there were hundreds of such groups who made no pretence to set up as major powers on their own but who followed the local chief and became members of his clan. Sometimes these smaller kindreds were widely spread and their branches could follow different Chiefs. And very often the same name could come from a whole range of unrelated sources, particularly in the case of Mac-names, or patronymics as they are called, which mean 'Son of'.

The nineteenth-century enthusiasm for clans, fostered for their own reasons both by the tartan manufacturers and by the Clan Societies, resulted in the attribution of as many names as possible to particular clans as septs – sadly only too often with ludicrous results. The idea that *all* Millers should belong to Clan Macfarlane or *all* Taylors to Clan Cameron is clearly untenable; this is not to say that the names were not used by members of those clans on occasion, but they are both work-names of trades carried on in practically every community across English-speaking Britain. Nor is the suggestion that all sons of Harry, Gib, Thomas or Arthur, to take four names as examples,

220

should descend from the same person of that particular name any more tenable. The same point needs to be made about names which derive from a place name and where the original form included 'de' or 'of', and which would be used by anyone, related or not, who came from the place in question. But every effort was made, often for the slimmest of reasons, to attach as many names as possible to the well-known clans. Some of these claims are based on nothing more than a lively imagination, while others depend entirely on one single recorded instance of a connection, this being judged enough to assign all holders of the name to one clan or another.

Our list of septs is by no means perfect; there are some names whose inclusion would seem to be due more to this sept-hunting enthusiasm than to historical accuracy and there are many names which loyally followed the Campbell Chiefs for centuries which have not been included. Quite who was responsible for the compilation of this list, or when, is unknown. But rather than encourage still further confusion, our Chief has said that he does not wish to make any alterations to the 'official' list of Campbell sept names which follows. Rather than do that, he said some years ago that he was prepared to accept as members of Clan Campbell all those of Scottish descent who were prepared to acknowledge him as their Chief. This very much follows what actually happened in past times when 'broken men' – those without a chief – attached themselves by his permission to a chief and became his men.

As will be seen, different versions of the same name which have a common origin are grouped together. Names appear here which also appear under other clans; this is quite proper since, as already explained, in many cases there were quite different, unrelated ancestors in different parts of the country who gave their name to their descendants. If, in modern times, people with a sept name which appears under more than one clan wish to show allegiance to a clan and have no idea from which area they originate, then they should choose *one* of the clans which is said to include their name. It is quite wrong to try to 'belong' to more than one clan.

Several septs have tartans assigned to them. This makes absolutely no difference to the status of the sept concerned and in no way implies that the name is a clan on its own. In cases where a sept quite properly appears under the name of more than one clan and is known to derive from more than one, unconnected source, the attribution of the tartan is actually misleading, and those of the sept name should wear the tartan of the parent clan.

Spelling was an uncertain art, and there is no significance in the various forms of spelling the same name. Nor is any significance to be taken from the various spellings of Mac, Mc, M', Mak or whatever. The same name occurs in different forms, and they have accordingly been grouped together where appropriate.

The 'Official' list of Clan Campbell septs is, in alphabetical order:

ARTHUR
BANNATYNE, BURNES, BURNESS, BURNETT, BURNS
CADDELL, CADELL, CALDER, CATTELL, CONNOCHIE, CONOCHIE
DENOON, DENUNE
GIBBON, GIBSON
HARRES, HARRIS, HASTINGS, HAWES, HAWS, HAWSON
ISAAC, ISAACS, IVERSON
KELLAR, KELLER, KISSACK, KISSOCK
LORNE, LOUDEN, LOUDON, LOUDOUN, LOWDEN, LOWDON
MACARTAIR, MACARTHUR, MACCARTER, MACCOLM, MACCOLMBE, MACCONACHIE, MACCONCHIE, MACCONNECHY, MACCONOCHIE, MACDERMID, MACDERMOTT, MACDIARMID, MACELLER, MACELVIE, MACEVER, MACGIBBON, MACGLASRICH, MACGUBBIN, MACGURE, MACISAAC, MACIVER, MACIVOR, MACKELLAR, MACKELVIE, MACKERLIE, MACKESSACK, MACKESSOCK, MACKISSOCK, MACLAWS, MACLEHOSE, MACNICHOL, MACNOCAIRD, MACONACHIE, MACORAN, MACOWEN, MACPHEDRAN, MACPHUN, MACTAUSE, MACTAVISH, MACTHOMAS, MACURE, MOORE, MUIR
OCHILTREE, ORR
PINKERTON
TAWESON, TAWESSON, THOMAS, THOMASON, THOMPSON, THOMSON, TORRIE, TORRY
URE

ARTHUR, MACARTAIR, MACARTHUR, MACCARTER

The name Arthur is a Celtic one of ancient Briton origin, *Artos* meaning a bear. Its most famous holder was Arthur, a leader of the Britons in the fight against the Anglo-Saxons around the year AD 500. There is little known of him from contemporary sources, but he was clearly someone of substance given the number of occasions on which his name was used by later generations. This use then faded until the thirteenth century when, in answer to the French *chansons de geste*, the fabulous tales of King Arthur and the Round

Table developed. Of more local interest was Arthur, son of Aidan, a Prince of the Scots who was killed in 596 when the Scots were in battle against the Pictish *Miathi*.

The name seems to have had strong connections with the Lennox, the area around Loch Lomond, part of the British Kingdom of Strathclyde, where it was used by such local clans as the Galbraiths and the MacArthurs of Darleith as well as by the Campbells, all of whom are reckoned to be of Lennox origin. The name occurs several times in *Ane Accompt of the Genealogie of the Campbells*, where Diarmid O'Duine's son is Arthur Armdhearg, who has no fewer than three sons called Arthur: Arthur *Urchanach* 'of the Orchy', Arthur Cruachan and Arthur Andrairan. This last Arthur Andrairan was said to have had two sons, Patrick Drynach from whom came the MacArthurs of Inistrynich on Loch Awe, and Duncan Darleith from whom came the MacArthurs of Darleith.[1]

As with so much in *Ane Accompt*, the compiler of the pedigree is using an impressionistic rather than a representational brush; what he is in fact admitting is that he realises there are various MacArthur families but does not know how they fit together, if at all. In fact, it is quite clear that various MacArthur families derive from more than one stem. The MacArthurs of Darleith have been identified by David Sellar as coming from the MacAulays of Ardencaple. In more modern times, there was a family of MacArthurs on Islay who were armourers to the Lords of the Isles; the tombstone of MacArthur of Proaig in Kildalton churchyard is unique for the period in substituting a musket for the more prevalent claymore. And a family of MacArthurs, possibly kin to the Islay armourers, were pipers to MacDonald of Sleat on Skye.

The pipers were said to have come to Skye from Ulva, off Mull, where they had a school of piping. Pennant's report of his visit to Lord MacDonald's piper in 1774 would imply that there was a school of instruction at Penigorm near Duntulm, where they held a croft for their services. The last hereditary piper of this line, according to Angus Mackay's account, was Angus, son of John Bane, whose brother Charles MacArthur was taught by Padruig Og MacCrimmon. Angus was the author of MacArthur's manuscript collection of pipe tunes, written at his dictation by John McGregor, around 1800. The collection is the earliest complete collection of pipe music on the stave. Where these MacArthurs came from is unknown, but it has been claimed that they were MacDonalds by descent as they certainly were by allegiance.

Loch Awe seems to have been early on the area from which various MacArthurs hail. The Arthur of Orchy in *Ane Accompt* would seem a likely reference to the connection of the MacArthurs with the north end of Loch

Awe, while the Drynach added as identification to Patrick Drynach is a reference to Inistrynich – the one-time island in the same loch. An early reference to MacArthurs here occurs in *The Manuscript History of Craignish*, where Dougall Campbell of Craignish, who is said to have succeeded his father around 1250,

> was nursed as his Father & Grandfather were, ever since the Maceachairns left Craiginsh by a principal Family of the MacArthurs on Lochow, & so the whole race continued to be nursed by them untill the unhallowed Christian gave that fatal blow to the Estate anno 1361.[2]

If this is an accurate statement, then the MacArthurs must have been on Loch Awe at least by the year 1200. Further references to members of the family are sparse at this early period, but those that exist imply that the family was a professional, learned one, one of the *Aes Dana*. *Cristinus Arthuri* – Christine MacArthur – is witness on a charter of the Campbell chief in 1403, and his son appears in a similar capacity in 1432.[3] *John MacArthua* (sic) Clerk, diocese of Argyll, of noble race on both sides, student in canon and civil law in Bologna and other universities, has the parish of Medulf (Melfort?), Argyll, for life and power of exchange in 1426,[4] while in 1440 *Dominus Gilbertus M'Arthour* appears on a charter of the Countess of Lennox to Colin Campbell of Glenorchy.[5] A Duncan MacArthur was also Prior of Ardchattan in 1514.

Towards the end of the 1400s, two names reappear on charters of the Earl of Argyll. John MacArthur appears several times in 1493 along with Archibald Uchiltree. It would seem that John died that year, for in 1494 he is replaced by Charles, presumably his son, who acts as witness in several instances alongside the aforesaid Archibald. On no fewer than twenty-six of the surviving Earl's charters between 1494 and 1523 he appears in one capacity or another, usually as a witness, and in places not only around Argyll but as far afield as Glasgow, Stirling, Inverness and Edinburgh. It is clear that he is acting as man of business for the Earl in days before lawyers as we know them existed.

An important change occurs around 1510. Prior to that date, Charles signs as Charles MacArthur, but after it he is always Charles MacArthur 'of Terivadich', having been granted that property by the Earl for his services. From now on, the MacArthurs could claim the status of Lairds, and, no doubt making full use of their legal expertise, the MacArthur landholdings spread around the north end of Loch Awe. As well as becoming owners of property, the MacArthurs appear to have maintained a strong foothold in the Church and the emerging legal profession. Between 1550 and 1560, there appear Master Niall MacArthur, Vicar of Muckairn, Finlay MacArthur, Priest of the Diocese of Lismore, Dougall MacArthur, Clerk to the Sheriffdom of Argyll, Duncan MacArthur, Clerk to the Sheriffdom of Argyll, and Dougall MacArthur, Servitor to the Earl of Argyll, all in the Argyll Transcripts.

Patrick MacArthur, son to Duncan MacArthur of Terivadich, was appointed Captain of the old Campbell Castle of Innischonnell on Loch Awe in April 1559.[6] This important post was held by successive members of the family until 1617 when the then incumbent was dismissed for theft, the post of Captain thereafter going to a younger son of MacLachlan of Craigenterive. In 1568, *Gilbert Makeane VcArthur* is referred to by the Earl of Argyll in a charter as his 'kindly servitor'. It should perhaps be explained that a servitor was a trusted personal assistant and no mere servant. 'Kindly' can mean 'of the same kindred' or 'by long inheritance'. The former meaning seems the intended one, particularly as a MacArthur had been appointed to the Captaincy of the old, principal Campbell place of strength, Innischonnell – a post of sufficient symbolic as well as actual importance as to make it unlikely that it would go to anyone regarded as being outside the Clan.

The rapid acquisition of land around the head of Loch Awe produced strained relationships with the leading family in the area, the MacConnochie Campbells of Inverawe. In 1567, Duncan MacArthur of Terivadich and his son Ian, together with several of their men, were drowned in a skirmish with these Campbells, who had previously held undisputed sway in the area. In 1569, the 5th Earl of Argyll issued a charter to John MacArthur of Terivadich of the office of Bailie on all the lands in Over Loch Awe belonging to Clan Arthur, thus settling the quarrel in favour of the MacArthurs. The lands are given as (modern spelling for identifiable sites) Barbreck, Auchnagum, Larach Ban, Terivadich, Mowey, Drummork, Capehin, Bocardie, Campurruck and Ardbrecknish. A MacArthur also held Drissaig at this time, while there were a number of lands around Innischonnell which went to support the Captain of the castle.[7]

By 1751, the MacArthur landholdings had dwindled once more. The most important was MacArthur of Inistrynich, who held lands rated at £30. 14s. 1d which put him in 75th position among the Argyllshire lairds. The only other MacArthur was MacArthur of Ardbrecknish, whose lands were valued at £5. 0s. 0d. The lands of Terivadich had been set in wadset to a MacCalman; their valuation was £8. 13. 2d. Patrick MacArthur of Terivadich sold the estate in 1771 and died in Jamaica; his only son Charles died on his way to India, leaving no issue, around 1787.

There has been endless confusion over the identity of the MacArthurs and the MacArthur Campbells of Strachur who descend from Bruce's Constable of Dunstaffnage Castle, Sir Arthur Campbell. (There never was a MacArthur who held this post.) Campbell of Strachur goes by the Gaelic title of *Mac-Artairr* – 'Son of Arthur' – while MacArthur of Terivadich is *Mac 'ic Artair* – 'Son of the son of Arthur'. So, too, the 'John MacArthur' executed by King James I in 1428 is in fact the descendant of Sir Arthur Campbell's younger son, also Arthur, who had a charter of her lands from Christina of Garmoran whom he may have been about to marry. Trouble had continued between the MacRuaris and the descendants of Arthur Campbell over the validity of the charter, and James I adopted the drastic expedient of executing both of the contestants in order to bring peace to the area.[8]

There were also MacArthurs in Lochaber who had gone there apparently along with the MacGlasrich Campbells after the MacDonald of Keppoch defeat at the hands of the Stewarts of Appin and the Maclarens in Glenorchy in 1497. One of the name murdered Stewart of Appin at the instigation of a member of the Keppoch family. The deed was done with his battleaxe, hence the Lochaber saying *Tuagh Bhearnach Mhic Artair* – 'The notched axe of MacArthur'. No fewer than five families emigrated to Glengarry in Canada from here in 1802.[9] The name was also common along both sides of Loch Tay, where the local name for the MacArthurs was on occasion *Mc a Chruim* and *McGilleChruim*.[10] From the number of names in Breadalbane of Argyllshire origin, the probability would seem to be that these MacArthurs were of Loch Awe stock. The most famous holder of the name is probably the US General of the Army Douglas MacArthur, Supreme Commander in the Pacific Campaign of the Second World War, whose family roots are in Argyll. His great-grandfather, Archibald MacArthur in Achantiobart, sailed for the USA in 1815.[11]

Recently, a *derbhfine* of MacArthurs was convened and petitioned Lyon for the appointment of a Commander of the Clan MacArthur until such time as the current Representor of MacArthur of Terivadich could be identified. The duly nominated Commander is Mr James MacArthur – formerly MacArthur-Moir – of Milton, Dunoon, descended of a family who were treasurers to Montrose. This new organisation now groups together all those of the name MacArthur, whatever their origins.

BANNATYNE

The name Bannatyne is said to be the same as Ballantine and to derive from Bellenden in Selkirk. The Campbell connection with this name refers only to the Bannatynes of Bute and later of Arran. There are many other Ballantynes and Bannatynes across Scotland who do not share this link. The head of the

CARN CHAILEIN By a lonely track over the hills north of Lochawich stands the pile of stones said to commemorate the spot where Sir Cailean Mor fell, shot in the back by a MacDougall arrow. Two of his descendants place fresh stones upon the cairn.

THE RED FORD *After an acrimonious meeting, the Campbells withdrew homewards over the Allt Dhtarg – the Red Burn. At the Red Ford, the MacDougalls caught up the Campbells and forced a fight in which they were bested. Sir Colin and his party continued on their way, following the track which winds its way up from the ford to the left of the picture, up the hill to the top where Sir Colin met his end. Both the burn and the ford are said to have been so named for the blood that flowed that day.*

CAISTEAL NA NIGHINN RUAIDHE 'Thick vegetation now hides the ruins of 'The Castle of the Red-haired Maiden' on its islet in Loch Avich – possibly the first castle base of the Campbells in Argyll.

INNISCHONNELL CASTLE It is uncertain whether the castle, which lies on an islet in Loch Awe and appears to date from the early 1200s, was built by the Campbells or by the MacDougall Lords of Lorne. From the time of King Robert the Bruce, however, it was the stronghold of the Campbell Chiefs until they transferred their base to Inveraray around the middle of the fifteenth century.

KILCHURN CASTLE (1) *A nineteenth-century engraving of Kilchurn Castle, original seat of the Campbells of Glenorchy, later Earls of Breadalbane, at the north end of Loch Awe. The castle was built in the middle of the fifteenth century by Sir Colin Campbell of Glenorchy, largely during his absence abroad, fighting the Infidel. The original tower house can be identified on the right while the range of buildings to the left is the late seventeenth-century barracks built in the time of John, 1st Earl of Breadalbane. Beyond the castle stretches Glenstrae, last remnant of the lands held by the MacGregor Chiefs.*

KILCHURN CASTLE (2) This view looking down on Kilchurn from the slopes of Ben Cruachan emphasises its strategic location, dominating as it does the north end of Loch Awe. In the background may be seen the entrances to Glenorchy and Glen Lochy – lands early in Campbell hands due to a fourteenth-century marriage with the heiress of Glenorchy – while on the slopes of Stronmilchan may be seen the smallholdings granted in the early 1800s to selected men of his regiment by Lord Breadalbane.

DUNSTAFFNAGE (1)   *Seen here from an unusual angle, Dunstaffnage was the chief stronghold of the Lordship of Lorne. An earlier fortress of which no traces remain was on the site, and it was from here that persistent legend claims that the Scottish King Kenneth MacAlpine moved east in the mid-800s, to take over his Pictish kingdom and to escape the increasing attacks by the Norsemen. The bay on the left provides an ideal anchorage for a galley fleet and is still in use today as a yacht marina. The chapel may be seen among the trees in the top left corner.*

*DUNSTAFFNAGE (2): THE CASTLE ENTRANCE The present castle was built by Duncan
(MacDougall), grandson of Somerled. It was captured by Robert the Bruce, who installed Sir
Arthur Campbell as Constable before a change of policy returned the castle to the MacDougall
Lords of Lorne. Together with the Lordship of Lorne it passed into the hands of the 2nd Earl
of Argyll in 1470. He appointed a kinsman to act as guardian, and, although the castle is now
a ruin, there is still a Campbell who lives nearby and carries out his ancient duties as
Hereditary Captain of Dunstaffnage.*

DUNSTAFFNAGE (3): THE CHAPEL Built at the same time as the castle, the magnificent Norman-style windows of the chapel are still to be seen. It was here, in 1463, that the unfortunate John Stewart, Lord of Lorne, eventually persuaded to make an honest woman of the mother of his illegitimate son Dougall, was killed, legend has it at the altar, by a MacDougall assassin. The Stewarts of Appin who descend from Dougall claim that the wedding had actually taken place, but this does not seem to have been the view at the time and the Lordship of Lorne in due course passed to the Campbell chiefs.

CASTLE SWEEN Said to be the oldest castle in Scotland, the castle is thought to have been built on the shores of Loch Sween at the end of the 1100s by Suibhne, head of the kindred of Anrothan who dominated Knapdale, Glassary and Cowal. The keepership of the castle was granted to Colin, Earl of Argyll in 1481.

CARRICK CASTLE Thought to have been built around the end of the 1300s for the Campbells of Lochawe, Carrick Castle stands on the shores of Loch Goil in Cowal. A branch of the Campbells of Ardkinglas were later installed as Captains of the Castle, which was used by the chiefly family as a convenient staging point on their way to and from the Lowlands.

CASTLE CAMPBELL. Perched on an outcrop of the Ochils, guarded on either side by the ravines of the Burn of Care and the Burn of Sorrow, Castle Campbell gazes out across the broad valley of the River Forth towards Edinburgh. It came into Campbell hands in 1470 as part of the deal with Walter Stewart of Innermeath and was used by the Campbell chiefs as a convenient staging post on the way to and from the capital and also as a dower house.

THE CHAPEL OF KILMUN Sir Duncan Campbell of Lochawe lies within the Argyll Mausoleum, part of the Collegiate Chapel of Kilmun on the Holy Loch, founded as the resting place built for his son Archibald who died around 1440. This became the place of burial for successive chiefs until the eleventh Duke, who followed his father Lord Walter Campbell and was buried on the Isle of Inishail in Loch Awe.

SIR DUNCAN CAMPBELL OF LOCHAWE *Sir Duncan's armoured effigy lies next to that of his wife, his helmeted head lying on his boar's-head crest. On his surcoat is embroidered his shield with the familiar device of gyronny of eight, borne on their arms by all armigerous Campbells.*

KILMARIE CHURCH, CRAIGNISH Built in the 1200s, possibly by the Campbells of Craignish, the mediaeval church of Kilmarie gazes as it has done for three quarters of a millennium over Loch Craignish and up Glen Domhain which leads through the hills to Loch Avich and the possible site of the earliest Campbell base of the Caisteal na Nighinn Ruaidhe – The Castle of the Red-haired Maiden.

TARBERT CASTLE The strategic importance of the narrow neck of land connecting Knapdale and Kintyre has long been recognised. Boats could be portaged across the isthmus. The earliest Scots arriving from Ireland in AD 500 had one of their chief strongholds here. Little now remains of the imposing castle renewed by King Robert the Bruce, but its extent may be judged from this aerial photograph which shows its domination of the East Loch anchorage. The custody of the castle was granted to the 2nd Earl of Argyll in 1504 by King James IV.

Bute Bannatynes was Bannatyne of Kames, a property on Bute which came to the family when Gilbert, son of Gilbert, received it in a charter of King Alexander III. The then head of the family signed a mutual bond with Stuart of Bute in 1547 in which each undertook to support the other against all-comers with the exception of the King and the Earl of Argyll. This followed a Bond of Manrent of 1538 in which Bannatyne had bound himself to the Earl. From then on, they seem to have followed the Campbell Chiefs loyally, with Bannatyne of Kames acting as a Campbell chieftain in all but name.

In the 1547 bond, Bannatyne is described as 'Chief of the MacAmelynes' – a scribe's botched attempt but one at a name which sounds a great deal more Gaelic in character and which may reflect the true origin of this kindred. A possible derivation for this name may be *Amhalghaidh*, possibly given on occasion as *Aulay*. Alwin, 2nd Earl of Lennox, had a son by the latter name who was a great-grandfather of Allan of Faslane.[12]

The arms of Bannatyne of Kames, in use prior to 1672, are *gules a chevron argent between three mullets or*.[13] At first sight, there seems to be no connection with the arms of the Earls of Lennox (*argent a saltire between four roses gules*), but on occasion the arms of *argent a chevron between four mullets gules* have been used by a Bannatyne. A chevron is of course the bottom part of a saltire, and it has been used by Lecky of that Ilk (*argent a chevron between three roses gules*),[14] whose ancestor was also a son of Alwyn, 2nd Earl of Lennox. *Mullets* (five-pointed stars) are not roses, but the shield as a whole to a heraldic eye might seem to have a possible connection. A link between the Bannatynes of Kames and the Earls of Lennox might well repay further investigation.

BURNES, BURNESS, BURNETT, BURNS

The inclusion of the name Burns as a sept of the Clan Campbell is based on very thin evidence and can only be classed as a prime example of optimism! The only link would seem to be a rumoured connection between Robert Burns, Scotland's national poet, and a particular family of Campbells who lived near Taynuilt. The family were almoners to the ancient Priory of Ardchattan on the far side of Loch Etive and guardians or *dewars* of a holy relic, the Staff of Saint Maol Rubha of Applecross. There is a signpost off today's main road just to the north of Taynuilt marked for Balindore or 'the Township of the Dewar' in Gaelic, which ties in with the story.[15]

According to the tale, the Campbells were set upon by a roving band of poets who could, according to ancient Highland custom, billet themselves on whomsoever they liked for as long as they liked, eating their involuntary hosts out of house and home. The son of the house was splitting a log of wood with a wedge one day when the voracious band of rhymers came strolling by. He invited them to help by pulling the log still further apart; but, with the next stroke of his hammer, instead of driving the wedge still further in, he knocked it right out so that the edges of the log sprang together, trapping the poets in agony by their crushed fingers. He kept them there until they had promised to leave his father's house without further ado, and then released them. They kept their promise with an ill-grace and managed to stir up so much annoyance locally at this disrespect for old custom that young Campbell was forced to leave home and take refuge on the other side of Scotland. Here, for added security, he changed his name. Taynuilt is *Tigh-an-Uillt* in Gaelic, or 'House of the Burn', so he is said to have adopted the name Burnhouse, an anglicised version of the same name, as an alias. This shortly became adapted to the local name of Burness – pronounced as having two syllables. Two generations or so later, the family moved south to Ayrshire where the name changed slightly again, this time to Burns, and this is the origin of Robert, the Bard of Scotland!

This story apparently originated with the Rev. Alexander Greig, minister of Stonehaven, who recounted it to the family. His mother was a member of the family. According to him, the episode which led to young Campbell's flight took place during the Civil Wars. There does not seem to be any supporting evidence apart from the place name Balindore; there is now no trace left of the family of dewars there, who are otherwise unrecorded.

But the family themselves believed it – at least for a time – and the records of Lord Lyon King of Arms still contain a detailed family tree showing the poet's descent from Walter Campbell which was deposited in Lyon Office by the family. When, in 1837, the poet's cousin, James Burnes of the Honourable East India Company, took out arms, Lyon granted him a shield of arms which contained the Campbell device of *gyronny of eight* which appears in it no fewer than three times. In 1851, he altered his arms and this time the Campbell reference was dropped – for what reason is unknown, although we do now know that a family called Burness were in Bogjordan much earlier than the reputed arrival of the poet's ancestor there and this knowledge may have been the reason for the change of opinion.

Whether true or not, this tale is of importance for those of the name of Burns since it appears to be the only reason for the statement that the name Burns in its various forms is a sept of the Clan Campbell. There would seem even less reason to include the name Burnett in the above list – because, it would appear, of the fancied resemblance between the names Burness and Burnett. But the Burnetts are a perfectly good clan of their own in the north-east with their Chief Burnett of Leys.

CADDELL, CADELL, CALDER, CATTELL

The name is geographical in origin, and it appears in various forms in various parts of Scotland: Calder in Caithness, Lanarkshire, Inverness, Ayrshire and Midlothian; Cadder in Glasgow; Cawdor in Nairn. It is the last which has the Campbell connection; elsewhere in this volume will be found the story of Muriel, heiress of Cawdor or Calder, whose removal for safe-keeping to Argyll as a child enabled her to marry John Campbell, younger son of the 2nd Earl of Argyll, and thereby to found the important branch of the Campbells of Cawdor whose head, the Earl Cawdor, still possesses the old family seat of Cawdor Castle today.

Muriel's family would seem to be probably one of the incoming southerners, most likely Flemish, planted in Moray during the twelfth century to subdue the local tribes who had a constant history of rebellion. Many of them were expelled as a result, but not all, and many of the incomers married into the families of the ancient possessors of the land to found new dynasties based upon the old. From an early stage the family held the position of Thane, although any connection with Shakespeare's *Macbeth* has immediately to be discounted.

First on contemporary written record is Donald, Thane of Cawdor in 1295.[16] Then in 1310, King Robert the Bruce granted a charter of the Thanage to William Thane of Cawdor 'as had been the custom in the days of the Lord Alexander, King of Scots, of Blessed Memory'.[17] With the arrival of Muriel and her Campbell husband, her uncles at first made trouble, but in due course all was dealt with and the Calders settled down under the new regime. Lord Cawdor, today, is still referred to, by friends of the family, as 'The Thane'.

CONNOCHIE, CONOCHIE, MACCONACHIE, MACCONCHIE, MACCONNECHY, MACCONOCHIE

MacConochie in its various spellings is the Gaelic for 'Son of Duncan'. It is in use in various parts of Scotland in various forms, notably by the Robertsons who usually spell the patronymic *MacDonachie*. In this particular case, the name was used by the descendants of a Duncan Campbell who was either the son of Dugald, younger son of Sir Neil Campbell of Lochawe as suggested in *Ane Accompt* or, rather more likely, the Duncan Skeodnish ('from Ardskeodnish') who was a younger brother of Colin Iongantach Campbell of Lochawe, who is also put forward as as an alternative in the same pedigree.

Nothing for certain is known of him nor of the intervening generations

until, in 1485, Colin, 1st Earl of Argyll, grants a charter of the fees of the
Wardenship of Over Lochow to his beloved cousin Dugald Campbell of
Inverawe. An undated charter by the 2nd Earl (who was killed at Flodden in
1513) is granted to

> Archibald, son and apparent heir to umquhile Dugald MacDonachadh
> Campbell of Inverawe macand mention the said umquhile Dugald in
> his lifetime obtenit ane chartour and seasings of said landis, salmond
> fishings etc. conform to the evidents of umquhile Archibald Campbell,
> father to the said umquhile Dugald . . .[18]

The patronymic of *MacConnochie* was also used by two related families, the
Campbells of Lerags, in Lorne, just south of Oban overlooking Loch
Feochan and the Campbells of Stronchormaig who became the Campbells
of Glenfeochan, also at the head of Loch Feochan. Duncan, son of the late
Duncan Campbell of Lerags, is on reecord in 1509 and John MacConnochie
of Stronchormaig in 1510. From the dates, it would appear most likely that
the elder Duncan and John are brothers of Dougall or *Dugald* of Inverawe.

It is thought that the Inverawe family were previously based on the island
of Fraoch Eilean in Loch Awe opposite the mouth of the Pass of Brander
where the towerhouse is first on record in a charter to MacNaughton in
1247. Lerags and Stronchormaig are both placed on an important route into
the heart of Campbell territory, and Inverawe is at the further end of the
equally important Pass of Brander. *Inver*, of course, means 'at the mouth
of', and the present house is a mile or so inland. At the actual mouth of the
river, however, is a *motte* or man-made mound which would once have had a
palisaded fort on its summit which dominates the river crossing of the Awe
where, until recent times, there was a ferry, operated for many generations by
a family named Turner, and also the crossing over Loch Etive. This is known
as 'The Dunan (or Little Fort) of Inverawe' and is clearly the site of the first
occupation by the MacConnochie Campbells before, some years later, they
decided to build themselves a more comfortable habitation.

The Campbells of Inverawe were a particularly ferocious branch of the
Clan. In 1587, their chieftain appears on *The Roll of the Names of the
Landlordis and Baillies of Landis in the Hielandis, quhair Broken Men hes
duelt and Presentlie duellis*[19] contained in an Act of Parliament, and the same
year the Campbells of Inverawe are included in *The Roll of the Clannis (in
the Hielandis and Iles) that hes Capitanes, Chieffis, and Chiftanes quhome on
thay Depend, oft tymes aganis the Willis of thair Landislordis: and of Sum
Speciale Personis of Branchis of the Saidis Clannis.*[20]

At the end of the sixteenth century, John Dubh Campbell, Tutor of

Inverawe, was the leader of the Scots Gallowglasses fighting in Ireland. Major Duncan Campbell of Inverawe was mortally wounded at the Battle of Ticonderoga in North America in 1762; he is the hero of a famous West Highland ghost story. He was alone at Inverawe, so the tale goes, when a frantic man burst in and rushed up to touch the hearth, claiming sanctuary and explaining that he had killed a man. Inverawe hid him in the upper part of the house, in a room which is there to this day; when the posse arrived, he was dismayed to find that the murder victim was his own foster-brother. The laws of Highland hospitality, however; held him firm and he did not give up his unwelcome guest. He did, however, transfer him to a cave on Cruachan. That night, the ghost of the murdered foster-brother appeared to Inverawe, telling him to give up the killer. This he refused to do. The same thing happened on the second night, and on the third the ghostly apparition bade him farewell, saying 'we meet again at Ticonderoga'. When he took food up to the cave, it was empty; the murderer had fled.

The years passed, and time dulled the memory. Duncan Campbell joined the army and rose to be second-in-command of his regiment, the Black Watch. The army were due to attack the heavily defended French position of Fort Carillon. The night before the engagement, Duncan saw again the ghost of his foster-brother; inquiry revealed that the Indian name for the fort was Ticonderoga and Duncan knew that his fate was sealed. The Black Watch were kept in reserve as the British troops flung themselves against the French, being cut down by the score. Eventually it was the turn of the Black Watch, who hurled themselves in vain at the thicket of cut-down trees that shielded the French palisade. Their casualties were heavier than any they were to suffer until the carnage of the First World War. Among them was Inverawe, heavily wounded and to die some ten days later, in fulfilment of his fate.

With his death and that of his only surviving son Alexander who died the following year, having failed to recover from his wounds sustained at the same battle, the lands of Inverawe passed to Duncan's daughter Janet who married a Captain Pitman, an Englishman. They sold Inverawe to Janet's maternal uncle, Campbell of Monzie, through which family the estate eventually passed through a daughter to the Campbells of Dunstaffnage. After various vicissitudes, the house at least is once more in Campbell hands, the present owner being Robert Campbell-Preston, heir male of the Campbell-Prestons of Ardchattan. The Representation of the family of Inverawe passed to the line of Duncan's brother, Alexander, who had pursued a prosperous career as Comptroller of Customs at Greenock. In 1908, Alastair Magnus Campbell of Auchendarroch, great-great-grandson of Alexander, was granted the undifferenced arms and recognised as Campbell of Inverawe by the Lord Lyon. His son, the present *MacConnochie*, Chieftain of Inverawe, is Alan Campbell, who lives in Yorkshire.

DENOON, DENUNE

Black in his *Scottish Surnames* notes the similarity between the various spellings of the names Denoon and Dunoon.[21] It would seem strange, therefore, that the Official List of Campbell septs should include the first and not the second, since Douglas in his *Baronage of Scotland* states clearly that the name derives from Dunoon in Argyll. The only other Denoon or Dunoon appears to be the farm of Denoon near Glamis, in Angus.[22] Douglas goes on to tell the tale 'handed down by their bards and sennachies' of a younger son of the House of Argyll who, having been appointed Hereditary Governor and Keeper of Dunoon Castle, was succeeded in due course by a descendant, one Duncan Campbell, who got into trouble for cattle-rustling. His kinsman the Earl of Argyll had him tried and condemned to death by drowning in the waters of Clyde, but he escaped and, with his brother, set off to the far north where they took their mother's name of Denune. Duncan's brother, Donald, became in due course Abbot of Fearn, in Ross. From Duncan descended the Denunes of Cadboll in Ross, this estate having been passed to his nephew by Abbot Donald.

The earliest mention of one of the family is given by Black as Walter de Dunoun, a witness on a charter of the Church of *Maleuille* to Dunfermline Abbey in 1255.[23] Alexander Dunon holds the lands of Neuyd, now Rosneath,[24] and as Alexander de Dunhon he serves on an inquest in Dumbarton in 1271.[25] Around 1285, he is granted the three-quarter carucate of Achencloy Nether 'which in Scots is called Arachor'.[26] *Arthur de Dunnon*, who appears on a Charter of James the Steward in 1294,[27] was among the magnates of Scotland who appear in Ragman Roll signing allegiance to Edward I of England. His seal is of particular interest, its blazon being given as *A shield, fesse chequy of three tracts, charges in chief obliterated, supported by two lions: 'S Arthuri de Dvnnovin'*,[28] while he is described as being *del conte de Ayr*. This would seem to indicate that by blood the Dunoons may have been Stewarts and agents of the latter's early dominance over the district of Cowal.

Donald, Abbot of Fearn, is on record as having been appointed around 1526 and to have died in 1540.[29] The editor of the *Calendar of Fearn* says that Abbot Donald's parentage is unknown. The *Calendar* includes an entry for 1534 which records the death at Cadboll of one David Dunowne, and in 1539 Abbot Donald, John Denoon of Davidston and William Denoon of

Pithogarty successfully claimed to be tenants-in-chief of the earldom of Ross.[30] Abbot Donald, as was not uncommon with churchmen of his day, was not exactly celibate and produced nine sons by two mothers; it is not entirely impossible that he and his brother could have produced the considerable number of Denunes who appear around this time in the area. Douglas says that Abbot Donald's nephew for whom he obtained Cadboll was Andrew, but this Andrew does not appear in the *Calendar*.

A final twist to the story is provided by the family of the Campbells of Denoon. Research carried out by the College of Arms in London traces them back to one David Campbell alias Denoon who lived at Hilton, Tain, and who died aged 65 in 1793 and was buried in the churchyard at Fearn. The family history which may or may not be true is that they descended from the original Campbells who took the name Denune and had fled from Arran to Ross-shire after the '15. This could only have happened if their forebears had returned south and had then followed the example of their earlier ancestors and had again taken refuge in Ross when things became difficult. Be that as it may, David's son, Andrew, went south to London, where he prospered as a goldsmith in the early 1800s. His grandson, William Branch Campbell, emigrated to Australia in 1850 and settled there, becoming a man of considerable substance. William Branch's grandson was Arthur Alfred Campbell, who, having taken out arms at the College of Arms in London, in 1838 had them matriculated at the Court of the Lord Lyon as 'Campbell of Denoon'. This strange territorial designation was apparently put forward by the future Lord Lyon Sir Thomas Innes of Learney in order to establish a new House within the Clan Campbell, the arms being those of an indeterminate cadet, that is to say one whose exact connection to the chiefly stem is unknown.

Dunoon Castle was captured from Balliol in 1334 by Robert Stewart and by Sir Colin Campbell of Lochawe or Dougall Campbell – accounts differ. It was thereafter held by a variety of constables until 1460/1 when Colin, 1st Earl of Argyll, received a life rent of the castle lands in return for garrisoning it and keeping it in good repair. In 1473 he received a charter giving him the hereditary custody of the castle with the power to appoint constables. In 1550, Archibald, Master of Argyll, later the 5th Earl, granted the keepership of the castle together with the twenty-seven merklands that went with it to Colin Campbell of Ardkinglas for the service of two boats. In 1571, Archibald, by then 5th Earl, granted the castle acre and the office of Baillie to Archibald Campbell, a cadet of the Ardkinglas family, as Captain of the Castle of Dunoon. From him descended the Campbells of Innellan and Dunoon. It would therefore seem, if this story is true, that the two brothers who fled to the north came from another family who held the post of Captain of Dunoon after 1473 and before about 1500, when it would seem likely they had to leave Argyll in a hurry.

GIBBON, GIBSON, MACGIBBON, MACGUBBIN

This is another collection of names popular across the English-speaking world, deriving ultimately from the Old English name Gilbert. According to Black, its popularity in Scotland is owing to its having been taken as the anglicised form of *MacGille Bride* – 'Son of the Servant of Saint Bride'. This evolved into many forms, not all of which are given here. As it is, there can be no suggestion that all those of the above names are automatically Campbells. Gibson is a late addition to our list. The other three names refer in all probability to a small Cowal tribe of MacGibbons of whom the leading family were the MacGibbons of Auchangarrane, who held lands in Glendaruel. These MacGibbon lairds were among the small lairds of the area who were wont to be referred to in popular parlance as 'Barons' – a possible reference to their once having held their properties, however small, directly from the Crown, or, more probably, from the Stewarts before they became Royal.

This appears to be an example, *Dungallus Gibbonsoun* of Auchingarne having resigned his lands into the hands of King James IV as tutor to his son, James, Prince of the Isles and Steward of Scotland. Young James having died shortly thereafter, his post as Steward reverted to his father King James. The King in 1508 granted the lands to Colin Earl of Argyll.[31] Thereafter the MacGibbons held of the Earls of Argyll until the earl passed the superiority of the lands to Campbell of Auchinbreck.[32] Christian MacGibbon of Achnangarn is on record in 1520 and Duncan MacGibbon of Auchnegarryn in 1525. Iain McGibboun of Auchangarrayn is on record in 1569 and in 1598.[33] Duncan Macgibbon of Auchnangarn appears in 1632 and 1648 – the latter date being when he and his brother were re-armed by Argyll, having lost their arms – and his brother's son at Stirling. Dougall MacGibbon of Auchnagarran is mentioned in 1683. He must have been dead by 1696 when Archibald MacGibbon appears as tutor to the Baron MacGibbon. Duncan MacGibbon of Auchnagarran – presumably the youthful baron aforementioned – appears in 1704 as a Commissioner of Supply for Argyll. In 1715, he appears on the list of Argyllshire lairds who sign an affirmation of loyalty to King George. In 1740, he sells land to John Macleod of Muiravonside, by which time he holds the position of Surveyor of HM Customs in Glasgow, and by 1751 he is out of the county since he does not appear in the Valuation Roll of that year.

HARRES, HARRIS, HAWES, HAWS, HAWSON

The attribution of these names to Clan Campbell is a puzzle. Frank Adam and Sir Thomas Innes of Learney in their *Clans, Septs and Regiments of the Scottish Highlands* include Hawes, Haws and Hawson as Campbell septs. Black, on the other hand, in his *Surnames of Scotland* only mentions Hawson of the above three names, while of Harris (of which Harres is presumably a variant) he merely says that it is a surname more English than Scottish. Hawson he says is probably English and a variant of Halson. All the above names derive from 'Son of Henry' – not a Campbell name. None of them appears in any record of Argyll that I have come across, and their inclusion remains a puzzle.

It may just be that an eager empire-builder has come across the name *M'Herries* or *M'herres* among those holding land from the Campbell chief and has seen this as justification for including the above. But if so, why the omission of Harrison? In any case, the derivation is false since *M'Herreis* or *McKerris* derives from *MacFhearguis* or 'Son of Fergus' and refers to the Fergusons of Glensellich, a small but ancient Cowal clan who look as if they were the ancient holders of Strachur and the surrounding lands until they were taken over by the Campbells, for whom they acted as Officers of Strachur. The last Chieftain of the *Clann Fhearghuis of Stra-chur* was a colourful individual who spent his latter days based in the Explorers' Club in New York, where he habitually wore Highland dress. He was a larger-than-life character who made extravagant claims both for himself and for his clan who, he claimed, were the oldest in Scotland, being directly descended from Fergus MacErc who was one of the founders of the Scottish Kingdom of Dalriada in AD 500. When Lord Lyon granted him arms, they included the supporters of an ancient chiefly family, while the arms themselves were the same as those given to the Fergussons of Kilkerran, Chiefs of the name of Ferguson, with the additional difference of a white wand through the buckle at the centre of the shield, a reference to their position as Officers or Stewards of Strachur. There is no blood connection between the two families.

Gilbarchan M'Kerras had sasine of the lands of Stronchrevich in 1542; in 1547 the Earl of Argyll confirmed these lands to his beloved servitor, *Iain Makane VcKerres of Kilcatrine* and *Gyllebarchane McKerres*, his natural son. In 1599, *Johne Makilleberchan Vecfergus of Ardeline* (Ardchyline) gives Stronchrevich to his natural son *Fergus M'Keane VcPhergus* and after him to *John Makeane Vc'illeberchan VicFergus*, reserving the life rent.[35] In 1603, *John M'Kerres of Ardeline* appears alongside *John Keyr M'Donchie VcDonnel VcErres in Glensellich* who by 1637 is described as *of Glensellich*, implying his progression from being the tenant of Glensellich to becoming its heritable owner.[36] The descent of *Iain Ciar* as given here, incidentally, by his patronymic, differs markedly from the pedigree claimed by the last Chieftain of Clannfhearguis.

HASTINGS

Once again, the reasons for attributing membership of all those of the name of Hastings to Clan Campbell seem remarkably tenuous. The name Hastings is English in origin. A branch of this distinguished family came to Scotland in the reign of William the Lion and was given land in Angus. John de Hastings was Lord of Duns and Sheriff and Forester of the Mearns in 1178. The only discernible Campbell connection comes with the marriage in 1804 of Flora Campbell, Countess of Loudoun, daughter and heir to James Mure Campbell, the 5th Earl of Loudoun, to Lord Rawdon. Lord Rawdon succeeded his mother as Earl of Moira and, among other titles, Baron Hastings of Hastings, as a result of which he added the name Hastings to his surname and became Rawdon-Hastings. The barony of Hastings of Hastings is an English title which dates back to 1461. A distinguished soldier who was Commander-in-Chief of the army in Scotland 1802–6, he was created a Knight of the Garter in 1812. He was Governor-General and Commander-in-Chief in India 1813–22, during which time he conquered Nepal and concluded a treaty with the Gurkha nation which endures to this day. In 1817 he was created Viscount Loudoun as a result of his marriage, Earl of Rawdon and Marquess of Hastings. He died in 1826, and the present Countess of Loudoun is his descendant through several marriages of heiresses. Her family surname is now Abney-Hastings. Quite why this should result in all those of the name of Hastings owing allegiance to Mac Cailein Mor is beyond the comprehension of this author, but it is the only connection he has been able to discern.

ISAAC, ISAACS, KISSACK, KISSOCK, MACISAAC, MACKESSACK, MACKESSOCK, MACKISSOCK

There are two possible origins for the name, the most prevalent one being *Mac Isaac* – 'Son of Isaac'. But another possible derivation is from *Mac-Gille-Kessock*, 'Son of the Servant of Saint Kessog', an early Celtic saint whose shrine was at Luss on Loch Lomond, where his relics were guarded by a family of Dewars who went by this latter name. A popular account of the name MacIsaac is that one of the name which was borne by a sept of the

Clanranald MacDonalds got into trouble and came south where he took service under the Campbells of Craignish, where, in 1544, John MacIsaac was appointed Sergeant and Mair of Craignish.[37] A Gillanders McYsac is witness on a Beauly Charter in 1231.[38]

There were for long a numerous tribe of MacIsaacs on South Uist, where they were known as the *Clann Mhic 'ille Riabhaich*. They are said to have come to Scotland as part of the dowry of O'Cain, the Irish Chieftain's daughter, when she married Angus Og, contemporary and erstwhile ally of King Robert the Bruce. Not all MacIsaacs in South Uist, appear, however, to be of this stock, since the name has also been borne as an alias by various MacQueens.[39] The name Isaac, possibly an anglicisation of Sitheigh,[40] is said to have been borne by a son either of Angus Og or of his brother Alexander. Contemporary opinion favours the latter, whose sons, Isaac among them, went to Ireland where they founded a tribe of MacDonald galloglasses, the MacSheehys.

We do not know the identity of the mysterious Squire, Thomas Isaac, later Sir Thomas, who married the Bruce's daughter Mathilda. Their daughter, Joanna Isaac, in due course was to marry John, Lord of Lorne.[41] In 1510, *Esaig M'Thome V'Esaig* is a witness on a sasine of the lands of Craignish to Archibald Earl of Argyll.[42] His father was almost certainly the Sir Thomas Esok, Canon of the Cathedral Church of Argyll in 1448.[43] But the MacIsaacs in Craignish would seem to go back much further in that part of the world than the sixteenth century; in a 1592 Craignish bond of manrent, *Malcolm Moir Makesaig* and his three sons are described as among the 'native men' of Craignish – in other words descended from the early inhabitants of the district, when they give their bond of manrent to Ronald Campbell of Barrichbeyan as their Chief.[44]

They share a common origin with the family who became the MacCallums and later the Malcolms of Poltalloch, who are said to descend from one of the six sons of a Baron MacKessock of Largie. One of the Largie properties was long known as Largie MacKessock to distinguish it from the other properties also using the same name.[45] In 1731, there was a row between the Malcolms of Poltalloch and the McKessocks of Slockavuillen over who owned the family burial ground in Kilmartin Churchyard (at this time, the Malcolms were mere bonnet lairds with none of the wealth they were later to amass in the West Indies). The Kirk Session[46] found in favour of the MacKessocks but pointed out that both sides were of the same stock. The statement by Black that the MacKissocks on the Moray Firth probably came there with Colin, 6th Earl of Argyll, who married the widow (not daughter as Black has it) of the Regent Moray, seems very unlikely.[47] Saint Kessog was venerated on the

Black Isle, where there are several sites dedicated to him and it would seem more probable that their name is in fact *MacGille Kessog* and that the family there were local devotees of the saint.

Isaac, of course, is a name of great importance in the Old Testament story and as such is likely to have been used by a number of people throughout the Highlands and the rest of Scotland. It appears frequently in the Isle of Man, where it is on record first. The name therefore is clearly one which stems from a variety of unrelated origins which no doubt includes those of purely Jewish blood who have settled here in Scotland. As far as being a Campbell sept is concerned, this obviously only applies to those MacIsaacs once settled in Craignish.

IVERSON, MACEVER, MACGURE, MACIVER, MACIVOR, MACURE, ORR, URE

The above are all variations of *Mac Iomhair*, meaning 'Son of Iver'. *Iver* or *Ivarr* was a popular Norse name and, as such, was found over most of Scotland, particularly in the Western Isles. There seems little or no likelihood of a common origin and of a single 'Clan MacIver', but the waters were considerably muddied by the efforts of Principal P. C. Campbell who wrote an anonymous book *Account of the Clan Iver*[48] seeking (unsuccessfully) to strengthen his petition to the Lord Lyon for the chiefship of such a Clan. There is a good deal of interesting information in the book but it has to be extracted with some care.

According to *Ane Accompt*, Iver was one of two illegitimate sons of *Colin Maol Math*, the other one being *Tavish Coir* from whom descended the MacTavishes.[49] Iver's mother was said by the same source to have been the daughter of Sween of Castle Sween who, as *Swineruo* or *Suibhne Ruadh*, was the leading chief of the kindred of Anrothan, possessors of the districts of Cowal, Glassary and Knapdale. This myth is further given credence by the existence of Dun Mor, at Kilmory, near Lochgilphead, a most impressive small fort which, according to legend, was a stronghold of the MacIvers.[50] The MacIvers' early possessions were said to have been in Glassary. First on written record is *Malcolm M'Ivyr*, who features in the list of magnates in Balliol's new Sheriffdom of Argyll/Lorne in 1292. 'The Lordship of MacIver', however, was further north in the area of country immediately south of the mouth of Loch Melfort near the site of the present-day Loch Melfort Hotel and Arduaine Gardens. The rocky spur by the road just to the south of the hotel is *Dun an Garbh-sroine*, site of a fortification thought to have been the MacIver base here from the fourteenth to the seventeenth century.

The leading family of the MacIver Campbells was MacIver of Lergachonzie and Stronshira. Lergachonzie is just south of *Dun an Garbh-sroine* and Stronshira is at the mouth of Glen Shira near Inveraray where a branch of the MacIvers were Captains of the Castle of Inveraray. The standing stone in the grounds of Inveraray Castle in the Winterland, the field on which the annual Inveraray Games are held, is said to have marked the boundary between the MacIver lands and those of the MacVicars. Other subsidiary branches include the MacIver Campbells of Ballochyle in Cowal, the Campbells of Kirnan in Glassary, the MacIvers later Campbells of Pennymore on Loch Fyne, south of Inveraray, and the Campbells of Ardlarach near Ardfern, Craignish. The inheritors of the main line were the MacIver Campbells of Asknish, the old name for the area in the old Lordship of MacIver now known as Arduaine. When the family moved to Loch Fyneside, they took the name of Asknish with them and gave it to their new house.

Less certain is the branch to which Principal Campbell belonged – the Campbells of Quoycrook in Caithness, allegedly descended from Lergachonzie in the persons of a Kenneth Buey MacIver and his brother Farquhar, claimed to have gone north to protect the interests there of the Countess of Argyll around 1575. From them, according to Principal Campbell, come the families of Campbell of Duchernan, of Thurso and Lochend and the Iverachs of Wideford away up in Orkney. Both the Iverachs and the Campbells of Duchernan display the Campbell gyronny in their arms. Much is made of the use by the MacIvers in their heraldry of the coat *quarterly or and gules, a bend sable*, which is claimed by Nisbet to be the ancient arms of MacIver in contrast to the Campbell gyronny. In fact, the coat is a popular one displayed by, among many others, the family of Eure as far back as 1300, and it would seem all too likely that this is a case of a fancied resemblance between that name and that of MacIver in its form 'Ure', resulting in its assignation to or adoption by the MacIvers in Argyll.

In June 1564, at Dunoon, Archibald 5th Earl of Argyll resigned to Iver MacIver of Lergachonzie, in return for certain sums of money, all calps paid to him by those of the name MacIver, reserving to himself the calp of Iver himself and his successors.[51] The significance of this act has been given various interpretations. It would also seem to be the case that after this date those of the name MacIver started to use the name Campbell in addition to or instead of their former one. It has been claimed that this was recognition of the MacIvers as a separate Clan and that the change of surname was part of the deal and in effect forced upon them. For this last there seems to be no actual proof whatever; what seems to be more likely is that the move was for administrative convenience. The various MacIvers in Argyll were now firmly placed under a chieftain who would be answerable for their actions to his Chief, Argyll, in whose hands his own calp very specifically remained. The move would seem to have been a popular one, and those affected appear keen to have stressed the continuation of their status as part of Clan Campbell by increasing their use of the name.

KELLAR, KELLER, MACELLER, MACKELLAR

The name MacKellar derives from the Gaelic *MacEalair*, 'Son of Hilary', a probable reference to the fourth-century Saint Hilary, Bishop of Poitiers. In 1422 at Dumbarton, *Eilar MacKellar* was a witness on a Duntroon charter. The name first appears in Argyll in 1432 when *Felanus Hilarii*, possibly a son of Eilar's, appears as witness on a charter by Duncan, 1st Lord Campbell, of the lands of Glenorchy to his son Colin.[52] He may be the same as the Patrick Mackellar who, the same year, witnesses a charter at Carnasserie.[53] In 1470, reference is made to *Cristinus McAlare de Ardare*, who has a precept addressed to him by Colin 1st Earl of Argyll.[54] Ardare is on the south bank of Loch Awe. Cristinus is the same as the *Gilchrist Makalare of Ardare* who in 1476 resigns Ardare into the King's hands, as does his wife Mariota MacIsaac her property of Craigmurell – also in Glassary – for a regrant of both estates to Gilchrist.[55] In 1489, a licence to trade in England on horseback or on foot is given to *Archibald Makelar of Argile* at the instance of Thomas Graham, merchant in London.[56]

The first reference to MacKellars in Cowal is the 1494 sasine to *Duncan Alarii* of the lands of Corrief, Glaslet and Drimsyniemore at Lochgoilhead.[57] It would have been his son who, as Archibald, son of Duncan MacKellar, had sasine of these lands around 1496.[58] How these MacKellars were connected is unclear, but it seems more than a coincidence that when, in 1528, a precept of sasine was granted by Campbell of Corvarron to infeft *Duncan M'Allar of Ardare* and his wife *Margaret Drumment* and their son *Patrick M'Callar* in the life rent and feu of the one merkland of Kilmun near Lochavich, the transaction should have taken place at Kenlochgoil (Lochgoilhead) with *Malcolm M'Callar* and *Duncan M'Gillepatrick M'Callar* as Corvarron's Baillies and *Maculin M'Callar Murche, piper* and *Sir Michael M'Callar* – obviously a churchman – among the witnesses. Kilmun had been in the hands of the Ardare family as early as 1520, when Campbell of Craignish had given a charter of it to Duncan M'Kellar.[59]

Duke Niall was of the opinion that the MacKellars had come to Cowal as Officers of Over Cowal for the Argyll family, an opinion borne out by both the 1558 letters of reversion by *Duncan M'Dowle V'Kellar* of half the lands of Glaslet and half the sergeandry of Lochgoilhead and by the 1583 sasine to Archibald MacKellar, 'an honest youth', who has sasine of the twenty shilling lands of Glaslet as nearest heir to the late Dougall MacKellar, *nepos fratris proavi*, and who is vested and seised in the said lands with the office of Serjeandrie of Over Cowal.[60] Duilettir in Glendaruel was also for a time a MacKellar possession; in 1587 *Duncan M'Eanmore VcKellar of Duisletir* sold the property to his 'liberall' or illegitimate son *Archibald M'Donachie VcEanmore VcKellar* with the consent of his eldest legitimate son *Gillepadrig*.[61]

Another branch of the family had possession of the lands of Cruachan on the opposite shore of Loch Awe to Innischonnell Castle. In 1560, Malcolm MacKellar is fiar of Corribuie; his father Gilbert has the three merkland of Cruachan Middle and the forty pennyland of 'Dirmaldony', wherever that may be. According to Dewar, one of the MacKellars of Cruachan was killed in a fight by the young sons of his neighbour, MacArthur of Barnaline, supposedly over his intention of exercising his right of *jus primae noctis*. The MacKellars took part in the infamous plot to murder Campbell of Cawdor in 1592. The fatal shot that killed him at Knipoch was fired from a hackbut by Patrick Og MacKellar who was later hanged; his brother Gillemartin was also involved.

Yet another MacKellar kindred is to be found in Glenshira, where they had the lands of Maam, Kilblaan and Stuckscarden. According to a letter written by Patrick MacVicar to the Duke's Chamberlain, James Ferrier, in 1802, soliciting lands or posts for his young MacKellar nephews, the MacKellars together with the MacVicars had long formed part of the *Leuchd-crios* or personal bodyguard of the Campbell chiefs; the MacKellars had also been their musicians, and the writer recalled seeing the harp in his grandfather's house – this would have been around the middle of the 1700s. According to him, the Harper's Ford in Glenshira is so named for the two family heads of Kilblaan and Maam who would sit on a summer's evening on either bank playing to each other.[62] There was also, it appears, a concentration of MacKellars on Loch Fyne, and in the late eighteenth century no fewer than twenty-five separate MacKellar families were living on the Knockbuy Estate.[63]

The Mackellars had, over the years, owned a number of small lairdships in Argyll. By the time of the 1751 Valuation, three small MacKellar lairdships remained, those of Dell, Kenchregan and the family of MacKellar in Kilmichael. Many had emigrated; the Glassary Mackellars seem to have gone to Canada, and those from around Inveraray and Loch Fyne to Australia, where they flourished. Many went to Glasgow, where they seem to have been numerous in the seafaring profession even to the extent of becoming shipowners. Descendants of this small Argyllshire kindred turn up in a wide variety of places and range from such kenspeckle figures as Kenneth Mackellar, the Scots singer, to Lt-Colonel George Mackellar, DSO, OBE, Commanding Officer of the 8th (Argyllshire) Battalion of the Argyll and Sutherland Highlanders in many a North African battle during World War II, and to the late Princess Dimitry of Russia, born a MacKellar.[64]

LORNE

Fergus, Loarn and Angus, the sons of Erc, are said to have been the leaders of the invasion of Argyll from Ireland which set up the Scottish Kingdom of Dalriada around AD 500. Loarn's portion was north Argyll, whence the title of the area around modern Oban where Loarn had his base at Dunollie. Somerled's rebellion carved out a new kingdom, and, after his death in 1164, the district of Lorne was included in the share of his eldest son Dougall whose descendants, the MacDougall chiefs, used the style of *de Ergadia* – 'of Argyll' – as a family surname and the title of 'Lord of Lorne'. The title passed out of the family to the Stewarts and from them, in turn, it went, in 1470, to the Campbell chiefs who ever after combined the Galley of Lorne with the Campbell gyronny of eight in their arms. The courtesy title of the Duke's son and heir has long been the Marquess of Lorne. As a surname, Lorne is of territorial origin. There is no means of knowing from what blood its users descend, and assignation of the name to Clan Campbell rests on the Campbell Chief's possession of the title which, as already stated, also belonged, at various times, to the MacDougalls and the Stewarts.

LOUDEN, LOUDON, LOUDOUN, LOWDEN, LOWDON

The name is geographical, from Loudoun in Ayrshire. In 1318, Sir Duncan Campbell, son of Donald, younger brother of Sir Neil Campbell of Lochawe, received a charter of the lands of Loudoun and Stevenson from King Robert I in a barony with Loudoun as its *caput*, for services of a knight. This was following his marriage to Susanna Crawford, heiress of Loudoun, with whom also came the office of hereditary Sheriff of Ayr. Thus started the important branch of the Campbells, later Earls of Loudoun. There is a complication in that early usage, following local pronunciation, often used Loudoun for Lothian – again for a geographical name but one with no Campbell connections.

MACCOLM, MACCOLMBE, MACLAWS, MACLEHOSE, MACTAUSE, MACTAVISH, MACTHOMAS, TAWESON, TAWESSON, THOMAS, THOMASON, THOMPSON, THOMSON

According to *Ane Accompt of the Genealogie of the Campbells*, the Clan Tavish – not, be it noted, the Clan MacTavish – descends from Taius or Tavis Coir, illegitimate son of Colin Maol Math, great-great-grandfather of Sir Cailean Mor, a man said to be of great courage and valour, who conquered Cowal from the Lamonts.[65] The name Tavis is anglicised as Thomas, and nearly all the names here grouped together from the 'official' sept list mean either Thomas or 'Son of Thomas'. The last two are exceptions; Maclehose derives from *Mc Gille Thamais* – 'Son of the Servant of (Saint) Thomas' – as does MacLaws, a variation of the same name and the name seems to have been found in Perthshire and Stirlingshire. It is a quite distinct name from MacTavish. Why two further variations of 'Son of Thomas' – *MacCombe* and *MacCombich* – have been left off the list is unknown and seems odd, since they are both to be found in Argyll, as is also the variation *MacOmish*.

It is quite wrong to suggest that all Sons of Thomas derive from the Argyllshire MacTavishes. Thomas or Tom was widely used as a Christian name across the English-speaking world, and a great number of totally unconnected users of the name exist including the Clan MacThomas, in Glenshee, who have a Chief of their own and who form part of the Clan Chattan confederation, while the MacTavishes in Stratherrick are considered a sept of the Frasers.[66]

If the evidence for *Tavis Coir* is uncertain, we can be quite sure about Sir Thomas Cambel, who appears in 1292 among the list of landowners in Balliol's new sheriffdom of Kintyre.[67] In 1296, he signed the oath of loyalty to King Edward I at Berwick (Ragman Roll) as *Thomas Cambel among king's tenants in Perthshire*,[68] and the following year he was liberated from imprisonment in the Tower of London. In 1308, he signed a letter to the French King.[69] In 1324, by which date it is probable he was dead, his probable son Duncan had a grant from the King of many lands in Argyll for the services of a ship.[70] He appears among 'the Barons of Argyll' at an inquest at Inverleckan in 1355 under the name of *Doncanus MacThamais* or MacTavish – 'Duncan Son of Thomas'.[71]

It would seem highly probable that this Sir Thomas was the ancestor of the later MacTavishes of Dunardry, the chief family of the name in Argyll, if not the actual eponym from which they took their name; the formation of clans as we know them today dates from this period, and only very seldom do they appear earlier. Sir Thomas was an important member of the Clan Campbell at a time when the Chiefship was not clearly established, and there is strong reason to think that the later MacTavishes took their name from him. It seems probable that later compilers of the Official Genealogy, *Ane Accompt*, did not know of Sir Thomas and were anxious to insert the MacTavishes into the account somehow. The dwelling place of Dunardry, of whatever it consisted, is no longer to be seen. It lay directly in the path of the Crinan Canal, where the name is still in use for the highest of the canal's locks.

The mausoleum in the churchyard of Kilmartin, which houses a number of stones formerly recumbent in the open air, includes one on which is the daunting figure of a warrior in his pleated warcoat and iron helmet, carrying sword and spear, across whose chest is carved *McTAVISH*. His identity is unknown, although it may be that of a Dunardry MacTavish who was so commemorated. The stone itself is thought to date from the fourteenth or fifteenth century, but of course the inscription may be a later addition, as is clearly the case on several neighbouring stones.[72]

In 1488, *Donald Duin MacTavish* gives up any claim to the two merkland of the south half of his toun of Sokachgaunan in the barony of Strachur, to which he had been given a charter by Evar Campbell of Strachur in return for the payment of forty merks Scots.[73] In 1490, *Allan* and *Duncan McTaus* are baillies on precepts by James Scrymgeour, Constable of Dundee. In 1493, following the succession of the 2nd Earl of Argyll, sasine was given to him in the various parts of his estates. Sasine was given to him at Otter on 8 May, and among the witnesses was *Thomas Mctavish* – obviously a local, since his name does not appear as a witness on the other sasines. *Ewin MacTavish* is thought to have died serving under the earl of Argyll at Flodden in 1513. In 1533, his grandson *Iain Makalister VcEwin McCaus* and *Dougal McAne* his son received a charter of feu farm from Archibald 4th Earl of Argyll of the three merkland of Dunardry, the two merklands of Dunans, the one merkland of Barderiche, the one merkland of Barloskin and the half merkland of Barindaif, extending to seven and a half merklands in Knapdale, Shire of Tarbert.[74]

From probably the early part of the sixteenth century comes the poem *Ciallach Duine Fioruasal*, in which the anonymous author boasts of his widespread connections. One of the verses, listing the various families with whom he is related, is translated as follows: 'Clan Lachlan and Clan Lamond, Clan Neill who study valour, Clan Tavish on the floor and on the brae of Glassary are kin to me'.[75] Duke Niall of Argyll wrote:

Though the MacTavishes were never a large or powerful clan, they have nevertheless been deemed a brave and honourable race and numbers of them still live in Argyll under their old patronymic . . . Though the clan as a whole never seem to have made the slightest sign of adopting the name Campbell, they followed always the bratach or banner of the Lords of Lochow in war and all hostings . . .[76]

The name was also to be found on Loch Tayside, and, notwithstanding the above statement by Duke Niall, the Rev. William Gillies specifically mentions that some of the name also used the name Campbell.[77] These patronymics give us four generations of the family which correspond with those given in a pedigree thought to be drawn up around 1790 by Lachlan MacTavish of Dunardry. This, however, does not connect as far back as Duncan, the son of Sir Thomas already mentioned, nor do its later generations correspond exactly with the pedigree published by Duke Niall in an article in the *Oban Times*.[78]

Donald MacTavish of Dunardry joined the 9th Earl of Argyll's Rebellion against King James VII in 1685 and eventually surrendered Carnasserie Castle where the last remnants of the defeated Earl's forces had taken refuge; his brother Alexander was subsequently executed. His grandson Dugald, however, went along with his friend and neighbour Campbell of Auchinbreck and became a Jacobite, following his leader into imprisonment for plotting to overthrow the government. He was released in 1747.[79] In the mid-1600s there had been a number of MacTavishes with small properties or as tenants, but by 1751 these had all reverted to the main family, and MacTavish of Dunardry was the only MacTavish landowner left in Argyll. His lands held a valuation of £53. 13s. 9d which placed him at 49th in a list of 248. The lands concerned were 3 mkl Dunardry, 1 mkl Barinloskin, 1 mkl Bardarroch, 4 mkl Dunoronsay, 2 mkl Dunans and 3 mkl Auchachoish.

The last of the family to hold his ancestral lands was Lachlan MacTavish of Dunardry, who sold the entire property on 31 December 1795, the purchaser being Colonel John Campbell of Barbreck.[80] MacTavish found a job as Assistant Surveyor General of Window and House Duty in the tax office in Edinburgh, a somewhat humdrum appointment but a welcome aid to keeping the wolf from the door. He died in 1796, his efforts to buy back at least part of his ancestral estates having come to nothing, although they nearly succeeded since Barbreck had put the lands on the market again in 1792 and MacTavish had made an agreement with Malcolm of Poltalloch to come in with him at least as far as the property of Dunardry was concerned. Sadly, had he survived, things might have turned out differently since help was at hand in the person of Simon McTavish, an eminently rich Canadian who had been one of the founders in 1783 of the North West Company, the principal rival of the Hudson's Bay Company until they eventually merged in 1821.

He paid off Malcolm of Poltalloch for the money promised and in 1799 became the owner of Dunardry. He sent Dugald, Lachlan of Dunardry's elder son, for training as a lawyer while gaining entry for John the younger son into the Hudson's Bay Company, where he prospered. Dugald also did well, becoming Sheriff of Campbeltown, where he built Kilchrist House (a handsome villa recently dignified by the present owner with the more grandiloquent title of 'Kilchrist Castle') where he lived with his wife. They had nine children who scattered round the world. William, the eldest son, became Governor of Red River, where he was Hudson's Bay Company Factor.[81]

When Simon MacTavish became Laird of Dunardry, Lachlan's two sons disponed to him their claim to the Chiefship of the MacTavishes, and Simon, who descended from a younger son of MacTavish of Gartbeg, a cadet branch of the main stem, became MacTavish of Dunardry. He died in 1804, and the designation of MacTavish of Dunardry was inherited by his elder son William. William died in 1818 without any children, and his younger brother Simon succeeded. He appears to have been totally disinterested in the position and offered it back to Sheriff Dugald, who also declined. In 1793, Lachlan MacTavish petitioned the Lord Lyon for arms, which were granted to him as follows:

> Quarterly first and fourth, gyronny of eight sable and or, second and third Argent a Buck's head cabossed Gules attired Or, on a chief engrailed Azure a Cross-crosslet fitched between two Mullets of the third.[82]

His crest was a boar's head erased or langued proper, and his motto NON OBLITUS – 'Not Forgetful'. These arms are of considerable import. The first and principal quarter displays the Campbell gyronny. The boar's-head crest copies that of the Campbell Chief, and the motto is a direct response to his demand NE OBLIVISCARIS – 'Do not Forget'. Heraldically speaking, the status of MacTavish of Dunardry as a member of Clan Campbell could hardly be stated more clearly. But in 1997 by Letters Patent, Edward Dugald MacTavish of Dunardry was recognised by the Lord Lyon King of Arms as 'MacTavish of Dunardry and Chief of the Clan MacTavish'.

The fact that there is now an officially recognised Clan MacTavish obviously raises questions in the minds of those of the name who had hitherto considered themselves as Campbells. It is suggested, however, that there is no real reason for confusion, since the Argyllshire MacTavishes were and are part of the same stock as the Campbells. It seems perfectly proper for those named MacTavish or any of the variations thereof, as far as Clan

Societies are concerned, to join both if desired. The position would be clearer if MacCailein Mor was to be recognised as High Chief of the various branches and branch clans which make up the Clan Campbell, as is the case with Lord MacDonald, and Mackintosh of Clan Chattan.

MACDERMID, MACDERMOTT, MACDIARMID

The name has a number of spellings all meaning 'Son of Diarmid'. It is reckoned to be the name of one of the earliest tribes inhabiting Glenlyon in Perthshire. As Glenlyon became a holding of the Campbells of Glenorchy, its inclusion as a Campbell sept seems appropriate. According to the Rev. William A. Gillies,[83] there were three branches of the MacDiarmids in Perthshire: the 'Royal' MacDiarmids who had the right of burial in Cladh Dobhi, Morenish; the *Dubh-bhusach* ('Black-lipped') MacDiarmids, and the Craiganie MacDiarmids, who went by the name of the 'Baron MacDiarmids'. It is, however, more likely that it has been listed due to the habit of referring to the Campbells as 'Clan Diarmid' and attributing their descent from the mythical *Diarmid O'Duine*.

The form MacDermott is an Irish rather than a Scottish form of the name, and, while *Dermot* is often given as a form of *Diarmid* in Ireland, its inclusion here seems inappropriate.[84] MacDermott of Moylurg was Chief of the race who descended from *Tadhg O'Connor*, King of Connacht in the eleventh century. The name does appear in other parts of Scotland, and, given the popularity of the name Diarmid (there were no fewer than eleven Irish saints of the name), a common ancestry seems unlikely.

MACELVIE, MACKELVIE

I can discern no reason for the inclusion of this name among the septs of Clan Campbell. Black, who derives the name from *Mac Shealbhaigh*, 'Son of Selbach',[85] gives various instances of the appearance of the name, but they would seem to centre on Galloway if anywhere. The local telephone directory gives five instances of the name in various parts of Argyll. Under Macelvie or Mackelwee, all forms of the same name, Black gives mention of the existence of the name M'Ilwee in Bute in 1656. The name also exists as McElwee.

MACGLASRICH

The name as above is said to derive from the Gaelic for 'The Son of the man from Glassary', the district by that name in mid-Argyll. According to Black, the name *MacGlasserig* was a Breadalbane one, the family dying out on Loch Tayside as the result of a curse by a witch. The name is also found in Brae Lochaber used by descendants of a Campbell who had to leave Argyll in a hurry. Neither his identity nor the circumstances are clear, but it seems that the reason for their hasty leaving had something to do with the imposition of *jus primae noctis* by their feudal superior on a new bride which was resented by her husband who took his revenge and then had to flee. Another version, that of the Rev. Somerled MacMillan, is that the Lochaber Campbells returned with the MacDonalds after their 1497 defeat in Glenorchy by the Stewarts of Appin and the MacLarens.

Be that as it may, the MacGlasrich Campbells are found as bodyguard to MacDonald of Keppoch in the sixteenth and seventeenth century, also acting on occasion as foster-parents to children of the Chief. Following the famous murder of Alexander of Keppoch in 1663, in which his uncle Alasdair Buidhe MacDonald was almost certainly implicated, the Campbell foster-father of Alasdair's eldest son Ailean Dearg killed his foster-son in a drunken skirmish and was hung for his crime. The Brae Lochaber Campbells asked Argyll to interpose but he, sensing the difficulties of becoming involved, offered all the Campbells in that area altenative tenancies instead. Most apparently chose to stay where they were. Several of the families held their lands in Lochaber from Argyll and subsequently from Breadalbane, and I have heard it suggested that some of the name MacGlasrich were MacDonalds after all but ones who, finding themselves on the Earl's side of the river, found it politic to adopt the Campbell identity.

There were other families by the name of MacGlasrich in Brae Lochaber – it was, it seems, a name also used by the MacGlashans, who were hereditary pipers to Keppoch. But they certainly regarded themselves as Campbells and were prepared to put themselves at risk in support of their ancient loyalties, as the following extracts from two letters show. The first letter is dated 29 May 1746 and is from John Campbell of Achalader to Donald Campbell of Airds.

> Some of the McIlasrichs of the Breas of Lochaber came here in order to be Advised, Directed, where and to whom, they should submit themselves and Deliver upp there Arms. You Know they are all Common Fellows, and tennant to Keppoch and its very well Known, that they Resisted being Concerned in this Rebellion, as much as they were able, or could well be Expected of a few poor men in the heart of a country all prone to Mischief. Their Choice would be to submit to General Campbell and some of them are gone to him to have his Directions

about it, and to Know from him whether he will chose to have them come to him wt there Arms, of if he will order them to Give them to some other that Lyes nearer them . . . There Misfortune is and what they are frighted for is this. They are Informed that some of of the Loos people in that country pretend to Keep theirArms, and it being surmisd that the Mc Glassrichs wanted to Submit, ther was threatning Messages sent them, that if they offered to Deliver there Arms there would be sever courses taken wt ther wives, Children and Catle. And what they beg is that when they are ordered to deliver their Arms they may be taken Immediately under the protection of the Government as they will be Defenceless, and cannot protect themselves or their families, from those who they Reckon Much more ther Enemies than the Kings troops, and mor so than ever, when they give upp there Arms. I need not tell yow how useful these poor fellowes us'd to be, to any of our Name, that went into the Breas of Lochaber, and what Endeavours they us'd to Keep themselves from being Ingag'd in the Rebellione as ye would hear of it formerlie. And you Know that when they coud do no more they positively Refused to wear White Cockades, and put upp Black and Yellow, which did not a litle vex ther Leaders, but they could not help it. I therfor Beg you would do them all the Service yow can in Representing ther case to Collonell Campbell . . . You Know very well that the familie of Breadalbine hes no particular concern in them, more than other Campbells have, yett I should be sorie, if such a faithfull few as they have always been to the name of Campbell should be destroyed, when their enmi is such as was not in their power to help . . .

The second letter, written shortly afterwards, is from Lieutenant-Colonel John Campbell, 'Colonel Jack', the future 5th Duke of Argyll, to General Campbell of Loudoun. From Strontian, he writes:

The bearer hereof is one Macglaserich, a Tribe consisting of about thirty families in the Braes of Lochaber who have sent this man desiring to deliver up their arms to the General. For as they look upon themselves to be Campbells they, in the highland way, thought themselvs obligd to deliver their arms to him rather than any other of his majesties officers. However as Your Lordship is more contiguous to their country & the General does not choose to indulge them in any of their clannish principles, he has directed them to deliver their arms to you or any other officer commanding in that part of the country. . .[86]

Some of these people were among the emigrants from Keppoch who went to

Nova Scotia, where they appear to use the name Campbell. A famous MacGlasrich was the late Archbishop of Glasgow, the Most Reverend A. Campbell, who was born in Brae Lochaber and who died in 1963.

MACKERLIE

This name derives from the Gaelic *MacThearlaich*, 'Son of Charles'; as such, it has been used on occasion by a number of totally unrelated persons. MacKerley and MacKerlich are other forms of the name. In this case, the name derives from a Charles Campbell, living at the beginning of the sixteenth century. While his origin as a Campbell of Craignish is beyond doubt, there are conflicting versions of his exact identity. One version says that Charles Campbell was an illegitimate son of Dougall Campbell of Craignish who died in 1527. His by-name was *Tearlach Eranich* – 'Irish Charles' – so-called from his having served in Ireland as a soldier under Archibald Campbell of Danna. Another makes him son of Archibald Campbell of Craignish. Charles was known from his size as *Tearlach Mor* and lived on the property of Corranmore in Craignish. Unfortunately, he had a furious temper and, having killed Gillies of Glenmore in a scuffle and wounded his cousin, he was 'obliged to retire' to Perthshire, where he and his family settled in Glenlyon. But his temper again got the better of him, and, after another unfortunate fight, he again was forced to remove, this time to Rannoch where he took the name of *MacVrachater* ('Son of the maltster'). Here he married again and sired another family.

Charles's descendant was Sir James Campbell of Inverneill, Hereditary Usher of the White Rod for Scotland, Member of Parliament for Stirling. In 1795, the heads of five related families signed a document declaring him to be the Chief of Clan Tearlach. They were representatives of the Clan M'Kater Campbells in Breadalbane, the Clan Tearlach Campbells in Breadalbane, the MacVrachater Campbells in Breadalbane and Glenlyon, the Clan Ich Kellegherne in Breadalbane and the Clan Haister Campbells in Rannoch. This claim was accepted by Lyon in 1875, when arms were matriculated by Campbell of Inverneill. He was given the single galley supporter of Craignish with a shield displaying the gyronny of eight, or and sable, with a border azure. His case is extremely unusual if not unique, since he has actually been recognised by Lyon as a Chief albeit of a Clan within a Clan. The late Chief of Clan Tearlach was the famous folklorist and historian John Lorne Campbell of Canna, whose younger brother was Colin Campbell, who by family arrangement took the designation of Campbell of Inverneill, younger, and who was a noted expert on heraldry.[87]

MACNICHOL

The name MacNichol in its various spellings and anglicised as Nichol or Nicolson is widespread in Scotland, and is particularly well known in the case of the Nicolsons or MacNeacails of Scorrybreac. The attribution of this name to Clan Campbell applies uniquely to the kindred of this name long settled in Glenorchy and in Glenshira. Their origin is unknown. Local tradition apparently had it that the family were originally MacPhees sprung from one Nicol McPhee who left Lochaber in the sixteenth century. There were indeed MacNichols in Lochaber. They descended from the MacPhees of Colonsay and had held their lands in Lochaber since before the 1493 forfeiture of the Lordship of the Isles.[88] The names in the MacNichol of Socach line repeat names commonly in use by the MacPhees.

Duke Niall of Argyll, on the other hand, noted that he thought they were MacNaughtons of Dunderave. This, however, may derive from a too-hasty reading of one of the unpublished Dewar Manuscripts which tells a tale of one *Thomas Ruadh Mac Sheumas Ruadh mhic Sheumais-dhuibh mhic Dhonachie Mhic Ghiobhaine-mhoire a Mhorara*, who came to a sticky end in a skirmish with the MacGregors. He was the ancestor of James MacNichol in Achalader and was said to have been of MacNaughton origin, but the crucial point which for once eluded Duke Niall is that he was apparently MacNichol's *maternal* ancestor.

Be that as it may, the MacNichols were long in Socach in Glenorchy. The first to settle there was Nicol, who married MacTavish of Dunardry's daughter. His brother Duncan settled in Achnafannich. In 1593, Nicol's son, *Gillepatrick mac Nicol mac Duncan Riabhach* in Socach, was given a charter of the lands of Elrigmore in Glenshira by MacNaughton of Dunderave. This property was taken on by Gillepatrick's younger son, Nicol Ban MacNichol.[89] The name *Elrig* denotes the narrow pass which formed the culmination of a deer drive where the fleeing beasts, collected together gradually over a period of days and a huge territory, were concentrated in a narrow pass where they faced the arrows and swords of the hunters waiting for them. The MacNichols also acquired the next-door Elrigbeg.

Famous in his day was the Gaelic scholar, the Reverend Donald MacNichol (1735–1802), minister of Lismore, whose spirited defence in his *Remarks on Dr. Samuel Johnson's Journey to the Hebrides* of the authenticity of the Poems of Ossian which had been rubbished by the great Doctor caused that worthy to 'growl hideously'.[90] A poet himself, with his family, the Glenorchy MacNichols, long celebrated for their knowledge of the ancient songs and poems of the Highlands, the Reverend Donald was a friend of the renowned bard, Duncan Ban Macintyre, whom he assisted in writing out his songs. This combination of the Church and a reputation for knowledge of and skill in poetry suggests that this family of MacNichols may have been a hereditary professional kindred. This may be further supported by mention in 1618 of *Donald M'ilpatrick Leiche M'Nycle* in Achnaraiff (*recte* Achnafannich?),[91] who is clearly the same as *Donald M'Gilpatrick Leiche*, servitor to George Loudoun, who has sasine of Inverliver the same year. This mention appears to combine both medical and clerical expertise, since a 'servitor' was much more of a personal assistant than his title might appear to imply.

MACNOCAIRD

The name derives from the Gaelic *Mac na Cearda* – 'Son of the Smith'. The smith in this case was a whitesmith rather than a blacksmith, skilled in working in brass and the lighter metals and producing ornaments and jewellery and household metalwork, goods much prized in early Celtic society. But in time, the craft was debased to the mere patching of pots and pans, and its practitioners became synonymous with travelling people or 'tinkers', whose modern reputation was not very salubrious. So it is that Black in his *Surnames of Scotland* records the fact that the MacNocairds frequently used the alternative name of Sinclair without perhaps realising that this was adopted as a very much more respectable name than 'Tinkler', which it closely resembles but without having any of the unfortunate associations of the latter.[92]

The name Caird is a shortened form of MacNocaird, and the compilers of sept lists might well have included it as well. The form MacNocaird is early found in Argyll and neighbouring areas, and Black gives several examples: *Gregor Makenkerd* appears in 1297, *Iain Mac nocerdych* is a witness in Lismore in 1525. *John M'Necaird* was tenant in Eyich in 1594 (Ewich, just between Tyndrum and Crianlarich); *Archibald M'Nokaird* is merchant burgess of Inveraray in 1695, and *Donald McNougard* is in Islay in 1741. *Gilfolen Kerd*, a sailor in the service of Alexander of Argyll, was arrested in Bristol in 1275 for being a suspected pirate; in the form Caird the name appears more widely across Scotland, as one might expect from a common work-name.

MACORAN

There is surprisingly little record of this name, which is not even recorded by Black, although he does give some reference to it under the heading of MacCorran.[93] According to family tradition, the name, more correctly

McCorran, was taken by young Campbell of Melfort who, during the later half of the seventeenth century, had to leave Argyll in a hurry, having killed a man named MacColl. He went to Menteith and took service under the Earl, who rewarded him with the farm of Inchanoch. He married a Miss Haldane, niece to Haldane of Lanrick and the family prospered. They were very much mindful of their Argyllshire connections and two of the farms they reclaimed from the Moss were named Easter and Wester Lorne. Once away from the area, members of the family resumed the name Campbell, among them being the families of Campbell of Tullichewan and of Campbell Adamson of Stracathro which included the British prime minister, Sir Henry Campbell-Bannerman. Apparently the local people used to say 'there was never a Campbell in the Inchanoch or a McOran out of it'.[94] Dugald M'Corran appears in Fernoch, Kilmelfort, in 1698.

MACOWEN

In *The Clans, Septs and Regiments of the Scottish Highlands*, Frank Adam and Lord Lyon Sir Thomas Innes of Learney state that 'MacOwen was the name of the family who were the sennachies to the Campbells of Argyll' – a reference to the name described elsewhere as MacEwan.[95] Black, however, gives another version, a more likely one deriving MacOwan or MacCowan from *Mac Gille Chomgain* – 'Son of the Servant of Saint Comgan'. In this form, the name may originate with a family who served the shrine of the saint concerned or from someone who, being born on that Saint's Day, has been named for his servant.

Saint Comgan inherited the throne of Leinster in 715, only to take up the mantle of the Christian missionary two years later. He is said to have first settled on Loch Alsh but then moved east to Aberdeenshire, where he became Abbot of the monks at Turriff. When he died, tradition has it that his nephew, Saint Fillan, took his body for burial at Iona. His stay in Wester Ross is marked by a number of churches dedicated to his memory by the use of his name in the form Kilchoan. The name occurs further south in Argyll, where there are Kilchoans in Ardnamurchan, on Islay, on Loch Melfort and near Poltalloch. At the last, there was a family of dewars or guardians of a holy relic, the MacLucases, who held the lands for their services, but the nature of the relic they looked after is unknown.[96] The name *MacGille Chomgain* appears notably in Argyll, further north on the west coast and around Dingwall. The cross in the main street of Inveraray has an inscription which declares that it commemorates the noblemen Duncan *Meicgyllichomgnan*, his son Patrick, and Maolmore, Patrick's son, who caused the cross to be made. It has been suggested that the cross may have originally stood in the nearby cemetery of Kilmalew, but it may have come from much further away.

The existence at one time of a noble kindred of the name is further underlined by the appearance as witnesses on a charter of around 1355 by John Campbell, lord of Ardscotnish, to Gilbert of Glassary, of Roderick and Iver, 'sons of *M'Gillecoan*' – the style M'Gillecoan without any further qualification denoting a chief.[97] Apparently, according to the MacDonald historians, John, Lord of the Isles, had a strong standing force to protect Lochaber from incursion under the command of Hector More Macillechoan.[98] *Donald Mcillichoan* was in 1595 among the 'native men' of Craignish – the early inhabitants – who gave their bond of manrent to Ronald Campbell of Barrichbeyan as their Chief.[99] The name also appears as MacIlhone or MacElhone.

MACPHEDRAN

The name derives from the Gaelic form of Paterson – *MacPheaderain* – or 'Son of little Peter'. The original of the name is said to have been a MacAulay according to Buchanan of Auchmar. The family long held the lands of Sonachan on Loch Awe together with the lucrative office of ferrymen over Loch Awe from Portsonachan on the east side to Taychreggan on the west, the portership extending 'between Teatle Water and the rivulet called Beochlych on the east bank and the rivulet called Ganevan and the Water of Aw on the west side'.[100] The reason for this grant is given in two legends. In one, it was for MacPhederan's service in ferrying Robert the Bruce back to Scotland from his refuge on Rathlin Island; the other says it was for rescuing the son of the Campbell Chief after his galley capsized on Loch Awe and he nearly drowned. It is not impossible for both incidents to have been based on fact.

In 1439,[101] *Domenicus M'Federan* had confirmation from Sir Duncan Campbell of Lochawe of the one merkland of Sonachan and the ferry. In 1488 at Sonachan, a notarial transcript (official copy) was made for *Morich McFedren* of this charter. In 1501, *Gillemory M'Fedane* received a charter of confirmation from the 2nd Earl of Argyll. In 1590, *Duncan Glas McFederan* resigned the lands and office of Porter to the 7th Earl for a regrant in favour of his son *Gillemory*. The precept of sasine on this charter mentions that the family first had a grant of these from Sir Duncan Campbell of Lochawe in 1439 'as their evidents gave proof'.[102] This at first sight may support the tradition that it was saving Sir Duncan's son that earned them their position, although it is quite possible that this was the first *written* charter in the MacPhederans' possession.

The MacPhederans quarrelled bitterly with their neighbours and had a bloody skirmish with them at the burn between Upper Sonachan and Portsonachan. Eventually in 1619, the lands were handed over by *Duncan Glas McPhedren* to Ewin M'Corquodale of Phantilands acting as attorney for *Duncan Campbell M'Dowell V'Inryda* – Duncan Campbell, son of Dougald son of the Knight (of Cawdor) – in implementation of a contract of sale made by his grandson *Donald M'Gilmore V'Phedran*.[103] The family is said to have moved to Lochfyneside and to have become mariners.

Another family of MacFederans, possibly of the same kindred, were famous as smiths in Benderloch. They appear in the famous quatrain

Bogha dh'iubhar Easragain,	Bow of the yew of Easragan,
Ite fìrein Locha Treig,	Feather of the eagle of Loch Treig,
Ceir Bhuidhe Bhaile nan gaillean,	The yellow wax of Baille-nan-gaillean,
Smeoirn o'n cheard MacPheiderean.	Arrowhead from the craftsman MacPheidirean.

The MacPhederans had their forge at Ferlochan in Benderloch, near Barcaldine House. Their swords were said to be of outstanding finish and quality. The Burn of the Easragan is near Ardchattan Priory, further up Loch Etive.[104] It may well be one of this kindred who is buried further south down at Keills in Knapdale, where a tombstone of the fourteenth or fifteenth century is inscribed in Latin

Hic jacet Cormacus MacPhaterin   Here lies Cormac MacPhedran.

Both Keills and the Church at Kilmory on the other side of Loch Sween are particularly noted for the concentration of wealthy craftsmen buried there. They would appear to have originated there when Castle Sween was the base of the powerful MacSween Lords and to have remained in the area after the castle itself had changed hands. A smith would have been an essential part of such a community, and Cormac would seem to be a very likely candidate.[105]

MACPHUN

The name derives from Gaelic *Mac-Ghille-Mhund* or 'Servant of St Mund' and is the same as MacMunn, which, however, is not included in the 'official' list of Campbell septs. St Mund seems to have more than one claimant for his name, but the most likely in this case would appear to be a tenth-century saint who was Abbot of Glenorchy with his seat at Clachandysart – the old name for Dalmally.[106] He is said to be the patron saint of Clan Campbell.

In 1497, the sale was confirmed by John Colquhoun of Luss to Archibald Earl of Argyll of various lands at the foot of Loch Eck. These included *dime-dietate unius mercate terre (vocatus Pordewry) in territorio de Inverquhapil occupate per quendam procuratorem, cum baculo Sancte Munde, Scotice vocato* Deowray – 'the half merkland (called Pordewry) in Inverchapple occupied by a certain Guardian, with the staff of Saint Munde, called in Scots the *Deowray*'.[107] The keepers of this relic were supposed to be the MacMunns. In 1525, *Patrick* and *Ian McPune* are witnesses to a Strachur charter of the 3rd Earl.[108] In 1566, *Archibald Makyphunze* has a charter from the 5th Earl of the six merkland of Innernaodan in Strachur. This family was the chief branch of the MacPhuns. In 1685, the laird of Innernaodan was forfeited for taking part with the 9th Earl of Argyll in the latter's abortive Rebellion.

From this family sprang the younger branch of the MacPhuns of Drip, a property next door to Innernaodan. Of one of them the well-known tale is told of how, having been hung on the gallows at Inveraray for some crime, his apparently lifeless body was cut down and given to his young wife for burial. On the way back across the loch, she noticed some faint stirring and, by dint of mother's milk and brandy, succeeded in bringing her husband back to life!

MOORE, MUIR

The inclusion of the name Mure, Muir or Moore among Campbell septs is perhaps rather optimistic, since the family have a perfectly good Chief of their own in the person of Mure of Rowallan, in Ayrshire, one of Scotland's oldest and most historic families. There are however two instances of a Campbell connection on which, presumably, the attribution is based. James Mure Campbell, who succeeded his cousin as 5th Earl of Loudoun in 1782, had added the name Mure to his own on succeeding to the estates of Rowallan. These he inherited through his mother, who was the daughter of David Earl of Glasgow and Jean Mure, heiress of Rowallan. Members of the same family had been among the Presbyterian Lowlanders imported into Kintyre the previous century by the Marquess of Argyll in order to ensure the payment of rent from his estates there, and from the later 1600s onwards the name figures among the Earl's tenants in Kintyre.

OCHILTREE

Ochiltree is a name derived from a place near Linlithgow, West Lothian. Its users had nothing to do with the family called *MacUchtrie* or *MacUghtre* in Argyll, who on occasion anglicised their name to Uchiltree or Ochiltree. Like the MacArthurs on Loch Awe-side, the MacUchtries appear to have been a professional family. *Alan Oghtre, Vicar of Kilmun* and *William Oghtre* appear as witnesses on a notarial transumpt of 1432/3 at Kilmun, while *Sir David Ochtre* is Provost of Kilmun in 1466 and in 1470 is a notary public.[109]

In 1492, we find the first mention of *Archibald Uchiltree* on the sasine of his father's lands given to Archibald 2nd Earl of Argyll, along with Ian MacArthur, father of Charles MacArthur, later of Terivadich (see 'MacArthurs' above). Like MacArthur, Uchiltree travels the country clearly in charge of organising the Earl's charters. Between 1494 and 1524, *Archibald Uchiltree* appears on twenty of the extant forty charters of the Earl's. Archibald does not appear after 1524, but *Ian Uchiltre of Kildalvan* had already appeared in 1513. Whether he was the son of Archibald is not clear, nor is whether Kildalvan, which in 1497 was among the lands regranted to Gilchrist M'Lamont of Inverneilbeg, had then been transferred to the Uchiltrees in reward for their services as men of business to the Earl at the same time and for the same reason as the MacArthurs received Terivadich. Both suppositions, however, would seem reasonable.

There is then a gap until 1540, when Ian or *John Uchiltre of Kildalvan* signs nine times in seven years. In 1542, Ian is joined as a witness by Alan Uchiltre and by Alan's son, John. Again we are given no clue as to the relationship between Alan and Ian, but it would seem probable they are father and son since *Allan M'Ane Uchtre of Garvie* appears in 1573, Garvie being close to Kildalvan in Glendaruel. Allan would seem to have had a brother John Glas who appears as *John Glas M'Ane*. Another brother, Donald, appears in 1586. In 1587 we find *Ian Keir M'Allan Uchiltre, apparent of Garvie. Alan Ochiltree of Garvie*, who appears in 1599, is presumably his son or brother.[110] Thereafter there is no more mention, and by 1614 an *Archibald Campbell of Kildalvan* is in Garvie being appointed one of the Earl of Argyll Foresters in Cowal. He had previously appeared in Inveraray in 1610, where he is identified as a notary.[111]

Duke Niall, who made notes on this family of Campbells, suggests they are Ardkinglas cadets through either the Ardentinny or the Carrick branches. But their following generations concentrate on using the names Ian and Archibald, which, while quintessential Campbell names, also occur in the Uchiltree pedigree. The name of Uchiltree seems to vanish, while the fact that Archibald Campbell was also a notary suggests that either the line of Uchiltrees died out or the lands were tied to the post of the Earl's Man of Business. It is just possible, if Archibald had not married the Uchiltree heiress, that the Uchiltrees changed their name to Campbell and continued on in Kildalvan until the end of the eighteenth century at least. The name is now extremely rare.

PINKERTON

The surname Pinkerton comes from the place of the same name near Dunbar, in East Lothian. In 1483, Colin, 1st Earl of Argyll, 'for his faithful and gratuitous service', received a Royal Grant of the lands of Meikle and Little Pinkerton, forfeited by the Duke of Albany. The lands were by the same charter incorporated into the Barony of Pinkerton. In 1505, his disposition of these lands, together with those of Whyterig, in feu farm to Thomas Inglis, merchant in Edinburgh, was given Royal confirmation. It would seem that the superiority of the lands, the actual barony, remained in the possession of the Campbell Chiefs, since in 1542 it is listed among a number of lands 'previously incorporated by the King into the barony of Menstre . . .'. In 1571, it is among a number of baronies granted by his brother to Colin Campbell of Boquhan, who was to succeed him as 6th Earl of Argyll; but in 1663, on the restoration of the Argyll lands to the 9th Earl, there is no separate mention of it, and it is no doubt incorporated under the Barony of Menstrie, which continued among the possessions of the Chief's family. On the tenuous basis of the above, the name Pinkerton has been listed as a Campbell sept. The most famous holder of the name is the well-known nineteenth-century American detective, Allan Pinkerton.

TORRIE, TORRY

According to Black, there are places by this name in Kincardineshire and in Fife,[112] although Torrie of that Ilk had his seat in Dumfries. But the name is found widely across Scotland. Some of them settled at Cawdor, where George Torrie 'in Cawdor' is mentioned in 1639 and 1642.[113] He appears to have been servitor to John Campbell, fiar of Cawdor, in 1626 before the unfortunate young man was declared insane and the affairs of the family were undertaken by his brothers Colin and then George, as tutors.[114] Some of the name went with Cawdor to the Isle of Islay, acquired by the Campbells in 1614, and there are two of the name listed among the tenants on the island in 1686.[115] For the same reason, no doubt, their name is also to be found on the island of Kerrera. There were Torries in Islay as late as the 1830s; the name does not appear in the telephone directory there any more, although there are one or two scattered elsewhere in Argyll.

APPENDIX 4

The Clan Tartans

(The following article is a repeat of the 1985 publication 'Campbell Tartan' by the author.)

1. AUTHORISATION OF A CLAN TARTAN

Authority for saying what is or is not the tartan of a clan lies entirely with the Chief of that Clan. Further authentication may be achieved by its registration in Lyon Court Books, subject to the Lord Lyon's approval, which is based on the recommendation of his Advisory Committee on Tartan. Other bodies act as recorders – no more – such as the Scottish Tartans Society.

2. THE HISTORICAL BACKGROUND

While it is not the purpose of these notes to go exhaustively into the entire question of the origin of 'Clan' tartans, a brief summary is useful in putting what follows into perspective. One school of thought which I think can fairly be termed the 'Romantic' one would have us believe that from the earliest times the Highlanders were all immediately recognisable from the pattern of their plaids. Some of these patterns, but by no means all, were preserved through the period of the Proscription of Highland Dress, to be lovingly resurrected when the wearing of the 'Garb of Old Gaul' was once more permitted.

Although it is fair to say that on at least one occasion, in 1703, the Laird of Grant did order his clan to take the field in plaids of red and green – portraits of the time reveal that they nevertheless managed to do so in a wide variety of patterns – and that it seems probable that there were a number of patterns which were very popular in certain areas which did allow a degree of recognition, the overwhelming evidence is that the assignation of 'Clan' significance to tartan is of much later date – little if at all earlier than the beginning of the nineteenth century.

Two important examples can be quoted against the 'Romantic' view. One is the well-known picture by David Morier, which hangs in the Palace of Holyroodhouse, of Barrell's Regiment resisting the Jacobite charge at Culloden (cf. John Telfer-Dunbar, *The History of Highland Dress*, Plates 26 and 27). This is a contemporary record, the Highland figures being modelled by prisoners-of-war in captivity at Carlisle; they are all wearing several different setts, none of which appears to be the same as and few of which bear any recognisable resemblance to any of today's Clan tartans. The other comes in the reminiscences of one James Ray, who served in the government forces at the same battle. Shortly after the end of the engagement, he came up against a Highlander who cried 'Hold your hand, I'm a Campbell!' To quote Ray:

> On which I asked him 'Where is your Bonnet?' He reply'd 'Somebody hath snatched it off my head!' I only mention this to show how we distinguished our loyal clans from the Rebels: they being dress'd and equipped all in one way, except the Bonnet; ours having a Red or Yellow cross or ribbon; theirs a white cockade.

This would seem pretty clear evidence against any significance for 'Clan' tartans at this date.

Certainly, what early portraits there are showing tartan would strongly support the view that, while tartan itself is of early date, until comparatively recently what pattern was worn depended not on any 'Clan' significance but on what was available locally and what took the wearer's fancy. The whole idea of uniformity in tartan most probably had a military origin. There is evidence to suggest that as early as 1725 the Independent Highland Companies may have been all clothed in the same sett. Indeed, it is difficult to overstate the influence of the military on the survival and the development of tartan and indeed all Highland dress as we know it today.

The performance of the Highland regiments had much to do with raising popular esteem for the Highlanders in general, and a wave of romanticism built up which reached a peak in 1822 with the Royal Visit to Edinburgh of King George IV. It was a few years prior to this, in 1816, that the Highland Society of London, which had organised the campaign for the repeal of the Act of Proscription, put together a collection of tartans, signed and sealed by the Chiefs concerned as being that of their Clans. Contemporary correspondence reveals that in many cases the Chiefs had no idea what their tartan should be, which was hardly surprising in the circumstances – but as always, the tartan manufacturers had no difficulty in providing something suitable.

The idea of a Clan tartan is a very attractive one, and it found ready acceptance. During the nineteenth century, examples proliferated, and they have continued to do so, receiving, as is only to be expected, every encouragement from the manufacturers. This has, of course, led to the appearance of many tartans which are now attached to names which have never been – could never have been – Clans in their own right, as well as the continuing production of perfectly properly authorised new Clan tartans. All of this is quite in order provided that unjustified claims are not made for the historic provenance of Clan tartan in general and specific setts in particular. There is a great deal of difference in my view between the tartan of a Clan, authorised by that Clan's Chief and perhaps dating back to the commencement of the nineteenth century, and the all-too-frequent examples which have been produced for purely commercial reasons within the last couple of decades without any authorisation at all.

If this difference were made plain in every reference to a particular sett, that is, the date and place of its first recorded appearance together with the fact of whether or not it has the approval of the Chief concerned, then the true state of affairs would be very much more apparent and much of the utter nonsense currently aired on the subject of tartans would be avoided.

3. DESCRIPTION OF TARTANS

I have used the current thread-count method, by which one starts from a pivot point and counts through to the other pivot point, where the process is then reversed. Early users of this method, such as Wilson's and Logan, in fact varied it slightly, but to minimise any confusion I have converted their count to what is the standard method of today. The tartans are also illustrated by drawings which are, I hope, reasonably accurate in scale. I have, however, been unable to reproduce the actual tones and shades of colour of the various examples mentioned, which anyway for present purposes are not important beyond indicating where the dark form of the plain tartan is being referred to. It should, however, be pointed out straight away that there is no real difference at all between the plain 'Campbell' tartan and its darker version known as '42nd', 'Black Watch', 'Government' or whatever.

There are often several minor variations in the proportions of the most popular setts, depending on which manufacturer is involved. I have given in these cases one typical thread-count only. With the actual construction of the sett, rather against my will, I have gone into much detail since it would appear today that such a minor change as the existence of black guard-lines edging a white stripe is considered sufficient to change a sett from 'Lamont' to 'Forbes'. While the drawings are to scale, this does not reflect the size of the sett, which can of course vary provided that the proportions of the various colours it contains remain the same. In general, earlier tartans were often much smaller in size than that which is normal today.

In giving the thread-counts, I have used obvious abbreviations for the colours: Bk = black; Bl = Blue; Gr = green; R = red; Y = yellow; W = white; Az = azure or light blue; LD = light drab; LP = light pink; DP = dark pink; DBl = dark blue; LBl = light blue; Br = brown; and O = ochre. In cases where I have taken a tartan from a portrait by observation, I have not attempted to produce a thread-count, which can be deduced sufficiently accurately from the drawing.

4. THE APPROVED CAMPBELL SETTS

MacCailein Mor has authorised the following setts:

(a)   CAMPBELL – see illustrations No. 1 and 2

Bl	Bk	Bl	Bk	Bl	Bk	Gr	Bk	Gr	Bk	Bl	Bk	*Bl*
24	4	4	4	4	20	24	6	24	20	22	4	4

This is the basic sett which may be worn by all Campbells. This is the tartan worn by the Duke and his family.

(b)   CAMPBELL OF CAWDOR – see illustration No. 3

Az	Bk	Gr	Bk	Bl	Bk	*R*
4	2	16	16	16	2	4

This tartan may be worn, if desired, by Campbells of the Cawdor branch.

(c)   CAMPBELL OF BREADALBANE – see illustration No. 4

Bk	Bl	Bk	Gr	Y	Gr	*Bk*
2	8	8	8	2	8	8

To be worn, if desired, by Campbells of the Breadalbane or Glenorchy branch of the Clan.

(d)   CAMPBELL OF LOUDOUN–see illustration No. 8

Bl	Bk	Bl	Bk	Gr	Bk	*Y/W*
4	2	24	24	24	2	4

This tartan may be worn, if desired, by Campbells of the Loudoun branch; the sett is not often seen and may be difficult to obtain.

5. HISTORY OF THE APPROVED SETTS

(a)   CAMPBELL – see illustrations No. 1 and 2

The origin of this sett is almost certainly military. From 1678 onwards, at various times, Independent Highland Companies were raised as units of the British army to keep the peace in the Highlands. In 1725 there were six companies and, for the first time, it appears that their dress was standardised and that they were all clothed in the same tartan. Three of the six companies were Campbell ones, being commanded by the lairds of Skipness, Lochnell and Carrick; the other three companies were commanded respectively by Fraser of Lovat, Grant of Ballindalloch and Munro of Culcairn. It would appear that this sett, or one very like it, was the one appointed for the Highland Companies in 1725 and became the tartan adopted by the Black Watch as they are now known today, when the six companies were regimented to form that famous military unit in 1739.

This is why this tartan, usually in darker tones, is known as 'Government', 'Military', 'Black Watch' or '42nd'. It is today worn by a number of regiments, notably the Black Watch and the Argyll and Sutherland Highlanders. This is a dark version, but there is evidence from pictures that in earlier times some of the several Highland regiments who wore the sett did so in tones identical to those used in the present-day lighter-version Campbell tartan. It is also known as 'Sutherland'; this too has a military origin, as it was the tartan worn by the 93rd Sutherland Highlanders and by the three regiments of Sutherland Fencibles raised earlier in the eighteenth century during periods of national emergency in 1759, 1779 and 1793. It is from these military connections that the tartan is worn on occasion by Grants, Munros and Sutherlands. Such a practice can be identified elsewhere; certain Highland regiments differenced the basic sett by the addition of coloured lines, and, in at least two examples, those of the Gordons and the Mackenzies, the regimental tartan in due course became the 'Clan' tartan of the clan most closely connected with the original regiment.

There are two theories on the origin of this tartan: one has it that the tartan of the majority of the men was adopted by the rest and that they were clothed in Campbell tartan; the other that the sett was specially invented for the companies, and, when 'Clan' tartans came into vogue, the Campbells adopted the sett which, because of their military service, was already being worn by so many members of the clan. Much of interest on the subject is to be found in H. D. MacWilliam's 'The Black Watch Tartan', including contemporary correspondence on the subject of the clothing for the Highland Companies which effectively refutes the unusually confused and confusing account of the origin of the Black Watch tartan given by General Stewart of Garth in his 'Sketches of the Highlanders', where he claims that the tartan was specially created for the 42nd when they were regimented in 1739. Mr MacWilliam comes down on the side of the regiment having adopted the Campbell tartan; rather reluctantly, I am drawn to the opposite conclusion. In my view, 1725 is too early for the existence of 'Clan' tartans, as the variety of different patterns worn by the subjects of portraits of the period testifies. The practice of clans adopting the tartan of 'their' regiment has already been referred to, and the fact that the green, black and blue sett is also worn by the Grants, Munros and Sutherlands would seem to argue pretty conclusively that it has a military rather than a clan origin. One need hardly speculate, if perchance clan tartans had existed at that date, as to what would have been the reaction of the other three companies if they had been told to put on the tartan of the Campbells! All this is now no more than of historical interest, since successive Dukes of Argyll have made their views on what is Campbell tartan abundantly clear.

What would appear to be the earliest recorded example of this tartan being worn in a civilian rather than a military capacity is the portrait of Robert Grant of Lurg, painted as a very old man in the 1760s, according to Telfer-Dunbar. Lurg apparently served in the Highland Company commanded by his Chief and was retired on account of age in 1739. He is said to have worn throughout his life the garb of his youth and is represented as wearing coat and plaid of the green, black and blue sett in the tones of today's Campbell tartan (cf. Telfer-Dunbar, Plate 45). A copy of this portrait hangs at Inveraray with the original version of the tartan replaced by a carefully rendered version of what is now taken to be the normal Grant sett.

From the early 1760s, too, comes what is, I believe, the first detailed representation of military use of the tartan. A rather primitive portrait thought to be of John Campbell of Melfort, an officer in the Black Watch, shows clearly, as does Lurg's picture, the now familiar 2/4 arrangement of the black lines on the blue. This picture hangs in the Black Watch Museum, Balhousie Castle, Perth. The earliest reference to the plain sett having a specific Campbell significance that I have found is on a label on a sample of the tartan in the Cockburn Collection of c. 1810–20 (see below).

In 1816, the Highland Society of London put together a collection of tartans, sealed and signed by the Chiefs of the Clans involved. The only example with any Campbell connection is a tartan labelled 'Breadalbane', which was worn by the Breadalbane Fencibles whose First Battalion was raised in 1793. In June 1822, the Secretary of the Highland Society of London, John Wedderburn, was in Edinburgh, and the National Museum of Antiquities there has some half-dozen pieces of tartan named, sealed and signed with the date and the place by him. It includes the pattern we are discussing which bears a label describing it as *Cadath Ghranntaich* – Grant Tartan. A later hand than Wedderburn's has added that this is the 42nd tartan in the 'old tones'. There is also a sett labelled 'Campbell' whose details will be described shortly.

The use of this tartan by Clan Campbell has continued to stir up controversy among 'experts' on tartan who ignore the fact that the Chief's dictum is now taken as the final one. In our case, the argument is over the addition of lines to the basic sett, a practice followed by the 6th and 7th Dukes of Argyll. This is discussed in more detail below. Frank Adam, author of *The Clans, Septs and Regiments of the Scottish Highlands*, who was apparently no lover of our Clan, makes much of the story that a later Duke attempted to have the stripes on the portraits of his predecessors painted out. This is, it would seem, founded on fact; our present Chief has told me that it is a well-known family story. No less a figure than the President of the Royal (Scottish?) Academy was invited to stay at Inveraray to undertake a commission. Much delighted, he arrived and at once started to examine the lines of the Duke's face as the light fell on it from various angles; on learning that his real task was to paint out the offending lines in the portraits, his chagrin was such that he packed his bags and left on the spot!

The continued practice of writers on tartan insisting on saddling the Clan with an unauthorised overstriped tartan and ignoring the views of the Chief is a source of real annoyance. Fortunately, this practice shows signs of becoming less prevalent although it still occurs. But the position of the blue, black and green tartan is perfectly clear: it is *the* Campbell tartan, to be worn by all members of the Clan unless they belong to a branch which has its own sett that they prefer. It has been worn as such by successive Chiefs of Clan Campbell for well over 100 years, and their example has been followed by most of the leading members of the Clan.

(b) CAMPBELL OF CAWDOR – see illustration No. 3

The first mention I have seen of this sett is in the pre-1820 books of Wilson's of Bannockburn, the well-known tartan manufacturers, where it first appears under the title of 'Argyle', or 'No. 230'. The Scottish Tartans Society have noted it as appearing in correspondence from the same makers as early as 1798, under the name of 'Argyle'. The tartan was confirmed as being his by

Earl Cawdor in 1850 for the publication of their book on tartans by the Smiths of Mauchline. So they claimed, although Lord Cawdor sometime later was sure he had given it no such accolade. Writing to Lord Archibald Campbell in 1883, Lord Cawdor says: 'I certainly have no recollection of having selected the so-called Cawdor Campbell with a red stripe, and my impression is that I first saw it in a book of patterns shown me by MacDougal . . .', and, again, a day or two later: 'I should be very much obliged if you would tell me whether the Cawdor Campbells are entitled to a tartan of their own and if so . . . of what pattern or whether they ought to wear the Campbell (which) I believe is the same as the 42d'.

When, in 1864, the 91st Regiment were once more clothed in tartan, as they had originally been when they were raised as the Argyllshire Highlanders, there was great uncertainty as to the sett they had originally worn, and in the end it was this one, erroneously as it happens, which was adopted as being the old pattern. It seems extraordinary that the memory of the plain sett in which they had actually been raised should have faded so fast, since the regiment dated back no further than 1794.

There is some interesting correspondence on the subject in Dunn and Pattison's *History of the 91st Highlanders*, somewhat confused by the fact that the authors were writing at a time when the idea of 'Clan' tartans had become much more firmly established than it had been at the period of events they were discussing. Colonel Walter Campbell of Skipness, whose opinion was sought by the Duke, was influential in the final choice. He would have been referring to this tartan when he wrote to the Duke: 'I have known the Campbell tartan with the red stripe for many years, and always wear it. I believe it to be the proper *Argyll* tartan; that of the Breadalbane Campbells having a yellow, instead of a red stripe.' It is also significant that, at about this time, the various Companies of Volunteers in the county were being organised into a proper battalion and were to be dressed in the kilt. The tartan they adopted was this one. This was already in wear by one of the Companies, the 10th Tayvallich Corps, which had been raised by Campbell of Inverneill in 1860 and which wore it in the form of a tartan band around their shakos.

At Inveraray there is a portrait of the Marquis of Lorne as a young man which must also date from this period and which shows him wearing this sett. Lady Elizabeth Campbell, sister to the 10th Duke, said that the Marquis's father, the 8th Duke, also had a kilt of this pattern and was himself painted in it but later had the overstripes painted out. All this would suggest that the tartan with the red and blue stripes had at first an Argyll rather than specifi-cally Campbell connotation, which might account for its being recorded as worn by the McCorquodales, who are of course an Argyllshire clan. Whether it is in fact an old 'District' tartan or not I do not know, but the entry in Wilson's book as 'No. 230' would rather suggest that it may have started life as an attractive pattern which had to be given a name. Although probably of relatively little significance, it is perhaps worth recording that the War Office suffered no such hesitation, and the Official Instructions for the reclothing of the 91st state unequivocally that it was to be 'in Campbell tartan'. There are sometimes slight variations in the pattern; some manufacturers show the red stripe without black guard-lines. There is also considerable variation in the tone, which can approach that of the military tartan on occasion.

(c) CAMPBELL OF BREADALBANE – see illustration No. 4

It would seem that the first recorded appearance of this pattern is in Wilson's pattern books pre-1820, where it is shown both as 'Breadalbane' and also as 'Abercrombie with yellow'. A similar sett, only with white lines instead of yellow, is given as 'Abercrombie'; this is now known as 'Graham of Montrose'. It seems that other early descriptions of the tartan illustrated here refer to it simply as 'Fancy'. Similar patterns, but with other colours replacing the yellow, have been given various clan attributions. In 1850, it appears in the Smith's book as 'The Breadalbane Campbell' with the blessing of the Marquess. Five years later, in 1855, *The Black Book of Taymouth* was published. I am the fortunate possessor of one of the few copies specially produced for close members of the family with the inside covers bound in silk tartan of this pattern, which is now the accepted form of Campbell of Breadalbane tartan. As such, it has taken over from the tartan originally worn by the Breadalbane Fencibles, raised in 1793. This was as follows; see illustration No. 5.

Bl	Bk	Bl	Bk	Y	Gr	Y	Bk	Bl	Bk	Bl	Bk	*Bl*
2	2	16	16	2	28	2	16	2	2	2	2	16

As already mentioned, this is the only sett with any Campbell connection in the Highland Society of London's Collection of 1816. As it happens, my notes, taken when I had occasion to examine this collection some years ago, show yet another small but marked difference from the pattern shown elsewhere. I should like to double-check this, but what I have in my notebook is as follows; see illustration No. 6.

Bk	Bl	Bk	Bl	Bk	Bl	Bk	Y	Gr	Y	Bk	Bl	Bk	*Bl*
8	38	8	8	8	8	42	8	70	8	46	46	8	8

The Highland Society collection is now in the National Museum of Antiquities, in Edinburgh. As bad luck would have it, this particular sett appears to be missing and my attempt to verify this variation has been frustrated. The military pattern of Breadalbane tartan is shown by Logan (1831), Smibert (1850), D. W. Stewart (1893) and as late as 1950 by his son, D. C. Stewart. MacIan shows it with only single 'tramlines' on the blue, and the Scottish Tartans Society have a note that it is shown in this form in Provost MacBean's collection in Inverness where, almost certainly due to fading, azure has replaced the green; see illustration No. 7.

(d) CAMPBELL OF LOUDOUN – see illustration No. 8

The first appearance of this pattern would appear to be in James Grant's *The Tartans of the Clans of Scotland* in 1886. Some manufacturers produce a version in which the black guard-lines are omitted; see illustration No. 9.

6. OTHER SETTS WITH CAMPBELL CONNECTIONS

(a)   THE YELLOW AND WHITE STRIPE – see illustration No. 10

Bl	Bk	Bl	Bk	Gr	Bk	W/Y	Bk	Gr	Bk	Bl	Bk	Bl	Bk	*Bl*
2	2	16	16	16	2	4	2	16	16	2	2	2	2	16

This tartan continues to arouse controversy. In spite of very clear views expressed by successive Dukes of Argyll as to what is *the* Campbell tartan, it is this pattern which is continually quoted as the principal tartan of the Clan with the alternative name of 'Campbell of Argyll' or, as Stewart says, sometimes 'Campbell of Lochawe'. This has caused some embarrassment with the number of members of the Clan who have, in all good faith, purchased articles made with this pattern of tartan. It was with this in mind that, when the brochure on the Clan Campbell was produced for the Clan Gathering in 1977, MacCailein Mor asked that the statement, that he was 'quite happy' that members of the Clan who so wished should wear this version, should be included. It should be understood, however, that this is *not* a pattern which has the Chief's approval as an official Campbell tartan, and purchasers should avoid it if they wish to be correct.

The history of this particular pattern is confused by the existence, which does not appear to be generally known, of another sett which, although superficially the same, differs in one important respect in that the yellow and white stripes on the green, instead of alternating with each other, follow the pattern yellow/yellow white/white, as shown in illustration No. 11. I first came across this particular variation in the National Museum of Antiquities of Scotland, where it is one of the pieces of tartan signed and sealed by John Wedderburn, Secretary of the Highland Society of London. The label in his handwriting is as follows:

Cadath Mhic Chailein Mhoir, agus
Chlainn Dhiarmaid
John Wedderburn, Secretary
Edinburgh, June 1822.

This sett also appears in the pre-1820 Wilson's of Bannockburn pattern books where, however, a note has been added – I suspect very probably later – to the effect that the white and yellow stripes should alternate, which in the pattern they manifestly do not. General Cockburn's Collection, on the other hand, which is said to have been formed between 1810 and 1820 contains a sample where the yellow and white stripes do alternate.

A few years later, in 1824, an order was received by Wilson's for a quantity of 'Campbell (Argyll) tartan' from merchants called McCallum of Glasgow. A very careful drawing accompanies the order, specifying the colours and proportions required. Once again, the stripes follow the sequence yellow/yellow white/white, but the blue is replaced by the description 'purple'. One can only surmise that the McCallums had copied what they wanted from an existing piece of tartan which had faded, blue into purple being a by no means infrequent metamorphosis with the early dyes which were not particularly stable, and where red, I am told, was often added to tone down an overbright blue dye. This letter is also in the National Museum of Antiquities collection. It should be noted that in the yellow/yellow white/yellow version, the changes of colour is on either side of the blue square containing single tramlines only.

James Logan, in his *The Scottish Gael* published in 1831, actually gives the thread-count of the yellow/yellow white/white version; subsequent authors appear, however, to have missed this and give the alternating yellow and white stripe version when they illustrate or refer to this tartan, MacIan (1845) and James Grant (1883), however, showing it without black guard-lines to the yellow and white stripes; see illustration No. 12. The 6th Duke (born 1766, succeeded 1806, died 1839) did wear a yellow and white striped tartan. He may, however, have seen this as his own personal sett and not that of the Clan as a whole. His portrait was painted in full Highland dress by Sir Thomas Lawrence; the stripes are clearly shown. The picture was, unfortunately, lost in the 1975 fire at Inveraray and, although black and white reproductions exist, we may now never know the order of the stripes that he wore.

As a final footnote on this tartan, it is interesting to see that it figures in the *Vestiarum Scotticum*, that splendid work of fiction by the dubious Sobieski Stuart brothers, who, it will be remembered, claimed to be the grandsons of Prince Charles Edward and whose work on clan tartans was based on mysterious copies of a medieval manuscript which somehow was never available for inspection by historians of repute. Their description of the Campbell tartan is as follows:

> Clan Cambell. The Clannoduine of the auld: he has settis of blewe and settis of grene & ye dark sett bath fyrst ain bordure or lyste of blak, & near to ye ynwarde syd yroff tua sprangis of blak of four threiddis, neverthelesse, ye haille blewe settis be not of ye lyk pattron, bot ylk ither ane lakethe ye sprangis be ye lystis, and hathe twa yegidder through ye mydward of ye sett, for ye greine settis yi have ilk ane ae sprang of zello & ilk ither ane ae spraing of quhite of aucht threidis or ten.

Somehow the authors have managed to translate this into the pattern as in illustration No. 13 with what appears to be a disproportionate amount of blue and green as compared with black and no guard-lines on the white and yellow stripes. Its thread-count is as follows:

Bl	Bk	Bl	Bk	Bl	Bk	Gr	Y/W	Gr	Bk	Bl	Bk	*Bl*
48	2	2	2	4	16	40	4	40	16	30	2	4

This splendid work of the imagination enjoyed much popular success, and it says a lot for the historic authenticity of 'clan' tartans that a surprising number of those currently in use saw the light of day in this remarkable volume. Although any statement by the Sobieski Stuarts has to be treated with some caution, it would appear almost certain that it was they who invented the sett with the yellow and white stripes. A letter to J. F. Campbell of Islay, signed 'Jan Sobieski, Conte d'Albanie', is in the collection of Campbell's papers in the National Library of Scotland, in one of his notebooks entitled 'Clan Tartans'. Dated from Stanley Street, 19 March 1871, it reads in part as follows:

> As to the Campbell sett worn by the Duke. The Duke always wore the 42nd until after 1824 when I last saw him in the kilt and I think He afterwards, but some years later adopted the bright sprainges from my information as in 1824 he had no knowledge of such a tartan until I told him of the tradition of the very old Campbell woman on Loch Awe side who in 1819 told my brother and me that this was the old Campbell sett . . . I remember very well the 'authority' for the opinion that the bright stripes were for the chief and his house only. This arose as a

common bruit in Argyllshire after the Duke appeared in such a Tartan at Inverara, the people and the Cean Tighe such as the Sonachans, Lochnell, Airds, etc. never having seen it before and ignorant of the traditions which I have mentioned confirmed by 3 or 4 old people, thought the 'newe gyne' of the Duke was a distinction only lawful for Mac Chalainn Mor and his immediate house.

The significance of this is extremely important; the story is vintage Sobieski Stuart, with its rumours of ancient sages, unknown to anyone else, all recounting even more ancient legends. The date just fits into the story told above, and I think, personally, that there is little doubt that the tartan with the yellow and white stripe, so beloved by successive experts on the subject of tartan, is no more than fabrication by the ingenious brothers who were the source of so many of today's 'Clan' tartans. In particular, it should be noted that the Duke 'had no knowledge of such a tartan' until informed of it by the egregious brothers; that before then he had been wearing the plain sett and that the leading members of the Clan regarded the new practice with suspicion, from which it seems fair to suggest that they, too, like their Chief, were wearing the plain blue, black, and green tartan.

(b) THE WHITE STRIPE

The 7th Duke of Argyll (born 1777, succeeded 1839, died 1847) on occasion wore a tartan with a white stripe in it. He was presumably following what is said to be a traditional practice that a Chief thus differenced his personal sett. There are, in fact, several variations of this pattern. J. F. Campbell of Islay says that his father certainly regarded the sett with white overstripes as belonging to the Ducal House alone; this is also mentioned in Sobieski Stuart's letter, which implies that other Campbell lairds continued to wear the plain tartan.

The Smiths of Mauchline in 1850 showed Campbell of Argyll as being the tartan shown in illustration No. 14, for which they obtained the Duke's authorisation. Its thread-count is:

Bl	Bk	Bl	Bk	Gr	*W*
4	4	24	22	24	4

A variation on this theme is shown by the piece of tartan on display at Inveraray which is said to be part of a plaid belonging to Captain Archibald Campbell of Ardslignish and later of Lochnell, who was one of the original officers of the 91st Highlanders when the regiment was raised in 1794. There is also mention of a portrait of him painted around 1820 in which he is wearing a sett with a white stripe. This may be the reason why the noted military artist, Harry Payne, committed the 'howler' of depicting the early tartan of the 91st as having a white stripe, Duncan Campbell of Lochnell having raised the regiment. This tartan was never, in fact, worn by the 91st; but it may be that the Lochnells, as nearest family in line to that of the Chief's, felt that they too should wear the white stripe as today they wear the silver salmon for buttons as immediate members of the entail of MacCailein Mor. The piece of Ardslignish's plaid, which was given to Lord Archibald Campbell, is shown in illustration No. 15.

There is also at Inveraray a portrait by Briggs of the 7th Duke. He is shown full-length, clad in ordinary tweed jacket and trousers with his gun under his arm and a tartan plaid over his shoulders. The sett this time has white lines on each alternate green only, the others being dissected by a black stripe, while no tramlines at all are visible on the blues; they may have been omitted, but the detail of the picture as a whole is considerable. The tartan is shown in illustration No. 16. Finally, the Castle also contains a small water-colour of the same Duke in full Highland dress wearing a tartan which resembles the Ardslignish sett but without the black guard-lines; see illustration No. 17. This number of variations on a simple theme merely goes to show that the niceties of minor detail gone into so painstakingly today were deemed of little account by our predecessors.

(c) THE 'RED CAMPBELL TARTAN'

There are a number of references to this tartan, which, however, is never described in detail. It derives, I am quite sure, from the number of portraits of Campbells in red tartans. From the facts that these portraits predate 'Clan' tartans as such, that their subjects are shown wearing more than one pattern of red tartan at the same time, and that there is no shortage of pictures of members of other clans also wearing red setts, I have little hesitation in saying that there has never been a red 'Campbell Tartan' as such, although there is plenty of evidence that Campbells not infrequently wore red tartans. So did a lot of other people; Dr Micheil MacDonald of the Scottish Tartans Society has told me that such tartans were quite difficult and expensive to obtain, as the dye necessary to produce the best colour had to be imported and the resulting tartan was therefore much prized by those that could afford it.

In its simplest form, this tartan is made up of a plain red and black check in equal proportions; see illustration No. 18. This tartan was worn by Pryse Campbell, 18th Thane of Cawdor, who had his picture painted in 1762 by Francis Cotes. The portrait hangs in Cawdor Castle and shows him wearing no fewer than three tartans, all different; his coat is made from this sett.

Around the beginning of the nineteenth century, the tartan manufacturers christened it 'Rob Roy'; on this dubious historical basis it appears to have been taken up by the Macgregors as their Clan tartan, and it is now firmly established as such! Tartan weavers, however, composed many elaborations of this very basic pattern in red and black, and a number of Campbell wearers are listed below.

The earliest representation of a Campbell wearing a red kilt that I know of occurs in the Genealogical Tree of the Campbells of Glenorchy. It was painted in 1635 and depicts at the foot of the tree Sir Duncan Campbell of Lochow, 1st Lord Campbell, from whom this branch of this family sprang. The artist, George Jamesone, was of course painting some centuries after the death of his subject, so that the picture cannot be classed as any sort of hard evidence. Sir Duncan is shown wearing what appears to be a belted plaid and hose. On his head is a Baron's Cap of Dignity. The material of his kilt is plain red. The original of this painting is to be found in the Scottish National Portrait Gallery; there is a coloured reproduction of it in R. W. Munro's *Highland Clans and Tartans* and there is also a black and white version of it in Lord Archibald Campbell's *Records of Argyll*.

A red grounded tartan was worn by Loudoun's Highlanders, raised by John Campbell, Earl of Loudoun, in 1745. This was a regular line regiment of the British army. Lord Loudoun was painted in full regimentals by Allen Ramsay; a coloured reproduction of this picture is also to be found in R. W. Munro's book, and in black and white it is in both John Telfer-Dunbar and in Lady Hesketh's *Tartans*. The date must be around 1747. Edinburgh University possess a portrait of General Sir John Reid, the composer of *The Garb of Old Gaul*, as a Lieutenant in this regiment with a waistcoat made in what appears to be this tartan. While these are military portraits, it is likely that the portrait of Lord Loudoun has played a part in suggesting the existence of a red Campbell tartan.

The sett of the tartan in Lord Loudoun's picture is not easy to make out. Ruaridh Halford-MacLeod has made a close study of the original portrait and says that the dark bands and stripes on the red ground are not black but very dark blue and green. He has kindly allowed me to repeat his reconstruction of the sett of Lord Loudoun's plaid as featured in his article in *The Proceedings of the Scottish Tartans Society*, Series 3, No. 1, as follows; see illustration No. 19.

Bl	R	Bl	R	Gr	R	Gr	R	Bl	R	Bl	R	Bl	R	Bl	R	Bl	R
2	8	10	20	20	28	8	6	2	2	2	6	28	36	2	2	6	2

Bl	R	Bl	R	Bl	R	Bl
2	6	18	6	2	2	6

This sett is not easy to decipher; I have notes by the late A. E. Haswell Miller, former Keeper of the Scottish National Portrait Gallery and a noted portrayer of and expert on Highland dress, who describes Lord Loudoun's tartan as 'red; all lines black or dark blue. No green or other colours.' Halford-MacLeod has also discovered a most interesting letter and tartan sample among the Loudoun Papers in the Huntington Library, Los Angeles, which show that the original tartan of this regiment was not a red one but based on the familiar blue, black and green pattern with red and yellow overstripes as in illustration No. 36. Although the sample is an irregular one, the thread-count would appear to be the following:

R	Bk	Gr	Bk	Bl	Y
8	6	48	43	41	6

This pattern is very akin to one now known as a MacLeod tartan, and appears to be the first but by no means the last example of the creation of a regimental tartan by the addition of coloured overstripes to the basic 42nd pattern which, in this case, is in a remarkably light tone. It is interesting to speculate whether a claim would have been made for it as 'Campbell of Loudoun' had its origin been more widely known to an earlier generation, and had the MacLeods not got there first!

Lord Loudoun, it may be remembered, was actually a Breadalbane Campbell in the male line, and two other cadets of this branch of the Clan also appear in red tartan at an early date. The first, whose portrait is in the Scottish National Portrait Gallery, is Charles Campbell of Lochlane, a son of Campbell of Monzie. He became Sheriff-Depute of Selkirk after the '45 and died in 1751. His picture is an interesting one as it shows, for the first time, kilt and plaid as separate garments. Again, a coloured reproduction is to be found in Munro's *Highland Clans and Tartans*. Having spent some time studying the original, I estimate the tartans he is wearing to be as follows, the sett of the kilt not being visible:

Coat: see illustration No. 20.
Plaid: see illustration No. 21.

In Cawdor Castle, as already mentioned, there is the portrait of Pryse Campbell, the 18th Thane, painted in 1762. He is wearing no fewer than three different tartans. His coat of the 'Rob Roy' sett has already been described. His kilt is also in a variation of the red and black theme and appears to be as depicted in illustration No. 22.

The second Breadalbane cadet to be found wearing a red tartan is John Campbell of the Citadel, 'John of the Bank' from his position as first Cashier of the Royal Bank of Scotland in whose boardroom his splendid portrait hangs and where I was allowed to inspect it. John Campbell wears a belted plaid and tartan coat, with a sword and dirk belted on him. On the table beside a bag of golden sovereigns lie his bonnet, pistol and powderhorn. In the bottom left-hand corner is the inscription 'John 1777'. It appears that the tartans he is wearing are:

Coat: see illustration No. 23.
Belted plaid: see illustration No. 24.

The Scottish Tartans Society has produced notes on this picture from Mr John Cargill which are very inaccurate; they state *inter alia* that the warp and the weft of the tartan are different and that coat and belted plaid are of the same sett, neither statement being the case.

In the Scottish National Portrait Gallery there is a picture by Sir David Wilkie which shows the Duke of Hamilton proffering the keys of the Palace of Holyrood to King George IV during the famous Royal Visit of 1822. It includes a kilted figure said to be that of the Duke of Argyll. The picture is too small to allow any accurate detail of the various tartans worn, but that worn by MacCailein Mor would appear to have a good deal of red in it. A larger version hangs in Holyrood, but no more detail is shown. It was, incidentally, in honour of this visit that Sir Walter Scott is said by his son-in-law and biographer, Lockhart, to have donned a pair of Campbell tartan trews thanks to some female ancestor. It would be most interesting to know if a portrait exists of the great man so attired and what sett he is wearing. There is, as it happens, a sett in Wilson's pre-1820 pattern book labelled 'Sir Walter Scott' – most probably only as a trade name – which is shown in illustration No. 26.

Bk	Purple	Bk	Bl	Gr	*Bk*
4	14	18	4	16	4

The fact that it apparently contains blue and purple means that the former cannot have faded into the latter, and there is no apparent similarity between this sett and any Campbell one.

Mention is made of a red tartan by J. F. Campbell of Islay writing to Lord Archibald Campbell in 1882, when, referring to the Dewar Manuscripts, he says 'as far as I can remember, there is but one instance in which a man was recognised by his tartan. An Earl, or some other Argyll Chief, was recognised, according to the story, on the opposite side of a Loch by his red plaid' (*Records of Argyll*, p. 437). Lord Archibald later castigates Islay for his opinions, summed up as 'The result is, that tartans are old Highland dresses – very old – but that uniform clan tartans are not older than regiments' (ibid., p. 445). This did not please Lord Archie, who was firmly a member of what I have already called 'the Romantic School'. But if Islay was right, as I am quite sure he was, then the true significance of the red plaid in Dewar's story can easily be seen. Of course people can be recognised by their clothes, as today one might recognise at a distance someone wearing, say, a yellow anorak; this does not mean to say that the yellow anorak itself has any special significance.

Similarly, Lord Archibald's tale of Sir Alexander Campbell of Dunstaffnage turning out a lumber-room around 1836 or 1840 and finding no trace of the present-day Campbell tartan among several old plaids, one of which at least was largely red with green and yellow stripes, really has little significance as pointed out by Dr Archie Campbell in his article in the Summer 1984 issue of the *UK Clan Campbell Magazine*. But another reference exists to a red sett: in Elizabeth Grant of Rothiemurcus's 'Reminiscences of a Highland Lady'; she mentions a servant, Betty Campbell, and says 'a red plaid of the Campbell tartan, spun and dyed by herself, was thrown around her when she went out'. The date of this would be around 1814. Readers may draw what conclusion they wish from this.

A sett under the title of 'New Loudoun' appears in Wilson's pattern books – No. 4 of pre-1820. Whether its name has any significance beyond being a handy means of reference, I do not know. But I do not know of any grounds for the statement in the Scottish Tartan Society's notes that it is a Campbell of Loudoun sett nor that it is 'the elusive red Campbell tartan'. Illustrated as No. 25, its thread-count is:

LD	W	LP	DP	R	Bk	R	DP	LP	W	Gr	W	LD	DBl	LBl
18	4	4	4	10	4	10	4	4	4	24	4	10	4	4
LD	W	*R*												
10	4	50												

What, then, gave rise to this myth of the red tartan? The answer seems clear enough with the number of portraits of Campbells wearing setts of black and red. But even if one were a dedicated believer in the antiquity of tartans with a specific clan significance, it would be hard to explain away the relatively large number of portraits of members of other Highland clans wearing similar setts. Finally, the multiplicity of patterns of these black and red tartans worn by Campbells seems to argue conclusively against any one of them being a 'clan' tartan, the portraits of John of the Bank, Cawdor and Lochlane collectively displaying no fewer than six variations! I have not the slightest hesitation in saying that I do not believe that there was ever such a thing as the 'Red Campbell Tartan'.

(d) CAMPBELL OF DUNSTAFFNAGE – see illustration No. 1

The Scottish Tartans Society notes refer to this coming from Anderson's in Edinburgh and to derive from an old coat found at Dunstaffnage and later copied. It is the plain Campbell sett in a small scale and in fairly pale colours. The late Captain of Dunstaffnage described the circumstances to me in a letter of 1976 as follows: 'My grandfather, while having a well dug, discovered three skeletons with remains of plaids of some odd-looking tartan. This was examined by experts who said it was the old vegetable dyes.' Writing in 1907 to the *Oban Times*, Lord Archibald Campbell also referred to this plain sett:

> A complete cuff of this same tartan, 200 years old, was dug out of a peat moss at Dunstaffnage. The late Duke of Argyll, who was an authority on the age of peat mosses, reckoned that at the depth at which this fragment was found it must be 200 years old. This I caused to be copied by Mr Maclachlan, Clan Tartan Warehouse, Oban, so as the sett should be noted.

This is obviously the origin of the name 'Campbell of Dunstaffnage' for the tartan which otherwise has little significance, apart from being, as will be discussed shortly, an early occasion in recent times on which the attraction of early dyes was brought to the attention of those who were not familiar with them. Although the Duke knew a great deal about agriculture, his method of dating could hardly be classed as scientific, and even if it were correct (and he probably wasn't all that far out) no very definite conclusions can be drawn from the find. The story, however, is not without interest. A piece of this tartan, authenticated by Dunstaffnage as being a true copy and dated 1934, is in the Highland Society of London collection.

(e) CAMPBELL VARIATION – see illustration No. 27

Bl	Bk	Bl	Bk	Gr	*Bk*
6	6	18	18	22	5

The variation is to be seen in Kenneth Macleay's *Highlanders of Scotland* published in 1870. The illustration of Colin Campbell, Farmer, Ceanmore, Lochfyne, portrays him wearing a bonnet, kilt and hose. This is the tartan of his kilt, which is most carefully delineated, as is Macleay's work in general, so it seems possible that this variation with only single black 'tramlines' on the blue is what he actually saw. It is also given in one of the early Wilson pattern books according to the Scottish Tartans Society, labelled as '42nd'.

(f) CAMPBELL OF LOCH AWE – see illustration No. 28

Bk	Bl	Bk	Gr	*Bk*
4	22	52	22	4

This sett, so called, is from Anderson's of Edinburgh. As shown above, there is a large proportion of black in the tartan and only single lines through green and blue. This pattern appears quite often in the manufacture of various articles, but I do not think it is any more than a manufacturer's convenience noted by the Scottish Tartans Society. A painting of the Medical Officer of the 42nd c. 1770 appears to show this simplified pattern.

(g) CAMPBELL OF GLENLYON – see illustration No. 29

Bl	Bk	Bl	Bk	*Gr*
4	2	14	12	14

The pattern above was produced by Messrs Romanes and Paterson, Edinburgh, and noted by the Scottish Tartans Society.

Bk	Bl	*Gr*	repeated, not reversed
8	8	8	

This sett is displayed under the same title in the Highland Folk Museum, Kingussie. It is on a very small scale, as were most early tartans, and is said to come from Wilson's of Bannockburn. It also appears in the Provost MacBean collection in the Inverness Museum under the title of 'Glenlyon' alone; see illustration No. 30.

(h) CAMPBELL OF ISLAY – see illustration No. 1

A small-scale version of the normal Campbell tartan from the collection of Messrs Anderson, the Edinburgh tailors. In 1881, J. F. Campbell of Islay wrote to Lord Archibald Campbell:

> When I was first tartaned, more than 50 years ago, I was taken by John Campbell, piper, to the shop of his brother William, in Glasgow, to be tailored. So far as I can remember, the Campbell tailor called the tartan 42nd. Both piper and tailor were sons of a Lorne Campbell who was a piper of a family of pipers, of whom one was at Culloden. If any of these Campbells had knowledge of any Campbell tartan, I should have been adorned with that device. I have worn 42nd all my life.

(i) HUNTING CAMPBELL – see illustration No. 34

Bl	Bk	W	Bk	Y	Grey	Brown	Bk	Brown	*R*
8	2	4	6	2	24	2		24	24	8

This splendid concoction is noted by the Scottish Tartans Society as originating in Toronto. One can only assume that a Canadian Campbell must have decided to cut a dash in a tartan of his own devising, though what he was hunting in such gaudy plumage somewhat baffles the imagination.

j) CAMPBELL (BROWN)–see illustration No. 35

W	Bk	Br	Gr	DBl	Gr	DBl	Gr	DBl	Gr	Br	Bk	*Y*
18	2	62	60	72	6	6	6	72	60	62	2	18

An example of this tartan is held by the Scottish Tartans Society in their MacGregor-Hastie collection. It was apparently specially made for a Captain Campbell of the Blythswood family. Older dyes faded in sunlight in due course, often with most pleasing results. Modern dyes are less likely to do so, and manufacturers nowadays sometimes offer versions of tartan which seek to reproduce the effect of age by interposing a brown thread after each coloured one, the result being marketed under such soubriquets as 'Muted' or 'Weathered' Campbell or whatever.

Aficionados of the work of the late Compton Mackenzie will recall his splendid characters Donald Macdonald of Ben Nevis and Hugh Cameron of Kilwhillie. Kilwhillie was a noted expert on Highland dress who used to consider every new kilt required to be buried in a peat bog for a period in order to reduce its brightness to a level where it could, with decency, be worn. What Kilwhillie would have made of 'Muted Cameron' can only be surmised. It is a fact, I have been told, that Compton Mackenzie modelled Kilwhillie on the real-life Angus, Captain of Dunstaffnage.

A further variation on this theme has recently come my way in the form of a mail-order catalogue from a well-known firm in the USA. This includes articles of clothing in five different Campbell-related patterns, of which one is correct. They include the following, under the title of 'Weathered Campbell'; see illustration No. 47.

W	O	W	O	W	O	W	O	W	Bk	Y	Bk
4	6	16	2	4	2	16	6	4	16	2	

The sett is then repeated, not reversed. Although of no real significance, I have included this sett as an example, yet again, of manufacturers' malpractice. There is nothing wrong with the pattern itself, but to label it as 'Campbell' of any description is wilfully misleading and could, in Britain at any rate, lead to action under the Trades Descriptions Act.

(k) 'LORNE' AND 'LOUISE'

Tartans under these names were 'brought out by Mr. M'Kissock, of Girvan' and approved by the Marquis of Lorne. They were used on various articles by Messrs Smith of Mauchline. The pattern was described as 'a combination of the Argyll and Hunting Stuart tartans'. They were produced to take commercial advantage of the publicity surrounding the wedding of the Marquis of Lorne to Her Royal Highness the Princess Louise in 1871, as was the little book *The Clan Campbell and the Marquis of Lorne* from which these details are taken. The 'Lorne' tartan is *not* a district pattern, as has erroneously been asserted.

'LORNE' – see illustration No. 37

Bl	Bk	Gr	Bk	Gr	Bk	Gr	Bk	Bl	Bk	Bl	Bk	Bl	Bk	*Gr*
2	1	8	2	2	2	2	8	2	2	2	2	8	1	2

'LOUISE' – see illustration No. 39

Bl	R	Gr	Bk	Gr	Bk	Gr	Bk	Bl	Bk	Bl	Bk	Bl	Bk	*Gr*
2	1	8	2	2	2	2	8	2	2	2	2	8	1	2

The Lorne tartan above was in fact adopted as the regimental tartan by the 5th Royal Scots of Canada on assuming a Scottish identity for the whole regiment in 1880. By 1883 the unit had become a kilted one, but enormous difficulty was found in getting a standard shade for the different shipments of tartan, no two of which looked alike, so that the battalion presented a very patchy appearance on parade. Because of this, the decision was eventually taken to switch to the Government 42nd pattern where supplies gave no difficulty. Adoption of the Lorne tartan had been in deference to the Marquis, by then Governor-General of Canada, and in his honour the regiment displayed the boar's head and *Ne Obliviscaris* on their accoutrements. In due course, the regiment became 'The Black Watch (Royal Highland Regiment) of Canada', under which title it flourishes today.

W. & A. K. Johnston Ltd, in their *Tartans of the Clans and Septs of Scotland* published in 1906, display a different version of the above 'Louise'.

'LOUISE' – see illustration No. 40

Gr	Bk	Bl	Bk	Gr	Bl	Gr	Bl	Gr	R	*Bl*
2	1	14	12	2	2	2	2	8	1	2

The Provost MacBean collection in the Inverness Museum contains a sample of another sett no doubt made up for the same occasion under the title of 'Marquis of Lorne'. This is one of various 'Campbell' tartans purchased in the course of a walk down Regent Street in London by J. F. Campbell of Islay in 1871 and included in his notebook on *Clan Tartans* in the National Library of Scotland, where this particular sett is labelled simply as 'Lorne'.

'MARQUIS OF LORNE'–see illustration No. 38

BP	Bk	Gr	Bk	Gr	Bk	Gr	Y	Gr	W	Gr	R	Gr	Bk	Gr	Bk	Gr	*Bk*
6	6	4	22	3	3	32	3	3	3	3	3	32	3	3	22	4	6

The sett is repeated, not reversed. BP = Bright Purple.

(l) DRESS CAMPBELL

'Dress' tartans are a manufacturers' invention. These are usually versions of tartan in which the base and predominant colour is white. It is claimed that women's *arisaids*, or cloaks, in earlier times often showed this preponderance of white or grey-white, although long before the attribution of any clan significance to a particular sett. This grey-white was no more than undyed, natural wool, which no doubt represented a worthwhile saving in time and money. There is early mention of plaids made solely in grey and white as well as in tartan; the *arisaid* patterns would appear to be somewhere between the two. But a plague of Clan 'Dress' tartans has proliferated in recent times. These showy, some might say garish, setts are much loved by tourists and Highland dancers, to say nothing of professional 'Scottish' entertainers. A large number of varieties exist under the title of 'Dress Campbell' or 'Dress 42nd or Black Watch', the 'Campbell' so-called setts containing the yellow and white lines. 'Dress Black Watch' is a particular abomination – the regiment has *never* worn such a sett, although a piece of one of these patterns is displayed in a showcase in the Regimental Museum, Balhousie Castle, Perth.

I have noted the following:

'CAMPBELL (DRESS)' – W. & A. K. Johnston, 1906 – see illustration No. 41

W	Bl	W	Bl	W	Bk	Gr	W	Gr	Bk	Bl	Bk	Bl	Bk	Bl
4	1	8	3	4	4	6	1	6	4	4	1	2	1	4

Bk	Gr	Y	Gr	Bk	W	Bl	W	*Bl*
4	6	1	6	4	4	3	8	1

This pattern is repeated and does not reverse.

'DRESS CAMPBELL' – USA mail order catalogue, 1984 – see illustration No. 42

W	Bk	W	Bk	W	Bk	W	Bk	W	Bl	Bk	Bl	Bk	Bl	Gr
2	16	2	2	2	16	2	2	16	2	2	2	16	16	2

Bk	W/Y	Bk	*Gr*
2	2	16	2

and repeat, alternating, however, the yellow and white overstripes.

'DRESS CAMPBELL' – USA mail order catalogue, 1984 – see illustration No. 43

W	Grey	W	Grey	W	Grey	W	Grey	W	Grey	W	Grey	Y	Grey
2	2	8	2	2	2	8	2	2	4	3	30	3	4

This pattern is repeated and not reversed.

The Scottish Tartans Society quote Mr Adam Geddes of Anderson's, the Edinburgh outfitters, as saying: 'Campbell of Lochnell tartan is identical to Dress Campbell but with black guards to the yellow lines'. The Society also possesses a sample of 'Dress Cawdor' in their Coulson Bonner collection. Neither of these setts is here illustrated; as can be seen, this whole sector is one where fancy 'trade-checks', as Sir Thomas Innes of Learney would describe them, abound, fanciful patterns given dignity by even more fanciful names. Our Chief has made his views on these tartans abundantly and pungently clear; in no way do they have his authorisation, and they should be avoided by anyone seeking to purchase a Campbell tartan.

The sett at the Black Watch Museum is as follows:

'42nd DRESS TARTAN 1870–80' Balhousie Castle – see illustration No. 44

W	Bl	W	Bl	W	Bk	Gr	Bk	C	Bk	Bl	Bk	*Bl*
6	4	30	6	6	14	16	4	16	14	16	2	4

This sett, according to Mr MacGregor-Hastie's notes in the Scottish Tartans Society collection, was also produced in the 1930s by Forsyth's, the Edinburgh outfitters, at the behest of Lt-Colonel John Macrae-Gilstrap of Eilean Donan, a former officer of the regiment. It was never worn, however, as has already been pointed out, as a regimental tartan.

Messrs W. & A. K. Johnston also included a version in 1906:

'FORTY-SECOND "BLACK WATCH" (DRESS)' – see illustration No. 45

Bl	Bk	Bl	Bk	W	Bl	W	Bl	W	Bl	W	Bl	W	Bk	Gr	*Bk*
4	2	10	12	2	4	18	2	4	2	18	4	2	12	10	4

This pattern is repeated and not reversed.

Another version is to be found in the Provost MacBean collection, Inverness:

'FORTY SECOND' – see illustration No. 46

W	Bl	W	Bl	W	Bl	W	Bl	W	Bk	Gr	Bk	Gr	Bk	Bl
4	4	28	2	6	2	28	4	4	16	22	4	22	16	20

Bk	Bl	Bk	Bl	*Bk*
4	4	4	20	16

This pattern is repeated and not reversed.

7. PRE-1800 CAMPBELL PORTRAITS IN TARTAN

Although family portraits going back to the seventeenth century and even beyond are far from uncommon, it surprises many people to find that the occasions on which their subjects are shown wearing tartan are relatively few and far between. This does not mean that they never wore tartan clothes, but it was seldom that their best suit, in which they would naturally want to be painted, was made of this material. In the seventeenth and early eighteenth centuries, it was very often the practice to be painted in a steel breast-plate over a velvet or fine cloth jacket. Early portraits, therefore, do not provide us with much information on the subject of tartans.

Archibald, 7th Earl of Argyll – succeeded 1584. There is a magnificent full-length portrait of this nobleman that hangs on the wall at Inveraray, showing him in what appears to be the uniform of Spain in whose service he saw action in the Low Countries. At the shoulder, down the front of his doublet, and above the knee are displayed arrangements of ornamental striped ribbons of green and white. It is this portrait which caused Lord Archibald Campbell to write to the *Oban Times* in 1907 claiming that these ribbons were of Campbell tartan. With due respect to Lord Archibald, he was a man known for his enthusiasms, and in this case I am forced to the conclusion that his heart was ruling his head, or rather his eye, when he made this statement. After prolonged and careful study of this picture at short range, I am reluctantly but quite clearly of the opinion that there is *no* tartan at all depicted; the ribbons are merely of striped silk.

It is all too easy for the eye to see what the brain wants it to see. At the risk of digressing, what appears to be a similar piece of 'wishful thinking' is revealed by lecture notes belonging to Lady Elspeth Campbell, sister of the 10th Duke, among the Inveraray Castle Papers. She speaks of a portrait of the 2nd Duke, known as 'Red John of the Battles', painted around 1720 wearing armour and standing in front of a tartan curtain which she likens to the present Gordon tartan as it has a single yellow overstripe running through it. There are three portraits of the 2nd Duke at Inveraray Castle; the present Duke and I have examined them in detail and can find *no* trace of tartan in any of the pictures, let alone the yellow stripe described by Lady Elspeth!

'A Highland Chieftain' by John Michael Wright. Thought to date from around 1660, this picture hangs in the Scottish National Portrait Gallery. Considerable doubt exists over the identity of the sitter, who is said by some to be one Lacey, a favourite actor of the King's, who possessed portraits of him in various roles including one as 'Sawney the Scot' (reproduced in Lord Archibald Campbell's 'Records of Argyll'). But to me, at any rate, the picture has a power and authority which I find difficult to believe comes from a theatrical posing. It balances Wright's other magnificent portrait of Sir Neil O'Neil in his dress as an Irish Chieftain. For many years it was in the possession of the Campbells of Glenorchy, and, while it may never be proved beyond doubt, there is a distinct possibility that the subject may be 'Slippery John', 1st Earl of Breadalbane. This opinion is held by Sir Iain Moncreiffe 'for various reasons' (cf. *The Highland Clans*). The tartan depicted is a very complex and apparently irregular one, as was very often the case with early tartans, and is impossible to reproduce, being a multiplicity of thin dark lines on a buff/brown/dirty yellow background.

John Campbell, eldest son of John, Lord Glenorchy, 1708. There are several copies of this picture, but its subject is beyond doubt, being inscribed as above. John Telfer-Dunbar suggests that the artist is either Kneller or Charles Jervas. He describes the tartan of the version formerly in Taymouth Castle, seat of the Breadalbane family, as a 'complex striped tartan of greyish-white, viridian, bright red and black lines'. An earlier description by John Sobieski Stuart gives 'white tartan in very wide setts, crossed by numerous stripes of red, green, purple and light blue'. Not having seen the original, I can make no attempt to reproduce the tartan, but it clearly bears no resemblance to any later 'Campbell' sett.

Charles Campbell of Lochlane – pre-1751. This portrait with its red tartans has already been described.

Pryse Campbell, Thane of Cawdor, father of the first Lord Cawdor. This is one of three family portraits at Cawdor Castle painted by Francis Cotes in 1762. Neither of the other two displays any tartan. Cawdor's kilt, plaid and coat are all of different setts. Apart from the 'Rob Roy' pattern of his coat and the red and black tartan of his kilt, both of which have already been described, his plaid displays the sett illustrated as No. 33. To my shame, I failed to proof-read my article on tartans properly in the 1977 Clan Campbell brochure and inadvertently transposed the coloured stripes which are, however, as shown here.

John Campbell of the Bank, 1777. This portrait has already been described. There is a mention in Lady Hesketh's book *Tartans* of a portrait of a tartan-clad Duke of Argyll whom she calls the 2nd Duke, painted in 1789. The 2nd Duke was long dead by then, and neither our present Chief nor the Scottish National Portrait Gallery has any idea of what this may refer to. I have talked with Lady Hesketh, who is unable to trace her source for this mention, and it looks as if it may be the work of one of those gremlins who entrap even the most meticulous of authors every now and then.

8. THE EVOLUTION OF 'CAMPBELL TARTAN'

What follows is merely of academic interest. I have attempted to place, in some sort of chronological order, the various setts for which a Campbell connection was claimed by various authorities, these being successive Chiefs of the Clan and those who wrote on the subject. The picture that emerges is a very confused one, perhaps not to be wondered at with the relatively recent advent of the whole idea of 'Clan' tartans, and almost inconceivable if in fact one still believes that specific tartans had been rigidly adhered to by individuals of each clan for centuries. Other factors still further muddy the waters. Clan Chiefs in the early days did not necessarily pronounce on or even wear their 'Clan' tartan. Indeed, it appears that some of them deliberately went out of their way to difference their own personal tartan from that worn by their followers. In more than one case, this difference took the form of a white stripe added to the general tartan of their clan; from correspondence on the subject, it seems possible that the white stripe preferred by the 7th Duke of Argyll originated as his own personal sett. But the idea of following their Chief's choice appealed to some people and hence an obvious source of confusion.

If one adds to that a growing demand for 'Clan' tartans only equalled by the manufacturers' determination that those who sought should find, then confusion is assured. A tartan was found for everyone, bearing his name, and hopefully – but not always – the same tartan would be supplied to anyone else of the same name who asked for 'his' tartan. The efforts of the Sobieski Stuarts did not make the situation any easier, as they often produced a different sett for a Clan who thought they already had one. Such would appear to be so in the case of Clan Campbell. Actually, the tartan manufacturers managed to maintain a remarkable degree of consistency, and only rarely does one get a situation where the same tartan was allocated to several clans at once. Such an example was that of the tartan of the 74th Highlanders, who had added a white stripe of their facing colour to the military tartan, the result being claimed at one and the same time by the Lamonts, the Forbes and the Campbells for whom small differencing details had hurriedly to be found. A tartan could go through several metamorphoses in this way, such a one being the present Breadalbane tartan which, in its day, has been known as 'Fancy', 'Abercrombie with yellow' and, finally, by the name it enjoys today.

I have been very sparing with the various letters published on the subject, particularly those of the 'my grandfather always said' type. The writer's memory is seldom all that it might be, and grandfather has as likely as not got it wrong in the first place. Hence a careful selection to avoid adding still further confusion. Alas! The picture that emerges is far from clear, which is hardly surprising. But it is hopefully not without interest if only to make one wonder why so many modern writers, while subscribing to the idea that it is the Chief of the Clan who says what his clan tartan should be, still persist in ascribing to Clan Campbell a totally different sett from that worn by and subscribed to by our Chiefs for well over a century.

The lost portrait of the 6th Duke by Sir Thomas Lawrence has already been mentioned, and I do not know its exact date. It looks very much as if it might have been painted around 1822 at the time of the Royal Visit. It will be remembered that this picture shows the Duke wearing tartan with yellow and white stripes in it, following the dictum of the Sobieski Stuarts. Prior to their invention, it will be remembered, he always wore the plain blue, black, and green sett.

The Highland Society of London began its collection in 1816. The only tartan in it with Campbell connections is the Breadalbane tartan of the military pattern worn by the Breadalbane Fencibles at the close of the eighteenth century.

'Breadalbane' – see illustration No. 6

It may well have been because of omissions that John Wedderburn, Secretary of the Society, signed and sealed a further selection of tartans in Edinburgh, in 1822, shortly before the Royal Visit. Among these tartans in the Museum of Antiquities are the following. I should have explained that, in each case, I have put the actual title by which the tartan concerned is named by each illustration in order to show the various titles employed.

'Duke of Argyll and Clan Campbell' – see illustration No. 11
'Grant' – see illustration No. 1

The interesting feature of the yellow/yellow white/white progression of the stripes has already been pointed out. It also appears that the date of 1824 given by the 'Conte d'Albanie' in his letter may be rather too late.

The exact chronology of the next two sources is not easy to establish. They were both spread out over a number of years, and exact dating is impossible. Lieutenant-General Sir William Cockburn of Cockburn, Bart, was a member of the Highland Society of London. His collection is said to have been made between 1810 and 1820 and is located, in the shape of fifty-six specimens of hard tartan mounted in a large book, in the Mitchell Library, Glasgow. It contains three setts of Campbell interest:

'Black Watch or Government'; 'Sutherland'; 'Campbell of Argyle'; 'Munro';
'Grant of Grant' – see illustration No. 1
'Campbell' – see illustration No. 10
'Breadalbane' – see illustration No. 4

Most of the tartans have a small handwritten label pinned to them. The first four specimens as mounted in the book are all plain blue, green and black, described on the facing page in each case as being 'Black Watch or Government Tartan'. The name of the clan is on the handwritten label attached to each specimen. The commentary on the page opposite states that the labels were written 'in 1815' – a suspiciously exact point between 1810 and 1820. In each case, even allowing for fading, the sett is much lighter than today's regimental sett and more nearly resembles the tones of what is now usually sold as 'Campbell'. It is particularly interesting as being the earliest example I have so far found of a specific Campbell label on the plain sett. The fact that it occurs at the same time as the tartan is attributed to the other clans is also interesting.

The dating of the next source is spread over a period which also cannot be specified exactly, although it is known to predate 1820. The Society of Antiquaries of Scotland owns a series of notebooks containing extracts made by the late Mr Pittendrigh MacGillivray from early pattern books of the famous tartan manufacturers, Wilson's of Bannockburn. Unlike the Cockburn collection, where one cannot tell the order in which the collection was put together, here at least one can be pretty sure that the contents of book No. 1, for instance, are earlier than those of, say, book No. 4. The contents are most interesting and show clearly how the naming of early tartans owed as much to commercial reasons, to put it politely, as to historical ones. The setts of Campbell interest are as follows.

Books Nos 1 and 2: 'Royal Highland Regt.; 42nd; 93rd' – see illustration No. 2
Books Nos 1 and 2: 'No. 230; Argyle' – see illustration No. 3
Book No. 3: 'Campbell' – see illustration No. 11
Book No. 3: 'Breadalbane' – see illustration No. 5
Book No. 4: 'Breadalbane; Abercrombie' – see illustration No. 4

Although the thread-count for the 'Campbell' quite clearly indicates the stripes as shown here, an added note says that the yellow and white should always be alternate. There was obviously considerable confusion over this point; I do not know the date of this note and whether it is a later addition. The earlier military Breadalbane is now joined by the civilian fancy pattern. Abercrombie was usually given white stripes, but a version in book No. 4 states that the stripes may be white or yellow.

In 1824, we again meet with the yellow/yellow white/white version of the stripes in Messrs McCallum's order. The fact that their carefully executed drawing specifies purple rather than blue is due, I am sure, to the fading of the model from which their drawing was made.

'Campbell (Argyll)' – see illustration No. 11

James Logan brought out his *Scottish Gael* in 1831. If followed to the letter, his thread-counts give:

'The Duke of Argyll & Campbells of Lochow' – see illustration No. 11
'The Earl of Breadalbane & his Clan' – see illustration No. 5
'Sutherland' – see illustration No. 1

The Sobieski Stuarts eventually produced their *Vestiarum Scotticum* in 1842. The tartan plate, based on the description given earlier in their version of medieval English, makes the sett look ill-proportioned. There are no black guard-lines to the white and yellow stripes.

'Clan Cambell' – see illustration No. 13

George, 7th Duke of Argyll, born in 1777, succeeded his brother in 1839 and himself died in 1847. He is recorded wearing three different setts. I do not know the dates concerned. As well as tartan with a white stripe, he is known to have worn the plain blue, black and green sett. The setts he wore are illustrated in Nos 1, 15 and 17.

In 1845, R. R. MacIan published his famous *Costumes of the Clans* with text by James Logan. Although his illustrations are really of costume as a whole rather than of specific tartans, the Campbell setts he illustrates are clearly identifiable. There are two Campbell figures, neither of whom is wearing the plain sett, which is, however, shown as Sutherland. MacIan has also produced a variation in the Breadalbane military sett. The tartans concerned are:

'Campbell of Argyle' – see illustration No. 12
'Campbell of Breadalbane' – see illustration No. 7
'Sutherland' – see illustration No. 27

The Sutherland sett shown by MacIan has single tramlines only through the blue.

Thomas Smibert, in his *The Clans of the Highlands of Scotland* (1850), gives:

'Clan Campbell (Breadalbane)' – see illustration No. 5
'Clan Campbell (Argyle)' – see illustration No. 10

In the same year, the Smiths of Mauchline, producers of 'Mauchlineware', brought out their *The Authenticated Tartans of the Clans and Families of Scotland*. This is interesting in that, for what appears to be the first time, the authors of such a work approached the Chiefs for their views. They included the following:

'Campbell' – see illustration No. 10
'The Argyll Campbell' – see illustration No. 14
'The Breadalbane Campbell' – see illustration No. 4
'Cawdor Campbell' – see illustration No. 3
'Sutherland or 42nd' – see illustration No. 2

'Cawdor' and 'Sutherland' were authenticated by the Earl of Cawdor and by the Duke of Sutherland respectively. Lord Cawdor, however, writing some thirty years later, could not recall ever having been approached on the subject. Of the 'Campbell' sett, the authors had this to say:

> We have every reason to believe the annexed tartan is the original 'Campbell tartan' and we know that it is worn both by the Loudoun family and by General Campbell of Lochnell.

The 'Argyll Campbell' sett with its succession of single tramlines apparently received the blessing of the Duke of Argyll. Could this, I wonder, be the 7th Duke, who had died three years before the book's publication? Of 'The Breadalbane Campbell' sett, the authors write: 'This specimen is what we would call a Family and not a Clan tartan . . .'. It was authorised by the Marquis of Breadalbane, and from now on the older, military sett virtually disappears from the scene, apart from the support given it by the Stewarts,

father and son. The personal family copies of *The Black Book of Taymouth*
produced for the Marquis of Breadalbane in 1855 have the inside covers
bound in the tartan seen illustrated as No. 4.

In 1864, the 91st Regiment, the old 91st Argyllshire Highlanders, who
had lost the kilt in 1809, were once more to be clad in the tartan. The Duke,
it will be remembered, was involved in the discussion over which tartan the
regiment had originally worn. The correspondence recorded in Dunn-
Pattison throws an interesting light on the views of the time. Writing in
November 1863 to Lt-Col. Bertie Gordon, the Commanding Officer of the
91st, the Duke had this to say: 'Because if tartan is to appear at all in the uniform, it probably would be the Campbell tartan, which is dark green and
blue.' In December he wrote again: 'There is no doubt that the tartans called
Campbell and Sutherland have become so confounded as to be nearly
identical. I believe that it used to be considered a rule that the chief of each
clan added a white stripe to his ordinary clan tartan.' The regimental tailors
were consulted, as was Colonel Walter Campbell of Skipness. Meyer &
Mortimer, the tailors, produced a sample of the Cawdor or 'Argyll' sett,
claiming (erroneously, since they had worn the plain sett) that it was the
original tartan of the 91st. Skipness wrote:

> I have known the Campbell tartan with the red stripe for many years
> and always wear it. I believe it to be the proper Argyll tartan . . . I
> believe all tartans have, or ought to have, a distinguishing stripe; and
> that the 42nd tartan (which I am aware is claimed and worn by many
> Campbells) is not a clan tartan at all.

The Duke did not like the red stripes, which reminded him of those ancient
foes of his house, the Atholemen. 'I have never been accustomed to consider
these colours as Campbell and I am pretty sure that it is now called the
Athole tartan'. His reservations were overcome, however, and his suggestion
of the addition of a white stripe to the red to make the 'Ninety-First Argyll
Tartan' was not followed. The 91st were clothed in the Cawdor sett, and it
was not until their amalgamation with the 93rd Sutherland Highlanders,
whose uniform they adopted in 1881, that they found themselves once more
in the tartan they had worn at their birth.

The above episode has a number of interesting facets. It reveals a remarkable state of ignorance on the uniform of the 91st of only some fifty years
earlier. The Duke's immediate reaction that the Campbell tartan should be
the plain sett is to be noted, as is the fact that the Cawdor tartan was clearly
seen as a general Campbell/Argyll pattern by others. The desire to rationalise
and make rules for everything connected with tartan is also seen at an early

date: it is clearly nothing new. Let His Grace have the last word, from the letter to Colonel Gordon: 'The whole subject of tartans has got into hopeless confusion; if indeed (which I doubt) it was ever anything else but a very uncertain and varying custom'.

The 8th Duke (born 1823, succeeded 1847, died 1900) himself seems to have worn the plain blue, black and green sett. There is a portrait of him in full Highland dress at Inveraray, painted by Angeli in 1876. The Duke's tartan is a dark one; on his coat are the salmon buttons and the Star of the Order of the Thistle. Earlier, his granddaughter Lady Elspeth records, he had also worn the sett now known as 'Cawdor'. His son, the Marquis of Lorne, later 9th Duke and husband of Queen Victoria's daughter, the Princess Louise, is also portrayed at Inveraray (born 1845, succeeded 1900, died 1914). There is a full-length picture of him as a young man in tweed jacket, kilt and plaid, with a shotgun under his arm: from the subject's youth, the picture must have been painted in the mid-1860s. His tartan, as also in a 'Spy' cartoon of around the same time, is shown to be the Cawdor or 'Argyll' sett. In later life, however, the 9th Duke, as he in due course became, appears to have reverted to using the plain blue, black and green sett as later pictures of him reveal, and it appears that his Cawdor kilt was in fact that of the Inveraray Volunteers, in which he was an officer. It was probably the 8th Duke who attempted to have the stripes in his forebears' portraits painted out; a further reference to this will be found in Frank Adam's *The Clans, Septs and Regiments of the Scottish Highlands*. From this period on, the views and preferences of the Dukes of Argyll would seem to be clear! Macleay's *Highlanders of Scotland*, published in 1870, showed, possibly but not necessarily due to the artist's error, a sett with single 'tramlines', as in illustration No. 27.

Writing in 1882 to Lord Archibald Campbell, J. F. Campbell of Islay recalls the wedding of Lord Lorne to Princess Louise in 1871 to which he, along with a very small number of Campbell immediate family and close friends, was invited. 'When Lorne was to be spliced and we were ordered to parade in our Clan Tartan. We paraded accordingly at Windsor in four different tartans White stripe, Red stripe, (Yellow I think) and Black Watch.' Correspondence immediately prior to the publication of Lord Archibald Campbell's *Records of Argyll* in 1885 produces a unanimous view that the 'Campbell' and 'Black Watch' tartans are one and the same, although the historical arguments for this advanced by Lord Archibald owe more, perhaps, to his heart than to his head. John Campbell of Islay supports this view in contrast to his first cousin, Walter Campbell of Skipness, quoted above. Dunstaffnage says he was ordered by his father 'never to wear anything except the black, blue and green' and recollects a letter of his grandfather's saying that the same thing had been said to him by his father, a statement which if accurate might date back to the end of the eighteenth century. Dunstaffnage also says that the Campbells of Inverawe and those of Melfort, however, all wear the white and yellow stripe, which, if true then, has certainly not been the case for some time now.

James Grant produced *The Tartans of the Clans of Scotland* in 1886 and shows:

'The Clan Campbell of Argyll' – see illustration No. 12
'Campbell of Breadalbane' – see illustration No. 4
'Campbell of Cawdor' – see illustration No. 3
'Campbell of Loudoun' – see illustration No. 8
'Sutherland' – see illustration No. 2

This appears to be the first occasion on which the present 'Campbell of Loudoun' is featured. D. W. Stewart in 1893 then produced his *Old and Rare Scottish Tartans*, a work distinguished by the use of actual tartan material to illustrate the limited number of setts that it dealt with, and by the fact that the author makes a serious attempt to describe the origin of each one. The old military Breadalbane sett is the only Campbell tartan shown, being labelled as 'Campbell of Breadalbane' and not just 'Breadalbane' alone; see illustration No. 5.

In 1906, Messrs W. & A. K. Johnston Ltd produced what must rank as the ultimate in comprehensive books, listing in their *Tartans of the Clans and Septs of Scotland* a weird and wonderful selection of setts which include:

'Campbell (Chief)' – see illustration No. 12
'Campbell (Dress)' – see illustration No. 41
'Campbell (Breadalbane) – see illustration No. 4
'Campbell of Cawdor' – see illustration No. 3
'Campbell (Loudoun)' – see illustration No. 8
'42nd'; 'Sutherland as 42nd' – see illustration No. 2
'Lorne' – see illustration No. 37
'Louise' – see illustration No. 40
'Forty-Second 'Black Watch' (Dress)' – see illustration No. 45

There is also a 'Sutherland – old' shown, which is in fact the pattern invented by the Sobieski Stuarts. Also featured is a 'MacDiarmaid' tartan which I do not recall ever having seen elsewhere. The above is the last printed source I propose to go through in detail. Confusion continued on the subject of Campbell tartan and does so today, most of the tartan books displaying the alternate yellow and white stripe in spite of the ever-increasing clarity and forcefulness of views expressed by successive Clan Chiefs. Honourable mention, however, must be made of Robert Bain, City Librarian, Glasgow, who in 1938 produced *The Clans and Tartans of Scotland* and showed the plain sett as 'Campbell, Ancient', omitting the yellow and white striped variety. I have the copy he gave to my grandmother and a letter in which he says: 'I thank you for your complimentary reference to my clan tartan book. The Campbell tartans illustrated in it have earned criticism, but the illustrations are correct.' After the war, a new edition was brought out and its editor, Miss Margaret McDougall, saw fit to remove the plain sett, replacing it yet again by the striped one and adding 'there is also a dress tartan'. Other writers seem insistent on the same pattern with its dubious origins, although Ian Grimble's *Scottish Clans and Tartans* does add the plain sett as an extra under 'Campbell, old colours'. All this in spite of the generally held agreement that it is the Chief's word that determines the Clan Tartan!

Let us give the last word to Niall, 10th Duke of Argyll, who, in a letter to Ian Campbell of Fraochyllan, later author of *The Campbells of Inverawe*, wrote in 1928:

> A marvellous lot of blathering has I perceive lately appeared in the *Oban Times* and other newspapers about lines and stripes. As an Inverawe, you should wear the ordinary Campbell tartan such as I and my father, all my uncles, grandfather and grandsire always did, which is the same as Kilberry, Inverneill, Lochnell, Jura, Succoth, Auchendarroch, etc. all wear. It should have no white or yellow lines in it, nothing but greens and blues enter into its sett.

9. LIGHT AND DARK SHADES: MILITARY USAGE

Faced with a multitude of users of the plain sett who do not belong to Clan Campbell, there has been a tendency to suggest that the darker version as worn by the military is a different tartan from that in a lighter shade as now worn by the Duke. Such, however, is not the case. There is nothing, apart from the strength and type of dye used, which dictates what tone a tartan should have. It is, however, quite possible to have two tones of the same colour in a sett, specified as such, but it is their relation to each other that matters, not their individual depth of tone. A clear example of this is given by the Cawdor tartan, where the stripe on the green is given as 'light blue' or azure by contrast to the darker blue of the alternating base. Two shades of

Cawdor tartan are commonly sold, and the 'light blue' of the darker version more or less corresponds with the 'dark blue' of the lighter tartan. This is demonstrated in illustrations 52 and 53. Indeed, there is considerable evidence, in the shape of contemporary portraits, to show that the eighteenth-century military tartan was often light and lively in tone; from the brightness of the colours, I would suggest it is very definitely not due to fading of the darker tartan. To mention two easily accessible examples, I would quote E. Daye's portrait of a Black Watch Officer and Copley's picture of the Earl of Eglinton, both of which appear in Telfer-Dunbar's book.

The light and darker forms of Campbell tartan both seem to have been worn by leading members of the Clan; in the earlier decades of the twentieth century it was very often the darker pattern that was most usually seen. The discovery of the tartan buried at Dunstaffnage aroused interest once more in the use of the old, lighter, dyes. In his letter of 1977, Dunstaffnage says that his uncle, Angus, Captain of Dunstaffnage, along with his family, promoted it in the 1920s and 1930s together with Duke Niall and some others. He says that at that time Campbell tartan was the only one available in these soft, attractive colours. My family were also clothed in it, my grandfather and Duke Niall having shared in the purchase of a bolt of this tartan.

The question of dyestuffs is dealt with in an interesting fashion by J. D. Scarlett in the introduction of his *The Tartans of the Scottish Clans*, first published in 1975. According to the author, the early vegetable dyes were gradually replaced by 'improved' synthetic dyes whose general effect was to enhance harsh brightness in yellows and reds while darkening blues and greens almost to black; the resulting tartans, or more accurately, shades of tartans, were known as 'modern'. It is not clear exactly what date is involved; certainly when Queen Victoria came to visit her daughter at Inveraray in 1875, the approach to the castle was lined by halberdiers 'dressed in Campbell tartan kilts with brown coats turned back with red, and bonnets with a black cock's tail and bog-myrtle (the Campbell badge)', as the Queen recorded in her journal. The late Sir George Campbell of Succoth had in his possession one of these kilts, which my father recalls as being of hard tartan but of a light hue, with no overstripes on the blue, green and black basic sett. Scarlett says that it was at the end of the First World War that a return was seen to softer, brighter colours, the result being termed 'old' or 'ancient' tartan. Dunstaffnage's letter might imply a rather later date. Finally, after the Second World War, a fashion was introduced for duller colours, in imitation of a piece of tartan dug up on the field of Culloden and referred to as 'Reproduction' or 'Muted'.

When Niall, 10th Duke of Argyll, died in 1949, a number of Campbell

Lairds attended his funeral. Contemporary photographs show the split between those still wearing the dark '42nd' version of the tartan and those with the lighter sett. Stonefield, Craignish, Succoth, Arduaine and Inverneil are all wearing the former; Dunstaffnage, Airds and young Succoth the light. But the important thing to realise is that the usage of such terms as 'Ancient', 'Modern' or 'Reproduction' have nothing to do with the antiquity or otherwise of the tartan concerned as most people think, so much as with the style of its colouring.

But ever since its first appearance as the tartan of the six Independent Highland Companies in 1725, the Crown has made much use of the blue, black and green sett. It has always been the military tartan, and a large number of the Highland Corps raised in the eighteenth century, Line, Fencible, Militia, Volunteer and Local Militia, all wore it. It has formed the basis for a host of other regimental tartans with the addition of stripes in various combinations, and several of these resulting patterns have subsequently been turned into 'Clan' tartans. When, in 1881, the Lowland Scots Regiments were taken out of the normal Line uniform they had worn for centuries and were clothed in tartan trews, it was this tartan that they were given initially, before, a few years later, they each adopted a distinctive sett of their own choice.

It is not always easy to keep pace with military reorganisations, but within recent years it has been worn by regiments around the world, including the New Zealand Scottish, the Byron Scottish in Australia; the Black Watch of Canada, the Argyll and Sutherland Highlanders of Canada, the Calgary Highlanders and the Lanark and Renfrew Scottish in Canada. At home, it is, of course, the tartan of those pre-eminently Campbell regiments the Black Watch (Royal Highland Regiment) and the Argyll and Sutherland Highlanders. It is interesting to note, too, that in Canada, the Lorne Scots wear the lighter version of this tartan under the title of 'Campbell of Argyll' – without, be it noted, any addition of white or yellow stripes, this title having received the official imprint of the Canadian Government! In its dark form, the tartan is enormously popular and is worn all over the world, simply as an attractive patterned material. Nothing will ever change that, and indeed I believe this practice is no more than history repeating itself, so that one can afford to take a relaxed view of a recent pronouncement from the Court of the Lord Lyon on the wearing of tartan, where it is stated that 'Black Watch or 'Government' tartan in its exact Regimental form, or one of the modified forms' should be worn by those without a Clan Tartan but who are of Scottish descent 'of Hanoverian or Whig ancestoral proclivities'.

10. DISTRICT TARTANS

It is currently popular to suggest that, if clan tartans cannot claim great antiquity, 'District' tartans, those named after an area rather than a clan, have a much stronger chance of doing so. Certainly logic would support the idea of certain patterns selling better than others and thereby becoming common in the areas where they were produced. This would also go far towards explaining the oft-quoted statement by Martin Martin, in his *Description of the Western Islands of Scotland*, of c. 1695, that a man's residence was detectable by his plaid.

But I very much doubt whether there was ever such a clear-cut system, as is too often suggested. Even when a tartan bears the name of a District, that does not necessarily mean that that is due to anything more than a nineteenth-century manufacturer's desire for a name that would identify and might sell. 'New Loudoun' and 'Breadalbane', which we have already discussed, do not fall into the category of proper 'District' tartans which their names might imply. I am not sure of 'Argyll'/Campbell of Cawdor, for there are, as will have been seen, indications that it was used as a District tartan, if only in the nineteenth century, even if its origin was only a manufacturer's fancy. 'Lorne', in spite of suggestions to the contrary, is quite clearly not a 'District' tartan. Nor am I much clearer on the origins of the following whose names, however, might imply a Campbell connection.

'Glenlyon' – see illustration No. 31

Bk	Gr	R
12	10	4

According to the Scottish Tartans Society, this is a Wilson's of Bannockburn sett of pre-1820. Another horse from the same stable is the pattern shown in Wilson's pre-1820 pattern books as 'GLENLYON' or 'MULL' or 'No. 53'; see illustration No. 32.

Az	Gr	Bk
4	6	10

Provost MacBean's collection, Inverness, also includes a sett with the name 'GLENLYON'; see illustration No. 30. This pattern's thread-count has already been given under 'CAMPBELL OF GLENLYON'; it is identical with the tartan of that name as displayed in the Highland Folk Museum, Kingussie.

D. C. Stewart gives two setts under the alternative names of 'MacIntyre or

Glenorchy' and a third whose alternate title is 'Cumming', all of which date back to the beginning of the nineteenth century:

'Glenorchy'; 'MacIntyre' – see illustration No. 48

Bk	Gr	R	Bl	R	Gr	R	Az	Bl	R	Gr	R	Bk	*Gr*
4	4	6	36	4	12	8	2	12	6	36	6	4	4

'Glenorchy'; 'MacIntyre' – see illustration No. 49

Az	R	Gr	R	Bl	R	Gr	R	Bl	R	Gr	R	Bl	R	*Az*
2	4	4	8	32	4	2	8	2	4	32	8	4	4	2

'Glenorchy'; 'Cumming' – see illustration No. 50

Gr	R	Bl	Az	R	Gr	R	Bl	R	Bl	Az	R	Bl	R	Gr
66	6	24	2	16	24	6	40	6	6	2	6	40	6	24

R	Az	Bl	R	Gr	R	*Bl*
16	2	24	6	44	6	6

There is also a Glenorchy sett which is different again and which comes from Wilson's pre-1820 pattern book:

'Glenorchy' – see illustration No. 51

Gr	R	LP	DBl	R	Gr	R	Az	DBl	R	Gr	R	LP	DBl	*Az*
10	8	2	72	8	30	16	2	70	8	72	8	2	10	2

Finally, it is interesting to note that there was apparently an Inveraray Tweed dating back to the mid-nineteenth century. It is recorded by E. S. Harrison in *Our Scottish District Checks* as follows; it will be noticed that the form of the thread-count is different, to represent the different weave involved.

Inveraray Check

White	2	1	1	
Red/Brown	2	2 1	1	
Red	4			Total 78

11. CONCLUSION

In spite of the fact that the reader has every right by now to feel exhausted, to say nothing of the state of the author, this appendix on the subject of the Campbell tartan lays no claim to be exhaustive. There is work still to be done on the late eighteenth-century correspondence of the tartan manufacturers, and there must be other early paintings in tartan which have not been mentioned here. Tartan has enormous attraction: it is bright, it is colourful, it allows us to show a legitimate pride in the family to which we belong. To an extent it has a history, albeit not as long as many people would like to believe. It is sad, therefore, that so much nonsense tends to be talked on the subject and so many fanciful shibboleths proclaimed, when in fact our ancestors until recently treated tartan much less seriously and with none of the rules and regulations laid down so assiduously today. The story told here is indeed complicated and may come as somewhat of a surprise to some. It is, however, typical of most, if not all, of today's Clan tartans. I have tried to make it as comprehensive as possible. But, in spite of all the cheapjack tomfoolery, the blatant commercialisation and the weird and wonderful myths propagated by the 'experts', there is still something about the tartan which catches the throat, and it is a poor heart indeed that does not beat just a little faster at the sight of the colours of the Clan.

APPENDIX 5

Crystal Balls and Brooches: Highland Charmstones

There are a number of crystal balls held by various Highland families, a surprising number of whom are Campbells. They share common magical properties such as the miraculous cure of humans and animals and the guarantee of safe return from travel or war. None is very large, two inches in diameter at most; some are or have been mounted in metal and some are unadorned. One or two are displayed as the centrepiece in large and complicated silver brooches.

Their origin is a mystery. According to G. F. Black (Letter to *Oban Times*, 30 April 1938), the crystals date from the Late Iron Age. They originate from China and have always had occult powers; some of them have later been 'turned' by the Church to Christian purposes and incorporated in reliquaries. Around twenty examples have been found in graves in England mostly of the Anglo-Saxon period and three or four in Ireland. There have been examples in Denmark, Germany and France.

How they got here is unknown for certain, and why they should be clustered in the Highlands, particularly the West Highlands, and why so many should be in Campbell hands is very strange. It is tempting to see the Middle East and the Crusades as a possible way for them to have found their way here, but this would not fit with the statement that the English examples dated from the Anglo-Saxon period, and when I asked Sir Steven Runciman, the great authority on the Crusades, whether he had ever come across anything of the kind, his answer was a decided 'no'.

In fact, in two cases the stones are said to come from the Middle East. The Ardvorlich stone is said by Simpson to have been brought back by an ancestor from the Crusades – this would have to have been one of the early Stewarts of what was to become the Royal Line, unless of course it was through the distaff side – and the Breadalbane stone was said to have been brought back from Rhodes by Sir Colin Campbell, which was after the end of the Crusades as such. Known examples in Scotland include the following.

(1)   The *Clach na Bratach* of the Robertsons of Struan. Before a battle, it showed a different colour depending on what the outcome of the battle was to be. The flaw in the stone was first discovered on the eve of Sheriffmuir in 1715. Last to use the stone was Alexander, the 16th Chief – 'The Slim Captain' – who fought in the American War. He used to dip the stone in water from a 'Fairy Spring' and then distributed the water to clansmen who in many cases had travelled far to take advantage of its powers. The fortunes of the House of Struan are said to have gone into decline ever since the flaw in the stone was first discovered.

(2)   *A' Clach Bhuidhe* of the Campbells of Glenlyon, said to be round or oval in shape and set in silver. Was dipped in water by the Laird in order to be effective (Simpson). Also said to bring safe home those who drank from a glass with the stone in it. A tailor who failed to take this precaution was the only man in the Glenlyon contingent to fall at Culloden (Fraser, *The Lairds of Glenlyon*).

(3)   Charmstone of the Campbells of Ballochyle. This included a large crystal and was used for the cure of people and cattle (Lt-Col. W. R. Campbell of Ballochyle's talk to the Glasgow Cowal Association 1873 and *PSAS*). It is now in the possession of the National Museum of Scotland.

(4)   Charmstone belonging to John Campbell, the Ledaig Bard. This was apparently an agate used for curing sick cattle. If touched by the index finger of the right hand, the stone became ineffective (*TGSI*, 35; J. E. Scott, *Benderloch*).

(5)   The Lochnell Charmstone – a small, rather cloudy crystal sphere with a hole in it – obviously for mounting purposes. On display at Inveraray Castle.

(6)   The Breadalbane charmstone. Claimed to cure ills, protect its devotees and bring them safe home. Some years ago, I was sent a small notebook by Miss Thelma Lewis, lately companion to Armorer, Countess of Breadalbane. It contained an amount of material on the family including the sad tale of a young man in the 6th Black Watch during the First World War. On the eve of his departure, he went up to the castle to pay his respects to Lord Breadalbane, who got out the charmstone and, according to ancient custom, dipped it in a glass of water from which they both drank to the young man's safe return. On this occasion, the charm did not work. Breadalbane had previously taken the stone with him as a good-luck talisman on his tour of South Africa in 1896–7. It is probably the stone said to have been brought back with him from fighting the infidel by Sir Colin Campbell

of Glenorchy, who was known from his exploits as 'Colin of Rhodes'. In a seventeenth-century inventory, it was described as 'ane stone of the quantitye of a hen's eg set in silver, which Sir Coline Campbell first Laird of Glenurchy woir when he fought in battell at Rhodes agaynst the Turks, he being one of the Knychts of Rhodes . . .' (*Black Book of Taymouth* and *In Famed Breadalbane*, 116).

(7)   The *Clach Dearg* or 'Yellow Stone' of Ardvorlich. Said to have been brought back from the Crusades by a fourteenth-century ancestor and to provide a cure for cattle sickness. As noted before, this ancestor, if in the male line, would have to have been of the Royal House of Stewart, if indeed the stone came back from the Crusades.

(8)   The Nether Lochaber Talisman. In the possession of Angus McDonnell of Insh, who emigrated to Australia c. 1854 and took it with him.

(9)   A stone belonging to the Gordons of Carrall.

(10)   Crystal charmstone of the Stewarts of Ardsheal. Mounted in silver with a chain, it had healing properties, being dipped in water which was then drunk as a protection against disease or death (National Museums of Scotland).

(11)   Two crystal stones belonging to the MacDougalls of Dunolly. Mentioned in the *Statistical Account* of 1845 'about the size of pigeons' eggs'. They were stolen in 1969. One of them is described as a spherical ball with an internal crack reflecting rainbow hues – supposedly caused by its being dropped at the lochside at the String of Lorne. One of these balls was traditionally in the MacDougall family, believed to have been brought back from the Crusades by an ancestor, possibly Duncan who built both Ardchattan and Dunstaffnage. The other stone was smaller, more of an oblong oval with a slightly domed top and a flattened base. (These details were kindly given to me in 1997 by Miss Hope MacDougall of MacDougall.)

(12)   Charmstone of the Campbells of Inverliever. This may be the crystal ball now in the Royal Irish Academy, Dublin. It is $1\frac{1}{2}$ inches in diameter and was sold by Campbell of Craignish in 1855. A bond of manrent of 1610 mentions 'ane precious stone' in possession of Ronald Campbell of Barrichbeyan – Craignish's ancestor – but belonging to Angus Campbell of Inverliver.

(13)   Small crystal ball found in a grave in Fife.

(14)   Crystal ball of the Murrays of Fingask. No clue as to its origin. Now in the National Museum of Scotland.

(15)   Crystal ball of the Campbells of Ardeonaig and Lochend. Mentioned by Fraser, but no other details. There are a number of this family in Australia including Sir Walter Campbell, lately Governor of Queensland, but he knew nothing of the stone and its present location.

(16)   The Raasay Charmstone. Another crystal ball with the power of curing sick cattle. It was long in the possession of the Stewarts of Ensay and went with the descendants of that family to South Africa (Shaw of Tordarroch, *N & Q, SWHIHR*, October 1977, p. 20).

(17)   The Auchmedden stone, in the possession of the Bairds of Auchmedden since 1174 but then passed through marriage to the Frasers of Findrack (Simpson).

(18)   Saint Columba's Curing Stone, mentioned in his *Life* by Adomnan (Simpson).

(19)   The Clan Chattan stone – the eponym of Clan Chattan was said to be Saint Cattan, a contemporary of Saint Columba and in the household of Saint Patrick as 'Catan the Presbyter', who had a Holy Stone described as green in colour and the size of a goose egg. According to Martin Martin, this stone was in the possession of Saint Moluag. Presumably it then passed to Gillechattan Mor as the Coarb of Saint Cattan, and was said to have 'come from Ardchattan' on Loch Etive, although whether this means it originated there or merely was held there for a time is unclear. The Mackintosh chiefs inherited the chiefship of Clan Chattan through the marriage in 1291 of Angus, 6th of Mackintosh, to Eva the heiress of Clan Chattan. Martin also claims that it was the *vexillum* or standard of the Lords of the Isles, whose foes would flee before it. It, too, was possessed of curative powers (*Loyal Dissuasive*, Martin).

There are also three brooches with a silver ornamented surround enclosing a crystal ball; they are the Ugadale Brooch, the Lochbuie Brooch and the Brooch of Lorne. The Brooch of Lorne is held by the MacDougalls of Dunollie. It is said to have belonged to Robert the Bruce and to have been taken from him by force in 1304 in a skirmish with the Lord of Lorne's men at Dalrigh just by modern Tyndrum. Here he was surprised and attacked by a superior party. Three men who, according to Barbour, went by the name of *Mackyne Drosser* (an attempt to reproduce *Mac Ian* and a Gaelic descriptive), attacked the Bruce, who could only break free by leaving his brooch in their hands. It was kept for several centuries by the MacDougall Chiefs until it was taken from Gylen Castle in 1647, surrendered to Campbell of Inverawe and his forces. The actual taker appears to have been Campbell of Bragleen, in whose family the brooch now resided. According to a letter in the *Oban Times* of 28 March 1903 from J. A. Campbell of Barbreck, Major Campbell of Bragleen had died early in the nineteenth century, and his children's affairs were placed in the hands of trustees who purchased the brooch from their charges and handed it over as a trophy which was presented to Admiral William MacDougall of MacDougall at a brilliant meeting of the County in 1825. (Miss Hope MacDougall: 'It was handed to Captain John MacDougall, later Admiral – but not William, his father Patrick, 24th Chief, being too old to make the journey.') It now rests in the possession of his descendant, the present Madam MacDougall of MacDougall. The National Museum of Scotland dates it as probably the earliest of the three, from the mid-fifteenth century (*Angels and Unicorns*, p. 58).

Stories proliferate around it. It was said to have been given to Queen Victoria, who was certainly shown it as she was rowed down Loch Tay in 1842. It is also linked with the Campbells of Inverawe, who may have been in command of the expedition against Gylen. Dr Douglas Simpson, in conjunction with European researchers, held that the brooch was not a Highland brooch of Celtic origin but that it should be traced to the decorative work of the Ottoman periods of the Roman Empire. The crystal in the brooch has a slight, dulled mark on it; this, I was told by Miss Hope MacDougall of MacDougall, was caused by a jeweller to whom her father once showed the brooch, who claimed he could deduce the origin of the ball. He took out a tool and scratched it, at which her father hastily recovered the brooch; but the jeweller's mark remains.

The Ugadale Brooch is also supposed to have connections with Bruce, being said to have been presented by that monarch to Mackay of Ugadale for having given him help and hospitality in his early days when he was still in search of the throne. Mackay of Ugadale was a chieftain of a very ancient family in Kintyre and on Islay – they have nothing at all to do with the Strathnaver Mackays – and acted as Mair of Fee, effectively the administrator, of North Kintyre for successive overlords, probably following a frequent pattern in which the original owner steps down when overcome by a superior power for whom he then becomes the agent. Certainly the concentration of fortified sites near Ugadale of various periods would indicate that it has long been a centre of power in the area. The Mackays died out with an heiress who married Macneal of Lossit, who took the designation of Ugadale, and the brooch is now in possession of their descendant Lieutenant-Colonel Hector Macneal of Lossit, OBE, TD, DL. It has had a somewhat chequered career, being long lost before being found walled up in a recess, no doubt for reasons of safe-keeping. Like the other two, it is made up of a crystal surrounded by a circular silver mount decorated by filigree work out of which rise a number of turrets set with coral and pearls. The lid opens to reveal a recess for a relic behind the crystal. No indication remains as to what the contents may have been.

The third brooch belonged to the Maclaines of Lochbuie in Mull. The original is now in the British Museum, but the family have a reproduction in their possession. There was an inscription attached to the back of the brooch stating that it was 'made by a tinker from silver found on the estate of Lochbuie around the year 1500'. It eventually went to a daughter and was afterwards sold. It passed through various hands before coming into the possession of the British Museum. Like the Ugadale brooch, it has a lid under which there is a recess for relics which added to the magic powers ascribed to the stone. This Christianising of the older, disreputable religion is of course a well-known tactic. The term 'tinker' is a modern description for a craftsman who was once highly regarded as a whitesmith and jeweller, whose function later degenerated into the mere mending of pots and pans. The Gaelic work-name for this craft was *MacNocaird*, anglicised to Caird from the Gaelic *Ceard*. The most noted family in this part of the world who practised in this fashion were the MacNabs of Barachastelain, near Dalmally.

These three brooches are clearly of the same genre and are, presumably, roughly of the same date. It is difficult to avoid the conclusion that the stone in each case is the important part of the brooch with magical powers, and that in these three cases the silver surround is a later addition. This would seem to be the view of the National Museum of Scotland. But the mystery of these magical crystals remains. Where did they come from, when did they arrive, and why are so many to be found in the West Highlands, particularly in the hands of so many Campbell families?

Notes

Chapter 1 Out of the Mists

1. T. C. Smout, *A History of the Scottish People, 1560–1830*, Collins/Fontana, London, 1972, p. 43.
2. Robert Douglas, *The Peerage of Scotland*, Edinburgh, 1764, p. 34.
3. W. F. Skene, *The Highlanders of Scotland* (first published 1836), ed. Alexander Macbain, Eneas Mackay, Stirling, 1902, p. 356.
4. Sir Thomas Innes of Learney, *The Tartans of the Clans and Families of Scotland*, W. & A. K. Johnston, Edinburgh, 1947, p. 90.
5. George Douglas, 8th Duke of Argyll, *Scotland as It Was and as It Is*, 2nd edn, Edinburgh, 1887, p. 34.
6. Beryl Platts, *Scottish Hazard: The Flemish Nobility and Their Impact on Scotland*, Procter Press, London, 1985, pp. 144–6.
7. Miranda J. Green, *Dictionary of Celtic Myth and Legend*, Thames and Hudson, London, 1992, pp. 80–1.
8. W. F. Skene, *Celtic Scotland*, 3 vols (first published 1880), repr. New York, 1971, vol. 3, pp. 458–9.
9. The Iona Club (ed.), *Collectanea de Rebus Albanicis*, Thomas G. Stevenson, Edinburgh, 1847, p. 55.
10. W. D. H. Sellar, 'The Earliest Campbells: Norman, Briton or Gael?', *Scottish Studies*, vol. 17 (1973), pp. 109–24 (p. 117).
11. SRO GD/112/57/8/21.
12. Scottish History Society, *Highland Papers*, vol. 2, p. 74.
13. Sellar, 'The Earliest Campbells'.
14. Alexander Campbell, 'The Manuscript History of Craignish' (ed. Herbert Campbell), *Miscellany*, vol. 4, Scottish History Society, Edinburgh (1926), pp. 187–299 (pp. 190–1).
15. Donald Campbell, *Treatise of the Language, Poetry and Music of the Highland Clans*, D. R. Collie and Sons, Edinburgh, 1862.
16. W. F. Skene, *Chronicles of the Picts, Chronicles of the Scots and Other Memorials of Scottish History*, HM General Register House, Edinburgh, 1867, p. 310; John Bannerman, *Studies in the History of Dalriada*, Scottish Academic Press, Edinburgh, 1974, pp. 84–5.
17. Skene, *The Highlanders of Scotland*, pp. 356–7.

18. Unpublished notebooks containing material collected by John Dewar, Argyll Archives.
19. Sellar, 'The Earliest Campbells', p. 112.
20. Ibid., p. 120, quoting *Glasgow Registrum*, 1:87.88, *Kelso Liber*, 1:181, *Lennox Cartularium*, pp. 25, 26.
21. Kenneth Jackson, *Gaelic Notes on the Book of Deer*, Cambridge University Press, Cambridge, 1922, pp. 31, 35n.
22. *Regesta Regum Scottorum*, 8 vols, Edinburgh University Press, Edinburgh, vol. 6, pp. 454–5.

Chapter 2   Setting the Scene

1. A. O. Anderson, *Early Sources of Scottish History*, 2 vols, Oliver and Boyd, Edinburgh, 1922, vol. 1, pp. 83–5.
2. Ibid., vol. 2, p. 112.
3. Sir Iain Moncreiffe of that Ilk, *The Highland Clans*, rev. edn, Barrie and Jenkins, London, 1982, pp. 117, 157 and rear endpapers.
4. Rev. Paul Walsh, *Leabhar Chlainne Suibhne*, Dollar, Printinghouse, Dublin, 1920, p. 5.
5. Dunbar, John, 'The Medieval Architecture of the Scottish Highlands', *The Middle Ages in the Highlands*, p. 44.
6. Donald E. Meek, 'The MacSween Poem in *The Book of the Dean of Lismore*', *West Highland Notes and Queries*, vol. 25, pp. 3–11.
7. RCAHMS, *Inventory of Argyll*, passim.
8. Niall, 10th Duke of Argyll, *Argyll Transcripts* [hereafter *A/T*].
9. Simpson and Webster, 'Charter Evidence and the Distribution of Mottes in Scotland', *Essays on the Nobility of Mediaeval Scotland*, pp. 1–24; RCAHMS, *Inventory of Argyll*, passim.
10. C. Innes (ed.), *Origines Parochiales Scotiae*, Bannatyne Club, Edinburgh, 1865, vol. 2, p. 225, quoting *Rotuli Scotiae*, vol. 1, pp. 31–2.
11. Sir William Fraser, *The Red Book of Menteith*, 2 vols, Edinburgh, 1880, vol. 1, p. 49; *Acts of Parliament of Scotland* [hereafter *APS*], vol. 1, p. 603.
12. George Watson, *Bell's Dictionary and Digest of the Law of Scotland*, Bell and Bradfute, Edinburgh, 1882, p. 157.
13. *APS*, vol. 1, p. 372.
14. W. F. Skene (ed.), *John of Fordun's Chronicle of the Scottish Nation*, 2 vols (first printed 1872 as part of the Historians of Scotland series), repr. Llanerch, Lampeter, 1993, vol. 2, p. 284.
15. R. Andrew McDonald, *The Kingdom of the Isles*, Tuckwell Press, East Linton, 1997, pp. 88–91; A. A. M. Duncan and A. L. Brown, 'Argyll and the Isles in the Earlier Middle Ages', *Proceedings of the Society of Antiquaries of Scotland*, vol. 90 (1956–7), pp. 192–220 (pp. 200–2).
16. The title of 'King' was used in what appears to be remarkable numbers to today's eyes. It appears to have been more of a personal ranking than an office. In Ireland there were some 150 'Kings'.
17. Anderson, *Early Sources*, vol. 2, p. 625.

18. Family tradition.
19. *Celtic Monthly*, vol. 9, p. 54.

Chapter 3   Companion to the King

1. John Stuart, George Burnett and J. G. Mackay (eds), *The Exchequer Rolls of Scotland*, 23 vols, HM General Register House, Edinburgh, 1878 onwards, vol. 1, p. 24.
2. J. Dowden, *Chartulary of the Abbey of Lindores, 1193–1479*, Edinburgh, 1903, p. 8.
3. *Scots Peerage*, vol. 1, p. 319.
4. Ibid., vol. 2, p. 426.
5. Sellar, 'The Earliest Campbells', p. 116; MacQueen, 'The Kin of Kennedy'; Alexander Grant and Keith J. Stringer, *Mediaeval Scotland: Crown, Lordship and Community*, Edinburgh University Press, Edinburgh, 1993, pp. 282, 284.
6. McEwen, *West Highland Notes and Queries*.
7. Geoffrey W. S. Barrow, *Robert Bruce and the Community of the Realm of Scotland*, Edinburgh University Press, Edinburgh, 1988, p. 289.
8. A. Martin Freeman (ed.), *The Annals of Connacht*, Dublin Institute for Advanced Studies, Dublin, 1970, p. 127.
9. Barrow, *Bruce*, p. 37.
10. Ibid., p. 289. The evidence for Colin's son Neil may be doubtful; see Stones and Simpson, *Edward I and the Throne of Scotland*, vol. 2, p. 82, n. 6.
11. Marion Campbell of Kilberry and Mary Sandeman, 'Mid Argyll: An Archaeological Survey', *Proceedings of the Society of Antiquaries of Scotland*, vol. 95 (1961–2), pp. 1–125 (p. 52).
12. George F. Black, *The Surnames of Scotland: Their Origin, Meaning and History*, The New York Public Library, New York, 1946.
13. Joseph Bain (ed.), *Calendar of Documents Relating to Scotland*, 4 vols, HM General Register House, Edinburgh, 1881–8, vol. 2, p. 742.
14. Ibid., vol. 2, p. 464; vol. 4, p. 434.
15. *Scot. Rolls Ed. I, Yr 25, Tower of London; A/T*.
16. *A/T*; Joseph Stevenson, *Documents Illustrative of the History of Scotland*, 2 vols, HM General Register House, Edinburgh, 1870, vol. 2, p. 175.
17. *APS*, vol. 1, pp. 289, 447; Bain, *Cal. Doc. Scot.*, vol. 2, p. 675.
18. *Cartularium comitatus de Levenax ab initio seculi decem tertii usque ad annum 1398*, Edinburgh, 1833, p. 21; *Scots Peerage*, vol. 1, p. 319.
19. Sir William Fraser (ed.), *Registrum Monasterii S. Marie de Cambuskenneth*, vol. 4, Grampian Club, Edinburgh, 1872, p. 70.
20. *A/T*.
21. Stevenson, *Documents*, vol. 2, p. 112.
22. *Scots Peerage*, vol. 1, p. 320, no source given.
23. *A/T*.
24. Ibid.
25. The Iona Club (ed.), *Collectanea*, p. 291.
26. *A/T*.

27. Barrow, *Bruce*, p. 289, quoting *Rotuli Scotiae*, vol. 1, p. 32a.
28. Bain, *Cal. Doc. Scot.*, vol. 2, pp. 196, 199, 200, 202, 204, 211.
29. Barrow, *Bruce*, p. 129.
30. Bain, *Cal. Doc. Scot.*, vol. 2, p. 328.
31. *A/T*, quoting *Wardrobe Book, Documents Relating to Scotland*, p. xxxix, n. 7.
32. *Scots Peerage*, vol. 1, p. 322.
33. *A/T*, quoting *Chancery Miscellaneous Portfolios, Documents Relating to Scotland, 1406*.
34. Bain, *Cal. Doc. Scot.*, vol. 4, p. 434.
35. Ibid., vol. 2, pp. 1437, 377.
36. Ibid., vol. 5, p. 408.
37. Ibid., vol. 5, p. 514.
38. *A/T*, quoting Stevenson, *Patent Rolls*, p. 443.
39. *A/T*, quoting *Calendar of Patent Rolls*.
40. *Scots Peerage*, vol. 1, p. 323.
41. McDonald, *The Kingdom of the Isles*, p. 164, quoting *Rotuli Scotiae*, vol. 1, p. 31.
42. The actual text says 'Ronald'. I am indebted to David Sellar, who points out that 'Ronald' is certainly 'Roland', the frequent anglicisation of 'Lachlan'.
43. Stevenson, *Documents*, vol. 2, p. 187.
44. Ibid., p. 189.
45. Ibid.
46. Ibid., vol. 2, p. 477.
47. Bain, *Cal. Doc. Scot.*, vol. 2, p. 853.
48. Ibid., vol. 5, p. 152.
49. Stevenson, *Documents*, vol. 2, p. 101.
50. Freeman (ed.), *The Annals of Connacht*, p. 199.
51. *Annals of the Four Masters*, 9 vols, de Burca Rare Books, Dublin, 1990, p. 471.
52. John Barbour, *The Bruce*, ed. A. A. M. Duncan, Canongate Press, Edinburgh, 1997, p. 117.
53. Bain, *Cal. Doc. Scot.*, vol. 3, p. 118.
54. Ibid., p. 29.
55. Ibid., p. 80; Barrow, *Bruce*, p. 179.
56. Barbour, *Bruce*, p. 362.
57. *Scots Peerage*, vol. 1, p. 320.
58. *APS*, vol. 1, p. 289.
59. Bain, *Cal. Doc. Scot.*, vol. 3, p. 95.
60. Ibid., p. 191.
61. McDonald, *The Kingdom of the Isles*, p. 181, quoting *Rotuli Scotiae*, vol. 1, pp. 90, 93, 99.
62. E. B. Fryde et al. (eds), *A Handbook of British Chronology*, 3rd edn, Royal Historical Society, London, 1986, p. 136.
63. Bain, *Cal. Doc. Scot.*, vol. 3, p. 101; *Scots Peerage*, vol. 1, p. 323.
64. Lost original, quoted in *Regesta Regum Scottorum*, vol. 5, p. 129.
65. *Regesta Regum Scottorum*, vol. 5, p. 315.
66. *RMS*, vol. 1, Appendix 2, p. 364.
67. *A/T*; *Scots Peerage*, vol. 1, p. 321; Stuart et al. (eds), *Exchequer Rolls*, vol. 1, p. 52.

68. Bain, *Cal. Doc. Scot.*, vol. 5, p. 590. Full text of this in *Regesta Regum Scottorum*, vol. 5, p. 329.

Chapter 4   The Springboard is Established

1. John Dewar, *The Dewar Manuscripts*, ed. Rev. John Mackechnie, William Maclellan, Glasgow, 1964, p. 59.
2. Per W. D. H. Sellar.
3. Frank Adam and Sir Thomas Innes of Learney, *The Clans, Septs and Regiments of the Scottish Highlands*, 2nd edn, W. & A. K. Johnston, Edinburgh, 1955, p. 540. See also the note on MacArthurs in Appendix 3 below.
4. The original is in the possession of the Faculty of Procurators, Glasgow.
5. Skene, *The Highlanders of Scotland*, p. 357.
6. *Regesta Regum Scottorum*, vol. 5, no. 46, p. 333.
7. Alexander Campbell, 'Craignish', *Misc.*, vol. 4, SHS, p. 207.
8. Scottish History Society, *Highland Papers*, vol. 2, p. 82.
9. *A/T.*
10. *RMS*, vol. 1, Appendix 2, p. 351.
11. Ibid., p. 695.
12. Ibid., pp. 353, 368, 642.
13. *Regesta Regum Scottorum*, vol. 5, p. 639; 'dl' is an abbreviation for 'pennyland', a method of land valuation.
14. *RMS*, vol. 1, Appendix 2, p. 620.
15. *Regesta Regum Scottorum*, vol. 5, p. 398; William Robertson, *Index of Charters*, Murray and Cochrane, Edinburgh, 1798, p. 6.
16. *RMS*, vol. 1, Appendix 2, p. 660.
17. Innes (ed.), *OPS*, vol. 2, p. 154; *RMS*, vol. 1, Appendix 2, p. 660.
18. *RMS*, vol. 1, Appendix 2, p. 351.
19. Sean Duffy, 'The Anglo-Norman Era in Scotland', in T. M. Devine and J. F. McMillan (eds), *Celebrating Columba: Irish–Scottish Connections 597–1997*, John Donald, Edinburgh, 1999, pp. 15–34.
20. Colin McNamee, *The Wars of the Bruces*, Tuckwell Press, East Linton, 1997, p. 169.
21. Barbour, *Bruce*, p. 587.
22. Freeman (ed.), *Annals of Connacht*, p. 253.
23. Stuart et al. (eds), *Exchequer Rolls*, vol. 1, p. 52.
24. Barbour, *Bruce*, pp. 779–81.
25. Barrow, *Bruce*, p. 234.
26. *Regesta Regum Scottorum*, vol. 5, pp. 366, 617; *A/T.*
27. *A/T.*
28. Scottish History Society, *Highland Papers*, vol. 2, p. 90.
29. *A/T.*
30. Ibid.
31. *Regesta Regum Scottorum*, vol. 6, p. 97; *A/T*, p. 54. The varied spellings are as given.

32. *Regesta Regum Scottorum*, vol. 6, p. 109, quoting *1680 Inventory of Charters*, Argyll Archives.
33. Scottish History Society, *Highland Papers*, vol. 2, p. 91.
34. *Regesta Regum Scottorum*, vol. 6, p. 113.
35. Ibid., p. 114.
36. Ibid., p. 507.
37. Ibid., p. 136; Scottish History Society, *Highland Papers*, vol. 2, p. 136.
38. Ranald Nicholson, *Scotland: The Later Middle Ages*, vol. 2, The Edinburgh History of Scotland, Oliver and Boyd, Edinburgh, 1978, p. 146, quoting the *Chronicle of Lanercost*, p. 347.
39. Bain, *Cal. Doc. Scot.*, vol. 3, pp. 1,489, 1,504.
40. *Scots Peerage*, vol. 5, p. 491.
41. *Regesta Regum Scottorum*, vol. 6, p. 442; *RMS*, vol. 1, pp. 77, 95, 620.
42. Nicholson, *Scotland: The Later Middle Ages*, p. 148.
43. *A/T*.
44. Scottish History Society, *Highland Papers*, vol. 2, p. 140.
45. *A/T*.
46. Innes (ed.), *OPS*, vol. 2, p. 168, quoting Sir David Dalrymple of Hailes, Bart, *Annals of Scotland*, 3 vols, Edinburgh, 1819, vol. 3, p. 331.
47. Gregory, *History*, p. 28; Robertson, *Index*, p. 30.
48. Jean Munro and R. W. Munro, *Acts of the Lords of the Isles*, Scottish History Society, Edinburgh, 1986, p. 5.
49. Bain, *Cal. Doc. Scot.*, vol. 3, p. 1,606.
50. *RMS*, vol. 1, Appendix 2, pp. 867–8.

Chapter 5 Laying the Foundation

1. *A/T*.
2. Ibid.
3. Ibid.
4. Fraser, *The Red Book of Menteith*, pp. 239–46.
5. *A/T*; *Regesta Regum Scottorum*, vol. 6, pp. 326–7.
6. *A/T*.
7. Colin MacDonald, *The History of Argyll*, Holmes (Books), Glasgow, n.d., p. 166, quoting *APS*, vol. 1, pp. 498–9.
8. *RMS*, vol. 1, Appendix 2, p. 1,182.
9. MacDonald, *Argyll*, p. 167, quoting *APS*, vol. 1, p. 500.
10. *Regesta Regum Scottorum*, vol. 6, p. 454.
11. Stuart et al. (eds), *Exchequer Rolls*, vol. 2, p. 425.
12. *A/T*.
13. Ibid.
14. Ibid.
15. *RMS*, vol. 1, p. 484.
16. Scottish History Society, *Highland Papers*, vol. 4, p. 17.
17. *A/T*.
18. Ibid.

19. *RMS*, vol. 2, p. 187; Sir Robert Douglas of Glenbervie, *The Baronage of Scotland*, Edinburgh, 1798, p. 291.

20. Douglas, *Baronage*, p. 291.

21. William Fraser, *The Lennox*, 2 vols, Edinburgh, 1874, vol. 2, p. 47.

22. Fraser, *Red Book of Menteith*, vol. 1, p. lviii.

23. Scottish History Society, *Highland Papers*, vol. 4, pp. 17–18.

24. W. D. H. Sellar, 'Spens Family Heraldry', *West Highland Notes and Queries*, vol. 22, p. 25.

25. *Scots Peerage*, vol. 1, p. 327; Scottish History Society, *Highland Papers*, vol. 2, p. 91.

26. *Scots Peerage*, vol. 5, p. 39.

27. Ibid., p. 340.

28. Edmund Dwelly, *The Illustrated Gaelic-English Dictionary*, 9th edn, Gairm Publications, Glasgow, 1977 (first published 1901–11), p. 553.

29. Archibald Brown, *History of Cowal*, Greenock, 1908, p. 55.

30. Scottish History Society, *Highland Papers*, vol. 2, p. 92.

31. Robertson, *Index*, p. 44; *Scots Peerage*, vol. 1, p. 326; *A/T*, p. 76.

32. *A/T*, p. 89.

33. *A/T*.

34. Alexander Campbell, 'Craignish', *Misc.*, vol. 4, SHS, p. 216.

35. Ibid., pp. 216–17.

36. *A/T*.

37. Ibid.

38. Ibid.

39. Scottish History Society, *Highland Papers*, vol. 2, pp. 93–4.

40. *A/T*.

41. James B. Johnston, *Place-Names of Scotland*, John Murray, London, 1934, p. 217.

42. *Inventory of Argyll*, vol. 7, pp. 281, 552; *A/T*, 1422, 1448.

43. *A/T*.

44. Ibid.

45. *Scots Peerage*, vol. 1, p. 329.

46. Stephen Boardman, *The Early Stewart Kings*, Tuckwell Press, East Linton, 1996, p. 282, quoting SRO GD/124/1/129; Michael Brown, *James I*, Canongate Press, Edinburgh, 1994, p. 12ff.

47. *Scots Peerage*, vol. 7, p. 241ff.

48. Walter Bower, *Scotichronicon*, ed. D. E. R. Watt, Aberdeen University Press, Aberdeen, 1987, vol. 8, p. 77.

49. *A/T*; Alexander Campbell, 'Craignish', *Misc.*, vol. 4, SHS, p. 223.

50. Alexander Campbell, 'Craignish', *Misc.*, vol. 4, SHS, pp. 224–6.

51. *A/T*.

Chapter 6   The Arrival

1. *RMS*, vol. 1, p. 630.

2. *A/T*.

3. Ibid.

4. Bain, *Cal. Doc. Scot.*, vol. 4, pp. 960, 961, 964.
5. Brown, *James I*, p. 57.
6. Ibid., p. 58.
7. Gregory, *History*, p. 33.
8. Bower, *Scotichronicon*, p. 259; Brown, *James I*, pp. 97–8.
9. Bower, *Scotichronicon*, p. 261.
10. McDonald, *The Kingdom of the Isles*, p. 176.
11. Innes (ed.), *OPS*, vol. 2, p. 79; *A/T*.
12. Bower, *Scotichronicon*, p. 261.
13. Rev. A. MacDonald and Rev. A. MacDonald, *The Clan Donald*, 3 vols, Northern Publishing Co., Inverness, 1896, vol. 1, pp. 172–9.
14. Simon Kingston, 'Trans-Insular Lordship in the Fifteenth Century', in T. M. Devine and J. F. McMillan (eds), *Celebrating Columba: Irish–Scottish Connections 597–1997*, John Donald, Edinburgh, 1999, p. 36.
15. *APS*, vol. 2, p. 19.
16. Wallace Clark, *The Lord of the Isles' Voyage*, The Leinster Leader Ltd, Naas, Co. Kildare, 1993, passim.
17. Brown, *James I*, p. 187.
18. *A/T*.
19. Ibid.; *Scots Peerage*, vol. 1, p. 332.
20. *RMS*, vol. 3, p. 2,306.
21. *Scots Peerage*, vol. 1, p. 331; *A/T*, quoting *Register of Supplications [Petitions]*, vol. 375, fo. 124, Vatican Archives; *CSSR*, vol. 4, no. 791.
22. *Inventory of Argyll*, vol. 7, pp. 174–86.
23. Hector McKechnie, *The Lamont Clan*, Neill & Co., Edinburgh, 1938, pp. 70–1.
24. Angus McLean, unpublished manuscript.
25. Alexander Carmichael, *Carmina Gadelica*, 6 vols, Oliver and Boyd, Edinburgh, 1928, vol. 2, p. 270.
26. Scottish History Society, *Highland Papers*, vol. 2, pp. 152, 158.
27. Ibid., pp. 161, 162.
28. Ibid., p. 165.
29. Ibid., p. 175.
30. Ibid., p. 178.
31. Ibid., p. 179.
32. Moncreiffe, *Highland Clans*, p. 215.
33. MacDonald, p. 209.
34. Christine McGladdery, *James II*, John Donald, Edinburgh, 1990, p. 53.
35. Alexander Grant, *Independence and Nationhood: Scotland 1306–1469*, The New History of Scotland, Edward Arnold, London, 1984, p. 123.
36. *A/T*.
37. Ibid.
38. Ibid.
39. William Gillies, 'Some Thoughts on the Toschederach', *Scottish Gaelic Studies*, vol. 17, Special Volume, *Feill Sgribhinn do Ruaraidh MacThomais – Festschrift for Derick Thomson*, p. 128.
40. *A/T*.

Chapter 7   The Greatest Power in the West Highlands and Isles

1. *Scots Peerage*, vol. 1, p. 331.
2. *A/T*.
3. *The Black Book of Taymouth*, p. 10; *Scots Peerage*, vol. 2, p. 176; *A/T*.
4. *A/T*.
5. Ibid.
6. *Scots Peerage*, vol. 2, p. 177.
7. Alan Macquarrie, *Scotland and the Crusades, 1095–1560*, John Donald, Edinburgh, 1985, pp. 93–5.
8. *The Black Book of Taymouth*, pp. 346–7.
9. *RMS*, vol. 2, p. 195; *A/T*.
10. *A/T*; Thomas Thomson (ed.), *The Auchinleck Chronicle*, privately printed, Edinburgh, 1819, pp. 58–9.
11. *A/T*.
12. Ibid.
13. Ibid.
14. Ibid.
15. Munro and Munro, *Acts of the Lords of the Isles*, pp. 111–16.
16. *A/T*.
17. *RMS*, vol. 2, p. 1,168.
18. Norman MacDougall, *James III: A Political Study*, John Donald, Edinburgh, 1982, p. 122; *A/T*; *RMS*, vol. 2, p. 287.
19. MacDougall, *James III*, p. 123.
20. MacDonald and MacDonald, *The Clan Donald*, vol. 1, p. 251.
21. MacDougall, *James III*, p. 123, quoting *APS*, vol. 12, p. 115.
22. Gregory, *History*, pp. 50–1.
23. *A/T*.
24. Ibid., quoting Lauderdale Charters.
25. *A/T*.
26. MacDougall, *James III*, p. 167, quoting Innes (ed.), *OPS*, vol. 2, p. 144, quoting untraced Breadalbane charter.
27. *Scots Peerage*, vol. 1, p. 335.
28. MacDonald and MacDonald, *The Clan Donald*, vol. 1, pp. 269–70.
29. Gregory, *History*, pp. 52–5.
30. Ibid., pp. 55–7.

Chapter 8   Triumph and Disaster

1. *Scots Peerage*, vol. 1, p. 334.
2. *Annals of the Four Masters*, vol. 5, p. 1,565.
3. Norman MacDougall, *James IV*, Tuckwell Press, East Linton, 1997, pp. 102–3.
4. MacDonald and MacDonald, *The Clan Donald*, p. 289.
5. Gregory, *History*, p. 89.
6. MacDougall, *James IV*, p. 116.

7. *A/T*.
8. Ibid.
9. Ibid.
10. Ibid.
11. Ibid.
12. Ibid.
13. *RSS*, vol. 1, p. 242.
14. MacDougall, *James IV*, p. 177.
15. *A/T*.
16. Ibid.; *RSS*, vol. 1, p. 520.
17. C. Innes (ed.), *The Book of the Thanes of Cawdor*, Spalding Club, Edinburgh, 1859, p. 94.
18. MacDougall, *James IV*, p. 102.
19. Innes (ed.), *Cawdor*, pp. 95–6.
20. Ibid., pp. 99–102.
21. Ibid., p. 115.
22. Ibid., p. 125.
23. MacDougall, *James IV*, p. 178.
24. *A/T*.
25. Ibid.
26. Ibid.
27. Dr Steve Boardman, unpublished paper.
28. Stuart et al. (eds), *Exchequer Rolls*, vol. 12, pp. 247–8.
29. MacDougall, *James IV*, p. 183.
30. *APS*, vol. 2, p. 241.
31. MacDougall, *James IV*, p. 183; Gregory, *History*, pp. 98, 100–1.
32. Gregory, *History*, p. 100.
33. *A/T*.
34. Gregory, *History*, p. 102.
35. Stuart et al. (eds), *Exchequer Rolls*, vol. 12, p. 704ff.
36. *A/T*.
37. *The Black Book of Taymouth*, p. 15.
38. MacDougall, *James IV*, p. 157.
39. *A/T*.
40. MacDougall, *James IV*, p. 158.
41. *Scots Peerage*, vol. 2, p. 179; *RMS*, vol. 2, p. 688.
42. *RMS*, vol. 2, pp. 690, 788, 838.
43. MacDougall, *James IV*, p. 271.
44. William J. Watson (ed.), *Scottish Verse from the Book of the Dean of Lismore*, Scottish Gaelic Texts Society, Edinburgh, 1937, p. 159.
45. MacDougall, *James IV*, p. 272, quoting *Letters and Papers Henry VIII*, vol. 1, part 2, nos 2,279, 2,283.
46. Viv. 1502, Dunstaffnage Papers; 1517, Airds Writs.
47. Archibald Campbell alias MacConochie of Inverawe has charter 1493 as heir to his father; witnesses bond of manrent, 1520. *A/T*.
48. Herbert Campbell, *Pedigrees*; 'Campbell of Dunstaffnage', *Burke's Landed Gentry*.

Chapter 9 The Clan: An Overall Survey

1. Dwelly, *Dictionary*, p. 204.
2. *The Oxford Book of Quotations*, Oxford University Press, London, 1959, pp. 24, 386.
3. Scottish History Society, *Highland Papers*, vol. 2, pp. 80, 82.
4. Fergus Kelly, *A Guide to Early Irish Law*, Dublin Institute for Advanced Studies, Dublin, 1988, passim.
5. *A/T*; Angus Matheson, 'Bishop Carswell', *Transactions of the Gaelic Society of Inverness*, vol. 42 (1953–9).
6. *A/T*.
7. *West Highland Notes and Queries*, vol. 11, n. 23.
8. Note by Duke Niall in manuscript pedigree of MacLachlans, Argyll Archives.
9. Watson, *Scottish Verse*, p. 166.
10. Bundle 696, Argyll Archives.
11. *A/T*.
12. *Oban Times*, 25 March 1999; Alastair Campbell of Airds, yr, *Two Hundred Years: The Highland Society of London*, Highland Society of London, London, 1983, p. 29; 'The Campbell Canntaireachd', *Piping Times*, n.d.
13. Duke Niall's note.
14. Tombstone in Kilbrandon churchyard, Seil.
15. John Bannerman, 'The MacLachlans of Kilbride and their Manuscripts', *Scottish Studies*, vol. 21 (1977), pp. 1–34.
16. John Bannerman, *The Beatons*, John Donald, Edinburgh, 1986, pp. 144–9; D. McNaughton, 'The O'Connachars of Lorne', *The Scottish Genealogist*, vol. 16, no. 3 (September 1969), pp. 65–6.
17. Bannerman, *The Beatons*, pp. 150–1.
18. Derick S. Thomson (ed.), *The Companion to Gaelic Scotland*, Blackwell, Oxford, 1983, p. 188.
19. *A/T*.
20. *Scots Law Times*, 29 December 1951, p. 5.
21. *CSP*, vol. 1, p. 92.
22. John Dewar, unpublished manuscript.
23. Per Sarah, Mrs Campbell of Dunstaffnage.
24. Carmichael, *Carmina Gadelica*, vol. 2, p. 359.
25. K. A. Steer and J. W. M. Bannerman, *Late Medieval Monumental Sculpture in the West Highlands*, RCAHMS, Edinburgh, 1977, p. 146.
26. John Dewar, unpublished manuscript.
27. Rev. John MacInnes, 'West Highland Sea Power in the Middle Ages', *Transactions of the Gaelic Society of Inverness*, vol. 48, p. 527.
28. Scottish History Society, *Highland Papers*, vol. 2, p. 257; *West Highland Notes and Queries*, vol. 14, pp. 3–9.
29. Garrett, 'Wood Engravings and Drawings by Iain Macnab of Barachastlain', pp. 7–13.
30. Alasdair Maclean, 'Notes on South Uist families', reprint, 1985, from *Transactions of the Gaelic Society of Inverness*, vol. 53, pp. 491–518.

31. T. B. Johnston and James A. Robertson, *Historical Geography of the Clans of Scotland*, W. & A. K. Johnston, Edinburgh, 1899, pp. 3–6, 7–8.
32. Argyll Archives, bundle 1073.
33. Argyll Archives, bundle 1093; *A/T*.
34. Argyll Archives, bundle 1078.
35. *A/T*.
36. Dr Steve Boardman, unpublished paper.
37. *A/T*.
38. *CSP, Scotland and Mary Queen of Scots, 1547–1603*, vol. 13, part 2, p. 717.
39. Jane Dawson, 'The 5th Earl of Argyle, Gaelic Lordship and Political Power in Sixteenth-century Scotland', *Scottish Historical Review*, vol. 67:1, no. 183 (April 1988), pp. 1–27.
40. Johnston and Robertson, *Historical Geography*, pp. 31, 35.
41. Moncreiffe, *Highland Clans*, p. 55.
42. Donald Campbell, *Treatise of the Language, Poetry and Music of the Highland Clans*, D. R. Collie and Sons, Edinburgh, 1862, p. 133.
43. Sir James Turner, *Memoirs of His Own Life and Times*, n.p., Edinburgh, 1829, p. 48.
44. John MacInnes, 'The Panegyric Code in Gaelic Poetry and its Historical Background', *Transactions of the Gaelic Society of Inverness*, vol. 50 (1976–8), pp. 435–98 (p. 442).

Appendix 3 Septs

1. Scottish History Society, *Highland Papers*, vol. 2, p. 80.
2. Alexander Campbell, 'Craignish', *Misc.*, vol. 4, SHS, p. 209.
3. *A/T*.
4. Scottish History Society, *Scottish Supplications to Rome*, 1423–8, p. 140.
5. *A/T*.
6. Ibid.
7. Scottish History Society, *Highland Papers*, vol. 4, p. 54.
8. Skene, *The Highlanders of Scotland*, p. 358; Bower, *Scotichronicon*, vol. 16, p. 261.
9. Rev. Somerled MacMillan, *Bygone Lochaber*, privately published, 1971, p. 158.
10. Rev. William A. Gillies, *In Famed Breadalbane*, Munro Press, Perth, 1938, p. 359.
11. Alexander Fraser, *Lochfyneside*, The Saint Andrew Press, Edinburgh, 1971, p. 66.
12. Per W. D. H. Sellar; *Scots Peerage*, vol. 5, pp. 329, 330.
13. Sir James Balfour Paul (ed.), *An Ordinary of Arms Contained in the Public Register of All Arms and Bearings in Scotland*, William Green and Sons, Edinburgh, 1903, p. 56.
14. John Burke and John Bernard Burke, *Encyclopedia of Heraldry, or General Armory of England, Scotland and Ireland*, Henry G. Bohn, London, 1844; this is set out alphabetically, and no page numbers are given.
15. Carmichael, *Carmina Gadelica*, pp. 269–70.
16. Innes (ed.), *Thanes of Cawdor*, pp. xiii, 3.
17. Ibid., p. 3.

18. Undated charter. *A/T*.
19. *Roll of the Names*. Johnston and Robertson, *Historical Geography of the Clans of Scotland*, pp. 3–6.
20. *Roll of the Clannis*. Ibid., p. 7.
21. Black, *Surnames of Scotland*, pp. 205–6, 231.
22. Douglas of Glenbervie, *The Baronage of Scotland*, p. 456.
23. *Reg. de Dunfermelyne*, p. 206.
24. Stuart et al. (eds), *Exchequer Rolls*, vol. 1, p. 30.
25. *Reg. Mon. Passelet*, p. 191.
26. HMC 2 Rep., Appendix, p. 166.
27. *Reg. Mon. Passelet*, p. 96.
28. Bain, *Cal. Doc. Scot.*, vol. 2, p. 591.
29. R. J. Adam (ed.), *The Calendar of Fearn: Text and Additions 1471–1667*, Scottish History Society, Edinburgh, 1991, pp. 79–82.
30. Ibid., p. 14.
31. *RMS*, vol. 2, p. 3,213.
32. Innes (ed.), *OPS*, vol. 2, p. 57.
33. NDC notes.
34. Adam and Innes, *Clans, Septs and Regiments*, p. 554. Black, *Surnames of Scotland*, pp. 344, 349.
35. *A/T*.
36. Argyll Archives, NE6.
37. Adam and Innes, *Clans, Septs and Regiments*, p. 299.
38. Rev. Reginald Kissack, *The MacIsaacs: Possible Origins of a Scots-Manx Surname*, Manx Heritage Foundation, Isle of Man, 1990, p. 4.
39. Maclean, 'Notes on South Uist Families', p. 506.
40. Per W. D. H. Sellar.
41. *Scots Peerage*, vol. 1, p. 8.
42. *A/T*.
43. Ibid.
44. The Iona Club (ed.), *Collectanea*, p. 198.
45. Notes (1844) by W. Forbes Skene, sent by Dugald Malcolm in New Zealand to his namesake Captain Dugald Malcolm CMG, CVO, TD, to whom my thanks.
46. Kilmartin Kirk Session Book, 23 November 1731, Argyll and Bute Council Archives.
47. Black, *Surnames of Scotland*, p. 527.
48. Principal P. C. Campbell ('Anon.'), *Account of the Clan-Iver*, privately printed, n.d.
49. Scottish History Society, *Highland Papers*, vol. 2, pp. 80, 82.
50. Marion Campbell of Kilberry and Mary Sandeman, 'Mid Argyll: An Archaeological Survey', *Proceedings of the Society of Antiquaries of Scotland*, vol. 95 (1961–2), pp. 1–125 (p. 52).
51. *A/T*.
52. Ibid.
53. *Poltalloch Writs*.
54. *A/T*.

55. Ibid.
56. Ibid.
57. Ibid.
58. Argyll Archives, bundle 114.
59. NDC note on Fisher pedigree.
60. Alexander Campbell, 'Craignish', *Misc.*, vol. 4, SHS, p. 295.
61. *A/T.*
62. Argyll Archives, bundle 696.
63. Duncan Beaton, quoting Miss Marion Campbell of Kilberry.
64. Per Duncan Beaton.
65. Scottish History Society, *Highland Papers*, vol. 2, p. 82.
66. Black, *Surnames of Scotland*, p. 566.
67. *APS*, vol. 1, p. 91.
68. Bain, *Cal. Doc. Scot.*, vol. 2, p. 202.
69. *APS*, vol. 1, p. 13.
70. *A/T.*
71. Scottish History Society, *Highland Papers*, vol. 2, pp. 138–9.
72. RCAHMS, *Inventory of Argyll*, vol. 7, p. 137.
73. *A/T.*
74. Ibid.
75. Watson, *Scottish Verse*, pp. 238–9.
76. Duke Niall of Argyll.
77. Gillies, *In Famed Breadalbane*, p. 359.
78. E. F. Bradford, *MacTavish of Dunardry*, privately printed, 1991, p. 176; *Oban Times*, 22 December 1909.
79. Sir James Fergusson of Kilkerran, *Argyll in the Forty-Five*, Faber and Faber, London, 1951, pp. 43, 57.
80. Bradford, *MacTavish of Dunardry*, p. 7, quoting NDC.
81. Bradford, *MacTavish of Dunardry*, passim.
82. Grant of arms. Balfour Paul, *An Ordinary of Arms*, pp. 212, 228.
83. Gillies, *In Famed Breadalbane*, p. 360.
84. Woulfe, *Irish Surnames*, p. 349.
85. Black, *Surnames of Scotland*, pp. 524–5.
86. Both these letters are among the Campbell of Loudoun papers in the Huntington Library, San Marino, California. My thanks to Professor Allan MacInnes.
87. Colin Campbell of Inverneill, yr, 'The Origins of the Campbells of Inverneill', *The Scottish Genealogist*, vol. 35, no. 2 (June 1988), pp. 63–72; Innes of Learney, *Tartans of the Clans*, pp. 34–5.
88. MacMillan, *Bygone Lochaber*, p. 96.
89. Gillies, 'Some Thoughts on the Toschederach', p. 340.
90. W. David H. Sellar and Alasdair Maclean, *The Highland Clan MacNeacail*, Maclean Press, Lochbay, Isle of Skye, 1999, pp. 25–6.
91. Herbert Campbell, *Argyll Sasines*, 2 vols, W. Brown, Edinburgh, 1951, vol. 2, p. 9.
92. Black, *Surnames of Scotland*, p. 552.

93. Ibid., p. 477.

94. Margaret Olivia Campbell, *A Memorial History of the Campbells of Melfort*, 2 vols, Simmons and Botten, London, 1882 and 1894, vol. 1, p. 8, vol. 2, pp. 75–81.

95. Adam and Innes, *Clans, Septs and Regiments*, p. 300; Black, *Surnames of Scotland*, p. 510.

96. Edwin Sprott Towill, *The Saints of Scotland*, The Saint Andrew Press, Edinburgh, 1983, pp. 51–4; David Hugh Farmer, *The Oxford Dictionary of Saints*, Oxford University Press, Oxford, 1992, p. 109.

97. Scottish History Society, *Highland Papers*, vol. 2, p. 14.

98. Ibid., vol. 1, p. 25.

99. The Iona Club (ed.), *Collectanea*, p. 198.

100. Argyll Archives, bundle 1098.

101. Black (*Surnames of Scotland*, p. 557) has made a slip and gives the date as 1349.

102. *A/T*.

103. Ibid.

104. Carmichael, *Carmina Gadelica*, vol. 2, p. 359.

105. Steer and Bannerman, *Late Medieval Monumental Sculpture*, p. 146.

106. Angus McLean, unpublished manuscript.

107. *A/T*.

108. Ibid.

109. Ibid.

110. Ibid.

111. Duke Niall's genealogical notebooks.

112. Black, *Surnames of Scotland*, pp. 775–6.

113. Innes (ed.), *Thanes of Cawdor*, pp. 285, 301.

114. Ramsay, *Book of Islay*, pp. 374, 379.

115. Ibid., pp. 519, 520.

Bibliography

Books

Adam, Frank and Sir Thomas Innes of Learney, *The Clans, Septs and Regiments of the Scottish Highlands*, 2nd edn, W. & A. K. Johnston, Edinburgh, 1955, 554.

Adam, R. J. (ed.), *The Calendar of Fearn: Text and Additions 1471–1667*, Scottish History Society, Edinburgh, 1991.

Alcock, Leslie, *Arthur's Britain*, Allen Lane, London, 1971.

Anderson, A. O., *Early Sources of Scottish History*, 2 vols, Oliver and Boyd, Edinburgh, 1922.

Annals of Connacht [see Freeman].

Annals of the Four Masters, 9 vols, de Burca Rare Books, Dublin, 1990.

Anon., *Clan Campbell, House of Argyll*, John Tweed, Glasgow, 1871.

Argyll, George Douglas, 8th Duke of, *Scotland as It Was and as It Is*, 2nd edn, Edinburgh, 1887.

Argyll, Niall, 10th Duke of, *Argyll Transcripts* [*A/T*].

Ashe, Geoffrey, *From Caesar to Arthur*, Collins, London, 1960.

Ashe, Geoffrey (ed.), *The Quest for Arthur's Britain*, Paladin/Granada, London, 1971.

The Auchinleck Chronicle [see Thomson, Thomas].

Bain, Joseph (ed.), *Calendar of Documents Relating to Scotland*, 4 vols, HM General Register House, Edinburgh, 1881–8.

Balfour Paul, Sir James (ed.), *An Ordinary of Arms Contained in the Public Register of All Arms and Bearings in Scotland*, William Green and Sons, Edinburgh, 1903, 212, 228.

Bannerman, John, *Studies in the History of Dalriada*, Scottish Academic Press, Edinburgh, 1974.

Bannerman, John, *The Beatons*, John Donald, Edinburgh, 1986.

Barbour, John, *The Bruce*, ed. A. A. M. Duncan, Canongate Press, Edinburgh, 1997.

Barrow, Geoffrey W. S., *Robert Bruce and the Community of the Realm of Scotland*, Edinburgh University Press, Edinburgh, 1988.

Bell's Dictionary and Digest of the Law of Scotland [see Watson, George].

Black, George F., *The Surnames of Scotland: Their Origin, Meaning and History*, The New York Public Library, New York, 1946.

'Blind Harry', *Wallace*, trans. William Hamilton of Gilbertfield, Luath Press, Edinburgh, 1998.

Boardman, Stephen, *The Early Stewart Kings*, Tuckwell Press, East Linton, 1996.

Bower, Walter, *Scotichronicon*, ed. D. E. R. Watt, Aberdeen University Press, Aberdeen, 1987.

Bradford, E. F., *MacTavish of Dunardry*, privately printed, 1991.

Brogger, A. W. and Haakon Shetelig, *The Viking Ships: Their Ancestry and Evolution*, Dreyers Forlag, Oslo, 1971.

Brown, Archibald, *History of Cowal*, Greenock, 1908.

Brown, Michael, *James I*, Canongate Press, Edinburgh, 1994.

Burke, John and John Bernard Burke, *Encyclopedia of Heraldry, or General Armory of England, Scotland and Ireland*, Henry G. Bohn, London, 1844.

'G. E. C.' (ed.), *The Complete Peerage*, 6-volume reprint, Allan Sutton, Gloucester, 1987.

Cameron, Rev. Alexander, *Reliquiae Celticae*, ed. Alexander Macbain, 2 vols, The Northern Counties Newspaper and Publishing and Printing Co., Inverness, 1894.

Campbell of Airds, Alastair, yr, *Two Hundred Years: The Highland Society of London*, Highland Society of London, London, 1983.

Campbell, Lord Archibald, *Records of Argyll*, William Blackwood and Sons, Edinburgh, 1885.

Campbell, Donald, *Treatise of the Language, Poetry and Music of the Highland Clans*, D. R. Collie and Sons, Edinburgh, 1862.

Campbell, Herbert, *Argyll Sasines*, 2 vols, W. Brown, Edinburgh, 1951.

Campbell, Margaret Olivia, *A Memorial History of the Campbells of Melfort*, 2 vols, Simmons and Botten, London, 1882 and 1894.

Campbell, Principal P. C. ('Anon.'), *Account of the Clan-Iver*, privately printed, n.d.

Carmichael, Alexander, *Carmina Gadelica*, 6 vols, Oliver and Boyd, Edinburgh, 1928.

Cartularium comitatus de Levenax ab initio seculi decem tertii usque ad annum 1398, Edinburgh, 1833.

Clark, Wallace, *The Lord of the Isles' Voyage*, The Leinster Leader Ltd, Naas, Co. Kildare, 1993.

Cock, Matthew, *Dunderave Castle and the MacNachtans of Argyll*, Dunderave Estate, Argyll, 1998.

Dalrymple of Hailes, Sir David, Bart, *Annals of Scotland*, 3 vols, Edinburgh, 1819. [Referred to as *Hailes' Chronicles*]

Dewar, John, *The Dewar Manuscripts*, ed. Rev. John Mackechnie, William Maclellan, Glasgow, 1964.

Douglas, Robert, *The Peerage of Scotland*, Edinburgh, 1764.

Douglas of Glenbervie, Sir Robert, *The Baronage of Scotland*, Edinburgh, 1798.

Dowden, J., *Chartulary of the Abbey of Lindores, 1193–1479*, Edinburgh, 1903.

Dwelly, Edward, *The Illustrated Gaelic–English Dictionary*, 9th edn, Gairm Publications, Glasgow, 1977 (first published 1901–11).

The Exchequer Rolls of Scotland [see Stuart et al.].

Farmer, David Hugh, *The Oxford Dictionary of Saints*, Oxford University Press, Oxford, 1992.

Fergusson of Kilkerran, Sir James, *Argyll in the Forty-Five*, Faber and Faber, London, 1951.

Fraser, Alexander, *Lochfyneside*, The Saint Andrew Press, Edinburgh, 1971.

Fraser, William, *The Lennox*, 2 vols, Edinburgh, 1874.

Fraser, Sir William (ed.), *Registrum Monasterii S. Marie de Cambuskenneth*, Grampian Club, vol. 4, Edinburgh, 1872.

Fraser, Sir William, *The Red Book of Menteith*, 2 vols, Edinburgh, 1880.

Freeman, A. Martin (ed.), *The Annals of Connacht*, Dublin Institute for Advanced Studies, Dublin, 1970.

Fryde, E. B., D. E. Greenway, S. Porter and I. Roy (eds) *A Handbook of British Chronology*, 3rd edn, Royal Historical Society, London, 1986.

Garrett, A., *Wood Engravings and Drawings by Iain Macnab of Barachastlain*, Midas Books, Tunbridge Wells, 1973.

Gillies, Rev. William A., *In Famed Breadalbane*, Munro Press, Perth, 1938.

Grant, Alexander, *Independence and Nationhood: Scotland 1306-1469*, The New History of Scotland, Edward Arnold, London, 1984.

Grant, Alexander and Keith J. Stringer, *Mediaeval Scotland: Crown, Lordship and Community*, Edinburgh University Press, Edinburgh, 1993.

Grant, I. F., *The Social and Economic Development of Scotland before 1603*, Oliver and Boyd, Edinburgh, 1930.

Grant, James, *British Battles on Land and Sea*, Cassell, London, 1897.

Green, Miranda J., *Dictionary of Celtic Myth and Legend*, Thames and Hudson, London, 1992.

Gregory Smith, G. (ed.), *The Book of Islay*, privately printed, 1895.

Henderson, George, *The Norse Influence on Celtic Scotland*, James Maclehose and Sons, Glasgow, 1910.

Highland Papers [see Scottish History Society].

Innes, C. (ed.), *The Book of the Thanes of Cawdor*, Spalding Club, Edinburgh, 1859.

Innes, C. (ed.), *Origines Parochiales Scotiae*, Bannantyne Club, Edinburgh, 1865.

Innes, Cosmo (ed.), *Registrum de Dunfermelyn*, Edinburgh, 1842.

Innes, Cosmo (ed.), *Registrum monasterii de Passelet*, Edinburgh, 1832.

Innes of Learney, Sir Thomas, *The Tartans of the Clans and Families of Scotland*, W. & A. K. Johnston, Edinburgh, 1947.

The Iona Club (ed.) *Collectanea de Rebus Albanicis*, Thomas G. Stevenson, Edinburgh, 1847.

Jackson, Kenneth, *Gaelic Notes on the Book of Deer*, Cambridge University Press, Cambridge, 1922.

Johnston, James B., *Place-Names of Scotland*, John Murray, London, 1934.

Johnston, T. B. and James A. Robertson, *Historical Geography of the Clans of Scotland*, W. & A. K. Johnston, Edinburgh, 1899.

Kelly, Fergus, *A Guide to Early Irish Law*, Dublin Institute for Advanced Studies, Dublin, 1988.

Kissack, Rev. Reginald, *The MacIsaacs: Possible Origins of a Scots-Manx Surname*, Manx Heritage Foundation, Isle of Man, 1990.

Lamont of Knockdow, Sir Norman (ed.), *An Inventory of Lamont Papers*, Skinner & Co., Edinburgh, 1914.

Loomis, Roger Sherman (ed.), *Arthurian Literature in the Middle Ages*, Oxford University Press, Oxford, 1969.

MacDonald, Rev. A. and Rev. A. MacDonald, *The Clan Donald*, 3 vols, Northern Publishing Co., Inverness, 1896.

MacDonald, Colin, *The History of Argyll*, Holmes (Books), Glasgow, n.d.

McDonald, R. Andrew, *The Kingdom of the Isles*, Tuckwell Press, East Linton, 1997.

MacDougall, Norman, *James III: A Political Study*, John Donald, Edinburgh, 1982.

MacDougall, Norman, *James IV*, Tuckwell Press, East Linton, 1997.

McGladdery, Christine, *James II*, John Donald, Edinburgh, 1990.

McKechnie, Hector, *The Lamont Clan*, Neill & Co., Edinburgh, 1938.

MacLean of Dochgarroch, Loraine (ed.), *The Middle Ages in the Highlands*, Inverness Field Club, Inverness, 1981.

MacMillan, Rev. Somerled, *Bygone Lochaber*, privately published, 1971.

McNamee, Colin, *The Wars of the Bruces*, Tuckwell Press, East Linton, 1997.

McNaughton, Duncan, *The Clan McNaughton*, Albyn Press, Edinburgh, 1977.

MacPherson, Alan G., *The Posterity of the Three Brethren*, Alliance Press, Newmarket, Ontario, 1976.

Macquarrie, Alan, *Scotland and the Crusades, 1095–1560*, John Donald, Edinburgh, 1985.

Moncreiffe of that Ilk, Sir Iain, *The Highland Clans*, rev. edn, Barrie and Jenkins, London, 1982.

Morris, John, *The Age of Arthur*, 3 vols, Phillimore & Co., Chichester, 1977.

Munro, Jean and R. W. Munro, *Acts of the Lords of the Isles*, Scottish History Society, Edinburgh, 1986.

Nicholson, Ranald, *Scotland: The Later Middle Ages*, vol. 2, The Edinburgh History of Scotland, Oliver and Boyd, Edinburgh, 1978.

Nisbet, Alexander, *A System of Heraldry, Speculative and Practical*, 2nd edn, Alex. Lawrie, Edinburgh, 1804.

O'Hart, John, *Irish Pedigrees*, 2 vols (first published 1892), Genealogical Publishing Co., Baltimore, 1989.

O'Rahilly, Thomas F., *Early Irish History and Mythology*, Dublin Institute for Advanced Studies, Dublin, 1984.

The Oxford Book of Quotations, Oxford University Press, London, 1959.

Papworth, John W., *An Ordinary of British Armorials*, T. Richards, London, 1874 (repr. Heraldry Today, London, 1985).

Platts, Beryl, *Scottish Hazard: The Flemish Nobility and Their Impact on Scotland*, Procter Press, London, 1985.

Regesta Regum Scottorum, 8 vols, Edinburgh University Press, Edinburgh.

Robertson, William, *Index of Charters*, Murray and Cochrane, Edinburgh, 1798.

Ross, Stewart, *Monarchs of Scotland*, Lochar Publishing, Moffat, 1990.

Royal Commission on Historical Manuscripts, *Second Report and Appendix*, Eyre and Spottiswoode, London, 1871.

Sanger, Keith and Alison Kinnaird, *Tree of Strings*, Kinmor Music, 1992.

Scottish History Society, *Highland Papers*, vols 1–4, Edinburgh, 1914–34.

Sellar, W. David H. and Alasdair Maclean, *The Highland Clan MacNeacail*, Maclean Press, Lochbay, Isle of Skye, 1999.

Seymour, William, *Battles in Britain, 1066–1746*, Sidgwick and Jackson, London, 1989.

Skene, W. F. (ed.), *Chronicles of the Picts, Chronicles of the Scots and Other Memorials of Scottish History*, HM General Register House, Edinburgh, 1867.

Skene, W. F., *The Highlanders of Scotland* (first published 1836), ed. Alexander Macbain, Eneas Mackay, Stirling, 1902.

Skene, W. F., *Celtic Scotland*, 3 vols (first published 1880), repr. New York, 1971.

Skene, W. F., *Arthur and the Britons in Wales and Scotland*, repr. Llanerch, Lampeter, 1988.

Skene, W. F. (ed.), *John of Fordun's Chronicle of the Scottish Nation*, 2 vols (first printed 1872 as part of the Historians of Scotland series), repr. Llanerch, Lampeter, 1993.

Smout, T. C., *A History of the Scottish People, 1560–1830*, Collins/Fontana, London, 1972.

Steer, K. A. and J. W. M. Bannerman, *Late Medieval Monumental Sculpture in the West Highlands*, RCAHMS, Edinburgh, 1977.

Stevenson, Joseph, *Documents Illustrative of the History of Scotland*, 2 vols, HM General Register House, Edinburgh 1870.

Stones, and Simpson, *Edward I and the Throne of Scotland*, 2 vols.

Stringer, K. J. (ed.), *Essays on the Nobility of Mediaeval Scotland*, John Donald, Edinburgh, 1985.

Stuart, John, George Burnett and J. G. Mackay (eds), *The Exchequer Rolls of Scotland*, 23 vols, HM General Register House, Edinburgh, 1878 onwards.

Thomson, Derick S. (ed.), *The Companion to Gaelic Scotland*, Blackwell, Oxford, 1983.

Thomson, Thomas (ed.), *The Auchinleck Chronicle*, privately printed, Edinburgh, 1819.

Tolstoy, Nicolai, *The Quest for Merlin*, Hodder and Stoughton (Coronet), 1985.

Towill, Edwin Sprott, *The Saints of Scotland*, The Saint Andrew Press, Edinburgh, 1983.

Turner, Sir James, *Memoirs of His Own Life and Times*, n.p., Edinburgh, 1829.

Tytler, Patrick Fraser, *The History of Scotland* 4 vols, William P. Nimmo, Edinburgh, 1864.

Walsh, Rev. Paul, *Leabhar Chlainne Suibhne*, Dollar, Printinghouse, Dublin, 1920.

Watson, George, *Bell's Dictionary and Digest of the Law of Scotland*, Bell and Bradfute, Edinburgh, 1882.

Watson, William J. (ed.), *Scottish Verse from the Book of the Dean of Lismore*, Scottish Gaelic Texts Society, Edinburgh, 1937.

Woulfe, Rev. P., *Sloinnte Gaedheal is Gall*, Dublin, 1923.

Articles

Anon. [Sheriff J. R. N. Macphail], 'The Genealogie of the Campbells', *Highland Papers* vol. 2, Scottish History Society, Edinburgh (1916), 70–111.

Bannerman, John. 'The MacLachlans of Kilbride and their Manuscripts', *Scottish Studies*, vol. 21 (1977), 1–34.

Campbell of Airds, A. and D. C. McWhannell, 'The Mac Gille Chonnels – A Family of Hereditary Boat-builders', *Society for West Highlands and Islands Historical Research, Notes and Queries*, Series 2, 14, 3–9.

Campbell, Alexander, 'The Manuscript History of Craignish' (ed. Herbert Campbell), *Miscellany*, vol. 4, Scottish History Society, Edinburgh (1926), 187–299.

Campbell of Inverneill, Colin, yr, 'The Origins of the Campbells of Inverneill', *The Scottish Genealogist*, vol. 35, no. 2 (June 1988), 63–72.

Campbell of Kilberry, Marion and Mary Sandeman, 'Mid Argyll: An Archaeological Survey', *Proceedings of the Society of Antiquaries of Scotland*, vol. 95 (1961–2) 1–125.

Dawson, Jane, 'The 5th Earl of Argyle, Gaelic Lordship and Political Power in Sixteenth-century Scotland', *Scottish Historical Review*, vol. 67:1, no. 183 (April 1988), 1–27.

Duffy, Sean, 'The Anglo-Norman Era in Scotland', in T. M. Devine and J. F. McMillan (eds), *Celebrating Columba: Irish–Scottish Connections 597–1997*, John Donald, Edinburgh, 1999, pp. 15–34.

Dunbar, 'The Medieval Architecture of the Scottish Highlands', *The Middle Ages in the Highlands*.

Duncan, A. A. M. and A. L. Brown, 'Argyll and the Isles in the Earlier Middle Ages', *Proceedings of the Society of Antiquaries of Scotland*, vol. 90 (1956–7), 192–220.

Garrett, 'Wood Engravings and Drawings by Iain Macnab of Barachastlain'.

Gillies, William, 'Some Thoughts on the Toschederach', *Scottish Gaelic Studies*, vol. 17, Special Volume, *Feill Sgribhinn do Ruaraidh MacThomais – Festschrift for Derick Thomson*.

Henderson, George, 'Lamh-Sgriobhainnean Mhic-Neacail', *Transactions of the Gaelic Society of Inverness*, vol. 27 (1908–11).

Kingston, Simon, 'Trans-Insular Lordship in the Fifteenth Century', in T. M. Devine and J. F. McMillan (eds), *Celebrating Columba: Irish–Scottish Connections 597–1997*, John Donald, Edinburgh, 1999.

Loomis, Roger Sherman, 'Scotland and the Arthurian Legend', *Proceedings of the Society of Antiquaries of Scotland*, vol. 89 (1955–6), 1–21.

MacInnes, John, 'The Panegyric Code in Gaelic Poetry and its Historical Background', *Transactions of the Gaelic Society of Inverness*, vol. 50 (1976–8), 435–98.

MacInnes, Rev. John, 'West Highland Sea Power in the Middle Ages', *Transactions of the Gaelic Society of Inverness*, vol. 48.

Maclean, Alasdair, 'Notes on South Uist Families', reprint, 1985, from *Transactions of the Gaelic Society of Inverness*, vol. 53, 491–518.

McNaughton, D., 'The O'Connachars of Lorne', *The Scottish Genealogist*, vol. 16, no. 3 (September 1969), 65–6.

MacQueen,

Matheson, Angus, 'Bishop Carswell', *Transactions of the Gaelic Society of Inverness*, vol. 42 (1953–9).

Meek, Donald E., 'The MacSween Poem in *The Book of the Dean of Lismore*', *West Highland Notes and Queries*, vol. 25, 3–11.

Sellar, W. D. H., 'The Earliest Campbells: Norman, Briton or Gael?', *Scottish Studies*, vol. 17 (1973), 109–24.

Simpson, and Webster, 'Charter Evidence and the Distribution of Mottes in Scotland', *Essays on the Nobility of Mediaeval Scotland*, 1–24.

Index